The Daily Telegraph

CRICKET YEAR BOOK 88

GW01451499

Michael Melford
Wendy Wimbush
Foreword by
Brian Johnston

Consultant Editor Michael Melford
Statistics Wendy Wimbush
Special articles E.W. Swanton, D.M. Green
Other contributors
Trevor Bailey, Rajan Bala (India), Mike Beddow,
Tony Cozier (West Indies), Rachael Flint, John Fogg,
Neil Hallam, Doug Ibbotson, David Leggat (New Zealand),
Michael Owen-Smith (South Africa), Qamar Ahmed
(Pakistan), D.J. Rutnagur, Alan Shiell (Australia), Sa'adi
Thawfeeq (Sri Lanka), A.S.R. Winlaw.

Editor Norman Barrett
Cover illustration Major Splash Ltd

Acknowledgements Thanks are due to David Armstrong and
Mike Gear for supplying the statistics for the Minor Counties
and Second XI championships, respectively, and to Brian
Langley and the TCCB for making the first-class fixtures
available. Young England statistics were provided by the
NCA. The Deloittes Ratings are published by kind
permission of Deloitte Haskins & Sells, with special thanks
due to Ted Dexter and Robert Eastaway.
  The photographs appearing in this book are reproduced by
kind permission of Patrick Eagar, All-Sport, Bill Smith,
Syndication International, and Bob Thomas.
  The editors particularly wish to thank Radford Barrett,
Sports Editor of The Daily Telegraph, for his generous help.

Published by Telegraph Publications
Peterborough Court, At South Quay,
181 Marsh Wall, London E14 9SR

6th edition
© The Daily Telegraph 1987

Typeset by Michael Weintroub Graphics Ltd,
Kenton, Middx.
Printed and bound in Great Britain by
Biddles Ltd, Guildford and King's Lynn

British Library Cataloguing in Publication Data

The Daily Telegraph cricket year book: a complete
    account of the . . . season.
    —88—
    1. Cricket—Periodicals
    796.35'8'05   GV911

ISBN 0-86367-177-2

Contents

Foreword

I have commentated on cricket either for TV or for Radio for the last 42 summers, covering 244 Tests in England or around the world. I am glad to say that I have never lost my love of cricket and still remain an optimist. Each spring, as I mow my lawn and get that delicious first sniff of new-mown grass, I think: 'This summer will be the best ever for both cricket and weather.' Of course, with exceptions such as 1947 and 1976, the weather usually lets me down, but there is always something good about the cricket.

The 1987 weather has earned the sobriquet of a 'Madame Butterfly summer' – i.e. one fine day. But in spite of some of the worst rains since records were kept, there have been compensations with the cricket.

It's not just because I married a Yorkshire girl that I am so pleased at the resurgence of Yorkshire – something which many of us thought would happen when they were once freed from their internal unhappiness. They deserve to do well because they are the only home-bred first-class team, although Kent are doing a fair job in trying to emulate them.

Similarly, it must be good for the game that the recent stranglehold on the various competitions by the 'South of Watford brigade' has been broken. Many congratulations therefore to Notts, Lancashire, and Northants as well as Yorkshire for their successes. And, of course, well done, Pakistan. They were a young and extremely talented team well led by Imran Khan, both on and off the field.

The other satisfactory features of the season are the ever increasing strength and popularity of club and village cricket and the tremendous efforts by county and other associations to counter the decline in school cricket. It is sadly true that far less cricket is played *at school* these days. But there are more and more chances for young boys to be coached and given opportunities to play during their holidays. They are a vital source of future Test cricketers.

That is the good news, but I have a few personal moans which I think will be shared by many:

1. Disappointing England

It was disappointing to see England fail to live up to the form they had shown in Australia. A glance at the Test averages will reveal some startling figures – main batsmen averaging under 30, main bowlers averaging over 50.

One of the reasons is that the England cricketers played so little before the first Test, not just because of the weather but also because of the fixture list. Because of the Benson & Hedges competition, they played few innings and bowled few overs in *first-class cricket* before the Old Trafford Test. The touring team has a tremendous advantage nowadays. They play regularly together *as a team* and, more important still, play three-day cricket. One other thing became very noticeable as the series progressed. England were still good stoppers, catchers, and throwers.

But with so many big men – most of them over or around 30 – they have lost their speed and mobility in the field.

In contrast, the young Pakistan team – some under 20 – sprinted and flung themselves about. It was particularly apparent at Edgbaston, where, when England were chasing runs in their second innings, they could run only one run to the deep fielders on the boundary. When England were fielding, the Pakistani batsmen had regularly been able to run two runs to the same position.

I hope Mike Gatting will not be too disappointed and disheartened. He did a splendid job both as captain and batsman, in spite of two doubtful decisions after winning the toss. Let's hope that the team spirit, which will be renewed during the winter tours, will put new life into the side.

2. Midsummer Madness

I would like to see one slight adjustment made immediately to the 1988 fixture list. It seems crazy that in midsummer during the Benson & Hedges final there was no first-class cricket scheduled for three days, which ironically were some of the best of the summer. It *should* be possible to arrange a full fixture list and then switch matches arranged for the two finalists to a later date.

3. Fielders in Helmets

I'm afraid that I am fed up with silly-points and short-legs in helmets crouching within a few feet of the batsman, waiting for the bat-pad catch. Not only is it dangerous, in spite of the helmets (e.g. Ijaz at the Oval), but their presence discourages the spin bowlers from attacking the batsmen with flighted spin. Instead, they bowl too flat with too little spin, resulting in a lot of maiden overs but few wickets. I am sure that this is the reason for the poor wicket-per-over rate of Emburey and Edmonds.

I would ban all helmets for fielders, in spite of the risk of legal action in case of injury. Without helmets, they would stand deeper. It would end the incessant and unnecessary appeals that create such bad feeling.

4. Unfriendliness

My next dislike follows the above. I am horrified by the unfriendliness that seems to be spreading between players and umpires, more in tests than in the county games, where there is a far better understanding. A lot of it is due to the action replay on television, which shows up umpires' errors that were never spotted in the days of umpires such as Chester, Buller, and Elliott. My wish is that, whenever possible, commentators should refrain from comment but just let viewers judge for themselves.

It is also a great pity that in 1987 the manager and eventually the captain of a touring team saw fit to criticize Test umpires in public. Nor do the players help with their all too obvious dissent at some decisions. One appreciates how difficult it must be with all the competition for places in a team and with a lot of money at stake. But if only they could wait until they get back to the dressing-room and then explain to manager or selector exactly what had really happened!

5. Aids to Umpires

I regret that the various aids to umpires invented by Professor Sir Bernard Lovell have proved too expensive to install at the Test grounds. His light meter at Old Trafford is a success in that it helps spectators to understand what is going on and to appreciate when the light is getting worse. But Sir Bernard has also developed gadgets that would give a buzz in the umpire's ear to indicate: (a) if the ball had touched wood instead of just pad; (b) whether the ball after hitting the pad would have gone on to hit the stumps (in the case of lbw); and (c) whether the batsmen had beaten the throw in a run-out. None of this would be taking the responsibility away from the umpires. It would merely be an extra aid to help their judgement.

6. Changes in the Laws

Finally, I would like to see several alterations in the Laws.

A. Quite definitely there should be only *one* bouncer allowed per over. What a joy it was in Australia during the one-day internationals to see any ball over the batsman's shoulder called a no-ball. The result was more strokes in front of the wicket and less unpleasant ducking and weaving by the batsmen.

B. No longer penalize a throw that hits the stumps and then ricochets off for overthrows. It should become dead on hitting the stumps and removing the bails.

C. Umpires should be asked to abide by the wording of Law 3.8 as has been applied to first-class matches in England. This concerns the decision to suspend play because of bad light. It says: 'The umpires will only suspend or continue to suspend play for bad light when they consider *there is a risk of serious physical injury to the batsman.*' They so often go off even when slow bowlers are bowling and there is more risk to fielders than to batsmen.

D. The Law regarding penalties needs clarifying. I was delighted when England were penalized five runs when the ball hit a fielders's helmet that had been placed behind the wicket-keeper. That is as it should be, and incidentally there were once two helmets behind the Pakistan wicket-keeper. But if the ball had hit them both, it would still have been only a five-run penalty, not ten, as the ball becomes dead as soon as it touches the first one.

But there is to my mind some doubt about the penalties given if a fielder, other than the wicket-keeper, uses a glove. This happened a few years ago when Sharp, the Northants wicket-keeper, ran after a ball down to fine-leg, discarding his glove as he ran. Steele seized the glove and put it on. When Sharp returned the ball, Steele took it in his glove and was penalized five runs. Fair enough, I suppose, as Law 41 says: 'The fieldsman may stop the ball with any part of his person but if he wilfully stops it otherwise, five runs shall be added to the score.'

But what about when the fielder stops the ball with his shin pads? And where in the Laws is there anything about who – even the wicket-keeper – can wear gloves?

Happy Memories of 1987

But enough of my moans. I am still enjoying the memories of one of the
happiest matches on which I have commentated, the Bicentenary Match
at Lord's – the cream of world cricket playing before capacity crowds at
Lord's looking its best.

MCC had had their little local difficulty during the early summer. But
this match made up for everything. The atmosphere was perfect and so
was the weather for most of the time. Old Test players and
administrators from every cricketing country were entertained by MCC
and renewed friendships made over many years of Test matches. And the
large crowds just sat and appreciated the feast of talent before them. No
chanting, cheering or rattling of beer cans. Just cricket-lovers enjoying
the skills of some players they may never see again. What better sight has
there been than the master batsman Gavaskar playing the world's fastest
bowler Marshall. And what about that fantastic run-out of Gooch by
Harper? It was all competitive but played in a wonderful spirit. And two
important points were proved. It *is* possible to start play before the
outfield is entirely dry without ill effect on the fielders. And so long as
there are only slow bowlers on, it is not dangerous to play in even
atrocious light, as they did on the Saturday evening.

The 1987 season may not have been the greatest ever, but this
Bicentenary Match ensured that it ended on a high note. And I am sure
that next spring – God willing – as I mow my lawn, I shall look forward to
1988 being the best season I have ever enjoyed.

Brian Johnston

1986-87

LOOKING BACK

Cloudy with Sunny Intervals

By Michael Melford

The English cricket-follower must have had a bumper year. In the winter he had the heady unexpected successes in Australia to cheer him. In the summer he was able to have a moan over the defeat by Pakistan - and there is nothing the English cricket public loves more than a good moan. In late summer came the MCC Bicentenary Match, which brought the best not only out of the players but out of the spectators. They did not chant, they did not clank cans, they did not rush on the field at the end of play to steal the stumps or knock the umpires about. Instead, they showed full appreciation of the technical excellence on view.

Here were most of the world's best players engaged in superb weather (on the first two days) and in a historic setting given an extra old world panache by the new Mound Stand. The misunderstandings of MCC's AGM in May and the bitter differences needing to be settled by a Special General Meeting in July seemed a lifetime away. The weather deteriorated, but the memory lingered on. The players did their stuff with a suitable degree of competitiveness, the crowd responded, the perfect atmosphere for the occasion was created.

To many this was something new or something that had been largely forgotten, a flash of sunshine not only in the wet summer but in the hurly-burly of the modern game with its ultra-competitiveness and, in the case of the limited-overs game, its bending of the Laws and crude defiance of the textbook. In this respect the nadir was probably reached during the one-day international at Edgbaston in May, not only in the disgraceful scenes off the field but in the bowling of the off-spinner Tauseef to Ian Botham. Pushing his line down the leg-side to the limits of one-day interpretations and occasionally beyond, Tauseef cheerfully accepted the not infrequent calls of wide. His line, after all, was not all that far away from that of other off-spinners in this form of cricket and he was clearly being successful. He could enjoy the sight of Botham pinned down and it was not for him to concern himself with the means that were being used to achieve the end.

The spectacle of Botham massively frustrated may have a certain macabre attraction, but from a strictly cricketing standpoint it was an unlovely episode that ended when Botham at last detected a ball on the stumps and mishit it. As it happened, Pakistan lost the match, but Tauseef had provided a connoisseur's example of the sort of negative bowling that limited-overs cricket inspires but which is often forgotten later in the excitement of a close finish.

The Test match at Edgbaston in July underlined the difference between the conventional and the limited-overs game. Under limited-over rules, England's task of making 124 in 18 overs would probably have been achieved nine times out of 10. Here, however, there were no limitations on field-placing, no special interpretations of what constituted a wide, and Imran Khan and Wasim Akram had the last word.

It would be nice to think that a Test match could not be saved by high, wide bowling, but here one runs into the perennial problem of how far it is right to curb the bowler's freedom of choice. Similarly, it would be popular with many if the local rule devised for one-day matches in Australia (making anything over shoulder-high a no-ball) could be introduced into first-class cricket. But to deprive the bowler altogether of the short ball and the batsman of the chance to hook strikes too much at the heart of the game for this to be hastily adopted, anyhow to the same degree. However, it may well be that if West Indies persist in packing their side with fast bowlers and refusing to bless any legislation that reduces the bouncer or improves the over-rate, the time may come when the call for action has to be answered.

Strain at the Top

Until financial returns increased and players and administrators became more money-minded, the TCCB had a sensible policy of keeping one winter in four clear of tours in order to give the leading players a rest from cricket. The last such sabbatical for England was in 1975-76. It is no surprise, therefore, that many England players of the present generation have shown signs of flagging and have begun to take winters off. In the autumn of 1987, too, the England selectors for the first time had to pick three different teams for the winter, one for limited-overs cricket alone, though even that would not necessarily avoid the unfortunate situation that developed in the later stages of last winter's tour of Australia.

One objective on every tour is to keep every player fit and in form. It is seldom easy, but in the past there were always minor matches between Tests in Australia in which the spare players would have match practice. In last winter's plethora of competitive one-day cricket, England were always in the position of having to field what they believed to be their strongest team, which meant that several members of the party went for weeks without playing. Some of the team were playing too much, some not enough, indeed not at all. High on the list of desirable changes must be a rearrangement of itineraries in Australia.

Limited-Overs Influences

When England are defeated and the suggestion is made that too much limited-overs cricket may have something to do with it, the question is usually asked – why does it not have the same ill effect on the opposition? Why, for example, did Pakistan bat and bowl so much better on a poor pitch at Headingley that, batting second, they won by an innings?

One answer certainly is that the present-day England batsmen have a more developed taste for adventure than many in past generations, who were leavened with solid, correct individuals with highly organized defences and abundant patience. The current heroes are thus more vulnerable to any eccentricities in the pitch. A stronger argument is that cricket in other countries where the climate is more accommodating and the season longer is more leisured. They do not have the concentrated cricket packed into four and a half months in England, where a player may have to change his method of batting or bowling once or twice each week. In England, too, the tourists' programme of recent years has usually provided them with more three-day cricket before the Test series started than has been available to home players.

The last opponents whom England beat at home were Australia, whose present plight can be attributed to the way in which the Sheffield Shield and Test series are pushed aside to accomodate one-day commercialism. This, it can be argued, is why in Melbourne in the other decisive Test match of the last year, also played on a poor pitch, England, batting second, beat Australia by an innings in three days.

Covering

Even in a wet summer the change to leaving pitches uncovered during the hours of play in the Britannic Assurance Championship was only a relatively small one, though there was one occasion in the past in a Trent Bridge Test match when this amount of uncovering was all-important. As the players came out to start the third day's play in 1978, the clouds in the relevant quarter left no doubt that it was about to rain heavily. But at the appointed hour the first drops had not fallen and the light was deemed adequate. The umpires allowed the fateful first ball to be bowled, though after two balls they decided that the light had faded and everybody went off. The pitch then remained open to several hours of rain, after which the unfortunate New Zealanders, who must have been looking forward to batting on the same excellent pitch on which they had done rather well to restrict England to 400, were bowled out twice and beaten by an innings. This hastened the arrival of full covering in Test matches in England.

There is little statistical evidence that the spinners profited from the relaxation of covering in 1987. If covering were wholly abolished now, it is, of course, by no means certain that it would be the spinners who benefited. Opinions have usually differed as to how it would affect the batsman. Some argue that leaving pitches uncovered throughtout extends the batsman's all-round range of strokes by requiring improvisation from him. An argument against it is that it prevents him from acquiring the confidence to play attacking strokes. In theory, the 1987 arrangement of leaving the pitches open only during the hours of play should provide odd opportunities of expanding his repertoire but without any loss of confidence.

Graeme Pollock Retires

A mournful event in 1987 was the retirement of Graeme Pollock, one of the world's great batsmen since his first tour of Australia in 1963-64 aged 19. One heard then of normally sophisticated, unexcitable, and patriotic Australians being on their feet cheering as Pollock and Eddie Barlow, himself only 23, made 341 together in four and three-quarter hours in a Test match in Adelaide.

Those present will not forget an hour after lunch on the first day of a Test match in Durban in 1970 when Pollock batted with Barry Richards and they made over 100 with brilliant effortless batting. Pollock went on to make 274 then. Three years before he had made an equally memorable 209, also against Australia, at Newlands, when confined to the back foot by a pulled muscle. Further back still, in 1965, on an overcast morning at Trent Bridge with the England bowlers right on top, he came in and played that extraordinary innings which put South Africa on the way to winning the match and the series – 125 out of 160 in two hours 20 minutes. 'One of the finest Test displays of all time,' said *Wisden*. And he was just 21.

For the past 17 years, since he last played in a Test match, he has gone on delighting those in South Africa who watched him, a left-hander of immense class combining power and charm. Yet the rest of the world has not seen him.

Those selecting the teams for the Bicentenary Match had the chance to pick him. Ideally they should have done so, but understandably they did not. This was eventually an occasion of peace and goodwill and they could not afford to risk threats to grounds, the withdrawal of other players by their Boards and so on. But what a way to treat a great player who really has done something to help produce the changes in his country which objectors elsewhere profess to want! What a sign of the times!

The Farewell of Rice and Hadlee

Not everyone is convinced of the value to English cricket of having overseas players taking up places in the county sides. But there are those players whose contribution stretches far beyond their performance on the field. Wayne Daniel, for one, has long seen his role for Middlesex as including helping the county's general and future cricket welfare, not just turning up and bowling. The influence of Clive Rice and Richard Hadlee has been vastly beneficial to Nottinghamshire, and there must be many in all parts of the country who were glad to see them go out on a note of triumph.

If a young bowler wanted a model, Hadlee was there to be watched, wasting no time and, with his short run-up and economical action, wasting no energy. The proof of his method and its effectiveness was that in the last year of his career in England at the age of 36 he was as successful as ever.

MCC Bicentenary

MCC's bicentenary had to overcome setbacks that could have destroyed less well organized celebrations, but overcome them it did, and by the end of the Bicentenary Match in August goodwill prevailed to a far greater extent than it had previously.

The first blow came from the weather and from the storm on the morning of 27 March, which blew down the marquee in which the Bicentenary Ball should have been held that night. Operations were shifted to the Pavilion and Tennis Court, and the evening was still successful enough for MCC to receive congratulations on their improvisation.

The resignation of the Secretary, J.A. Bailey, in January had already created unease about the internal workings of the Club and its moves to repair relations with the TCCB. At the AGM in May, a small section of members, not apparently understanding the issues involved, spread this unease so successfully that the Annual Report and Accounts were rejected. At the height of the season and with the main Bicentenary celebrations imminent, MCC with Lt-Col John Stephenson now confirmed as Secretary, had to stage a costly Emergency General Meeting at Central Hall, Westminster. It was preceded by a postal vote, and after a more peaceful meeting the protesters were defeated by 7,138 to 981.

By then, however, the President, Colin Cowdrey, was in hospital undergoing heart surgery which would keep him inactive for nearly all the rest of his year of office, ending on September 30. Under the MCC constitution, the Treasurer took his place, which meant that Hubert Doggart, already in charge of the Bicentenary celebrations, had to preside over the Emergency Meeting and the eve-of-match dinner at the Guildhall, not to mention the ICC meeting that preceded the match and the entertaining of many administrators and former players from overseas.

All this he accomplished with great success. The Dinner, at which Lord Home of The Hirsel and Clive Lloyd, manager of the Rest of the World team, were the speakers, hit the right note, as had the lunch in June in Dorset Square, site of Thomas Lord's first ground.

There remained the Bicentenary Match, for which the teams had been selected in May. MCC, captained by Mike Gatting, comprised the best players currently in English first-class cricket, irrespective of nationality. The Rest, captained by Allan Border, came from the best overseas players, though they could be augmented by up to three overseas players in England for whom the MCC selectors had not been able to find room. Vivien Richards preferred to play for his League club. Injuries kept Martin Crowe and Ian Botham out of the MCC team. The respective replacements were Dilip Vengsarkar, Graham Gooch, and Clive Rice.

In a wet summer, the match mercifully was granted a perfect first and second day, and though the third was shortened and the fifth washed out, the cricket played and the atmosphere in which it was played gave suitable lustre to a historic occasion.

Four-Day Cricket
by D.M. Green

The TCCB's decision to introduce four-day cricket into the 1988 County Championship is tacit recognition that there are areas of the county game, and through that English Test cricket, that are causing concern to administrators and even to some players.

In order to understand the thinking behind this experiment, under which each county will play three four-day matches in April and early May and three more in late August and September, with the total number of matches played in the Championship being reduced from 24 to 22, it may be helpful to trace the course followed by country cricket over the past three decades..

Until the 1960s, county pitches, apart from the bowler's landing area, were left open to the weather after the start of play, as were Test match pitches in England. Falling attendances at county matches in the sixties ushered in the era of sponsored one-day competitions, in which pitches were necessarily covered. Thereafter the covering of County Championship wickets was gradually extended until it reached the situation to which the legislators reverted last season, when pitches were covered overnight and also during the day if heavy rain caused early abandonment of play. At that time, however, bowlers' run-ups were not covered.

Meanwhile, in order to fall in line with other Test match countries, we had totally covered our Test pitches. It seemed, and still seems to many sound judges, to be ridiculous to play the highest class of cricket on protected surfaces while playing the stratum immediately below it, county cricket, on unprotected ones; so the stage was set for full covering of county pitches, which came in 1981.

High Expectations

The expectations aroused by the decision to cover fully were very high. We had long admired the stroke-making ability of batsmen from Australia, South Africa, and the West Indies who were brought up on hard, true surfaces, which also seemed to encourage fiery fast bowlers and clever spinners. A return to the Golden Age seemed at hand. Perhaps that near-Dodo, the leg-spinner, recalled so nostalgically by the middle-aged, might be sighted again.

The actuality, alas, was very different. Too many county captains, their thinking unduly coloured by the fact that they lead their sides in three highly lucrative one-day competitions as against only one three-day one, turned to defensive tactics when their bowlers failed to break through. Pitches, though now generally unhelpful to bowlers, were eminently suited to last-day chases; so, instead of the cut and thrust of battle over three days, what frequently happened was, after a little dart by the fielding side on the first morning, a virtual cessation of hostilities until the second evening, when the respective skippers would meet to establish the parameters of the next afternoon's play. 'If you set us 280 in 65 overs we'll go all the way.' 'OK, but if you want that many overs you will have to lob some up to us in the morning so we can score quickly enough.' This sort of travesty was all too prevalent and is no sort of way in which to breed Test cricketers.

Not all counties or all captains were equally guilty. Those with powerful bowling sides, such as Essex, Middlesex, and Notts, would have recourse to such jiggery-pokery only when rain had taken such a slice out of playing time that the only possible chance they had of victory was through reaching a mutually acceptable covenant with the opposition. Others, rather than encouraging their bowlers to counter the placid pitches by, say, getting the ball to swing – an art now largely lost – and posting a slip or two in case they found the edge, placed defensive fields, told their medium-pacers to aim at the middle of the bat, and hung on in there until the bargaining about the last innings started.

Sterile Approach

After six seasons of covered pitches, this sterile approach had become common enough, and its effect on the calibre of our cricket obvious enough, for the TCCB to agree last March, almost out of the blue, to return to partially uncovered wickets for the 1987 season. The rules would be those that had applied in 1980, i.e. pitches to be covered overnight and during the day after an abandonment of play. There was also one extension of the pre-1981 covering regulations, namely the area of bowlers' run-ups. This move, dictated by the increasing importance to counties' finances of sponsors, who evidently do not relish waiting for bowlers' approaches to dry, was to have important consequences.

Once again expectations were high. It was hoped that on surfaces enlivened by rain bowlers would be encouraged to attack and more matches would be won without recourse to contrivance. Spin bowling would surely benefit and batsmen whose techniques had become sloppy through a combination of easy-paced wickets and a general paucity of challenging bowling and field placings would have to tighten up if they were to continue to score heavily.

Again, the actuality was disappointing. Since more rain falls at night, when pitches are covered, than during the day, when they are not, there were few wet wickets, and, when they occurred, seam bowlers, operating off protected run-ups, tended to exploit them rather than spinners. In the seemingly continuous monsoon that we endured last summer, covers stayed on for days at a time. When the weather relented, they were removed to reveal a dry, benign surface which, with a day or two already lost, led inevitably to multiple forfeiture of innings and another one-day-type slog. In terms of Test cricket, we had the disturbing sight of Pakistan's batsmen playing markedly better in English conditions than our own, and their quicker bowlers giving ours lessons in how to swing the ball about.

So now four-day cricket is to be tentatively explored, presumably on covered pitches. The theoretical advantages are obvious: the additional playing time available means that interruptions by the weather should be less damaging; wickets will have an extra day's wear when the weather is good, which, since pitches tend to lose pace the longer they are played on, should aid the spinner rather than the faster bowler; again, the time available, and therefore the tempo, of four-day cricket will be closer to that of Test cricket and will therefore prepare our better players for international cricket more effectively than the three-day game.

Guarded Optimism

That, at any rate, is the theory. How will the practice turn out? As one who has long favoured a four-day County Championship, with the number of matches played reduced to 20 or, if necessary 16, I must profess a guarded optimism. This is based on a belief that in four-day cricket defensive tactics by the fielding side will be less effective, if indeed they are effective at all. This business of cutting off the fours and saving the ones is basically a one-day ploy, and even there I am not wholly convinced of its virtue. It succeeds in three-day games only because there is so often a pressure of time on the batsmen, who makes mistakes when trying to press on. Given fair weather, the addition of a day's play will remove that pressure from him.

Consider the following situation: a side loses the toss and fields first on a good pitch. The batting side will, if they can, look to bat until lunch on the second day at least, a matter of 150 overs. A policy directed at containment only, experience teaches us, leads to scoring rates of around 3 runs per over, giving the batting side some 450 runs. A nasty psychological barrier is set up by the realization that 300 runs are needed to avoid the follow-on. Moreover, the side fielding first will have to bat last on a pitch more worn that those to which they have been accustomed, all of which will make dismissing opponents as quickly as possible (which also tends to involve doing so very cheaply) eminently desirable.

It looks, therefore, as though four-day cricket should encourage attacking cricket by the fielding side, and I single out the fielding side purposely because bowlers dictate how batsmen play. (If you don't believe me, try to cover-drive an inswinger that starts on the line of your pads.) Our English game badly needs bowlers who aim to knock stumps out or find the bat's edge, and captains who will place fielders to catch the nick and not, as too many do, have no close men to penalize the false stroke but any number in the deep to prevent the good stroke from going for four.

Four-day county cricket is unlikely on its own to be a total panacea, but it seems to me that it may well have the effect of nudging some captains (and selectors) into more profitable paths.

The Daily Telegraph Schools Cricket Awards
by D.J. Rutnagur

Competition for The Daily Telegraph Schools Cricket Awards for 1987 was again most keen. The co-ordinator of the awards scheme, Cyril Cooper (Secretary of the English Schools Cricket Association), observed during his scrutiny of the claims of many candidates that an increasing number of boys were playing more cricket outside schools than in them, representing counties' second teams, colts sides, and league clubs. This pattern could be interpreted as a sign of our cricketers' maturing more quickly, which is a good thing. Yet, one asks if the non-participation of the better players will not detract from the general standard.

On the subject of maturity, the winner of the Under-19 batting award, **Neil Martin** (King Edward's, Birmingham), was seen to strike the ball with power beyond his 18 years. In one match, he hit four sixes off consecutive balls and, over the season, scored well over half his runs in boundary hits. Martin's cricket master, Martin Stead, describes his style as 'positively Bothamesque'. Although Martin batted with abandon – at the exciting rate of 95.58 per hundred balls – he had a three-figure average in accumulating 1,256 runs for his school. Above that, he scored 278 in six innings for Worcestershire Schools.

The winning of the bowling by **Nadim Shahid** (Ipswich) is a matter of general delight, for he is one of the much-loved, but dying, breed – the leg-spinner. For a bowler of his type, Shahid is remarkably accurate, and his cricket master, Phil Rees, says with great enthusiasm: 'Nadim is versatile. He bowls a good googly and a top-spinner.'

At a time when all-rounders are not in abundance, it is pleasing also to note that more than one player was in contention for both the batting and the bowling awards. Shahid, opening the batting for Ipswich, himself scored no fewer than 1,389 runs, besides taking 71 wickets. Runner-up for the Under-19 bowling award and finishing just two wickets behind Shahid was his schoolmate John Zagni, also a spinner. He, too, batted usefully, aggregating 899 runs.

Shahid's ability has already come to the attention of Essex and Kent. Hailing from an immigrant family, but born in England, Shahid developed his skills in club cricket, playing for Copdock. Until last year, he was at a comprehensive school which played no cricket to speak of.

Boys in the running for the Under-15 awards played more for their counties' junior teams than their schools. **Toby Radford** (Park House, Newbury) won the batting prize with an aggregate of 966 and a most impressive average of 120. He scored two centuries. John Crawley – whose brother, Mark, and school, Manchester GS, won the Under-19 batting award in 1986 – must get an honourable mention, for he ran Radford close and might have overtaken him had he not missed quite a few matches to play for England Schools.

Praise be, it was a spinner again, slow left-arm **Chris Hawkes** (Loughborough Grammar), who won the bowling award in the category, taking 38 wickets. He played for England Schools and shone in the match against Scotland, bowling as many as 45 overs and taking 5-52.

The Daily Telegraph Cricketers of the Year
by E.W. Swanton

Our international Cricketers of the Year are specially familiar to us this year as having all been seen, bar one, in last summer's English cricket, five of them at Lord's in the MCC Bicentenary Match. There would have been six if Martin Crowe had not had to pull out, to everyone's keen regret, with a broken finger. Looked at together, the eight reflect not only rare overall quality, but many of the arts and graces of the game, in the persons of Crowe, Imran, Roger Harper, Dilip Vengsarkar, and Dean Jones: probably too, in the less familiar Sri Lankan, Brendon Kuruppu.

The English choice, **Mike Gatting**, if not a stylist, exemplifies as well as anyone could the cardinal virtues of courage and determination. No attributes are more important to the captain of a side of what in the Test sense are limited talents exposed to the full spotlight of media attention. In the year under review, Gatting has followed his side's celebrated English success in Australia with another highly successful season with the bat (only Crowe, of those who have played the summer through, tops his average of 60), even though he could not prevent Pakistan taking the honours of the Test series. At the moment of writing, one can only hope that his side may come through with a fair degree of credit from their awesome winter programme. Being, like most hoary reactionaries, allergic to young men's beards, I must confess that Mike's does suggest the defiant British image of Sir Francis Drake.

The Australian choice for this select company was almost a formality. The advance of **Dean Jones's** reputation within six months from the first (tied) Test in Madras in September '86 to the last of the one-day Internationals in Sydney in February '87 was outstanding in itself and significant in that it was one of the few encouraging things in a bleak Australian picture. After his double-hundred against India, he finished as the leading Australian run-getter both in the Indian and in the England series, and in both the one-day affairs in Australia. Batting at No. 3 throughout, he had a combined aggregate of 1,505, averaging 56.

In South Africa's domestic cricket and in the representative games against an Australian XI, **Garth Le Roux** earns Michael Owen-Smith's vote as the outstanding performer. At the age of 31, Le Roux's fast-medium bowling was wonderfully consistent, and his relish for hard work plus emphasis on length and direction were an object lesson. His 6-53 for Western against Eastern Province in the Currie Cup semi-final was the match-winning effort. His latter-end hitting has always been a bonus to his side, not least last summer to Sussex, when, though unfit for a long while, he added to his 32 wickets a batting average of 37.

Tony Cozier makes an interesting West Indian choice in **Roger Harper** the Guyana and Northamptonshire all-rounder – interesting in that, although he was the only spin bowler in the party (apart from Richards with his occassional slows), he was sent home as not required for New Zealand after the tour of Pakistan. Harper's answer could hardly have been more emphatic, as Cozier puts it: 'He inspired Guyana to the Shell Shield championship by his leadership and personal example. In four first-class matches, he collected three centuries, all at vital times, and claimed 18 wickets at less than 20 each with his off-spin bowling. His fielding, as always, was breathtaking in its brilliance.' We saw the best possible evidence of that in Harper's running out of Gooch in the MCC v Rest of the World match. It is one of the sadder commentaries on current values that a young man of such all-round talent has to stand by for Northants for most of the summer while yet another West Indian fast bowler does his stuff.

At the age of 25, **Martin Crowe** has already equalled the seven Test hundreds achieved by Bevan Congdon and Glenn Turner. It was his batting and Richard Hadlee's bowling that enabled New Zealand to repeat on their own pitches against West Indies the success in a short rubber won seven years earlier. As a central figure in Somerset's stormy story at the end of 1986, the focus was very much on him last summer. It is history that he relished the implicit challenge by scoring 1,627 runs and topping the first-class averages with 67.79. It is also history that this popular young man had recommended himself to all when he previously played for Somerset in 1984. Long may he continue to do so!

Although **Dilip Vengsarkar** was overshadowed – as were all the others by Sunil Gavaskar's superb innings in the MCC Bicentenary Match at Lord's – his 1986-7 record marks him out without much argument as the premier Indian cricketer of the period. No one can dispute the scoring of 1,326 runs in 13 Tests at an average of 102, including six hundreds. Nor can anyone take away from his unique claim to three Test hundreds at Lord's, one in every Test played there. Following his 1986 126 not out, he earned even louder plaudits at Headingley when this tall, elegant young player clinched the rubber for India. On a pitch so difficult that no one else on either side could reach 40, he followed 61 in the first innings by taking out his bat for 102 in the second.

The names of **Imran Khan** and Pakistan have been synonymous in the summer of 1987, and the sensation would only have been if any other selection had been made. He has been not only a great natural all-rounder in his own right, but an inspirational leader – a virtue that not all Pakistani selectors have realized. It was his captaincy that lifted his side to the feat, hitherto unachieved, of success in the rubber against England, and he has preferred to go out of Test cricket at the top rather than struggle to live up to his own standards. It is good news that he will this summer assist Sussex in their one-day matches.

There remains a name largely unfamiliar here as the Sri Lankan nominee, **Brendon Kuruppu**, who wrote himself into the record books in no ordinary way at Colombo last April. When J.J. Crowe, New Zealand's new captain, invited the home side to bat, he discovered a tall young man coming in first in what was his first Test, although he had played in no fewer than 23 one-day internationals. Kuruppu took out his bat 777 playing minutes later for 201. It was the first Sri Lankan hundred on Test debut, the slowest double hundred in Test history, and incidentally third in Test length only behind Sir Leonard Hutton's and Hanif Mahommad's. He is a wicket-keeper also – clearly a man with a future.

1986-87

ENGLAND'S WINTER TOUR

England in Australia

For the cricket purists and others who care about the future of the greatest, grandest game of all, the now perennial, related topics of crowds and money overrode England's ecstasy and Australia's agony in the 1986-87 Ashes campaign. Consider this: 23 days of five Test matches, involving cricket's oldest rivals in supposedly the game's ultimate contest, attracted 334,417 spectators (an average of 14,540 a day), while 21 one-day internationals between England, Australia, the West Indies, and Pakistan drew 553,592 (26,362 a day). That's a staggering difference of 219,175. The 14 World Series Cup matches between England, Australia, and the West Indies had an aggregate crowd of 435,616 (31,115 a day). The seven Challenge Trophy matches between England, Australia, the West Indies, and Pakistan were attended by 117,976 spectators (16,854 a day).

One-day cricket has spawned a new breed of instant thrill-seekers, the majority of whom will be weaned on to the traditional game, according to Australian promoters. But crowd figures do not support their argument. The helter-skelter pace of the eighties and the all-seeing eye of television have drastically altered the attitudes of cricket's supporters and, indeed, sports fans everywhere. They are more selective about what they watch and, more importantly, what they will pay to watch. In Australia, many more of them are paying to watch the pyjama game instead of Test cricket and certainly Sheffield Shield cricket, at which you can just about count the number of spectators.

An Australian sporting columnist wrote recently: 'When you wake up to it – and a lot of the mob mentality is based on ignorance, so it can't last forever if you're even half-smart – the promises of limited-overs cricket make an empty and undeniable rattle.' And yet the sad fact remains that an England-Australia Test series, once cricket's showcase, has to be propped up financially, in Australia at least, by a bastardized version of the game. Australian cricket's promoters and programmers usually strive to get the five Tests out of the way, with rather indecent haste, in eight to nine weeks from early November to early January, before devoting most of the prime holiday month of January to a giddy, protracted procession of one-day internationals.

In the middle of this last Australian circus, Viv Richards, the West Indies captain, said he still enjoyed playing one-day cricket, but he thought there was 'too much' of it. 'Because of the continuity, you get a little bit tired playing all these games,' Richards said. 'After our short tour of Pakistan and now this, I'm really looking forward to going to New Zealand (the following month) because it will be a red ball again and you can start thinking properly again about playing some proper cricket. I think the one-day game is still the best salesman of cricket. We've all got to accept the fact that it's here to stay. But we've got to start thinking to ourselves: "Hey, are we playing a little too much one-day cricket?"' Indeed.

Mike Gatting's Englishmen certainly thought so. They had achieved their main mission – the retention of the Ashes – 11 weeks into their Australian tour, and still had to play one more Test and 14 one-day internationals over the remaining 6½ weeks. They lost the fifth Test by only 55 runs, but won 10 of their one-dayers to complete an unprecedented grand slam – the Ashes, the Challenge Trophy, and the World Series Cup. Sharing prize money of $A114,500 helped ease their exhaustion, caused more by regular travel than by too much cricket.

England deserved their hat-trick simply because they were the most professional and committed team of the four which shared the Australian summer. That England emerged so emphatically triumphant from all three competitions was a remarkable recovery for a side that had started their tour so unimpressively as to be given that now infamous 'can't bat, can't bowl, can't field' tag. Ian Botham's wonderful, belligerent century in the first Test at Brisbane knocked the stuffing out of the Australians, particularly as they felt Brisbane offered their best chance of winning one of the five Tests, as was subsequently reflected in Allan Border's angry, surly mood at his post-match Press conference.

The hard-fought draw at Perth, where the local hospitality again reigned supreme, and the dreary, Botham-less draw on a perfect pitch at Adelaide revived Australian hopes that the series wasn't over after all – except it suddenly was in three hectic days at Melbourne, where Gladstone Small took seven wickets, scored 21 not out, accepted the catch that clinched the Ashes and won the Player of the Match award – all in his first Test against Australia!

So Sydneysiders finally saw the Englishmen in the flesh for the first time on tour when the series had already been decided, and did they get their money's worth! – an unforgettable Test match and another Australian spin-inspired victory, with an over to spare, on the majestic Sydney Cricket Ground, where they had beaten Pakistan, the West Indies, and New Zealand in the previous three seasons. The enduring memory this time was Peter Taylor's Player of the Match debut – and the poignant scenes after the trophy presentation when he was hugged and kissed by his parents and sisters. All of them, 'Peter Who?' included, were crying. At the same place, 27 nights later, Gatting sipped champagne, eyed the just-won World Series Cup, and said with justifiable pride: 'It has been a 100 per cent professional effort. The lads did not let me down and I hope I didn't let them down.' He didn't, of course. Nor did his vice-captain John Emburey, team manager Peter Lush, cricket manager Micky Stewart, and physiotherapist Lawrie Brown, and the rest of a closely knit party, of which International Cricketer of the Year award-winner Chris Broad, a born-again batsman, and Graham Dilley, a born-again fast bowler, deserve special mentions for their consistent heroics.

From the Test series, the Australians sought consolation from Dean Jones's spectacular progress, Steve Waugh's exciting development, Geoff Marsh's courageous application, Border's being Border again, Bruce Reid's commendable accuracy, and, finally, the last-match-winning spin of Taylor and Peter Sleep. Border will take a wiser and tougher team to England in 1989.

First Test: Brisbane, 14, 15, 16, 18, 19 November.
England won by 7 wickets.

From their unpromising preliminaries, England advanced to better things almost from the start of the first Test. The very first stages showed no improvement, for Mike Gatting lost the toss and Australia, given a big advantage on recent form, put England in. At 15, Broad was out. But from the moment that Gatting came to the wicket, having promoted himself to No. 3, and took charge in a belligerent innings of 61, England were on top.

Athey batted through the four and a half hours' play possible that day and, at 198-2, the platform was in place for a healthy total. It looked wobbly next morning when Lamb and Athey were out without a run added, but Gower overcame a hazardous start and Botham, having laid a solid foundation, played one of his finest innings, 138 with 13 fours and four sixes, the highest and only the fourth Test hundred by an Englishman in Brisbane. On the second evening, England took Boon's wicket for 33 and next day Dilley took five wickets for the first time in his 23 Tests, forcing Australia to follow on 208 behind.

After the rest day, the pitch was rather slower and England had to work hard to take five wickets for 243. Geoff Marsh held one end all day, adding 108 not out to his first innings of 56. Next morning, however, Emburey and DeFreitas finished off the innings for only 39 runs and England needed only 75 to win.

Second Test: Perth, 28, 29, 30 November, 2, 3 December.
Match Drawn.

As if to confirm that their fortunes really had changed at last, England won the toss on a splendid pitch for batting and made 272 for two on the first day, with Broad 146 not out after an opening stand of 223 with Athey, 96. Next day both Gower and Richards made dashing hundreds, sharing in a sixth-wicket stand of 207, and Gatting was able to declare, leaving time for seven overs during which Boon was bowled by Dilley.

After three days, it was still not certain that Australia, 309-6, would reach the 393 needed to avoid the follow-on, an all-important landmark on this pitch which was unlikely to deteriorate. Waugh had played a fine innings of 71 and Border, given useful support by Ritchie and Matthews, was still there, 81 not out.

He continued after the rest day, avoiding the follow-on with his last partner, and England had to bat again leading by 191. Their efforts to press on quickly foundered against Waugh's accuracy. Gatting declared before the last day's play, 390 ahead, but despite the loss of Boon to the first ball of the innings, Australia batted comfortably through the day for a draw.

Third Test: Adelaide, 12, 13, 14, 15, 16 December.
Match Drawn.

England had to go into the third Test without the injured Botham, who was replaced by James Whitaker. This time they had no luck with the toss and spent the first day bowling as economically as they could on a blameless pitch.

Australia were kept to 207-2, one wicket each to Emurey and Edmonds, who bowled 53 overs between them for 80 runs. Boon made his fourth Test hundred, the only source of relief in what was to prove a disastrous series for him.

Next day Australia progressed quickly enough to declare at 514-5, all their batsmen making runs, but in the final eight overs no impression was made on Broad and Athey. On the third day, England went about their task at a great pace. An opening partnership of 112 was followed by a stand of 161 between Broad, who made 116, and Gatting, who reached a vigorous 100 off 140 balls.

At 273-2 England seemed poised to race up to Australia's score and beyond, but wickets were lost on the third evening, and next day their innings ended 59 short, leaving the match to peter out into an inevitable draw.

Fourth Test: Melbourne, 26, 27, 28 December.
England won by an innings and 14 runs.

The Melbourne Test was clearly going to be all-important for England because a finish seemed certain and they could not rely on the fifth Test in Sydney, where in previous years Australia had won isolated victories over both West Indies and New Zealand on turning pitches. Moreover, they had to take the field without the injured Dilley and with Botham not fit to bowl at full stretch.

Everything went right for England from the start. Gatting won the toss, put Australia in, and saw them bowled out for 141 in 54.4 overs, after which the batsmen finished off a perfect first day by reaching 95 for one in 31 overs. The pitch allowed movement off the seam, the Australian batting was often ill judged and the catches were held, nine of them. The wickets were shared equally between Small, who had replaced Dilley, and Botham.

Like many Melbourne pitches, this one was never entirely straightforward and England did not find the going easy next day, though Broad reached his third hundred in successive Tests. He and Gatting took the score past Australia's with only the one wicket down, but the middle order subsided swiftly, and England were grateful for the 60 runs added by Emburey, Edmonds, and Small for the last two wickets. On the third morning, Australia started their second innings – as at Brisbane, 208 behind – and by 20 minutes to five had been bowled out for 194. Having reached 153-3, they succumbed to the spin of Edmonds and Emburey. Once again England bowled and fielded very well.

Fifth Test: 10, 11, 12, 14, 15 January.
Australia won by 55 runs.

Far from being an anticlimax, the fifth Test, decided with only one over to spare, was voted a model of its kind, largely through the opportunity provided for the spinners by the curator. One of the Australia spinners, Peter Taylor, had played only six previous first-class matches, but he emerged with eight wickets and two useful innings as Man of the Match.

Winning the toss gave Australia an advantage, but with 236-7 on the first evening they were not obviously in command. However, Dean Jones, having had some luck early on, was still there, 119 not out, and next day he added another 107 runs with his last three partners. When England were 17-3 and still only 132-5 at the end of the second day, Australia were in a winning position.

But next day England's last four wickets produced 133 runs, most of them from Richards and Emburey, limiting the first innings deficit to 68, and after the rest day Emburey bowled them right back into the match. Once again Australia saved themselves, this time with an eighth-wicket stand of 98 between Waugh and Taylor. England were left to make 320, which seemed too much.

They were 29-1 overnight, and, at 102-5 just after lunch on the last day, seemed certain to be well beaten. On a worn pitch however, Gatting batted with great spirit, Richards supported him in a stand of 131, and in the second over of the final 20 England needed only 87 from five wickets. But after Gatting went, their effort petered out.

Australia v England 1986-87 1st Test

England won by 7 wickets
Played at Woolloongabba, Brisbane, 14, 15, 16, 18, 19 November
Toss: Australia. Umpires: A.R. Crafter and M.W. Johnson
Debuts: Australia – C.D. Matthews; England – P.A.J. DeFreitas, C.J. Richards

England

B.C. Broad	c Zoehrer b Reid	8	not out	35
C.W.J. Athey	c Zoehrer b C.D. Matthews	76	c Waugh b Hughes	1
M.W. Gatting*	b Hughes	61	c G.R.J. Matthews b Hughes	12
A.J. lamb	lbw b Hughes	40	lbw b Reid	9
D.I. Gower	c Ritchie b C.D. Matthews	51	not out	15
I.T. Botham	c Hughes b Walsh	138		
C.J. Richards†	b C.D. Matthews	0		
J.E. Emburey	c Waugh b Hughes	8		
P.A.J. DeFreitas	c C.D. Matthews b Waugh	40		
P.H. Edmonds	not out	9		
G.R. Dilley	c Boon b Waugh	0		
Extras	(B3, LB19, NB3)	25	(B2, NB3)	5
		456	(3 wkts)	**77**

Australia

G.R. Marsh	c Richards b Dilley	56	(2) b DeFreitas	110
D.C. Boon	c Broad b DeFreitas	10	(1) lbw b Botham	14
T.J. Zoehrer†	lbw b Dilley	38	(8) not out	16
D.M. Jones	lbw b DeFreitas	8	(3) st Richards b Emburey	18
A.R. Border*	c DeFreitas b Edmonds	7	(4) c Lamb b Emburey	23
G.M. Ritchie	c Edmonds b Dilley	41	(5) lbw b DeFreitas	45
G.R.J. Matthews	not out	56	(6) c & b Dilley	13
S.R. Waugh	c Richards b Dilley	0	(7) b Emburey	28
C.D. Matthews	c Gatting b Botham	11	lbw b Emburey	0
M.G. Hughes	b Botham	0	b DeFreitas	0
B.A. Reid	c Richards b Dilley	3	c Broad b Emburey	2
Extras	(B2, LB8, W2, NB6)	18	(B5, LB6, NB2)	13
		248		**282**

Australia	O	M	R	W	O	M	R	W
Reid	31	4	86	1	6	1	20	1
Hughes	36	7	134	3	5.3	0	28	2
Matthews, C.D.	35	10	95	3	4	0	11	0
Waugh	21	3	76	3				
Matthews, G.R.J.	11	2	43	0	7	1	16	0

England	O	M	R	W	O	M	R	W
DeFreitas	16	5	32	2	17	2	62	3
Dilley	25.4	7	68	5	19	6	47	1
Emburey	24	11	66	0	42.5	15	80	5
Edmonds	12	6	12	1	24	8	46	0
Botham	16	1	58	2	12	0	34	1
Gatting	1	0	2	0	2	0	2	0

Fall of Wickets

Wkt	E 1st	A 1st	A 2nd	E 2nd
1st	15	27	24	6
2nd	116	97	44	25
3rd	198	114	92	40
4th	198	126	205	–
5th	316	159	224	–
6th	324	198	262	–
7th	352	204	266	–
8th	443	239	266	–
9th	451	239	275	–
10th	456	248	282	–

Australia v England 1986-87 2nd Test

Match Drawn
Played at WACA Ground, Perth, 28, 29, 30 November, 2, 3 December
Toss: England. Umpires: R.A. French and P.J. McConnell
Debuts: nil

England

B.C. Broad	c Zoehrer b Reid	162		lbw b Waugh	16
C.W.J. Athey	b Reid	96		c Border b Reid	6
A.J. Lamb	c Zoehrer b Reid	0	(4)	lbw b Reid	2
M.W. Gatting*	c Waugh b C.D. Matthews	14	(3)	b Waugh	70
D.I. Gower	c Waugh b C.D. Matthews	136		c Zoehrer b Waugh	48
I.T. Botham	c Border b Reid	0		c G.R.J. Matthews b Reid	6
C.J. Richards†	c Waugh b C.D. Matthews	133		c Lawson b Waugh	15
P.A.J. DeFreitas	lbw b C.D. Matthews	11		b Waugh	15
J.E. Emburey	not out	5		not out	4
P.H. Edmonds	did not bat				
G.R. Dilley	"				
Extras	(B4, LB15, W3, NB13)	35		(B4, LB9, NB4)	17
	(8 wkts dec)	592		(8 wkts dec)	199

Australia

G.R. Marsh	c Broad b Botham	15	(2)	lbw b Emburey	0
D.C. Boon	b Dilley	2	(1)	c Botham b Dilley	49
S.R. Waugh	c Botham b Emburey	71			
D.M. Jones	c Athey b Edmonds	27	(3)	run out	69
A.R. Border*	c Richards b Dilley	125	(4)	c Lamb b Edmonds	16
G.M. Ritchie	c Botham b Edmonds	33	(5)	not out	24
G.R.J. Matthews	c Botham b Dilley	45	(6)	not out	14
T.J. Zoehrer	lbw b Dilley	29			
G.F. Lawson	b DeFreitas	13			
C.D. Matthews	c Broad b Emburey	10			
B.A. Reid	not out	2			
Extras	(B9, LB9, NB11)	29		(B9, LB6, NB10)	25
		401		(4 wkts)	197

Australia	O	M	R	W	O	M	R	W
Lawson	41	8	126	0	9	1	44	0
Matthews, C.D.	29.1	4	112	3	2	0	15	0
Reid	40	8	115	4	21	3	58	3
Waugh	24	4	90	0	21.3	4	69	5
Matthews, G.R.J.	34	3	124	1				
Border	2	0	6	0				

England	O	M	R	W	O	M	R	W
Botham	22	4	72	1	7.2	4	13	0
Dilley	24.4	4	79	4	15	1	53	1
Emburey	43	9	110	2	28	11	41	1
DeFreitas	24	4	67	1	13.4	2	47	0
Edmonds	21	4	55	2	27	13	25	1
Gatting					5	3	3	0
Lamb					1	1	0	0

Fall of Wickets

Wkt	E 1st	A 1st	E 2nd	A 2nd
1st	223	4	8	0
2nd	227	64	47	126
3rd	275	114	50	142
4th	333	128	123	152
5th	339	198	140	–
6th	546	279	172	–
7th	585	334	190	–
8th	592	360	199	–
9th	–	385	–	–
10th	–	401	–	–

Australia v England 1986-87 3rd Test

Match Drawn
Played at Adelaide Oval, 12, 13, 14, 15, 16 December
Toss: Australia. Umpires: A.R. Crafter and S.G. Randell
Debuts: Australia – G.C. Dyer; England – J.J. Whitaker

Australia

G.R. Marsh	b Edmonds	43	(2) c & b Edmonds		41
D.C. Boon	c Whitaker b Emburey	103	(1) lbw DeFreitas		0
D.M. Jones	c Richards b Dilley	93	c & b Dilley		2
A.R. Border*	c Richards b Edmonds	70	not out		100
G.M. Ritchie	c Broad b DeFreitas	36	not out		46
G.R.J. Matthews	not out	73			
S.R. Waugh	not out	79			
G.C. Dyer†	did not bat				
B.A. Reid	"				
M.G. Hughes	"				
P.R. Sleep	"				
Extras	(LB2, NB15)	17	(B4, LB6, NB2)		12
	(5 wkts dec)	**514**	(3 wkts dec)		**201**

England

B.C. Broad	c Marsh b Waugh	116	not out		15
C.W.J. Athey	b Sleep	55	c Dyer b Hughes		12
M.W. Gatting*	c Waugh b Sleep	100	b Matthews		0
A.J. Lamb	c Matthews b Hughes	14	not out		9
D.I. Gower	lbw Reid	38			
J.E. Emburey	c Dyer b Reid	49			
J.J. Whitaker	c Matthews b Reid	11			
C.J. Richards†	c Jones b Sleep	29			
P.A.J. DeFreitas	not out	4			
P.H. Edmonds	c Border b Sleep	13			
G.R. Dilley	b Reid	0			
Extras	(B4, LB14, W4, NB4)	16	(B2, LB1)		3
		455	(2 wkts)		**39**

England	O	M	R	W	O	M	R	W
Dilley	32	3	111	1	21	8	38	1
DeFreitas	32	4	128	1	16	5	36	1
Emburey	46	11	117	1	22	6	50	0
Edmonds	52	14	134	2	29	7	63	1
Gatting	9	1	22	0	2	1	4	0

Australia	O	M	R	W	O	M	R	W
Hughes	30	8	82	1	7	2	16	1
Reid	28.4	8	64	4				
Sleep	47	14	132	4	5	5	0	0
Matthews	23	1	102	0	8	4	10	1
Border	1	0	1	0				
Waugh	19	4	56	1	3	1	10	0

Fall of Wickets

Wkt	A 1st	E 1st	A 2nd	E 2nd
1st	113	112	1	21
2nd	185	273	8	22
3rd	311	283	77	–
4th	333	341	–	–
5th	368	341	–	–
6th	–	361	–	–
7th	–	422	–	–
8th	–	439	–	–
9th	–	454	–	–
10th	–	455	–	–

Australia v England 1986-87 4th Test

England won by an innings and 14 runs
Played at Melbourne Cricket Ground, 26, 27, 28 December
Toss: England. Umpires: A.R. Crafter and R.A. French
Debuts: nil

Australia

G.R. Marsh	c Richards b Botham	17	(2) run out		60
D.C. Boon	c Botham b Small	7	(1) c Gatting b Small		8
D.M. Jones	c Gower b Small	59	c Gatting b DeFreitas		21
A.R. Border*	c Richards b Botham	15	c Emburey b Small		34
S.R. Waugh	c Botham b Small	10	b Edmonds		49
G.R.J. Matthews	c Botham b Small	14	b Emburey		0
P.R. Sleep	c Richards b Small	0	run out		6
T.J. Zoehrer†	b Botham	5	c Athey b Edmonds		1
C.J. McDermott	c Richards b Botham	0	b Emburey		1
M.G. Hughes	c Richards b Botham	2	c Small b Edmonds		8
B.A. Reid	not out	2	not out		0
Extras	(B1, LB1, W1, NB7)	10	(LB3, W1, NB2)		6
		141			**194**

England

B.C. Broad	c Zoehrer b Hughes	112
C.W.J. Athey	lbw b Reid	21
M.W. Gatting*	c Hughes b Reid	40
A.J. Lamb	c Zoehrer b Reid	43
D.I. Gower	c Matthews b Sleep	7
I.T. Botham	c Zoehrer b McDermott	29
C.J. Richards†	c Marsh b Reid	3
P.A.J. DeFreitas	c Matthews b McDermott	7
J.E. Emburey	c & b McDermott	22
P.H. Edmonds	lbw b McDermott	19
G.C. Small	not out	21
Extras	(B6, LB7, W1, NB11)	25
		349

England	O	M	R	W	O	M	R	W
Small	22.4	7	48	5	15	3	40	2
DeFreitas	11	1	30	0	12	1	44	1
Emburey	4	0	16	0	20	5	43	2
Botham	16	4	41	5	7	1	19	0
Gatting	1	0	4	0				
Edmonds					19.4	5	45	3

Australia	O	M	R	W	O	M	R	W
McDermott	26.5	4	83	4				
Hughes	30	3	94	1				
Reid	28	5	78	4				
Waugh	8	4	16	0				
Sleep	28	4	65	1				

Fall of Wickets

Wkt	A 1st	E 1st	A 2nd
1st	16	58	13
2nd	44	163	48
3rd	80	198	113
4th	108	219	153
5th	118	251	153
6th	118	273	175
7th	129	277	180
8th	133	289	185
9th	137	319	189
10th	141	349	194

Australia v England 1986-87 5th Test

Australia won by 55 runs
Played at Sydney Cricket Ground, 10, 11, 12, 14, 15 January
Toss: Australia. Umpires: P.J. McConnell and S.G. Randell
Debuts: Australia – P.L. Taylor

Australia

Batsman	1st innings		2nd innings	
G.R. Marsh	c Gatting b Small	24	(2) c Emburey b Dilley	14
G.M. Ritchie	lbw b Dilley	6	(1) c Botham b Edmonds	13
D.M. Jones	not out	184	c Richards b Emburey	30
A.R. Border*	c Botham b Edmonds	34	b Edmonds	49
D.McD. Wellham	c Richards b Small	17	c Lamb b Emburey	1
S.R. Waugh	c Richards b Small	0	c Athey b Emburey	73
P.R. Sleep	c Richards b Small	9	c Lamb b Emburey	10
T.J. Zoehrer†	c Gatting b Small	12	lbw b Emburey	1
P.L. Taylor	c Emburey b Edmonds	11	c Lamb b Emburey	42
M.G. Hughes	c Botham b Edmonds	16	b Emburey	5
B.A. Reid	b Dilley	4	not out	1
Extras	(B12, LB4, W2, NB8)	26	(B5, LB7)	12
		343		**251**

England

Batsman	1st innings		2nd innings	
B.C. Broad	lbw b Hughes	6	c & b Sleep	17
C.W.J. Athey	c Zoehrer b Hughes	5	b Sleep	31
M.W. Gatting*	lbw b Reid	0	(5) c & b Waugh	96
A.J. Lamb	c Zoehrer b Taylor	24	c Waugh b Taylor	3
D.I. Gower	c Wellham b Taylor	72	(3) c Marsh b Border	37
I.T. Botham	c Marsh b Taylor	16	c Wellham b Taylor	0
C.J. Richards†	c Wellham b Reid	46	b Sleep	38
J.E. Emburey	b Taylor	69	b Sleep	22
P.H. Edmonds	c Marsh b Taylor	3	lbw b Sleep	0
G.C. Small	b Taylor	4	c Border b Reid	0
G.R. Dilley	not out	4	not out	2
Extras	(B9, LB3, W2, NB2)	16	(B8, LB6, W1, NB3)	18
		275		**264**

England	O	M	R	W	O	M	R	W
Dilley	23.5	5	67	2	15	4	48	1
Small	33	11	75	5	8	2	17	0
Botham	23	10	42	0	3	0	17	0
Emburey	30	4	62	0	46	15	78	7
Edmonds	34	5	79	3	43	16	79	2
Border	1	0	2	0	2	2	0	0

Australia	O	M	R	W	O	M	R	W
Hughes	16	3	58	2	12	3	32	0
Reid	25	7	74	2	19	8	32	1
Waugh	6	4	6	0	6	2	13	1
Taylor	26	7	78	6	29	10	76	2
Sleep	21	6	47	0	35	14	72	5
Border					13	6	25	1

Fall of Wickets

Wkt	A 1st	E 1st	A 2nd	E 2nd
1st	8	16	29	24
2nd	58	17	31	91
3rd	149	17	106	91
4th	184	89	110	102
5th	184	119	115	102
6th	200	142	141	233
7th	232	213	145	257
8th	271	219	243	257
9th	338	270	248	262
10th	343	275	251	264

Test Match Averages: Australia v England 1986-87

Australia

Batting and Fielding	M	I	NO	HS	R	Avge	100	50	Ct/St
D.M. Jones	5	10	1	184*	511	56.77	1	3	1
G.R.J. Matthews	4	7	3	73*	215	53.75	–	2	6
A.R. Border	5	10	1	125	473	52.55	2	1	4
S.R. Waugh	5	8	1	79*	310	44.28	–	3	8
G.R. Marsh	5	10	0	110	429	42.90	1	2	5
G.M. Ritchie	4	8	2	46*	244	40.66	–	–	1
D.C. Boon	4	8	0	103	144	18.00	1	–	1
T.J. Zoehrer	4	7	1	38	102	17.00	–	–	10
C.D. Matthews	2	3	0	11	21	7.00	–	–	1
P.R. Sleep	3	4	0	10	25	6.25	–	–	1
M.G. Hughes	4	6	0	16	31	5.16	–	–	2
B.A. Reid	5	7	4	4	14	4.66	–	–	–

Also batted: G.F. Lawson (1 match) 13, 1ct; C.J. McDermott (1 match) 0, 1, 1ct; P.L. Taylor (1 match) 11, 42; D.McD. Wellham (1 match) 7, 1, 3ct. G.C. Dyer (2ct) played in one match but did not bat.

Bowling	O	M	R	W	Avge	Best	5wI	10wM
P.L. Taylor	55	17	154	8	19.25	6-78	1	–
B.A. Reid	198.4	44	527	20	26.35	4-64	–	–
P.R. Sleep	136	43	316	10	31.60	5-72	1	–
S.R. Waugh	108.3	26	336	10	33.60	5-69	1	–
C.D. Matthews	70.1	14	233	6	38.83	3-95	–	–
M.G. Hughes	136.3	26	444	10	44.40	3-134	–	–

Also bowled: A.R. Border 16-6-32-1; G.F. Lawson 50-9-170-0; C.J. McDermott 26.5-4-83-4; G.R.J. Matthews 83-11-295-2.

England

Batting and Fielding	M	I	NO	HS	R	Avge	100	50	Ct/St
B.C. Broad	5	9	2	162	487	69.57	3	–	5
D.I. Gower	5	8	1	136	404	57.71	1	2	1
M.W. Gatting	5	9	0	100	393	43.66	1	3	5
C.J. Richards	5	7	0	133	264	37.71	1	–	15/1
J.E. Emburey	5	7	2	69	179	35.80	–	1	3
C.W.J. Athey	5	9	0	96	303	33.66	–	3	3
I.T. Botham	4	6	0	138	180	31.50	1	–	10
P.A.J. DeFreitas	4	5	1	40	77	19.25	–	–	1
A.J. Lamb	5	9	1	43	144	18.00	–	–	6
G.C. Small	2	3	1	21*	35	17.50	–	–	1
P.H. Edmonds	5	5	1	19	44	11.00	–	–	2
G.R. Dilley	4	4	2	4*	6	3.00	–	–	1

Also batted: J.J. Whitaker (1 match) 11, 1ct.

Bowling	O	M	R	W	Avge	Best	5wI	10wM
G.C. Small	78.4	23	180	12	15.00	5-48	2	–
G.R. Dilley	176.1	38	511	16	31.93	5-68	1	–
I.T. Botham	106.2	24	296	9	32.88	5-41	1	–
P.H. Edmonds	261.4	78	538	15	35.86	3-45	–	–
J.E. Emburey	315.5	86	663	18	36.83	7-78	2	–
P.A.J. DeFreitas	141.4	24	446	9	49.55	3-62	–	–

Also bowled: M.W. Gatting 23-7-39-0; A.J. Lamb 1-1-0-0.

Statistical Highlights of the Tests

1st Test, Brisbane. England ended a run of 11 Tests without a win (8 defeats and 2 draws). Botham's 138, his 14th Test 100 and 4th against Australia (passed 1,500 runs against them), included 22 in one over from Highes (2,2,6,4,4,4) and was highest by England batsman at Brisbane. Dilley's 5-68 was his first 5-wicket haul in a Test innings. Australia forced to follow on for 27th time against England. Marsh made his 3rd Test 100. Emburey's 5-80 was his 5th in Tests and included his 100th wicket (38th Test).

2nd Test, Perth. England's 592-8 dec was their highest score in Perth. Broad's 162 was his 1st 100 (7th Test) and highest by England batsman at Perth, and 223 partnership with Athey the best for any wicket by England at Perth. Gower scored his 14th Test 100, 6th against Australia. Richards's 133 was his first Test 100, his highest first-class score, and his 207 partnership with Gower was a 6th-wicket record for England in Australia. Border's 125 was his 20th Test 100, his 6th against England, and the 200th for Australia against England. He also passed 2,000 runs (101) against England. Waugh took his 1st 5-wicket haul. Botham caught Boon off the 1st ball of the last day to register his 100th Test catch. The 126 partnership between Marsh and Jones was a record for the 2nd wicket for Australia against England at Perth.

3rd Test, Adelaide. Only the 4th draw in 24 Australia-England Tests at Adelaide. Boon made his 4th Test 100, his 1st against England. The Matthews/ Waugh unbeaten 146 partnership was a record for the 6th wicket for Australia against England at Adelaide. Gatting scored his 7th Test 100, his 3rd against Australia and the 1st by an England captain at Adelaide. Border made his 21st Test 100 (equals Harvey), his 7th against England. Only the 19th time both captains scored 100 in a Test, 5th in Ashes.

4th Test, Melbourne. England retained the Ashes, just 61 balls being bowled after tea on the 3rd day. 5-wicket hauls for Small (1st) and Botham (27th, 9th v Australia), who took his 50th catch against Australia. Richards took 5 catches in innings to equal England record against Australia (Parks, Taylor). Broad's 3rd 100 in successive Tests – 4th England player to do so against Australia after Hobbs, Hammond, and Woolmer. McDermott took 50th wicket in 17th Test. Gatting was the 3rd England captain to retain the Ashes in Australia (Hutton 1954-55, Brearley 1978-79).

5th Test, Sydney. Australia won with 1 over to spare, ending a run of 14 Tests without a win (4 lost, 9 drawn, 1 tied). Jones's 184 not out was his 2nd Test 100. Small achieved his 2nd 5-wicket haul, Taylor his 1st (6-78) in his debut Test, with his best first-class bowling in only his 7th first-class match! Emburey's 7-78 was his best Test analysis and his 6th 5-wicket tally. The Gatting/Richards 131 partnership was the best for the 6th wicket by England at Sydney. Sleep took his 1st 5-wicket haul. Border ended the series with 6,917 Test runs, the 3rd Australian after Greg Chappell (7,110) and Bradman (6,996).

England Tour of Australia 1986-87

First-Class Matches: Played 11; Won 5, Lost 3, Drawn 3
All Matches: Played 25; Won 15, Lost 7, Drawn 3

First-Class Averages

Batting and Fielding	M	I	NO	HS	R	Avge	100	50	Ct/St
N.A. Foster	4	6	2	74*	172	43.00	–	1	4
B.C. Broad	10	18	2	162	679	42.43	3	1	7
I.T. Botham	8	14	2	138	481	40.08	1	2	11
B.N. French	3	5	2	58	113	37.66	–	1	9/1
D.I. Gower	9	16	2	136	508	36.28	1	2	4
A.J. Lamb	10	18	1	105	534	31.41	1	3	11
J.J. Whitaker	5	7	0	108	214	30.57	1	–	2
M.W. Gatting	10	18	0	100	520	28.88	1	3	11
C.W.J. Athey	9	16	1	96	422	28.13	–	4	7
C.J. Richards	9	14	1	133	335	25.76	1	–	26/3
J.E. Emburey	9	14	3	69	279	25.36	–	1	6
W.N. Slack	5	9	0	89	184	20.44	–	1	5
P.A.J. DeFreitas	7	10	2	40	130	16.25	–	–	1
G.R. Dilley	6	6	3	32	39	13.00	–	–	1
G.C. Small	8	11	3	26	100	12.50	–	–	4
P.H. Edmonds	9	10	2	27	95	11.87	–	–	7

Bowling	O	M	R	W	Avge	Best	5wI	10wM
G.C. Small	258.4	72	626	33	18.96	5-48	3	–
M.W. Gatting	92	27	195	9	21.66	4-31	–	–
N.A. Foster	149	40	352	16	22.00	4-20	–	–
I.T. Botham	182.1	41	496	18	27.55	5-41	1	–
G.R. Dilley	231.1	44	685	21	32.61	5-68	1	–
J.E. Emburey	463.5	131	1023	31	33.00	7-78	3	–
P.A.J. DeFreitas	239	43	754	22	34.27	4-44	–	–
P.H. Edmonds	428.4	122	929	25	37.16	3-37	–	–

Also bowled: C.W.J. Athey 4-0-25-0; A.J. Lamb 1-1-0-0.

Perth Challenge

Ten days after having retained the Ashes at Melbourne, England added another jewel to their illustrious 1986-87 crown by winning the four-nation $A61,000 Benson & Hedges Challenge at Perth's handsomely refurbished WACA Ground. Unbeaten in their three qualifying matches, England defeated Pakistan by five wickets with 9.5 overs to spare in an anticlimactical final of the seven-match tournament, staged over nine days as cricket's contribution to the America's Cup Festival of Sport.

The Englishmen shared $A30,500 – $A9,000 from their first three victories, $A1,500 from three Man of the Match awards (Ian Botham, Graham Dilley, and Chris Broad) and $A20,000 from the final. The Pakistanis received $19,000, including $A10,000 from the final. Moreover, Pakistani batsman Javed Miandad won the Challenge Champion award – an 18-ct gold watch valued at $A15,000. He scored 53 against the West Indies, 7 against Australia, and 59 and 77 not out against England. The West Indians gained $A6,500 and the Australians took just $A5,000.

Ultimately, and this was indicative of their season's triumphs, England could point to an even team performance, in which every player contributed at some stage. The most startling feat was Botham's thunderous 68 off 39 balls against Australia. He hit seven fours and three sixes, and smashed 26 (4, 4, 2, 4, 6, 6) off an over from medium-pacer Simon Davis, watched by a WACA Ground record crowd of 27,125. Four of the matches (but not the final) were day/night fixtures, played under brilliant new floodlights. But one wonders about the future of televised night sport in Perth when, with Western Australia not on daylight saving time, 9.30 p.m. in Perth is 12.30 a.m. in Sydney and Melbourne and midnight in Adelaide.

Pakistan were involved in the two most thrilling matches, beating Australia by one wicket with only one ball to spare after recovering from 96 for five to 274 for nine, and losing to England by three wickets with two balls to spare in the last qualifying match, before which both teams had already qualified for the final. Winless Australia had to seek solace in Dean Jones's centuries on successive days against England and Pakistan and Steve Waugh's fine all-round effort against Pakistan – 82 and four wickets.

The biggest surprise was the early sluggishness of the West Indians, who had returned home to the Caribbean for a brief holiday after their arduous tour of Pakistan, and who lost to Pakistan by 34 runs in the opening match and to England by 19 runs in the fourth match. The West Indies thrashed Australia by 164 runs in the fifth match – and, only 11 days later, Australia beat England by 55 runs in the fifth Test at Sydney.

The West Indies fast bowlers believed they were unfairly restricted by one of the playing conditions for this series (and for the World Series Cup competition) – 'If the ball passes or would have passed above the shoulder height of the striker standing in his normal batting stance at the crease, either umpire shall call and signal "no ball" '. Asked by Tony Cozier if he thought age was beginning to catch up on his team, Viv Richards, the West Indies captain, said: 'Given some time to get match fit, these guys can play as well as they ever have. The way we move has a lot to do with it. You look at a West Indian who's 35 or 36 and he will move so much better than an Australian or an Englishman who is the same age.'

30 December. PAKISTAN beat WEST INDIES by 34 runs. Toss: West Indies. Pakistan 199-8 (50 overs) (Javed Miandad 53, Ramiz Raja 42; A.H. Gray 4-45). West Indies 165 (46.2 overs). Award: Mudassar Nazar (10-0-36-3).

1 January. ENGLAND beat AUSTRALIA by 37 runs. Toss: England. England 272-6 (49 overs) (B.C. Broad 76, I.T. Botham 68, A.J. Lamb 66). Australia 235 (48.2 overs) (D.M. Jones 104). Award: I.T. Botham (68, 10-0-52-1, and 1ct).

2 January. PAKISTAN beat AUSTRALIA by 1 wicket. Toss: Australia. Australia 273-6 (50 overs) (D.M. Jones 121, S.R. Waugh 82). Pakistan 274-9 (49.5 overs) (Qasim Omar 67, Asif Mujtaba 60*, Manzoor Elahi 48); Waugh 4-48. Award: D.M. Jones (121).

3 January. ENGLAND beat WEST INDIES by 19 runs. Toss: West Indies. England 228-9 (50 overs) (A.J. Lamb 71, C.J. Richards 50; J. Garner 5-47). West Indies 209 (48.2 overs) (A.L. Logie 51, I.V.A. Richards 45; G.R. Dilley 4-46). Award: G.R. Dilley (10-0-46-4).

4 January. WEST INDIES beat AUSTRALIA by 164 runs. Toss: Australia. West Indies 255-8 (50 overs) (C.G. Greenidge 100, M.A. Holding 53*; S.P. O'Donnell 4-65). Australia 91 (35.4 overs). Award: C.G. Greenidge (100 and 1ct).

5 January. ENGLAND beat PAKISTAN by 3 wickets. Toss: Pakistan. Pakistan 229-5 (50 overs) (Shoaib Mohammad 66, Javed Miandad 59). England 232-7 (49.4 overs) (B.C. Broad 97, C.W.J. Athey 42). Award: B.C. Broad (97).

Qualifying Table	P	W	L	Points
ENGLAND	3	3	0	6
PAKISTAN	3	2	1	4
West Indies	3	1	2	2
Australia	3	0	3	0

Final
7 January. ENGLAND beat PAKISTAN by 5 wickets. Toss: England. Pakistan 166-9 (50 overs) (Javed Miandad 77*). England 167-5 (40.1 overs) (M.W. Gatting 49, A.J. Lamb 47). Player of the Final: Javed Miandad (77*).

Benson & Hedges World Series Cup

Professionals to the end, England's battle-weary cricketers completed a unique treble when they won the Benson & Hedges World Series Cup for the first time. Successive victories over Australia, by six wickets with eight overs to spare at Melbourne and by eight runs at Sydney, in the scheduled best-of-three finals enabled the Englishmen to collect $A54,000 of the $A110,000 prize money available for the limited-overs competition, which comprised 14 matches at five venues in 26 days immediately after England had won the Challenge Trophy at Perth and had retained the Ashes. The Australians shared $A38,500, plus a $A12,000 bonus for qualifying for the finals, and the West Indians, winners of the cup at their four previous attempts, had to be content with $A17,500.

Ian Botham stamped the seal on England's all-round superiority, and was a deserved winner of the $A2,000 Player of the Finals award, with two match-winning performances – a brutal 71, with 11 fours and a six, off 52 balls as an opening batsman in the first final, and 25 and 3-26 off 10 overs (three of Australia's first four wickets) in the second final.

In their 10 matches, England could boast of four productive batsmen – openers Chris Broad and Bill Athey, Allan Lamb, and Botham – and three generally immaculate bowlers – openers Graham Dilley and Phillip DeFreitas and off-spinner John Emburey – backed by Botham's energetic medium-pacers and some often-brilliant fielding, particularly catching. In the fourth match, at Sydney, Lamb, who had endured a frustrating run in the Tests, produced one of the individual highlights of the summer by belting 18 (2, 4, 6, 2, 4) off the last over (from giant left-armer Bruce Reid) to propel England to an unlikely three-wicket win over Australia with just one ball to spare.

The Australians, who line-up usually was not as balanced or as potent as it could have been, because of selectors' whims, were well served by their key Test batsmen – Dean Jones, Geoff Marsh, and Allan Border – and they took heart from the significant all-round offerings of Steve Waugh and Simon O'Donnell and the off-spin bowling of Greg Matthews (who took some sensational return catches) and Peter Taylor.

The West Indians fielded with their customary magic, but their batting, without injured opener Gordon Greenidge, proved surprisingly vulnerable and their fast bowlers struggled to come to terms with the 'no-bouncer' law; one that prompted their captain, Viv Richards, to accuse administrators of waging 'a particular vendetta to cripple the West Indian style of cricket'.

Richards's winning of the Player of the Series award (six gold goblets and a gold tray) annoyed and bemused the Australian and English players. Border, the Australian captain, said: 'The voting's an absolute farce. I don't blame it on anyone in particular, but every time Viv turns up he wins something – and most of the time he doesn't deserve it.' England skipper Mike Gatting said: 'Perhaps it might be political, I don't know. Perhaps they want the West Indies to come back again.'

Richards polled 37 votes to win from three Australians – Waugh (34), Jones (28), and O'Donnell (21). Five Channel 9 commentators cast votes on a 3-2-1 basis in each of the 12 qualifying matches. Richards scored 266 runs (avge 38) – 0, 43, 69, 70, 58, 1 and 25 – and took 5-100 off 28.3 overs of off-spin.

Qualifying Rounds

17 January at Woolloongabba, Brisbane. ENGLAND beat WEST INDIES by 6 wickets. Toss: England. West Indies 154 (46.3 overs) (D.L. Haynes 48, A.L. Logie 46, G.R. Dilley 8.3-1-23-4). England 156-4 (43.1 overs) (B.C. Broad 49, D.I. Gower 42). Award: G.R. Dilley (8.3-1-23-4).

18 January at Woolloongabba, Brisbane. AUSTRALIA beat ENGLAND by 11 runs. Toss: Australia. Australia 261-4 (50 overs) (D.M. Jones 101, G.R. Marsh 93). England 250-9 (50 overs) (C.W.J. Athey 111). Award: D.M. Jones (101).

20 January at Melbourne Cricket Ground (floodlit). WEST INDIES beat AUSTRALIA by 7 wickets. Toss: West Indies. Australia 181-6 (50 overs) (A.R. Border 64*, S.P. O'Donnell 52). West Indies 182-3 (48.2 overs) (D.L. Haynes 67, A.L. Logie 44*). Award: D.L. Haynes (67).

22 January at Sydney Cricket Ground (floodlit). ENGLAND beat AUSTRALIA by 3 wickets. Toss: Australia. Australia 233-8 (50 overs) (D.M. Wellham 97, G.R. Marsh 47). England 234-7 (49.5 overs) (A.J. Lamb 77*, D.I. Gower 50, B.C. Broad 45). Award: A.J. Lamb (77*).

24 January at Adelaide Oval. ENGLAND beat WEST INDIES by 89 runs. Toss: West Indies. England 252-6 (50 overs) (C.W.J. Athey 64, B.C. Broad 55). West Indies 163 (45.5 overs) A.L. Logie 43), I.V.A. Richards 43, J.E. Emburey 10-0-37-4). Award: B.C. Broad (55 and 1 ct).

25 January at Adelaide Oval. WEST INDIES beat AUSTRALIA by 16 runs. Toss: Australia. West Indies 237-5 (50 overs) (R.B. Richardson 72, I.V.A. Richards 69, H.A. Gomes 43). Australia 221-9 (50 overs) (G.R. Marsh 94, D.M. Jones 40). Award: G.R. Marsh (94).

26 January at Adelaide Oval. AUSTRALIA beat ENGLAND by 33 runs. Toss: Australia. Australia 225-6 (50 overs) (A.R. Border 91, S.R. Waugh 83*, P.A.J. DeFreitas 10-1-35-4). England 192 (48.1 overs) (B.C. Broad 46, M.W. Gatting 46). Award: S.R. Waugh (83*, 10-1-30-2 and 1ct).

28 January at Sydney Cricket Ground (floodlit). AUSTRALIA beat WEST INDIES by 36 runs. Toss: Australia. Australia 194 (50 overs). West Indies 158 (46.1 overs) (I.V.A. Richards 70; S.P. O'Donnell 10-2-19-4). Award: S.P. O'Donnell (6, 10-2-19-4 and 1ct).

30 January at Melbourne Cricket Ground (floodlit). WEST INDIES beat ENGLAND by 6 wickets. Toss: England. England 147 (48.2 overs). West Indies 148-4 (48.3 overs) (I.V.A. Richards 58). Award: I.V.A. Richards (6.3-1-16-0 and 58).

1 February at Melbourne Cricket Ground. AUSTRALIA beat ENGLAND by 109 runs. Toss: England. Australia 248-5 (50 overs) (D.M. Jones 93, S.R. Waugh 49*, A.R. Border 45). England 139 (47.3 overs) (I.T. Botham 45). Award: S.R. Waugh (49* and 10-0-26-3).

3 February at Devonport. ENGLAND beat WEST INDIES by 29 runs. Toss: West Indies. England 177-9 (50 overs) (B.C. Broad 76). West Indies 148 (48 overs). Award: B.C. Broad (76).

6 February at Sydney Cricket Ground (floodlit). AUSTRALIA beat WEST INDIES by 2 wickets. Toss: West Indies. West Indies 192 (49 overs) (T.R.O. Payne 60). Australia 195-8 (49.1 overs) (T.J. Zoehrer 50). Award: T.J. Zoehrer (50 and 1ct).

Qualifying Table	P	W	L	Points
AUSTRALIA	8	5	3	10
ENGLAND	8	4	4	8
West Indies	8	3	5	6

Final Round Results

8 February at Melbourne Cricket Ground. ENGLAND beat AUSTRALIA by 6 wickets in a match reduced by bad light to 44 overs. Toss: England. Australia 171-8 (44 overs) (D.M. Jones 67, A.R. Border 42). England 172-4 (36 overs) (I.T. Botham 71, D.I. Gower 45).

11 February at Sydney Cricket Ground (floodlit). ENGLAND beat AUSTRALIA by 8 runs. Toss: England. England 187-9 (50 overs) (B.C. Broad 53). Australia 179-8 (50 overs) (S.P. O'Donnell 40*).
Player of the Finals award: I.T. Botham.

Leading Averages (Qual: 8 innings or 10 wkts)

Batting and Fielding	M	I	NO	HS	R	Avge	100	50	Ct
D.M. Jones (A)	10	10	0	101	396	39.60	1	2	3
B.C. Broad (E)	10	10	0	76	386	38.60	–	3	2
I.V.A. Richards (WI)	8	7	0	70	266	38.00	–	3	3
A.R. Border (A)	10	10	1	·91	321	35.66	–	2	4
G.R. Marsh (A)	10	10	–	94	354	35.40	–	2	2
S.R. Waugh (A)	10	10	3	83*	245	35.00	–	1	3
A.J. Lamb (E)	10	10	3	77*	243	34.71	–	1	4
A.L. Logie (WI)	8	8	2	46	199	33.16	–	–	2
S.P. O'Donnell (A)	10	9	4	52	144	28.80	–	1	4
I.T. Botham (E)	10	10	1	71	252	28.00	–	1	1

Bowling	O	M	R	W	Avge	Best	5wI
M.D. Marshall (WI)	62.2	9	214	13	16.46	3-30	–
G.R. Dilley (E)	64.3	10	217	13	16.69	4-23	–
P.A.J. DeFreitas (E)	92.5	12	292	17	17.17	4-35	–
G.R.J. Matthews (A)	91.1	8	313	14	22.35	3-27	–
S.R. Waugh (A)	85	4	345	15	23.00	3-26	–
S.P. O'Donnell (A)	84	6	346	14	24.71	4-19	–
J.E. Emburey (E)	90.3	3	407	16	25.43	4-37	–
C.A. Walsh (WI)	72.1	7	261	10	26.10	3-46	–
P.L. Taylor	82.1	4	337	12	28.08	3-29	–
R.A. Harper (WI)	79	1	300	10	30.00	3-49	–

1986-87

OVERSEAS CRICKET

India v Australia

The pulsating finish in a tie of the First Test – only the second tied Test in history – proved a false dawn to the three-match series, which petered out in anticlimax. The second Test was almost totally washed out and the third quickly assumed the look of an inevitable draw. It was the third consecutive rubber between the two countries to end inconclusively.

But for a brave challenge issued by Allan Border, asking India to make 348 in 87 overs, the first Test in Madras would also have had a drab finish, although, it must be said, it did not follow an unexciting course like its successors.

On a pitch much slower than is usually produced at Chepauk, Australia amassed their highest ever total in India. It included centuries by Boon and Border and a double century by Dean Jones, who, during much of his innings, suffered from heat exhaustion and frequently vomitted. Yet, he batted with facility and hit the ball with violent power. He spent that night in hospital and was restored with a saline drip.

Despite the blandness of the pitch and lack of fire in the bowling, the strong Indian batting faltered under the pressure of Australia's gigantic score. Not a few mistakes were brought about by errors of judgement and grave indiscretions. But they were saved from the follow-on by the depth to their batting and, principally, by a century of astonishing brilliance by the captain, Kapil Dev.

The Australians, leading by 177 runs, began their second innings shortly after lunch on the fourth day, and from 49 overs before the close scored 170-5. The ball was still turning only very slowly, but the bounce had become irregular enough to encourage the Australians to strike out for victory, which they did with a bold declaration.

Poor run-chasers in bygone days, India now possessed the expertise and the temperament to take up the challenge. Nor were they under-mined when one of their most lethal guns, Srikkanth, was stilled quite early. A superb innings of 90 by Gavaskar kept them in ballast and in range of their target.

At tea, India looked almost certain winners, needing 155 from 30 overs, with eight wickets standing – including Gavaskar's. That gap was narrowed to 118 at the start of the last hour and only one more casualty was suffered. Then wickets started to fall, the most crucial being Kapil Dev's, for only one.

But the Indians were not deterred. Shastri, who remained unbeaten with 48, headed the final charge against sprited bowling by the two spinners, Matthews and Bright, who took five wickets apiece. A stage was reached when brash slogging was no more required. Yet, the tail-enders rather lost their heads and the last man, Maninder Singh, joined Shastri with four runs required. Shastri made it his first priority to level the scores, which he did off the third ball of the final over. Maninder Singh survived one ball – and, attempting nothing more ambitious than a defensive prod at the next, fell leg before.

India v Australia 1986-87 1st Test

Tied
Played at M.A. Chidambaram Stadium, Chepauk, Madras, 18, 19, 20, 21, 22 September
Toss: Australia. Umpires: D.N. Dotiwala and V. Vikramju
Debuts: nil

Australia

D.C. Boon	c Kapil Dev b Sharma	122	(2) lbw b Maninder	49
G.R. Marsh	c Kapil Dev b Yadav	22	(1) b Shastri	11
D.M. Jones	b Yadav	210	c Azharuddin b Maninder	24
R.J. Bright	c Shastri b Yadav	30		
A.R. Border*	c Gavaskar b Shastri	106	(4) b Maninder	27
G.M. Ritchie	run out	13	(5) c Pandit b Shastri	28
G.R.J. Matthews	c Pandit b Yadav	44	(6) not out	27
S.R. Waugh	not out	12	(7) not out	2
T.J. Zoehrer†	did not bat			
C.J. McDermott	„			
B.A. Reid	„			
Extras	(B1, LB7, W1, NB6)	14	(LB1, NB1)	2
	(7 wkts dec)	574	(5 wkts dec)	170

India

S.M. Gavaskar	c & b Matthews	8	c Jones b Bright	90
K. Srikkanth	c Ritchie b Matthews	53	c Waugh b Matthews	39
M.B. Amarnath	run out	1	c Boon b Matthews	51
M. Azharuddin	c & b Bright	50	c Ritchie b Bright	42
R.J. Shastri	c Zoehrer b Matthews	62	(7) not out	48
C.S. Pandit	c Waugh b Matthews	35	(5) b Matthews	39
Kapil Dev*	c Border b Matthews	119	(6) c Bright b Matthews	1
K.S. More†	c Zoehrer b Waugh	4	(9) lbw b Bright	0
C. Sharma	c Zoehrer b Reid	30	(8) c McDermott b Bright	23
N.S Yadav	c Border b Bright	19	b Bright	8
Maninder Singh	not out	0	lbw b Matthews	0
Extras	(B1, LB9, NB6)	16	(B1, LB3, NB 2)	6
		397		347

India	O	M	R	W	O	M	R	W
Kapil Dev	18	5	52	0	1	0	5	0
Sharma	16	1	70	1	6	0	19	0
Maninder	39	8	135	0	19	2	60	3
Yadav	49.5	9	142	4	9	0	35	0
Shastri	47	8	161	1	14	2	50	2
Srikkanth	1	0	6	0				

Australia	O	M	R	W	O	M	R	W
McDermott	14	2	59	0	5	0	27	0
Reid	18	4	93	1	10	2	48	0
Matthews	28.2	3	103	5	39.5	7	146	5
Bright	23	3	88	2	25	3	94	5
Waugh	11	2	44	1	4	1	16	0
Border					3	0	12	0

Fall of Wickets

	A	I	A	I
Wkt	1st	1st	2nd	2nd
1st	48	62	21	55
2nd	206	65	81	158
3rd	282	65	94	204
4th	460	142	125	251
5th	481	206	165	253
6th	544	220	–	291
7th	574	245	–	331
8th	–	330	–	334
9th	–	387	–	344
10th	–	397	–	347

India v Australia 1986-87 2nd Test

Match Drawn
Played at Ferozeshah Kotla Stadium, New Delhi, 26(np), 27(np), 28(np), 29, 30 September
Toss: Australia. Umpires: V.K. Ramaswamy and P.D. Reporter

Australia

G.R. Marsh	c Pandit b Sharma	11
D.C. Boon	c Maninder b Shastri	67
D.M. Jones	st Pandit b Shastri	29
S.R. Waugh	not out	39
T.J. Zoehrer†	not out	52
A.R. Border*	did not bat	
G.M. Ritchie	,,	
G.R.J. Matthews	,,	
C.J. McDermott	,,	
R.J. Bright	,,	
D.R. Gilbert	,,	
Extras	(LB2, W4, NB3)	9
	(3 wkts dec)	**207**

India

S.M. Gavaskar	b Gilbert	4
K. Srikkanth	run out	26
M. Azharuddin	c Zoehrer b Waugh	24
D.B. Vengsarkar	not out	22
C.S. Pandit†	not out	26
M.B. Amarnath	did not bat	
R.J. Shastri	,,	
Kapil Dev*	,,	
C. Sharma	,,	
N.S Yadav	,,	
Maninder Singh	,,	
Extras	(LB5)	5
	(3 wkts)	**107**

India	O	M	R	W
Kapil Dev	14	5	27	0
Sharma	8	1	34	1
Shastri	21.4	4	44	2
Maninder	19	4	54	0
Yadav	13	1	46	0

Australia	O	M	R	W
McDermott	6	1	24	0
Gilbert	11	1	44	1
Waugh	6	0	29	1
Boon	2	1	5	0
Jones	1	1	0	0

Fall of Wickets

Wkt	A 1st	I 1st
1st	34	9
2nd	110	57
3rd	118	59
4th	–	–
5th	–	–
6th	–	–
7th	–	–
8th	–	–
9th	–	–
10th	–	–

India v Australia 1986-87 3rd Test

Match Drawn
Played at Wankhede Stadium, Bombay, 15, 16, 17, 18, 19 October
Toss: Australia. Umpires: J.D. Ghosh and R.B. Gupta
Debuts: India – R.R. Kulkarni

Australia

G.R. Marsh	c Gavaskar b Kulkarni	101	(2) b Shastri		20
D.C. Boon	c Gavaskar b Kulkarni	47	(1) c More b Shastri		40
D.M. Jones	c sub (L. Shivarama-krishnan) b Yadav	35	not out		73
A.R. Border*	st More b Maninder	46	not out		66
G.M. Ritchie	run out	31			
G.R.J. Matthews	b Yadav	20			
S.R. Waugh	b Yadav	6			
T.J. Zoehrer†	c & b Maninder	21			
R.J. Bright	lbw b Kulkarni	8			
D.R. Gilbert	c sub (L. Shivarama-krishnan) b Yadav	1			
B.A. Reid	not out	2			
Extras	(B5, LB12, NB10)	27	(B5, LB5, NB7)		17
		345	(2 wkts)		**216**

India

S.M. Gavaskar	c Ritchie b Matthews	103
K. Srikkanth	c Marsh b Bright	24
K.S. More†	c Jones b Matthews	15
M.B. Amarnath	c sub (M.R.J. Veletta) b Matthews	35
D.B. Vengsarkar	not out	164
M. Azharuddin	c sub (M.R.J. Veletta) b Matthews	10
R.J. Shastri	not out	121
R.R. Kulkarni	did not bat	
Kapil Dev*	,,	
N.S. Yadav	,,	
Maininder Singh	,,	
Extras	(B9, LB15, NB21)	45
	(5 wkts dec)	**517**

India	O	M	R	W	O	M	R	W
Kulkarni	23	2	85	3	6	0	29	0
Kapil Dev	6	1	16	0	6	1	24	0
Shastri	42	16	68	0	30	8	60	2
Yadav	41.4	8	84	4	23	7	52	0
Maninder	33	10	72	2	20	6	31	0
Srikkanth	2	0	3	0	3	0	10	0

Australia	O	M	R	W
Reid	32	5	81	0
Gilbert	24	3	75	0
Matthews	52	8	158	4
Bright	38	6	109	1
Border	10	3	29	0
Waugh	14	2	41	0

Fall of Wickets

	A	I	A
Wkt	1st	1st	2nd
1st	76	53	64
2nd	151	119	70
3rd	241	194	–
4th	252	205	–
5th	295	219	–
6th	304	–	–
7th	308	–	–
8th	340	–	–
9th	340	–	–
10th	345	–	–

Test Match Averages: India v Australia 1986-87

India

Batting and Fielding	M	I	NO	HS	R	Avge	100	50	Ct/St
R.J. Shastri	3	3	2	121*	231	231.00	1	1	1
S.M. Gavaskar	3	4	0	103	205	51.25	1	1	3
C.S. Pandit	2	3	1	39	100	50.00	–	–	3/1
K. Srikkanth	3	4	0	53	142	35.50	–	1	–
M. Azharuddin	3	4	0	50	126	31.50	–	1	1
M.B. Amarnath	3	3	0	51	87	29.00	–	1	–
K.S. More	2	3	0	15	19	6.33	–	–	1/1

Also batted: Kapil Dev (3 matches) 119, 1 (2ct); Maninder Singh (3 matches) 0*, 0 (2ct); C. Sharma (2 matches) 30, 23; D.B. Vengsarkar (2 matches) 22*, 164*; N.S. Yadav (3 matches) 19, 8. R.R. Kulkarni played in one match but did not bat.

Bowling	O	M	R	W	Avge	Best	5wI	10wM
N.S. Yadav	136.3	25	359	8	44.87	4-84	–	–
R.J. Shastri	154.4	38	383	7	54.71	2-44	–	–
Maninder Singh	130	30	352	5	70.40	3-60	–	–

Also bowled: Kapil Dev 45-12-124-0; C. Sharma 30-2-123-2; K. Srikkanth 6-0-19-0; R.R. Kulkarni 29-2-114-3.

Australia

Batting and Fielding	M	I	NO	HS	R	Avge	100	50	Ct/St
D.M. Jones	3	5	1	210	371	92.75	1	1	2
A.R. Border	3	4	1	106	245	81.66	1	1	2
D.C. Boon	3	5	0	122	325	65.00	1	1	1
S.R. Waugh	3	4	3	39*	59	59.00	–	–	2
G.R.J. Matthews	3	3	1	44	91	45.50	–	–	1
G.R. Marsh	3	5	0	101	165	33.00	1	–	1
G.M. Ritchie	3	3	0	31	72	24.00	–	–	3

Also batted: R.J. Bright (3 matches) 30, 8 (2ct); D.R. Gilbert (1 match) 1; B.A. Reid (2 matches) 2*; T.J. Zoehrer (3 matches) 52*, 21 (4ct). C.J. McDermott played in two matches but did not bat.

Bowling	O	M	R	W	Avge	Best	5wI	10wM
G.R.J. Matthews	120.1	18	407	14	29.07	5-103	2	1
R.J. Bright	86	12	291	8	36.37	5-94	1	–

Also bowled: D.C. Boon 2-1-5-0; A.R. Border 13-3-41-0; D.R. Gilbert 35-4-119-1; D.M. Jones 1-1-0-0; C.J. McDermott 25-3-110-0; B.A. Reid 60-11-222-1; S.R. Waugh 35-5-130-2.

Statistical Highlights of the Tests

1st Test, Madras. In only the second tied Test in history (with one ball left), Gavaskar became the first cricketer to play in 100 consecutive Tests. Australia's first innings (574) was their highest in India, and Jones's was the highest score by an Australian in a Test in India (503 mins, 27 fours, 2 sixes). Boon recorded his 3rd Test 100 and reached 1,000 Test runs at 70, Border his 19th Test 100, his 4th against India. Kapil Dev scored his 4th Test 100, and it was the first time that both captains made 100 since West Indies v India (Port-of-Spain) in 1982-83. Matthews took 5 wickets in an innings and 10 wickets in a Test for the first time, and Bright passed 50 Test wickets. Shastri achieved 2,000 runs and 100 Test wickets in his 44th Test. The aggregate 1,488 runs was the most in Tests between the two countries.

2nd Test, Delhi. Delay in starting the longest in any Test – only 6½ hours' playing time left. Vengsarkar became the 3rd Indian to score 5,000 Test runs, the 26th player in all.

3rd Test, Bombay. India's 517 was their highest score against Australia in India. Marsh made his 2nd Test 100, Gavaskar his 33rd (8th v Australia and 1,500 runs v Australia). Vengsarkar's 164 not out was his 12th Test 100 and his highest score in Tests, while Shastri's 6th Test 100 included 6 sixes (3 off 5 balls from Matthews), and their unbeaten 298 was a 6th-wicket record for India and a record for any wicket in Australia/India Tests.

One-Day Internationals

7 September at Sawai Mansinghe Stadium, Jaipur. INDIA won by 7 wickets. Toss: India. Australia 250-3 (47 overs) (D.C. Boon 111, G.R. Marsh 104). India 251-3 (41 overs) (K. Srikkanth 102, R.M. Lamba 64). Award: K. Srikkanth (102).

9 September at Shere-I-Kasmir Stadium, Srinagar. AUSTRALIA won by 3 wickets. Toss: Australia. India 222-8 (47 overs) (S.M. Gavaskar 52). Australia 226-7 (46 overs) (A.R. Border 90*). Award: A.R. Border (90*).

24 September at Lal Bahadur Stadium, Hyderabad. ABANDONED. Toss: India. Australia 242-6 (47 overs) (G.M. Ritchie 75, D.M. Jones 48). India 41-1 (10.4 overs).

2 October at Jawahal Nehru Stadium, New Delhi. INDIA won by 3 wickets. Toss: India. Australia 238-6 (45 overs) (S.R. Waugh 57*, G.C. Dyer 45*, D.M. Jones 43). India 242-7 (43.3 overs) (R.M. Lamba 74). Award: R.M. Lamba (74 and 1ct).

5 October at Sardar Patel Stadium, Ahmedabad. INDIA won by 52 runs. Toss: India. India 193 (47.4 overs) (R.J. Shastri 53). Australia 141 (43.3 overs) (A.R. Border 43, G.R. Marsh 43). Award: R.J. Shastri (53 and 9-2-23-2).

7 October at Municipal Stadium, Rajkot. AUSTRALIA won by 7 wickets. Toss: Australia. India 260-6 (48 overs) (R.M. Lamba 102, Kapil Dev 58). Australia 263-3 (46.3 overs) (A.R. Border 91*, D.M. Jones 55). Award: A.R. Border (91* and 2-0-10-0).

Australia Tour of India 1986-87

First-Class Matches: Played 7; Tied 1, Drawn 6
All Matches: Played 13; Won 2, Tied 1, Lost 3, Drawn 6, No Result 1

First-Class Averages

Batting and Fielding	M	I	NO	HS	R	Avge	100	50	Ct/St
D.R. Gilbert	5	4	2	117	152	76.00	1	–	–
G.C. Dyer	3	3	0	106	208	69.33	1	1	3
D.C. Boon	6	8	1	122	476	68.00	1	3	4
A.R. Border	5	6	1	106	320	64.00	1	2	4
S.R. Waugh	6	7	3	82	227	56.75	–	2	4
D.M. Jones	7	9	1	210	438	54.75	1	1	2
G.R.J. Matthews	6	6	1	99	263	52.60	–	1	1
G.M. Ritchie	6	6	0	124	291	48.50	1	1	7
G.R. Marsh	6	8	0	139	328	41.00	2	–	4
T.J. Zoehrer	5	4	1	52*	123	41.00	–	1	8/2
M.R.J. Veletta	3	4	1	29	76	25.33	–	–	3
C.J. McDermott	5	3	0	23	62	20.66	–	–	2
B.A. Reid	5	4	3	12*	18	18.00	–	–	–
R.J. Bright	7	6	1	30	66	13.20	–	–	3

Also batted: S.P. Davis (1 match) 0*, 3*, 1ct.

Bowling	O	M	R	W	Avge	Best	5wI	10wM
G.R.J. Matthews	179	29	601	20	30.05	5-103	2	1
D.R. Gilbert	107	23	367	11	33.36	4-92	–	–
S.P. Davis	48.4	12	175	5	35.00	3-52	–	–
S.R. Waugh	97	15	367	10	36.70	4-71	–	–
R.J. Bright	174.5	30	564	13	43.38	5-94	1	–
C.J. McDermott	99	13	355	7	50.71	3-85	–	–
B.A. Reid	116	18	394	7	56.28	2-34	–	–

Also bowled: D.C. Boon 2-1-5-0; A.R. Border 13-3-41-0; D.M. Jones 10-2-35-2;
T.J. Zoehrer 1-0-8-0.

Pakistan v West Indies

In a crowded six-week tour of Pakistan, the West Indies played three Test matches, three other first-class matches, and five one-day internationals. The Test series was one of the finest played in Pakistan. The two teams were equally balanced and produced exciting and entertaining cricket, winning one Test each. The decisive final Test at Karachi ended in an exciting draw after 11 mandatory overs had been bowled and bad light stopped play.

Though the Test series was evenly contested, the one-day series was won 4-1 by West Indies. Pakistan's only win was at Hyderabad, by 11 runs.

In a low-scoring series, none of the batsmen from either side made a century, only the third time in Test history that this had happened in a series of three or more matches. The only three-figure score of the whole tour was Jeff Dujon's 126 not out against the Punjab Governor's XI at Sahiwal. Pitches not conducive to stroke-making helped the bowlers, who dominated throughout. Only one stand of over 100 was made in the Tests from either side, Javed Miandad and Ramiz Raja putting on 111 for the third wicket in Karachi. Javed's 76 was the highest for Pakistan in the series, and Desmond Haynes's 88 not out at Karachi was the highest individual score of the series.

The first Test, at Faisalabad, resulted in a convincing victory for Pakistan. They won by 186 runs after bowling West Indies out in the second innings for 53, their lowest score in Tests. Leg-spinner Abdul Qadir demolished them by taking 6-16 in 9.3 overs in the second innings.

West Indies bounced back immediately winning the second Test, in Lahore, by an innings and 10 runs with more than a day to spare.

Pakistan captain Imran Khan led the side admirably and took 18 wickets. Abdul Qadir, too, bagged 18 and played a vital part. Wasim Akram and Tauseef Ahmed also bowled well, and in Saleem Jaffer, Pakistan found a useful left-arm medium-pacer.

Pakistan's opening batting kept on failing, and the middle order struggled after injury to their dependable batsman Salim Malik. The batting find was 18-year-old left-hander Asif Mujtaba, who played two fine innings against the tourists in the three-day games at Rawalpindi and Sahiwal, scoring 64 and an unbeaten 70.

The West Indian batting was a great disappointment. Vivian Richards failed repeatedly. Greenidge, Haynes, and Richardson played some useful knocks, but appeared below their best against the spinners. The most encouraging thing for West Indies was the performance of their young fast bowlers Courtney Walsh and Anthony Gray, who, with the experienced Marshall, extracted life out of the dead and slow pitches of Pakistan, taking 11 and 14 wickets respectively.

Neutral umpires, V.K. Ramaswamy and P.D. Reporter from India, officiated in the last two Tests.

Pakistan v West Indies 1986-87 1st Test

Pakistan won by 186 runs
Played at Iqbal Stadium, Faisalabad, 25, 27, 28, 29, 30 October
Toss: Pakistan. Umpires: Khizar Hayat and Mian Mohammad Aslam
Debuts: West Indies – A.H. Gray

Pakistan

Mohsin Khan	lbw b Marshall	2	(2) c Haynes b Walsh		40
Mudassar Nazar	c Richardson b Marshall	26	(1) c Haynes b Marshall		2
Ramiz Raja	lbw b Marshall	0	c Gray b Patterson		13
Javed Miandad	c Dujon b Patterson	1	(6) c sub (A.L. Logie) b Gray		30
Qasim Omar	hit wicket b Gray	3	lbw b Walsh		48
Salim Malik	retired hurt	21	(11) not out		3
Imran Khan*	c & b Gray	61	c Harper b Marshall		23
Abdul Qadir	c & b Patterson	14	lbw b Gray		2
Salim Yousuf†	lbw b Gray	0	(4) c Greenidge b Harper		61
Wasim Akram	c Richardson b Gray	0	(9) st Dujon b Harper		66
Tauseef Ahmed	not out	9	(10) b Walsh		8
Extras	(B1, LB11, NB10)	22	(B7, LB8, W2, NB15)		32
		159			**328**

Salim Malik retired hurt at 90-5

West Indies

C.G. Greenidge	lbw b Akram	10	lbw b Imran	12
D.L. Haynes	lbw b Imran	40	lbw b Imran	0
R.B. Richardson	b Tauseef	54	c Ramiz b Qadir	14
H.A. Gomes	c sub (Manzoor Elahi) b Qadir	33	b Qadir	2
P.J.L. Dujon†	c Ramiz b Tauseef	0	(6) lbw b Imran	0
R.A. Harper	c Yousuf b Akram	28	(7) c sub (Shoaib Mohammad) b Qadir	2
M.D. Marshall	c Yousuf b Akram	5	(8) c & b Qadir	10
I.V.A. Richards*	c Yousuf b Akram	33	(5) c Ramiz b Qadir	0
C.A. Walsh	lbw b Akram	4	(10) b Imran	0
A.H. Gray	not out	12	(9) b Qadir	5
B.P. Patterson	lbw b Akram	0	not out	6
Extras	(B9, LB8, NB12)	29	(LB2)	2
		248		**53**

West Indies	O	M	R	W	O	M	R	W
Marshall	10	2	48	3	26	3	83	2
Patterson	12	1	38	2	19	3	63	1
Gray	11.5	3	39	4	22	4	82	2
Walsh	5	0	22	0	23	6	49	3
Harper					27.5	9	36	2

Pakistan	O	M	R	W	O	M	R	W
Akram	25	3	91	6	3	0	5	0
Imran Khan	21	8	32	1	13	5	30	4
Qadir	15	1	58	1	9.3	1	16	6
Tauseef	22	5	50	2				

Fall of Wickets

Wkt	P 1st	WI 1st	P 2nd	WI 2nd
1st	12	12	2	5
2nd	12	103	19	16
3rd	19	124	113	19
4th	37	124	124	19
5th	37	178	208	20
6th	119	192	218	23
7th	120	223	224	36
8th	120	243	258	42
9th	159	247	296	43
10th	–	248	328	53

Pakistan v West Indies 1986-87 2nd Test

West Indies won by an innings and 10 runs
Played at Gadaffi Stadium, Lahore, 7, 8, 9, November
Toss: Pakistan. Umpires: V.K. Ramaswamy and P.D. Reporter
Debuts: Pakistan – Asif Mujtaba

Pakistan

Mohsin Khan	b Marshall	0	(2) lbw b Gray		1
Rizwan-uz-Zaman	c Richardson b Marshall	2	(1) b Marshall		1
Qasim Omar	lbw b Marshall	4	retired hurt		10
Javed Miandad	c Greenidge b Walsh	46	b Walsh		19
Ramiz Raja	b Gray	15	lbw b Gray		1
Asif Mujtaba	b Marshall	8	lbw b Richards		6
Salim Yousuf†	lbw b Walsh	8	(8) lbw b Gray		13
Abdul Qadir	run out	12	(9) b Walsh		2
Wasim Akram	lbw b Marshall	1	(11) c Harper b Walsh		0
Imran Khan*	not out	13	(7) c Dujon b Walsh		2
Tauseef Ahmed	c Dujon b Walsh	0	(10) not out		6
Extras	(B9, LB4, NB9)	22	(B4, LB9, W1, NB2)		16
		131			**77**

Qasim Omar retired hurt
at 26-2

West Indies

C.G. Greenidge	lbw b Qadir	75
D.L. Haynes	b Tauseef	18
R.B. Richardson	lbw b Qadir	4
H.A. Gomes	lbw b Imran	9
I.V.A. Richards*	c Yousuf b Qadir	44
P.J.L. Dujon†	b Imran	2
R.A. Harper	lbw b Qadir	6
M.D. Marshall	not out	13
C.G. Butts	c Yousuf b Imran	6
A.H. Gray	b Imran	10
C.A. Walsh	b Imran	8
Extras	(B15, LB5, NB3)	23
		218

West Inides	O	M	R	W	O	M	R	W
Marshall	18	5	33	5	8	3	14	1
Gray	13	0	28	1	17	7	20	3
Walsh	21.4	3	56	3	14.5	5	21	4
Harper	1	0	1	0				
Richards					5	2	9	1

Pakistan	O	M	R	W
Imran Khan	30.5	4	59	5
Akram	9	2	16	0
Qadir	32	5	96	4
Tauseef	19	8	27	1

Fall of Wickets

	P	WI	P
Wkt	1st	1st	2nd
1st	0	49	3
2nd	6	71	3
3rd	9	107	33
4th	46	153	44
5th	75	160	54
6th	95	172	64
7th	98	179	69
8th	99	189	71
9th	129	204	77
10th	131	218	–

Pakistan v West Indies 1986-87 3rd Test

Match Drawn
Played at National Stadium, Karachi, 20, 21, 22, 24, 25 November
Toss: West Indies. Umpires: V.K. Ramaswamy and P.D. Reporter
Debuts: Pakistan – Salim Jaffer

West Indies

C.G. Greenidge	c Yousuf b Mudassar	27	b Qadir	8
D.L. Haynes	lbw b Imran	3	not out	88
R.B. Richardson	c Mujtaba b Jaffer	44	c Ramiz b Qadir	32
H.A. Gomes	lbw b Qadir	18	lbw b Qadir	5
I.V.A. Richards*	c Ramiz b Tauseef	70	c Yousuf b Imran	28
P.J.L. Dujon†	c Yousuf b Qadir	19	c Yousuf b Jaffer	6
R.A. Harper	lbw b Imran	9	b Imran	4
M.D. Marshall	b Tauseef	4	lbw b Imran	0
C.G. Butts	lbw b Qadir	17	c Mohsin b Imran	12
A.H. Gray	c Imran b Qadir	0	b Imran	0
C.A. Walsh	not out	0	b Imran	0
Extras	(B14, LB11, W1, NB3)	29	(B7, LB13, W1, NB7)	28
		240		**211**

Pakistan

Mudassar Nazar	b Gray	16	(6)	lbw b Butts	25
Mohsin Khan	c Richards b Marshall	1	(1)	c Greenidge b Marshall	4
Ramiz Raja	c Harper b Butts	62	(4)	b Butts	29
Javed Miandad	run out	76	(5)	b Marshall	4
Imran Khan*	lbw b Butts	1	(8)	not out	15
Asif Mujtaba	c Dujon b Marshall	12	(7)	c Dujon b Walsh	6
Qasim Omar	c Richardson b Butts	5	(2)	c Dujon b Gray	1
Salim Yousuf†	c Walsh b Butts	22	(3)	c Haynes b Marshall	10
Tauseef Ahmed	c Richardson b Gray	3		not out	7
Salim Jaffer	b Gray	9			
Abdul Qadir	not out	8			
Extras	(B9, LB12, W1, NB2)	24		(B17, LB6, W1)	24
		239		(7 wkts)	**125**

Pakistan	O	M	R	W	O	M	R	W
Imran Khan	19	4	32	2	22.3	2	46	6
Jaffer	15	5	34	1	14	4	23	1
Mudassar	4	0	15	1				
Qadir	31.5	3	107	4	44	9	84	3
Tauseef	17	7	27	2	12	2	36	0
Mujtaba					3	2	2	0

West Indies	O	M	R	W	O	M	R	W
Marshall	33	9	57	2	19	5	31	3
Gray	21.1	6	40	3	14	7	18	1
Harper	7	0	31	0	1	0	1	0
Walsh	11	2	17	0	22	11	30	1
Butts	38	15	73	4	22	9	22	2

Fall of Wickets

Wkt	WI 1st	P 1st	WI 2nd	P 2nd
1st	14	19	36	3
2nd	55	29	109	16
3rd	94	140	128	19
4th	110	145	159	25
5th	172	172	171	73
6th	204	179	185	95
7th	210	215	185	95
8th	227	218	209	–
9th	234	222	211	–
10th	240	239	211	–

Test Match Averages: Pakistan v West Indies 1986-87

Pakistan

Batting and Fielding	M	I	NO	HS	R	Avge	100	50	Ct/St
Javed Miandad	3	6	0	76	176	29.33	–	1	–
Imran Khan	3	6	2	61	115	28.75	–	1	1
Ramiz Raja	3	6	0	62	120	20.00	–	1	5
Salim Yousuf	3	6	0	61	114	19.00	–	1	9
Mudassar Nazar	2	4	0	26	69	17.25	–	–	–
Wasim Akram	2	4	0	66	67	16.75	–	1	–
Qasim Omar	3	6	1	48	71	14.20	–	–	–
Tauseef Ahmed	3	6	3	9*	33	11.00	–	–	–
Abdul Qadir	3	5	1	14	38	9.50	–	–	1
Mohsin Khan	3	6	0	40	48	8.00	–	–	–
Asif Mujtaba	2	4	0	12	32	8.00	–	–	1

Also batted: Rizwan-uz-Zaman (1 match) 2, 1; Salim Jaffer (1 match) 9; Salim Malik (1 match) 21*, 3*.

Bowling	O	M	R	W	Avge	Best	5wI	10wM
Imran Khan	106.2	23	199	18	11.05	6-46	2	–
Wasim Akram	37	5	112	6	18.66	6-91	1	–
Abdul Qadir	132.2	19	361	18	20.05	6-16	1	–
Tauseef Ahmed	70	22	140	5	28.00	2-27	–	–

Also bowled: Asif Mujtaba 3-2-2-0; Mudassar Nazar 4-0-15-1; Salim Jaffer 29-9-57-2.

West Indies

Batting and Fielding	M	I	NO	HS	R	Avge	100	50	Ct/St
D.L. Haynes	3	5	1	88*	149	37.25	–	1	3
I.V.A. Richards	3	5	0	70	175	35.00	–	1	1
R.B. Richardson	3	5	0	54	148	29.60	–	1	5
C.G. Greenidge	3	5	0	75	132	26.40	–	1	3
H.A. Gomes	3	5	0	33	67	13.40	–	–	–
C.G. Butts	2	3	0	17	35	11.66	–	–	–
R.A. Harper	3	5	0	28	49	9.80	–	–	3
M.D. Marshall	3	5	1	13*	32	8.00	–	–	–
A.H. Gray	3	5	1	12*	27	6.75	–	–	2
P.J.L. Dujon	3	5	0	19	27	5.40	–	–	6/1
C.A. Walsh	3	5	1	8	12	3.00	–	–	1

Also batted: B.P. Patterson (1 match) 0, 6* (1ct).

Bowling	O	M	R	W	Avge	Best	5wI	10wM
C.G. Butts	60	24	95	6	15.83	4-73	–	–
A.H. Gray	99	27	227	14	16.21	4-39	–	–
M.D. Marshall	114	27	266	16	16.62	5-33	1	–
C.A. Walsh	97.3	27	195	11	17.72	4-21	–	–

Also bowled: I.V.A. Richards 5-2-9-1; R.A. Harper 36.5-9-69-2; B.P. Patterson 31-4-101-3.

Statistical Highlights of the Tests

1st Test, Faisalabad. West Indies set 240 to win, were all out 53, their lowest Test score, and the lowest for any innings at Faisalabad. It was only their 2nd defeat in 37 Tests (lost to Australia in January 1985 and previous loss to New Zealand 1979-80). In Pakistan's 2nd innings, Salim Malik played with a left arm (broken in 1st innings against Walsh) in plaster and survived 14 balls. Abdul Qadir's 6-16 was the best ever Pakistan bowling against West Indies and his 10th 5 wickets in a Test innings. Wasim Akram's 6-91 was his best in Tests. Imran Khan reached 269 Test wickets, passing Bedi's 266.

2nd Test, Lahore. Indian umpires were appointed for the rest of series. West Indies recorded their 3rd three-day win of 1986, and their 218 was the 3rd lowest Test score to win by an innings. Marshall's 5-33 was his 14th haul of 5 wickets in a Test innings and the best West Indies bowling against Pakistan in Pakistan. Qasim Omar retired hurt, hit in face by bouncer from Walsh. West Indies played two Test spinners for the first time since 1978-79, but between them they bowled only one over in the match! There were 11 lbws in the 29 wickets to fall.

3rd Test, Karachi. Series drawn – umpires took teams off with 9 of last 20 overs remaining. There was no 100 in the series; Haynes carried his bat for 88, the highest score in the series (3rd West Indian to carry bat, only the 2nd player to do so in Pakistan). West Indies remain unbeaten in 12 series, though this drawn series brought to an end their run of seven consecutive wins. Rameez Raja compiled the 3rd slowest Test 50 in history (318 mins). Imran Khan took 5 wickets in an innings for the 19th time and passed 50 wickets against Pakistan. Abdul Qadir played with a fractured bone in his left hand.

One-Day Internationals

17 October at Shahi Bagh Stadium, Peshawar. WEST INDIES won by 4 wickets. Toss: Pakistan. Pakistan 169-7 (49 overs). West Indies 165-6 (45.3 overs) (C.G. Greenidge 67). Award: C.G. Greenidge (67).

4 November at Municipal Stadium, Gujiranwala. WEST INDIES won on faster scoring rate. Toss: Pakistan. West Indies 196-7 (50 overs) (M.D. Marshall 66, P.J.L. Dujon 57*). Pakistan 155-6 (43.5 overs) (Javed Miandad 74*). Award: M.D. Marshall (66 and 8-2-18-2).

14 November at Jinnah Park Stadium, Sialkot. WEST INDIES won by 4 wickets. Toss: Pakistan. Pakistan 148-7 (45 overs). West Indies (44.3 overs). Award: P.J.L. Dujon* (1ct and 38).

17 November at Ibn-e-Qasim Bagh Stadium, Multan. WEST INDIES won by 89 runs. Toss: Pakistan. West Indies 202-5 (44 overs) (A.L. Logie 46). Pakistan 113 (38.2 overs) (A.H. Gray 9-0-36-4). Award: A.H. Gray (9-0-36-4)

18 November at Niaz Stadium, Hyderabad. PAKISTAN won by 11 runs. Toss: West Indies. Pakistan 202-6 (45 overs). West Indies 191-7 (45 overs) (R.B. Richardson 70, D.L. Haynes 59). Award: Imran Khan (27* and 9-1-37-2).

West Indies Tour of Pakistan 1986-87

First-Class Matches: Played 6; Won 2, Lost 1, Drawn 3
All Matches: Played 11; Won 6, Lost 2, Drawn 3

First-Class Averages

Batting and Fielding	M	I	NO	HS	R	Avge	100	50	Ct/St
D.L. Haynes	5	8	2	88*	259	43.16	–	2	5
I.V.A. Richards	6	8	0	70	276	34.50	–	2	4
R.B. Richardson	6	10	1	67	264	29.33	–	2	8
P.J.L. Dujon	5	7	1	126*	167	27.83	1	–	6/1
C.G. Greenidge	6	10	1	75	225	25.00	–	1	6
H.A. Gomes	5	7	0	66	133	19.00	–	1	–
C.G. Butts	5	6	1	57*	93	18.40	–	1	1
R.A. Harper	6	8	0	77	146	18.25	–	1	5
M.D. Marshall	4	6	2	16*	48	12.00	–	–	–
B.P. Patterson	3	4	1	9	18	6.00	–	–	1
A.H. Gray	4	6	1	12	28	5.60	–	–	2
C.A. Walsh	4	6	1	8	12	2.40	–	–	2

Also batted: W.K.M. Benjamin (3 matches) 38, 2, 92; A.L. Logie (2 matches) 4, 25, 29, 4ct;
T.R.O. Payne (2 matches) 0, 14, 4ct.

Bowling	O	M	R	W	Avge	Best	5wI	10wM
A.H. Gray	112	29	266	19	14.00	4-22	–	–
C.G. Butts	126.4	40	244	17	14.35	4-31	–	–
R.A. Harper	129.5	42	232	14	16.57	4-28	–	–
C.A. Walsh	117.3	29	265	14	18.92	4-21	–	–
M.D. Marshall	131	30	327	17	19.23	5-33	1	–
B.P. Patterson	54	11	173	8	21.62	3-34	–	–

Also bowled: W.K.M. Benjamin 34.2-3-120-3; I.V.A. Richards 14-3-35-1.

India v Sri Lanka

The Sri Lankan cricketers who toured India were something of a disappointment. They lost two of the three Test matches because their batting, though occasionally classy, was neither steady nor reliable. Subjected to pitches at Nagpur and Cuttack that were woefully under-prepared, they found Indian spin too much for them and were unable to handle pressure situations. Moreover, their bowling was far short of acceptable Test standard.

They played five limited-overs internationals, won the first rather surprisingly and sensationally, and lost the remaining four, though in the final encounter in Bombay they gave India a real fright. Unfortunately, they had a problem in the matter of attitude, giving the impression to one and all that they expected the worst from Indian umpires. Their griev-ances had some basis but some of their players needlessly allowed this to affect them. The obvious outcome was that they rarely gave of their best.

The side's leading batsmen generally performed poorly. Stroke-makers of the calibre of skipper Duleep Mendis and Roy Dias in a total of 10 innings between them managed an aggregate of 192 runs. Mohammed Azharuddin, who played just in the first Test (withdrawing from the other two because of injury), made 199 in the lone innings he got. Two Indians, the in-form Dilip Vengsarkar (376) and Kapil Dev (234), averaged over 100, while Sunil Gavaskar and Mohinder Amarnath averaged in the 80s. The difference in consistency and in performance was just too much.

For Sri Lanka, the only near success on the trip was makeshift opening batsman Ravi Ratnayake, who began his career as a medium-pace bowler. Ravi took the most wickets for his side (nine) as well as scoring the most runs (206), which included the best innings and the highest score for the rubber of 93. He also shared in an opening stand of 159 with Sidath Wettimuny (hero of Lord's), which is a record for Sri Lanka for this wicket against any country. Wettimuny, on his return home, announced his retirement from international cricket.

It was evident from the start of the tour that Sri Lanka were hoping that their batting would see them through the rubber. At Kanpur, in the opening Test match, they scored 420, their highest against India in Tests and their second highest overall. India replied with 676-7, their best in Tests. But Indian captain Kapil Dev apparently realized that the only way to get at the Sri Lankans was by having wickets made to order. Maninder Singh with his left-arm spin (18 wickets) and Shivlal Yadav with right-arm off-spin (11) made the most of the favourable conditions and sent the Sri Lankans on a spin. In the Tests, only two Sri Lankans, Ravi Ratnayake and vice-captain Arjuna Ranatunga, managed more than one half-century. But in the face of the mammoth scores by the Indians, the Sri Lankan efforts were totally inadequate.

India v Sri Lanka 1986-87 1st Test

Match Drawn
Played at Green Park, Kanpur, 17, 18(np), 20, 21, 22 December
Toss: Sri Lanka. Umpires: R.B. Gupta and V.K. Ramaswamy
Debuts: India – B. Arun, R.M. Lamba: Sri Lanka – G.F. Labrooy

Sri Lanka

S.D. Wettimuny	lbw b Sharma	79
J.R. Ratnayeke	lbw b Kapil Dev	93
P.A. De Silva	b Arun	26
A.P. Gurusinha	b Kapil Dev	19
R.L. Dias	c Azharuddin b Arun	50
L.R.D. Mendis*	lbw b Sharma	1
A. Ranatunga	lbw b Maninder	52
R.G. De Alwis†	b Maninder	13
A.L.F. De Mel	c Arun b Shastri	25
E.A.R. De Silva	lbw b Arun	21
G.F. Labrooy	not out	5
Extras	(B1, LB10, W6, NB19)	36
		420

India

S.M. Gavaskar	c Wettimuny b Labrooy	176
K. Srikkanth	c De Alwis b Ratnayeke	18
R.M. Lamba	run out	24
D.B. Vengsarkar	c Gurusinha b De Mel	57
M. Azharuddin	lbw b Ratnayeke	199
R.J. Shastri	lbw b Ratnayeke	6
Kapil Dev*	lbw b Ratnayeke	163
B. Arun	not out	2
Maninder Singh	did not bat	
C. Sharma	"	
K.S. More†	"	
Extras	(B1, LB11, W1, NB18)	31
	(7 wkts)	**676**

India	O	M	R	W
Kapil Dev	30	11	81	2
Arun	27	7	76	3
Sharma	31	4	122	2
Maninder	32	12	89	2
Shastri	17	6	37	1
Srikkanth	1	0	4	0

Sri Lanka	O	M	R	W
De Mel	31	4	119	1
Labrooy	35	4	164	1
Ratnayeke	37.1	2	132	4
De Silva	40	7	133	0
Ranatunga	15	4	58	0
Gurusinha	7	0	42	0
Wettimuny	2	0	16	0

Fall of Wickets

Wkt	SL 1st	I 1st
1st	159	50
2nd	217	100
3rd	217	217
4th	286	380
5th	292	399
6th	355	671
7th	355	676
8th	389	–
9th	394	–
10th	420	–

India v Sri Lanka 1986-87 2nd Test

India won by an innings and 106 runs
Played at Vidarbha CA Stadium, Nagpur, 27, 28, 30, 31 December
Toss: Sri Lanka. Umpires: R. Mehra and P.D. Reporter
Debuts: nil

Sri Lanka

S.D. Wettimuny	c Amarnath b Sharma	6		c Srikkanth b Kapil Dev	6
J.R. Ratnayeke	c Shastri b Kapil Dev	17		c Gavaskar b Maninder	54
A.P. Gurusinha	c Amarnath b Yadav	29		c & b Yadav	15
R.L. Dias	b Maninder	6		b Maninder	2
P.A. De Silva	lbw b Yadav	33		c sub (Arun Lal) b Maninder	6
A. Ranatunga	c Amarnath b Yadav	59	(7)	c Gavaskar b Maninder	5
L.R.D. Mendis★	c Srikkanth b Maninder	1	(6)	b Maninder	38
B.R. Jurangpathy	b Maninder	0		c Vengsarkar b Yadav	0
R.G. De Alwis†	c Vengsarkar b Yadav	1	(11)	c More b Maninder	0
R.J. Ratnayake	not out	32		not out	4
E.A.R. De Silva	c Shastri b Yadav	16	(9)	c Srikkanth b Maninder	0
Extras	(B2, LB1, NB1)	4		(B4, LB5, NB2)	11
		204			**141**

India

K. Srikkanth	c De Alwis by Ratnayeke	4
R. Lamba	c Jurangpathy b E.A.R. De Silva	53
M.B. Amarnath	c sub (R.S. Mahanama) b Jurangpathy	131
D.B. Vengsarkar	c Jurangpathy b Ratnayeke	153
S.M. Gavaskar	c E.A.R. De Silva b Gurusinha	74
Kapil Dev★	not out	11
R.J. Shastri	c sub (R.S. Mahanama) b Gurusinha	12
K.S. More†	did not bat	
Maninder Singh	"	
C. Sharma	"	
N.S. Yadav	"	
Extras	(LB4, W1, NB8)	13
	(6 wkts dec)	**451**

India	O	M	R	W	O	M	R	W
Kapil Dev	10	3	29	1	6	1	16	1
Sharma	5	0	26	1	5	0	14	0
Maninder	20	6	56	3	17.4	4	51	7
Yadav	19.1	4	76	5	14	6	21	2
Shastri	5	2	14	0	6	0	30	0

Sri Lanka	O	M	R	W	O	M	R	W
Ratnayake	35	4	139	2				
Ratnayeke	28	4	89	0				
Ranatunga	6	1	34	0				
De Silva	38	5	91	1				
Jurangpathy	21	3	69	1				
Gurusinha	1.5	0	25	2				

Fall of Wickets

Wkt	SL 1st	I 1st	SL 2nd
1st	7	5	15
2nd	38	131	42
3rd	52	304	47
4th	66	420	57
5th	105	428	122
6th	110	451	132
7th	110	–	137
8th	129	–	137
9th	160	–	141
10th	204	–	141

India v Sri Lanka 1986-87 3rd Test

India won by an innings and 67 runs
Played at Baribati Stadium, Cuttack, 4, 5, 6, 7 January
Toss: India. Umpires: R.B. Gupta and V.K. Ramaswamy
Debuts: nil

India

S.M. Gavaskar	lbw b Ratnayeke	5
K.Srikkanth	b Ratnayake	40
M.B. Amarnath	b Anurasiri	39
D.B. Vengsarkar	lbw b Ratnayeke	166
R. Lamba	lbw b Ratnayeke	24
R.J. Shastri	c E.A.R. De Silva b Ratnayeke	19
Kapil Dev*	b Anurasiri	60
B. Arun	c Ranatunga b Anurasiri	2
K.S. More†	not out	6
N.S. Yadav	st De Alwis b Anurasiri	3
Maninder Singh	lbw b Ratnayeke	2
Extras	(B8, LB19, NB7)	34
		400

Sri Lanka

S.D. Wettimuny	c Kapil Dev b Maninder	6		b Shastri	12
J.R. Ratnayeke	c Srikkanth b Yadav	20		c Srikkanth b Yadav	22
A.P. Gurusinha	c Lamba b Arun	40		c Arun b Yadav	10
E.A.R. De Silva	b Kapil Dev	1	(9)	st More b Yadav	19
L.R.D. Mendis*	b Kapil Dev	9		lbw b Shastri	27
A. Ranatunga	lbw b Kapil Dev	30		lbw b Maninder	2
R.L. Dias	c Kapil Dev b Maninder	49		b Shastri	9
P.A. De Silva	lbw b Maninder	21		c Shastri b Maninder	8
R.J. Ratnayake	lbw b Maninder	0	(4)	b Kapil Dev	24
R.G. De Alwis†	c Srikkanth b Kapil Dev	0		lbw b Shastri	0
S.D. Anurasiri	not out	0		not out	0
Extras	(B1, LB11, NB3)	15		(B2, LB5, NB2)	9
		191			**142**

Sri Lanka	O	M	R	W
Ratnayake	30	5	98	1
Ratnayeke	27.3	3	85	5
De Silva	40	6	114	0
Anurasiri	26	3	71	4
Ranatunga	4	2	5	0

India	O	M	R	W	O	M	R	W
Kapil Dev	26	3	69	4	16	4	36	1
Arun	13	5	26	1	2	0	14	0
Maninder	17.1	6	41	4	17	5	42	2
Yadav	15	6	21	1	13	3	32	3
Shastri	5	0	22	0	11	4	11	4

Fall of Wickets

Wkt	I 1st	SL 1st	SL 2nd
1st	18	27	35
2nd	70	33	45
3rd	164	38	51
4th	225	56	91
5th	272	95	94
6th	383	125	112
7th	385	188	121
8th	387	190	121
9th	397	191	124
10th	400	191	142

Test Match Averages: India v Sri Lanka 1986-87

India

Batting and Fielding	M	I	NO	HS	R	Avge	100	50	Ct/St
D.B. Vengsarkar	3	3	0	166	376	125.33	2	1	2
Kapil Dev	3	3	1	163	234	117.00	1	1	2
S.M. Gavaskar	3	3	0	176	255	85.00	1	1	2
M.B. Amarnath	2	2	0	131	170	85.00	1	–	3
R.M. Lamba	3	3	0	53	101	33.66	–	1	1
K. Srikkanth	3	3	0	40	62	20.66	–	–	6
R.J.Shastri	3	3	0	19	37	12.33	–	–	3

Also batted: B. Arun (2 matches) 2*, 2 (2ct); M. Azharuddin (1 match) 199 (1ct); Maninder Singh (3 matches) '2; K.S. More (3 matches) 6* (1ct, 1st); N.S. Yadav (2 matches) 3 (1ct). C. Sharma played in two matches but did not bat.

Bowling	O	M	R	W	Avge	Best	5wI	10wM
N.S. Yadav	61.1	19	150	11	13.63	5-76	1	–
Maninder Singh	103.5	33	279	18	15.50	7-51	1	1
R.J. Shastri	44	12	114	5	22.80	4-11	–	–
Kapil Dev	88	22	231	9	25.66	4-69	–	–

Also bowled: B. Arun 42-12-116-4; C. Sharma 41-4-162-3; K. Srikkanth 1-0-4-0.

Sri Lanka

Batting and Fielding	M	I	NO	HS	R	Avge	100	50	Ct/St
J.R. Ratnayeke	3	5	0	93	206	41.20	–	2	–
R.J. Ratnayake	2	4	2	32*	60	30.00	–	–	–
A. Ranatunga	3	5	0	59	148	29.60	–	2	1
R.L. Dias	3	5	0	50	116	23.20	–	1	–
A.P. Gurusinha	3	5	0	40	113	22.60	–	–	1
S.D. Wettimuny	3	5	0	79	109	21.80	–	1	1
P.A. De Silva	3	5	0	33	94	18.80	–	–	–
L.R.D. Mendis	3	5	0	38	76	15.20	–	–	–
E.A.R. De Silva	3	5	0	21	57	11.40	–	–	2
R.G. De Alwis	3	5	0	13	14	2.80	–	–	2/1

Also batted: A.D. Anurasiri (1 match) 0*, 0*; A.L.F. De Mel (1 match) 25; B.A. Jurangpathy (1 match) 0, 0 (2ct); G.F. Labrooy (1 match) 5*.

Bowling	O	M	R	W	Avge	Best	5wI	10wM
J.R. Ratnayeke	92.4	9	306	9	34.00	5-85	1	–

Also bowled: S.D. Anurasiri 26-3-71-4; A.L.F. De Mel 31-4-119-1; E.A.R. De Silva 118-18-338-1; A.P. Gurusinha 8.5-0-67-2; B.A. Jurangpathy 21-3-69-1; G.F. Labrooy 35-4-164-1; A. Ranatunga 25-7-97-0; R.J. Ratnayake 65-8-237-3; S.D. Wettimuny 2-0-16-0.

Statistical Highlights of the Tests

1st Test, Kanpur. Sri Lanka's 420 was their highest score against India, and the 1st-wicket partnership of 159 between Wettimuny and Ratnayeke the best against any country. India's 676 was their highest Test innings and the highest in India. Gavaskar scored his 34th Test 100, his 2nd against Sri Lanka. Azharuddin reached 1,000 Test runs (53) in scoring his 4th Test 100, while Kapil Dev's 163 was his 5th Test 100 and highest Test score; their 6th wicket stand of 272 was a record between the countries.

2nd Test, Nagpur. The 1st win in the 6 Tests between the countries, and India's 1st at home since England in Bombay, 1984-85. Yadev took 5 wickets in an innings for the 3rd time, Amarnath hit his 11th Test 100 and passed 4,000 runs (61) in his 61st Test. Vengsarkar's 153 was his 13th Test 100 and the highest at Nagpur. India's 451-6 dec was the highest Test score at Nagpur. Maninder Singh's 7-51 was his best Test analysis and his first 5 wickets in an innings, while his 10-107 in the match was the best for any bowler at Nagpur. He passed 50 wickets in his 24th Test.

3rd Test, Cuttack. Vengsarkar's 166 was his highest Test score and his 14th 100 in Tests. Ratnayeke took 5 wickets in a Test innings for the 2nd time, and his brother Ratnayake was Kapil Dev's 300th Test wicket, the day after the Indian captain's 28th birthday. He was the youngest player to reach this landmark, and the second to complete 3,000 runs and 300 wickets (after Botham). India's series win (2-0) was their first at home since England in 1981-82.

One-Day Internationals

24 December at Green Park, Kanpur. SRI LANKA won by 117 runs. Toss: India. Sri Lanka 195-8 (46 overs). India 78 (24.1 overs) (A. Ranatunga 6-1-14-4). Award: A. Ranatunga (31, 6-1-14-4, and 1ct).

11 January at Nehru Stadium, Gauhati. INDIA won by 8 wickets. Toss: India. Sri Lanka 145-8 (46 overs). India 146-2 (27.3 overs) (S.M. Gavaskar 70*, D.B. Vengsarkar 43*). Award: S.M. Gavaskar (70*).

13 January at Jawahal Nehru Stadium, New Delhi. INDIA won by 6 wickets. Toss: India. Sri Lanka 208-6 (44 overs) (A.P. Gurusinha 54, P.A. De Silva 51, A. Ranatunga 41). India 209-4 (41.3 overs) (R.M. Lamba 57*, D.B. Vengsarkar 56). Award: A. Ranatunga (41, 10-0-42-2, and 2ct).

15 January at Moti Bagh Stadium, Baroda. INDIA won by 94 runs. Toss: Sri Lanka. India 235-8 (43 overs) (S.M. Gavaskar 69, K. Srikkanth 63, G. Labrooy 5-57). Sri Lanka 141-9 (36.3 overs). Award: K. Srikkanth (63, 0.3-0-6-1, and 1ct).

17 January at Wankhede Stadium, Bombay. INDIA won by 10 runs. Toss: Sri Lanka. India 299-4 (40 overs) (M. Azharuddin 108, D.B. Vengsarkar 52, K. Srikkanth 46). Sri Lanka 289-7 (40 overs) (R.S. Mahanama 98, A.P. Gurusinha 52). Award: M. Azharuddin (108*).

Sri Lanka Tour of India 1986-87

First-Class Matches: Played 5; Won 0, Lost 2, Drawn 3
All Matches: Played 10; Won 1, Lost 6, Drawn 3

First-Class Averages

Batting and Fielding	M	I	NO	HS	R	Avge	100	50	Ct/St
S. Wettimuny	4	6	1	227*	336	67.20	1	1	1
R.S. Madugalle	2	2	1	39	54	54.00	–	–	–
P.A. De Silva	4	6	1	115*	209	41.80	1	–	–
J.R. Ratnayeke	4	6	0	93	244	40.66	–	2	–
A. Ranatunga	4	6	0	84	232	38.66	–	3	1
R.L. Dias	5	7	0	81	256	36.57	–	3	1
R.J. Ratnayake	3	4	2	32*	60	30.00	–	–	–
A.P. Gurusinha	4	6	0	59	172	28.66	–	1	1
A.L.F. De Mel	2	2	0	25	47	23.50	–	–	–
L.R.D. Mendis	5	7	0	65	156	22.28	–	1	–
B.R. Jurangpathy	3	3	1	27*	27	13.50	–	–	3
E.A.R. De Silva	4	5	0	21	57	11.40	–	–	2
R.G. De Alwis	5	6	0	13	27	4.50	–	–	4/1

Also batted: R.S. Mahanama (1 match) 91; S.D. Anurasiri (3 matches) 0*, 0*; G.F. Labrooy (2 matches) 5*, 0*.

Bowling	O	M	R	W	Avge	Best	5wI	10wM
A.P. Gurusinha	17.5	2	97	3	32.33	2-25	–	–
J.R. Ratnayeke	107.4	14	353	10	35.30	5-85	1	–
S.D. Anurasiri	64	8	207	5	41.40	4-71	–	–
G.F. Labrooy	68	8	301	5	60.20	4-137	–	–
B.R. Jurangpathy	37	3	134	2	67.00	1-65	–	–
R.J. Ratnayake	82	12	281	3	93.66	2-139	–	–
A.L.F. De Mel	60	7	213	2	106.50	1-94	–	–
E.A.R. De Silva	133	18	395	1	395.00	1-91	–	–

Also bowled: P.A. De Silva 7-0-35-0; R.L. Dias 6-0-39-0; R.S. Madugalle 4-0-17-0;
L.R.D. Mendis 6-0-20-0; A. Ranatunga 25-7-97-0; S. Wettimuny 2-0-16-0.

India v Pakistan

Reports from Lahore that the city went wild receiving Pakistan captain Imran Khan and his triumphant cricketers on their return from India, would give an idea of what victory or defeat means to the two countries in matches against each other.

Pakistan won the Test rubber (for the first time in India) 1-0 and took the six-match one-day series by the handsome difference of five matches to one. In the latter, it should have been a clean sweep but for the fact that at Hyderabad, with the scores level and Pakistan ahead in the rate of scoring, the experienced Qadir blundered by going for what should have been the winning second run and was run out. Pakistan, having as a result lost one more wicket than India, were adjudged according to the rules to have lost the match.

Four Test matches came and went without there being really any hope of a decision. The captains blamed the slow nature of the wickets, which left bowlers frustrated. Pakistan's main strength, the varied bowling, was really never in evidence, with Imran Khan and Abdul Qadir being treated roughly. Of all the bowlers on view, only India's Maninder Singh seemed to make any sort of impression.

Pakistan's batting, always regarded as being vulnerable, somehow found the inspiration and the determination to keep the Indian bowlers at bay. Imran, a disappointment as a bowler, proved himself to be a resourceful, and genuinely world-class, batsman, weathering many a storm with remarkable calm and control. The side's leading batsman, Javed Miandad, added to his reputation, while Rameez Raja showed that he could knuckle down and perform capably for the side.

India, on the other hand, always seemed to give the impression that at some point or other they would cut through. Yet the bowling lacked the 'teeth' to win Test matches. The batting looked extremely capable. Gavaskar missed the second Test at Calcutta, for 'personal reasons', but scored his 10,000th Test run in the fourth Test at Ahmedabad. There was much speculation that the final Test at Bangalore would be his last. But he made no statement to this effect. In fact, he went on to play his finest innings of his 125-Test-long career in defeat.

In a way, it was unfortunate that the Test rubber had to be decided on the basis of the final encounter. On a pitch that Gavaskar described as 'the worst I have ever played on', the spin bowlers called the tune. Off-spinner Tauseef, who was nearly unplayable, even managed to send down 'bouncers', as the ball either kicked or crept. Pakistan batted better in the crucial second innings after succumbing to Maninder Singh's wares in the first. Then Tauseef and the veteran left-arm spinner Iqbal Qasim (nine wickets apiece in the match), sent India, needing only 66 from the last five wickets, hurtling to a 16-run defeat.

India v Pakistan 1986-87 1st Test

Match Drawn
Played at M.A. Chidambaram Stadium, Chepauk, Madras, 3, 4, 6, 7, 8 February
Toss: Pakistan. Umpires: R. Mehra and V.K. Ramaswamy
Debuts: Pakistan – Ijaz Ahmed

Pakistan

Rizwan-uz-Zaman	c More b Maninder	1	(3)	not out	54
Shoaib Mohammad	lbw b Maninder	101		c Vengsarkar b Maninder	45
Ramiz Raja	c Srikkanth b Maninder	24	(1)	c Azharuddin b Kulkarni	14
Javed Miandad	run out	94		st More b Maninder	54
Salim Malik	b Maninder	19		not out	6
Ijaz Ahmed	c Vengsarkar b Maninder	3			
Abdul Qadir	c Azharuddin b Shastri	21			
Imran Khan*	not out	135			
Wasim Akram	c Gavaskar b Yadav	62			
Salim Yousuf†	c Kulkarni b Maninder	1			
Tauseef Ahmed	not out	13			
Extras	(LB11, W1, NB1)	13		(LB3, NB6)	9
	(9 wkts dec)	487		(3 wkts)	182

India

S.M. Gavaskar	c Tauseef b Qadir	91
K. Srikkanth	c Akram b Tauseef	123
M.B. Amarnath	run out	89
D.B. Vengsarkar	st Yousuf b Tauseef	96
M. Azharuddin	st Yousuf b Tauseef	20
R.J. Shastri	c Yousuf b Imran	41
Kapil Dev*	c Ramiz b Qadir	5
K.S. More†	lbw b Akram	28
R.R. Kulkarni	c Yousuf b Imran	2
N.S. Yadav	not out	6
Maninder Singh	not out	7
Extras	(B9, LB5, NB5)	19
	(9 wkts dec)	527

India	O	M	R	W	O	M	R	W
Kapil Dev	18	1	68	0	9	1	36	0
Kulkarni	7	0	41	1	5	0	15	1
Maninder	59	16	135	5	26	10	47	2
Yadav	41	3	127	1	15	4	29	0
Shastri	38	8	105	1	18	5	42	0
Srikkanth					3	0	6	0
Gavaskar					1	0	4	0

Pakistan	O	M	R	W
Akram	34	10	78	1
Imran Khan	27	4	103	2
Qadir	39	4	130	2
Tauseef	67	6	189	3
Shoaib	3	0	13	0

Fall of Wickets

	P	I	P
Wkt	1st	1st	2nd
1st	2	200	17
2nd	60	220	70
3rd	215	405	160
4th	237	424	–
5th	244	429	–
6th	257	453	–
7th	273	494	–
8th	385	498	–
9th	406	515	–
10th	–	–	–

India v Pakistan 1986-87 2nd Test

Match Drawn
Played at Eden Gardens, Calcutta, 11, 12, 14, 15, 16 February
Toss: Pakistan. Umpires: R.B. Gupta and R.D. Reporter
Debuts: nil

India

K. Srikkanth	c Malik b Akram	22	lbw b Imran		21
Arun Lal	c Tauseef b Jaffer	52	c Akram b Imran		70
M.B. Amarnath	run out	9	b Tauseef		31
D.B. Vengsarkar	c Yousuf b Akram	38	not out		41
M. Azharuddin	b Akram	141			
R.J. Shastri	b Qadir	5			
Kapil Dev*	c Miandad b Jaffer	66			
R.M.H. Binny	not out	52			
K.S. More†	run out	0			
R.R. Kulkarni	lbw b Akram	0			
Maninder Singh	b Akram	3			
Extras	(B1, LB8, W1, NB5)	15	(B4, LB12, NB2)		18
		403	(3 wkts dec)		**181**

Pakistan

Shoaib Mohammad	run out	24	(2) lbw b Binny		5
Ramiz Raja	c sub (S. Viswanath) b Shastri	69	(1) c More b Binny		29
Rizwan-uz-Zaman	b Kapil Dev	60	(4) b Shastri		8
Javed Miandad	c More b Binny	17	(5) not out		63
Salim Malik	lbw b Binny	0	(6) lbw b Kapil Dev		20
Imran Khan*	c Kapil Dev b Binny	1	(7) not out		5
Salim Yousuf†	lbw b Kapil Dev	33	(3) b Maninder		43
Wasim Akram	b Binny	1			
Abdul Qadir	b Binny	2			
Tauseef Ahmed	c Vengsarkar b Binny	0			
Salim Jaffer	not out	0			
Extras	(B4, LB4, W1, NB13)	22	(B1, LB2, W2, NB1)		6
		229	(5 wkts)		**179**

Pakistan	O	M	R	W	O	M	R	W
Imran Khan	27	2	93	0	7.1	0	28	2
Akram	31	5	96	5	18	4	46	0
Jaffer	36	2	115	2	7	0	33	0
Tauseef	10	1	39	0	18	2	50	1
Qadir	14	3	51	1	2	0	8	0

India	O	M	R	W	O	M	R	W
Kapil Dev	29	5	88	2	19	7	41	1
Binny	25.1	8	56	6	21	4	45	2
Maninder	20.1	11	21	0	16	6	30	1
Shastri	20.5	10	18	1	24	6	41	1
Kulkarni	13	1	38	0	7	2	19	0

Fall of Wickets

Wkt	I 1st	P 1st	I 2nd	P 2nd
1st	30	57	37	12
2nd	73	136	100	57
3rd	104	178	181	73
4th	144	178	–	116
5th	149	191	–	170
6th	292	195	–	–
7th	393	207	–	–
8th	393	215	–	–
9th	395	229	–	–
10th	403	229	–	–

India v Pakistan 1986-87 3rd Test

Match Drawn
Played at Sawai Mansinghe Stadium, Jaipur, 21, 22, 24 (np), 25, 26 February
Toss: India. Umpires: V. K. Ramaswamy and P.D. Reporter
Debuts: nil.

India

S.M. Gavaskar	c Miandad b Imran	0	c Ramiz b Tauseef	24
K. Srikkanth	lbw b Akram	45	c sub (Ijaz Ahmed)	
			b Qasim	51
M.B. Amarnath	b Imran	49	not out	15
D.B. Vengsarkar	c Qasim b Shoaib	30	not out	21
M. Azharuddin	c Yousuf b Tauseef	110		
R.J. Shastri	c Ramiz b Qasim	125		
Kapil Dev*	c Yousuf b Rizwan	50		
K.S. More†	c Miandad b Tauseef	22		
R.M.H. Binny	not out	6		
N.S. Yadav	not out	8		
G. Sharma	did not bat			
Extras	(B2, LB10, W1, NB7)	20	(LB2, BN1)	3
	(8 wkts dec)	**465**	(2 wkts)	**114**

Pakistan

Ramiz Raja	b Kapil Dev	114
Shoaib Mohammad	c Gavaskar b Amarnath	0
Rizwan-uz-Zaman	c More b Kapil Dev	10
Javed Miandad	lbw b Shastri	50
Younis Ahmed	c sub (Arun Lal) b Sharma	14
Salim Malik	c Srikkanth b Sharma	10
Imran Khan*	c Kapil Dev b Sharma	66
Salim Yousuf†	run out	14
Wasim Akram	c Kapil Dev b Yadav	11
Iqbal Qasim	c Srikkanth b Sharma	21
Tauseef Ahmed	not out	9
Extras	(B8, LB2, NB12)	22
		341

Pakistan	O	M	R	W	O	M	R	W
Imran Khan	35	7	93	2	5	2	8	0
Akram	36.3	5	88	1	5	1	17	0
Qasim	44	5	149	1	13	4	34	1
Tauseef	38	3	97	2	13	3	47	1
Shoaib	5	0	19	1	1	1	0	0
Rizwan-uz-Zaman	5	2	7	1				
Younis Ahmed					1	0	6	0

India	O	M	R	W	O	M	R	W
Kapil Dev	27	7	84	2				
Amarnath	8	4	15	1				
Shastri	36	12	79	1				
Yadav	25	8	65	1				
Sharma	32.5	3	88	4				

Fall of Wickets

	I	P	I
Wkt	1st	1st	2nd
1st	0	0	72
2nd	74	28	88
3rd	114	122	–
4th	156	162	–
5th	286	174	–
6th	384	228	–
7th	444	282	–
8th	451	302	–
9th	–	318	–
10th	–	341	–

India v Pakistan 1986-87 4th Test

Match Drawn
Played at Gujarat Stadium, Ahmedabad, 4, 5, 7, 8, 9 March
Toss: Pakistan. Umpires: R.B. Gupta and S. Ramachandra Rao
Debuts: nil

Pakistan

Ramiz Raja	b Kapil Dev	41	c Azharuddin b Maninder		21
Salim Yousuf†	st More b Amarnath	2			
Rizwan-uz-Zaman	c Kapil Dev b Maninder	5	(2) c Azharuddin b Sharma		58
Younis Ahmed	st More b Yadav	40	(3) not out		34
Salim Malik	c More b Yadav	20	(4) not out		14
Manzoor Elahi	c Kapil Dev b Yadav	52			
Imran Khan*	b Sharma	72			
Ijaz Fakih	lbw b Kapil Dev	105			
Abdul Qadir	b Kapil Dev	25			
Wasim Akram	not out	4			
Iqbal Qasim	c More b Yadav	0			
Extras	(B6, LB20, NB3)	29	(NB8)		8
		395	(2 wkts dec)		**135**

India

S.M. Gavaskar	lbw b Imran	63
K. Srikkanth	b Fakih	22
M.B. Amarnath	c & b Qasim	7
D.B. Vengsarkar	c Malik b Akram	109
K.S. More†	c Qasim b Qadir	23
M. Azharuddin	b Imran	12
R.J. Shastri	c Qasim b Manzoor	15
Kapil Dev*	not out	50
N.S. Yadav	b Akram	0
Maninder Singh	b Akram	0
G. Sharma	lbw b Akram	0
Extras	(B11, LB6, NB5)	22
		323

India	O	M	R	W	O	M	R	W
Kapil Dev	27	9	46	3	10	3	19	0
Amarnath	9	3	14	1	2	0	6	0
Maninder	54	21	106	1	23	16	13	1
Sharma	36	8	62	1	26	9	36	1
Yadav	48.3	13	109	4	14	4	18	0
Shastri	11	3	26	0	18	6	23	0
Srikkanth	2	0	6	0	2	0	5	0
Gavaskar					4	1	15	0

Pakistan	O	M	R	W	O	M	R	W
Imran Khan	17	6	41	2				
Akram	21.5	2	60	4				
Fakih	27	3	81	1				
Qasim	30	11	63	1				
Qadir	13	1	53	1				
Manzoor	3	2	8	1				

Fall of Wickets

Wkt	P 1st	I 1st	P 2nd
1st	2	34	43
2nd	23	46	107
3rd	62	157	–
4th	99	204	–
5th	149	218	–
6th	176	246	–
7th	330	306	–
8th	391	322	–
9th	394	322	–
10th	395	323	–

India v Pakistan 1986-87 5th Test

Pakistan won by 16 runs
Played at Karnataka State CA Stadium, Bangalore, 13, 14, 15, 17 March
Toss: Pakistan. Umpires: R.B. Gupta and V.K. Ramaswamy
Debuts: nil

Pakistan

Ramiz Raja	c Vengsarkar b Kapil Dev	22	b Yadav	47
Rizwan-uz-Zaman	b Kapil Dev	0	(3) b Shastri	1
Salim Malik	b Maninder	33	(4) b Kapil Dev	33
Javed Miandad	c Shastri b Maninder	7	(2) c Srikkanth b Shastri	17
Manzoor Elahi	c Azharuddin b Maninder	0	(7) c More b Maninder	8
Imran Khan*	c Amarnath b Maninder	6	c Srikkanth by Shastri	39
Wasim Akram	b Maninder	0	(8) lbw b Maninder	11
Salim Yousuf†	c & b Shastri	0	(9) not out	41
Iqbal Qasim	b Maninder	19	(5) c Srikkanth b Yadav	26
Tauseef Ahmed	not out	15	c Yadav b Shastri	10
Salim Jaffer	c Vengsarkar b Maninder	8	c Gavaskar b Maninder	0
Extras	(B2, LB1, NB3)	6	(B7, LB8, NB1)	16
		116		**249**

India

S.M. Gavaskar	b Tauseef	21	(2) c Rizwan b Qasim	96
K. Srikkanth	b Tauseef	21	(1) lbw b Akram	6
M.B. Amarnath	b Tauseef	13	c Yousuf b Akram	0
D.B. Vengsarkar	c Manzoor b Tauseef	50	b Tauseef	19
M. Azharuddin	c Manzoor b Qasim	6	(6) c & b Qasim	26
R.J. Shastri	c Malik b Tauseef	7	(7) c & b Qasim	4
Kapil Dev*	c Malik b Qasim	9	(8) b Qasim	2
R.M.H. Binny	c Tauseef b Qasim	1	(9) c Yousuf b Tauseef	15
K.S. More†	not out	9	(5) lbw b Tauseef	3
N.S. Yadav	b Qasim	0	b Tauseef	4
Maninder Singh	c Yousuf b Qasim	0	not out	2
Extras	(B4, LB4)	8	(B22, LB5)	27
		145		**204**

India	O	M	R	W	O	M	R	W
Kapil Dev	11	2	23	2	12	2	25	1
Binny	3	0	25	0				
Amarnath	3	1	7	0				
Maninder	18.2	8	27	7	43.5	8	99	3
Shastri	11	1	19	1	24	3	69	4
Yadav	3	0	12	0	15	3	41	2

Pakistan	O	M	R	W	O	M	R	W
Imran Khan	5	0	26	0				
Akram	2	0	9	0	11	3	19	2
Qasim	30	15	48	5	37	11	73	4
Tauseef	27	7	54	5	45.5	12	85	4

Fall of Wickets

Wkt	P 1st	I 1st	P 2nd	I 2nd
1st	3	39	45	15
2nd	39	56	57	15
3rd	60	71	89	64
4th	60	102	121	80
5th	68	126	142	123
6th	68	130	166	155
7th	73	135	184	161
8th	74	137	198	180
9th	98	143	249	185
10th	116	145	249	204

Test Match Averages: India v Pakistan 1986-87

India

Batting and Fielding	M	I	NO	HS	R	Avge	100	50	Ct/St
D.B. Vengsarkar	5	8	2	109	404	67.33	1	2	5
M. Azharuddin	5	6	0	141	315	52.50	2	–	5
S.M. Gavaskar	4	6	0	96	295	49.16	–	3	3
K. Srikkanth	5	8	0	123	311	38.87	1	1	6
R.M.H. Binny	3	4	2	52*	74	37.00	–	1	–
Kapil Dev	5	6	1	66	182	36.40	–	3	5
R.J. Shastri	5	6	0	125	197	32.83	1	–	2
M.B. Amarnath	5	8	1	89	213	30.42	–	1	1
K.S. More	5	6	1	28	85	17.00	–	–	7/3
N.S. Yadav	4	5	2	8*	18	6.00	–	–	1
Maninder Singh	4	5	2	7*	12	4.00	–	–	–

Also batted: Arun Lal (1 match) 52, 70; R.R. Kulkarni (2 matches) 2, 0 (1ct); G. Sharma (2 matches) 0.

Bowling	O	M	R	W	Avge	Best	5wI	10wM
R.M.H. Binny	49.1	12	126	8	15.75	6-56	1	–
Maninder Singh	260.2	97	478	20	23.90	7-27	2	1
G. Sharma	94.5	20	186	6	31.00	4-88	–	–
Kapil Dev	162	37	430	11	39.09	3-46	–	–
R.J. Shastri	200.5	54	422	9	46.88	4-69	–	–
N.S. Yadav	161.3	35	401	8	50.12	4-109	–	–

Also bowled: M.B. Amarnath 22-8-42-2; S.M. Gavaskar 5-1-19-0; R.R. Kulkarni 32-3-113-2; K. Srikkanth 7-0-17-0.

Pakistan

Batting and Fielding	M	I	NO	HS	R	Avge	100	50	Ct/St
Imran Khan	5	7	2	135*	324	64.80	1	2	–
Javed Miandad	4	7	1	94	302	50.33	–	4	3
Younis Ahmed	2	3	1	40	88	44.00	–	–	–
Ramiz Raja	5	9	0	114	381	42.33	1	1	3
Shoaib Mohammad	3	5	0	101	175	35.00	1	–	–
Rizwan-uz-Zaman	5	9	1	60	197	24.62	–	3	1
Tauseef Ahmed	4	5	3	15*	47	23.50	–	–	3
Salim Yousuf	5	7	1	43	134	22.33	–	–	8/2
Salim Malik	5	9	2	33	155	22.14	–	–	4
Manzoor Alahi	2	3	0	52	60	20.00	–	1	2
Wasim Akram	5	6	1	62	89	17.80	–	1	2
Iqbal Qasim	3	4	0	26	66	16.50	–	–	6
Abdul Qadir	3	3	0	25	48	16.00	–	–	–
Salim Jaffer	2	3	1	8	8	4.00	–	–	–

Also batted: Ijaz Ahmed (1 match) 3; Ijaz Fakih (1 match) 105.

Bowling	O	M	R	W	Avge	Best	5wI	10wM
Iqbal Qasim	154	46	367	12	30.58	5-48	1	–
Wasim Akram	159	30	413	13	31.76	5-96	1	–
Tauseef Ahmed	218.5	36	561	16	35.06	5-54	1	–
Imran Khan	123.1	21	392	8	49.00	2-28	–	–

Also bowled: Abdul Qadir 68-8-242-4; Ijaz Fakih 27-3-81-1; Manzoor Elahi 3-2-8-1; Rizwan-uz-Zaman 5-2-7-1; Salim Jaffer 43-2-148-2; Shoaib Mohammad 9-1-32-1; Younis Ahmed 1-0-6-0.

Statistical Highlights of the Tests

1st Test, Madras. Pakistan's 487 was their highest score in India, Shoaib Mohammad scoring his maiden Test century and Imran his third. Imran's 135 not out was his highest in Tests, and his 8th-wicket partnership with Wasim Akram was a record for Pakistan against India. Maninder took 5 wickets in a Test innings for the 2nd time. Srikkanth scored his second and highest Test hundred (123) and shared in a 200 partnership with Gavaskar, a record for the first wicket in Tests between the two countries.

2nd Test, Calcutta. Gavaskar refused to play because he had received threats to his safety, ending his run of 106 consecutive Tests. Azharuddin scored his 5th Test 100 and shared a record 6th-wicket partnership of 143 for India against Pakistan with Kapil Dev. Wasim Akram took 5 wickets in a Test innings for the 4th time, Binny for the 2nd time, with his best bowling of 6-56.

3rd Test, Jaipur. First Test played at Jaipur. Gavaskar was out to the first ball of the match. Rain seeping under cover on the rest day prevented any play on the third day. Azharuddin scored his 6th Test century, Shastri his 7th, and Ramiz Raja his 1st. India's Binny was injured and unable to bowl. Pakistan sent for Ijaz Fakih. Younis Ahmed, who had been sent for from London after the 1st Test, played his first test since 1969-70.

4th Test, Ahmedabad. Gavaskar became the first player to reach 10,000 Test runs (58). A large mob invaded the pitch to congratulate him and play was held up for 14 minutes. He announced that he would be retiring from Test cricket at the end of the series. Javed Miandad had a back injury and withdrew, as did Tauseef, who was taken ill immediately before the start. Fortunately, Ijaz Fakih had arrived from Pakistan the previous day, and he scored his 1st 100, reaching both 50 and 100 with a six. Vengsarkar scored his 15th Test 100, his 6th since June 1986. More was Abdul Qadir's 150th Test wicket. On the 4th day, Pakistan fielders were pelted with stones. Tea was taken, but 70 minutes' play was lost while order was restored and the boundary fielders then reappeared wearing helmets. The last day's play was described as 'extremely tedious', only 110 runs being scored from 85 overs.

5th Test, Bangalore. Gavaskar, in his last Test, tossed for India and lost. The pitch was described as 'treacherous' and Gavaskar's 2nd innings of 96 as 'one of his greatest, requiring a high degree of skill to survive'. Iqbal Qasim and Tauseef Ahmed bowled unchanged for 3 hours on the 4th day to give Pakistan the first victory by either side since 1982-83. Maninder's 7-27, including 4 wickets in 13 balls, was his best bowling and his third 5 wickets in an innings in Tests. His match analysis was 10-126. Pakistan's 1st-innings 116 was their lowest against India, who themselves lost their last 5 1st-innings wickets for 19 runs. Qasim took 5 wickets in an innings for the 6th time, Tauseef for the 3rd. Yadev reached 100 wickets in his 35th Test. Gavaskar finished with 79 scores of over 50 in Tests and reached his 2,000 runs against Pakistan.

One-Day Internationals

27 January at Nehru Stadium, Indore. PAKISTAN won by 3 wickets. Toss: Pakistan. India 196-7 (45 overs) (R.J. Shastri 50). Pakistan 200-7 (44 overs) (Mudassar Nazar 43). Award: Abdul Qadir (8-1-42-2 and 39).

18 February at Eden Gardens, Calcutta. PAKISTAN won by 2 wickets. Toss: Pakistan. India 238-6 (40 overs) (K. Srikkanth 123, M. Azharuddin 49). Pakistan 241-8 (39.3 overs) (Salim Malik 72*, Ramiz Raja 58, Younis Ahmed 58; R.J. Shastri 4-38). Award: Salim Malik (72*).

20 March at Niaz Stadium, Hyderabad. INDIA won by losing fewer wickets in a tied match. Toss: Pakistan. India 212-6 (44 overs) (R.J. Shastri 69*, Kapil Dev 59, R.M. Lamba 41). Pakistan 212-7 (44 overs) (Salim Malik 84).

21 March at Nehru Stadium, Pune. PAKISTAN won by 6 wickets. Toss: Pakistan. India 120-9 (42 overs). Pakistan 121-4 (37.2 overs). Award: Salim Jaffer (9-0-25-3).

24 March at Vidarbha CA Stadium, Nagpur. Pakistan won by 41 runs. Toss: India. Pakistan 286-6 (44 overs) (Javed Miandad 79, Imran Khan 73, Wasim Akram 48*). India 245-9 (44 overs) (S.M. Gavaskar 70, R.J. Shastri 52). Award: Wasim Akram (48* and 10-1-26-3).

26 March at Keenan Stadium, Jamshedpur. PAKISTAN won by 5 wickets. Toss: Pakistan. India 265-3 (44 overs) (M. Prabhakar 106, S.M. Gavaskar 69, D.B. Vengsarkar 54*). Pakistan 266-5 (43.2 overs) (Javed Miandad 78*, Ijaz Ahmed 72). Award: M. Prabhakar (106).

Pakistan Tour of India 1986-87

First-Class Matches: Played 8; Won 1, Drawn 7
All Matches: Played 14; Won 6, Lost 1, Drawn 7

First-Class Averages

Batting and Fielding	M	I	NO	HS	R	Avge	100	50	Ct/St
Younis Ahmed	3	4	2	103*	191	95.50	1	–	–
Manzoor Elahi	4	6	3	65*	215	71.66	–	3	6
Javed Miandad	5	8	1	151	453	64.71	1	4	3
Imran Khan	6	8	2	135*	343	57.16	1	2	–
Ramiz Raja	7	11	0	167	594	54.00	2	1	3
Rizwan-uz-Zaman	7	12	2	193	491	49.10	2	3	1
Ijaz Ahmed	4	5	0	131	229	45.80	1	1	1
Shoaib Mohammad	5	9	1	116	362	45.25	2	–	–
Abdul Qadir	5	5	0	103	177	35.40	1	–	–
Tauseef Ahmed	5	5	3	15*	47	23.50	–	–	3
Mudassar Nazar	3	4	1	31*	76	25.33	–	–	3
Salim Malik	8	14	2	53	304	25.33	–	1	4
Salim Yousuf	6	8	1	43	151	21.57	–	–	9/2
Wasim Akram	6	7	2	62	90	18.00	–	1	3
Iqbal Qasim	4	4	0	26	66	16.50	–	–	7
Salim Jaffer	4	5	3	8	13	6.50	–	–	–

Also batted: Asif Mujtaba (1 match) 13, 1ct; Ijaz Fakih (1 match) 105; Zakir Khan (2 matches) 21; Zulqarnain (4ct) played in two matches but did not bat.

Bowling	O	M	R	W	Avge	Best	5wI	10wM
Manzoor Elahi	30.4	3	131	5	26.20	3-65	–	–
Iqbal Qasim	191	51	454	17	26.70	5-48	2	–
Tauseef Ahmed	244.5	41	620	21	29.52	5-54	2	–
Wasim Akram	184.2	35	487	14	34.78	5-96	1	–
Salim Jaffer	90	13	322	9	35.77	3-57	–	–
Imran Khan	143.1	26	437	12	36.41	3-38	–	–
Abdul Qadir	117	18	386	7	55.14	2-44	–	–

Also bowled: Asif Mujtaba 5-1-24-0; Ijaz Fakih 27-3-81-1; Mudassar Nazar 14-1-34-1; Rizwan-uz-Zaman 7-2-13-1; Salim Malik 1-0-1-0; Shoaib Mohammad 14-2-41-1; Younis Ahmed 1-0-6-0; Zakir Khan 44-11-126-2.

New Zealand v West Indies

West Indies and New Zealand contested a close series which ended with honours even and both teams obviously facing a period of rebuilding. New Zealand fought back with characteristic determination from a sizeable first-innings deficit to draw the first Test; the West Indies beat the weather, and their opponents, by 10 wickets and a few minutes in the second; and New Zealand levelled the series with an emphatic victory in the third and final match.

Returning to New Zealand for the first time since their contentious tour of 1980, West Indies arrived from Australia dispirited after tasting rare defeat in the series of one-day internationals. After years of almost uninterrupted cricket, several of their ageing players could not find the enthusiasm necessary to maintain consistency of performance, and it showed in a spate of undisciplined strokes and dropped catches. The attitude was most evident when the great Michael Holding, the vice-captain, announced his retirement from Test cricket midway through the first Test and returned home.

New Zealand's problems centred on finding replacements for those who had formed the nucleus of their outstanding team of the early 1980s. They had to depend too heavily on too few players.

One batsman on each team virtually carried the batting – Gordon Greenidge for the West Indies and Martin Crowe for New Zealand. When they failed, their team failed: the West Indies were dismissed for 100 and 264 in the final Test, when Greenidge was out twice for less than 20, New Zealand for 228 in the first Test and 157 in the second when Crowe went similarly cheaply.

Greenidge, kept out of the last five matches in Australia by a strained hamstring muscle, was almost replaced by the West Indies selectors for the New Zealand tour, but, once there, batted with commanding authority. His double century in the second Test and his centuries in two one-day internationals were innings of a master batsman.

Crowe enhanced his reputation as one of the finest young batsmen of the day with big scores in all of the Tests, each compiled from the crisis of the loss of two early wickets.

In spite of pleas from New Zealand captain Jeremy Coney for dry pitches helpful to spinners, fast bowlers held sway in conditions which offered them some encouragement. There was a perceptible changing of the guard in the West Indies attack, in personnel if not strategy. Holding departed after a magnificent career with 249 Test wickets, Joel Garner missed the second Test through illness, and, for once, Malcolm Marshall found wickets hard to come by. This placed new responsibility on the two younger fast bowlers, and Courtney Walsh, in particular, with help from Tony Gray, took the opportunity eagerly.

The magnificent Richard Hadlee was again New Zealand's most important bowler, passing the landmark of 350 Test wickets at his home ground hn Christchurch. He was, as always, stoically supported by Ewan Chatfield and, in the final Test, by Martin Snedden.

New Zealand v West Indies 1986-87 1st Test

Match Drawn
Played at Basin Reserve, Wellington, 20, 21, 22, 23, 24 February
Toss: West Indies. Umpires: B.L. Aldridge and S.J. Woodward
Debuts: New Zealand – D.N. Patel

New Zealand

J.G. Wright	c Garner b Richards	75	c & b Gomes	138
K.R. Rutherford	c Logie b Garner	6	lbw b Garner	6
J.V. Coney*	c Logie b Marshall	3	c Richards b Garner	4
M.D. Crowe	lbw b Walsh	3	c Holding b Richards	119
D.N. Patel	c Garner b Walsh	18	b Walsh	20
J.J. Crowe	c Logie b Garner	37	not out	27
J.G. Bracewell	lbw b Garner	17	not out	28
R.J. Hadlee	not out	35		
I.D.S. Smith†	lbw b Garner	0		
S.L. Boock	c Garner b Marshall	3		
E.J. Chatfield	lbw b Garner	0		
Extras	(LB7, NB24)	31	(B10, LB10, NB24)	44
		228	(5 wkts dec)	**386**

West Indies

C.G. Greenidge	c Rutherford b Chatfield	78	c Rutherford b Boock	25
D.L. Haynes	b Bracewell	121	c Hadlee b Boock	13
H.A. Gomes	c Smith b Hadlee	18	not out	8
R.B. Richardson	b Boock	37	not out	0
I.V.A. Richards*	c Smith b Chatfield	24		
A.L. Logie	c Coney b Hadlee	3		
P.J.L. Dujon	c Smith b Chatfield	22		
M.D. Marshall	c & b Boock	30		
M.A. Holding	c sub (T. Ritchie) b Chatfield	0		
J. Garner	c Hadlee b Boock	0		
C.A. Walsh	not out	1		
Extras	(B1, LB8, W1, NB1)	11	(B3, LB1)	4
		345	(2 wkts)	**50**

West Indies	O	M	R	W	O	M	R	W
Marshall	22	3	57	2	20	6	43	0
Garner	27	5	51	5	30	9	72	2
Walsh	12	1	46	2	34	13	59	1
Holding	16	4	34	0	21	4	65	0
Richards	11	3	32	1	47	13	86	1
Gomes	1	0	1	0	21	6	37	1
Richardson					4	1	4	0

New Zealand	O	M	R	W	O	M	R	W
Hadlee	31	9	77	2	4	0	12	0
Chatfield	39	14	102	4	4	0	13	0
Coney	3	0	8	0				
Bracewell	14	5	47	1	7	2	13	0
Boock	35	14	76	3	7	4	8	2
Crowe, M.D.	3	1	13	0				
Patel	3	0	13	0				

Fall of Wickets

Wkt	NZ 1st	WI 1st	NZ 2nd	WI 2nd
1st	10	150	13	33
2nd	19	208	20	46
3rd	46	232	261	–
4th	107	278	301	–
5th	153	287	331	–
6th	181	289	–	–
7th	192	339	–	–
8th	192	343	–	–
9th	226	344	–	–
10th	228	345	–	–

New Zealand v West Indies 1986-87 2nd Test

West Indies won by 10 wickets
Played at Eden Park, Auckland, 27, 28 February, 1, 2, 3 March
Toss: West Indies. Umpires: F.R. Goodall and G.C. Morris
Debuts: nil

West Indies

D.L. Haynes	c M.D. Crowe b Hadlee	1	(2) not out	3
C.G. Greenidge	b Hadlee	213	(1) not out	10
H.A. Gomes	c Smith b Chatfield	5		
R.B. Richardson	c Smith b Hadlee	41		
I.V.A. Richards*	b Hadlee	14		
A.L. Logie	c M.D. Crowe b Hadlee	34		
P.J.L. Dujon†	b Boock	77		
M.D. Marshall	c J.J. Crowe b Boock	6		
C.G. Butts	not out	8		
A.H. Gray	lbw b Hadlee	8		
C.A. Walsh	did not bat			
Extras	(B4, LB3, NB4)	11		
	(9 wkts dec)	**418**	(0 wkts)	**13**

New Zealand

J.G. Wright	c Richardson b Marshall	11	c Logie b Walsh	7
K.R. Rutherford	b Marshall	12	c Richardson Marshall	5
J.J. Crowe	c Dujon b Walsh	1	c Gray b Walsh	21
M.D. Crowe	c Dujon b Marshall	10	c Logie b Gray	104
D.N. Patel	c Greenidge b Butts	21	lbw b Marshall	5
J.V. Coney*	c Logie b Gray	15	c Dujon b Gray	17
J.G. Bracewell	c Richardson b Gray	7	lbw b Gomes	43
R.J. Hadlee	c Dujon b Butts	0	c Richardson b Walsh	14
I.D.S. Smith†	not out	40	c Richards b Walsh	10
S.L. Boock	c Dujon b Gray	0	c Dujon b Walsh	4
E.J. Chatfield	c Logie b Marshall	4	not out	0
Extras	(B12, LB2, NB22)	36	(B7, LB8, NB28)	43
		157		**273**

New Zealand	O	M	R	W	O	M	R	W
Hadlee	41.4	7	105	6	1	0	9	0
Chatfield	37	14	88	1	0.3	0	4	0
Boock	25	6	96	2				
Bracewell	17	2	53	0				
Coney	11	2	22	0				
Crowe, M.D.	5	1	9	0				
Patel	6	0	38	0				

West Indies	O	M	R	W	O	M	R	W
Marshall	17	3	43	4	33	7	71	2
Walsh	14	5	34	1	30.2	6	73	5
Butts	12	4	21	2	26	6	61	0
Gray	10	1	45	3	18	4	44	2
Gomes					4	1	9	1

Fall of Wickets

Wkt	WI 1st	NZ 1st	NZ 2nd	WI 2nd
1st	7	30	10	–
2nd	14	38	14	–
3rd	109	39	83	–
4th	131	69	91	–
5th	219	81	126	–
6th	384	95	233	–
7th	400	101	250	–
8th	402	109	260	–
9th	418	118	269	–
10th	–	157	273	–

New Zealand v West Indies 1986-87 3rd Test

New Zealand won by 5 wickets
Played at Lancaster Park, Christchurch, 12 (np), 13, 14, 15 March
Toss: New Zealand. Umpires: G.C. Morris and S.J. Woodward
Debuts: New Zealand – P.A. Horne

West Indies

C.G. Greenidge	b Chatfield	2	c Smith b Hadlee	16
D.L. Haynes	b Hadlee	0	c Horne b Chatfield	19
R.B. Richardson	c M.D. Crowe b Hadlee	37	c M.D. Crowe b Hadlee	19
H.A. Gomes	c J.J. Crowe b Chatfield	8	c Coney b M.D. Crowe	33
I.V.A. Richards*	c Smith b Chatfield	1	c Smith b Snedden	38
A.L. Logie	c Coney b Hadlee	6	c J.J. Crowe b Snedden	19
P.J.L. Dujon†	c Coney b Hadlee	6	c M.D. Crowe b Snedden	39
M.D. Marshall	c Snedden b Chatfield	2	b Hadlee	45
J. Garner	c Coney b Hadlee	0	c Wright b Snedden	11
A.H. Gray	not out	10	c M.D. Crowe b Snedden	3
C.A. Walsh	b Hadlee	14	not out	8
Extras	(LB6, NB8)	14	(B2, LB4, NB8)	14
		100		**264**

New Zealand

J.G. Wright	c Richards b Walsh	6	c Richards b Gray	2
P.A. Horne	c Richards b Garner	9	c Gray b Walsh	0
J.J. Crowe	c Dujon b Gray	55	c Gray b Walsh	2
M.D. Crowe	b Marshall	83	not out	9
D.N. Patel	c Dujon b Gray	0	c Richardson b Walsh	9
J.V. Coney*	run out	36	c Gray b Garner	2
J.G. Bracewell	c Haynes b Garner	66	not out	2
R.J. Hadlee	not out	25		
I.D.S. Smith†	c Dujon b Garner	7		
M.C. Snedden	c Logie b Garner	7		
E.J. Chatfield	not out	1		
Extras	(B6, LB2, W1, NB28)	37	(NB7)	7
	(9 wkts dec)	**332**	(5 wkts)	**33**

New Zealand	O	M	R	W	O	M	R	W
Hadlee	12.3	2	50	6	23	2	101	3
Chatfield	18	8	30	4	16	3	42	1
Snedden	6	1	14	0	18.3	2	68	5
Bracewell					7	0	34	0
Crowe, M.D.					6	0	13	1

West Indies	O	M	R	W	O	M	R	W
Marshall	27	2	75	1				
Garner	19	2	79	4	1	0	3	1
Walsh	24.5	3	78	1	5.1	0	16	3
Gray	17	4	47	2	4	1	14	1
Richards	9	3	29	0				
Gomes	4	1	16	0				

Fall of Wickets

Wkt	WI 1st	NZ 1st	WI 2nd	NZ 2nd
1st	2	12	37	1
2nd	6	23	37	3
3rd	44	179	80	13
4th	56	180	129	27
5th	56	181	133	30
6th	64	270	160	–
7th	67	294	237	–
8th	70	307	241	–
9th	75	330	255	–
10th	100	–	264	–

Test Match Averages: New Zealand v West Indies 1986-87

New Zealand

Batting and Fielding	M	I	NO	HS	R	Avge	100	50	Ct/St
M.D. Crowe	3	6	1	119	328	65.60	2	1	6
J.G. Bracewell	3	6	2	66	163	40.75	–	1	–
J.G. Wright	3	6	0	138	239	39.83	1	1	1
R.J. Hadlee	3	4	2	35*	74	37.00	–	–	2
J.J. Crowe	3	6	1	55	143	28.60	–	1	3
I.D.S. Smith	3	4	1	40*	57	19.00	–	–	8
J.V. Coney	3	6	0	36	77	12.83	–	–	5
D.N. Patel	3	6	0	21	73	12.16	–	–	–
K.R. Rutherford	2	4	0	12	29	7.25	–	–	2
E.J. Chatfield	3	4	2	4	5	2.50	–	–	–
S.L. Boock	2	3	0	4	7	2.33	–	–	1

Also batted: P.A. Horne (1 match) 9, 0 (1ct); M.C. Snedden (1 match) 7 (1ct).

Bowling	O	M	R	W	Avge	Best	5wI	10wM
M.C. Snedden	24.3	3	82	5	16.40	5-68	1	–
R.J. Hadlee	113.1	20	354	17	20.82	6-50	2	–
S.L. Boock	67	24	180	7	25.71	3-76	–	–
E.J. Chatfield	114.3	39	279	10	27.90	4-30	–	–

Also bowled: J.G. Bracewell 45-9-147-1; J.V. Coney 14-2-30-0; M.D. Crowe 14-2-35-1; D.N. Patel 9-0-51-0.

West Indies

Batting and Fielding	M	I	NO	HS	R	Avge	100	50	Ct/St
C.G. Greenidge	3	6	1	213	344	68.80	1	1	1
P.J.L. Dujon	3	4	0	77	144	36.00	–	1	9
R.B. Richardson	3	5	1	41	134	33.50	–	–	5
D.L. Haynes	3	6	1	121	157	31.40	1	–	1
C.A. Walsh	3	3	2	14	23	23.00	–	–	–
M.D. Marshall	3	4	0	45	83	20.75	–	–	–
I.V.A. Richards	3	4	0	38	77	19.25	–	–	5
H.A. Gomes	3	5	1	33	72	18.00	–	–	1
A.L. Logie	3	4	0	34	62	15.50	–	–	8
A.H. Gray	2	3	1	10*	21	10.50	–	–	4
J. Garner	2	3	0	11	11	3.66	–	–	3

Also batted: C.G. Butts (1 match) 8*; M.A. Holding (1 match) 0 (1ct).

Bowling	O	M	R	W	Avge	Best	5wI	10wM
J. Garner	77	16	205	12	17.08	5-51	1	–
A.H. Gray	49	10	150	8	18.75	3-45	–	–
C.A. Walsh	120.2	28	306	13	23.53	5-73	1	–
M.D. Marshall	119	21	289	9	32.11	4-43	–	–

Also bowled: C.G. Butts 38-10-82-2; H.A. Gomes 30-8-63-2; M.A. Holding 37-8-99-0; I.V.A. Richards 67-19-147-2; R.B. Richardson 4-1-4-0.

Statistical Highlights of the Tests

1st Test, Wellington. Garner, who took 5 wickets in an innings for the 7th time and 7-128 in the match, took his Test haul to 254 (2nd West Indian behind Lance Gibbs – 309), passing Holding (249), who took 0-99, injured his back, announced his retirement from Test cricket, and returned home. Patterson was sent for. Smith became the 1st New Zealand wicket-keeper to reach 100 dismissals. Haynes scored his 9th Test 100, his 3rd against New Zealand, and shared with Greenidge their 10th opening 100 partnership. Wright and Martin Crowe made their 6th Test 100s and a record New Zealand 3rd-wicket partnership of 241.

2nd Test, Auckland. West Indies won with 4.3 overs to spare, their first Test victory in New Zealand since 1968-69 and only New Zealand's 2nd defeat in the last 24 home Tests. Greenidge made his 3rd Test 200 and 13th 100, hitting 20 fours and 7 sixes in his 213 off 384 balls. Hadlee's 6-105 was his 28th 5-wicket haul and moved him ahead of Botham again. Martin Crowe scored his 7th Test 100, equalling the New Zealand record shared by Glenn Turner and Bev Congdon, and passed 2,000 runs in his 34th Test. Walsh's 5-73 was his best bowling and his 1st 5-wicket haul.

3rd Test, Christchurch. After much rain before the Test, the pitch was officially described as 'underprepared'. The 1st day was washed out, and New Zealand won in 3 days, only West Indies' 5th defeat in 62 Tests between 1 January 1980 and 14 March 1987. Hadlee's 6-50 was his best against West Indies, his 29th 5-wicket haul in Tests, and he became the 3rd bowler to reach 350 Test wickets (351). Snedden's 5-68 was his best Test return and his 1st 5-wicket haul. Martin Crowe's 328 runs in the series was a record for New Zealand against West Indies in New Zealand. Coney retired from Tests with a record as captain of W5, L4, D6.

One-Day Internationals

18 March at Carisbrook, Dunedin. WEST INDIES won by 95 runs. Toss: New Zealand. West Indies 237-9 (50 overs) (I.V.A. Richards 119, C.L. Hooper 48). New Zealand 142 (42.1 overs) (I.V.A. Richards 5-41). Award: I.V.A. Richards (119 and 10-0-41-5).

22 March at Eden Park, Auckland. WEST INDIES won by 6 wickets. Toss: West Indies. New Zealand 213 (50 overs) (M.D. Crowe 53, J.V. Coney 52, J.G. Wright 45). West Indies 217-4 (49 overs) (C.G. Greenidge 104, D.L. Haynes 61) Award: C.G. Greenidge (104).

25, 26 March at Basin Reserve, Wellington. Abandoned without a ball bowled.

28 March at Lancaster Park, Christchurch, WEST INDIES won by 10 wickets. Toss: New Zealand. New Zealand 191-9 (50 overs) (M.D. Crowe 42). West Indies 192-0 (39.2 overs) (C.G. Greenidge 133*, D.L. Haynes 53*). Award: C.G. Greenidge (133*).

West Indies Tour of New Zealand 1986-87

First-Class Matches: Played 5; Won 1, Lost 1, Drawn 3
All Matches: Played 9; Won 4, Lost 1, Drawn 3, No Result 1

First-Class Averages

Batting and Fielding	M	I	NO	HS	R	Avge	100	50	Ct/St
C.G. Greenidge	4	7	1	213	383	63.83	1	1	3
D.L. Haynes	5	9	2	121	337	48.14	2	1	2
I.V.A. Richards	4	5	1	117*	194	48.50	1	–	5
R.B. Richardson	5	9	2	121	327	46.71	1	1	6
P.J.L. Dujon	4	6	1	77	223	44.60	–	2	13
C.A. Walsh	4	3	2	14	23	23.00	–	–	1
H.A. Gomes	5	8	1	73	147	21.00	–	1	1
M.D. Marshall	3	4	0	45	83	20.75	–	–	–
A.L. Logie	5	6	0	34	71	11.83	–	–	11
A.H. Gray	4	3	1	10*	21	10.50	–	–	4

Also batted: C.G. Butts (3 matches) 3*, 8*, 2ct; J. Garner (3 matches) 0, 0, 11, 3ct; M.A. Holding (2 matches) 34*, 0, 3ct; C.L. Hooper (2 matches) 19, 5, 69, 2ct; T.R.O. Payne (1 match) 0, 51, 1ct; B.P. Patterson (2ct) played in one match but did not bat.

Bowling	O	M	R	W	Avge	Best	5wI	10wM
J. Garner	96.5	18	265	17	15.58	5-51	2	–
H.A. Gomes	44.2	10	96	5	19.20	3-8	–	–
A.H. Gray	106	24	322	15	21.46	4-64	–	–
C.A. Walsh	156.2	37	397	15	26.46	5-73	1	–
M.D. Marshall	119	21	289	9	32.11	4-43	–	–
C.G. Butts	113	30	279	7	39.85	2-21	–	–

Also bowled: M.A. Holding 71-14-203-4; C.L. Hooper 7-0-50-0; B.P. Patterson 21-2-102-1; I.V.A. Richards 67-19-147-2; R.B. Richardson 4-1-4-0.

Sri Lanka v New Zealand

New Zealand's second official tour of Sri Lanka proved an abortive one, not by way of performance but by incidents unrelated to cricket.

On the final day of the drawn first Test, the tour was thrown into jeopardy by a bomb blast in Colombo that claimed more than a hundred lives. The incident took place barely two miles from where the New Zealand team were putting up at their five-star hotel, and the reaction from the players was quite understandable.

The tour, which had barely begun, was called off after only a three-day game at Galle and the first Test. The eight-match itinerary comprised a series of 3 Tests and 4 one-day internationals.

Sri Lanka, determined to prove themselves following a disappointing tour of India, began their 25th Test well, holding the Kiwis' attack, spearheaded by the redoubtable Richard Hadlee, for almost three days in compiling a total of 397-9 declared. They had been put in.

More than half this score came from the bat of Test debutant Brendon Kuruppu, who covered himself with glory by becoming the first Sri Lankan to make a century in his debut and only the third in Test history to begin with a double hundred. In fact it was Kuruppu's perseverance in the middle right throughout the Sri Lanka innings of 777 minutes that blunted the New Zealand attack on a good batting pitch.

Kuruppu established several batting records during his marathon stint, including the highest and longest innings by a Sri Lankan in Test cricket, eclipsing the 190 in 636 minutes by Sidath Wettimuny against England at Lord's in 1984. Primarily known as an attacking player, the 25-year-old wicket-keeper and opening batsman showed a great deal of patience, temperament, and skill in tackling Hadlee and Co.

Ranjan Madugalle marked his return to Test cricket in this match with a superbly struck 60, which preserved his excellent record against the Kiwis. He missed Sri Lanka's last six Tests after a ball from England B fast bowler Jonathan Agnew had damaged his hand and face and forced him out of international cricket for 15 months.

Hadlee always looked the danger man and his four wickets brought him level with Dennis Lillee's tally of 355 Test wickets and second only to Ian Botham's world record of 366 wickets. He followed it up by hitting a Test career best 151 not out that ensured New Zealand a draw after they had looked in danger of following on when 99-4.

Jeff Crowe marked his debut as captain with an unbeaten 120, and, with Hadlee, put on 246 runs for the sixth wicket, which is a New Zealand record against all countries.

Thus the incidents which ended the tour cut short what promised to be a closely contested series.

Sri Lanka v New Zealand 1986-87 1st Test

Match Drawn
Played at Colombo Cricket Club, Colombo, 16, 18, 19, 20, 21 April
Toss: New Zealand. Umpires: P.W. Vidanagamage and W.A.U. Wickramasinghe
Debuts: Sir Lanka – D.S.B.P. Kuruppu; New Zealand – A.H. Jones

Sri Lanka

R.S. Mahanama	c Smith b Chatfield	16
D.S.B.P. Kuruppu†	not out	201
A.P. Gurusinha	lbw b Hadlee	22
R.L. Dias	c Bracewell b Hadlee	25
A. Ranatunga	c Smith b Bracewell	15
L.R.D. Mendis*	c Bracewell b Hadlee	12
R.S. Madugalle	c Hadlee b Gray	60
J.R. Ratnayeke	c M.D. Crowe b Bracewell	12
R.J. Ratnayake	c Bracewell b Hadlee	17
S.D. Anurasiri	c Smith b Chatfield	1
A.K. Kuruppuarachchi	not out	0
Extras	(LB4, W1, NB11)	16
	(9 wkts dec)	**397**

New Zealand

K.R. Rutherford	c Madugalle b Ratnayake	11
P.A. Horne	c Kuruppu b Anurasiri	16
A.H. Jones	lbw b Ratnayeke	38
M.D. Crowe	c Mendis b Ratnayeke	27
J.J. Crowe*	not out	120
E.J. Gray	c Ranatunga b Kuruppuarachchi	31
R.J. Hadlee	not out	151
J.G. Bracewell	did not bat	
I.D.S. Smith†	,,	
M.C. Snedden	,,	
E.J. Chatfield	,,	
Extras	(LB2, W4, NB6)	12
	(5 wkts)	**406**

New Zealand	O	M	R	W
Hadlee	38.5	10	102	4
Chatfield	38	11	104	2
Crowe, M.D.	7	4	13	0
Snedden	16	4	41	0
Bracewell	47	14	98	2
Gray	17	12	35	1

Sri Lanka	O	M	R	W
Ratnayake	32	7	79	1
Kuruppuarachchi	20	3	64	1
Ranatunga	23	10	43	0
Ratnayeke	37	6	111	2
Anurasiri	36	13	67	1
Gurusinha	9	1	17	0
Madugalle	2	0	6	0
Dias	4	0	17	0

Fall of Wickets

	SL	NZ
Wkt	1st	1st
1st	29	20
2nd	70	51
3rd	129	90
4th	166	99
5th	210	160
6th	319	–
7th	342	–
8th	382	–
9th	383	–
10th	–	–

New Zealand Tour of Sri Lanka 1986-87

First-Class Matches: Played 2; Drawn 2
All Matches: Played 2; Drawn 2

First-Class Averages

Batting and Fielding	M	I	NO	HS	R	Avge	100	50	Ct/St
J.J. Crowe	2	3	2	120*	179	179.00	1	1	1
K.R. Rutherford	2	3	0	108	128	42.66	1	–	4
E.J. Gray	2	3	1	42	73	36.50	–	–	–
P.A. Horne	2	3	0	56	86	28.66	–	1	–
A.H. Jones	2	3	0	38	42	14.00	–	–	2

Also batted: J.G. Bracewell (2 matches) 1, 3ct; M.D. Crowe (1 match) 27, 1ct; R.J. Hadlee (1 match) 151*; E.B. McSweeney (1 match) 28, 1ct; D.K. Morrison (1 match) 3*, 1ct; D.N. Patel (1 match) 6, 9; I.D.S. Smith (2 matches) 54, 3ct/1st; M.C. Snedden (2 matches) 2. E.J. Chatfield played in one match but did not bat.

Bowling	O	M	R	W	Avge	Best	5wI	10wM
J.G. Bracewell	80.2	24	179	10	17.90	8-81	1	–
R.J. Hadlee	38.5	10	102	4	25.50	4-102	–	–

Also bowled: E.J. Chatfield 38-11-104-2; M.D. Crowe 7-4-13-0; E.J. Gray 46-19-76-2; D.K. Morrison 22-7-73-3; D.N. Patel 5-0-12-0; M.C. Snedden 33-9-103-0.

Statistical Highlights of the Tests

1st Test, Colombo. Kuruppu's unbeaten 201 set several records: 1st Sri Lankan on field throughout Test; longest innings for Sri Lanka, 778 min, 562 balls; slowest 200 in Tests (dropped 4 times – 31/70/165/181); 3rd player to make a 200 in 1st Test (Foster, Rowe). Hadlee reached 355 wickets in his 70th Test to equal Lillee's tally (also 70 Tests). Chatfield became the 6th New Zealander to take 100 wickets, in his 33rd Test. Jeff Crowe's 120 not out was his 3rd Test 100, the 3rd slowest Test 100 (515 min, 331 balls) and slowest for New Zealand, but he became the 13th player and 1st New Zealander to make 100 in 1st Test as captain. His unbeaten 246 partnership with Hadlee was a record for New Zealand's 6th wicket and the highest stand in Tests between the two countries. Hadlee's 151 not out was his 2nd Test 100 and highest Test score.

A bomb blast on 21 April near the players' hotel resulted in the cancellation of the remaining two Tests and the four one-day internationals, and New Zealand's team returned home.

England Young Cricketers in Sri Lanka

Judged strictly on results, the England Young Cricketers' tour of Sri Lanka was not blessed with much success. On the credit side there was just one victory – in the second of the three one-day international matches. But England played much good cricket in the three four-day internationals, all drawn, and in the second they made Sri Lanka follow on. Their single victory in the one-day series was won by a large margin, whereas the two defeats were each by only two wickets.

Overall, in fact, the tour proved a highly satisfactory exercise against strong opposition on mostly comfortable batting pitches. It confirmed the lofty reputations of some players, revealed the promise of others, and provided valuable experience for all 15. Tim Lamb, secretary of Middlesex, managed the party with Graham Saville, late of Essex and now an NCA coach, as assistant manager and coach.

The handicap under which every side coming from an English midwinter starts was faced with some success by the batsmen. The captain, Michael Atherton of Lancashire, led the way initially, was consistent throughout with the bat and took useful wickets with his leg-spin. In the second innings of the final match he shared in an unbroken opening stand of 208 with Mark Ramprakash of Middlesex, the youngest member of the party and the most effective batsman. In that last match Ramprakash made a hundred in each innings, the first determinedly, the second dashingly, and he averaged 58.70 for the whole tour, 80.25 in the Tests.

The other batsmen all made runs, notably Mark Alleyne (Gloucestershire) and Trevor Ward (Kent). Nasser Hussain (Essex) and Oliver Smith (Gloucestershire) both made hundreds during a fifth-wicket stand of 213 in the second four-day match. Harvey Trump of Somerset showed himself to be not only a reliable off-spinner but a robust batsman.

Of the bowlers, Martin Bicknell, so impressive for Surrey in 1986, used his exceptional height to defeat the not infrequent sluggishness of the pitches. He did not want for stamina, he was accurate, and in the four-day series he took 10 wickets for 141 runs.

In general, young English cricketers of 17 to 19 years of age are less developed physically and less experienced than their counterparts overseas, and this touring side's ability to hold its own did its members much credit.

The team was: M.A. Atherton (Lancashire) capt, M.W. Alleyne (Gloucestershire), M.P. Bicknell (Surrey), S.J. Brown (Northants), M.A. Crawley (Lancashire), A.G.J. Fraser (Middlesex), W.K. Hegg (Lancashire), N. Hussain (Essex), M.R. Newton (Hampshire), M.R. Ramprakash (Middlesex), O.C.K. Smith (Gloucestershire), M.P. Speight (Sussex), L. Tennant (Leicestershire), H.R.J. Trump (Somerset), T.R. Ward (Kent).

Four-day 'Tests'

3-6 February at Colombo CC, Colombo. MATCH DRAWN. Toss: England YC. England YC 214 (N. Hussain 42; D. Madena 4-58) and 208-8 dec (T.R. Ward 60, M.P. Bicknell 51*). Sri Lanka YC 173 (A. Allirajah 40; M.P. Bicknell 4-46, H.R.J. Trump 4-51) and 152-4 (C. Hathurusinghe 62*).

9-12 February at Asgiriya Stadium, Kandy. MATCH DRAWN. Toss England YC. England YC 451-7 dec (T.R. Ward 67, N. Hussain 170, O.C.K. Smith 105; D. Perera 6-162). Sri Lanka YC 260 (C. Mendis 96; M.P. Bicknell 4-37) and 261-6 (A. Allirajah 53; C. Unantanne 109*).

18-21 February at Galle Esplanade. MATCH DRAWN. Toss: England YC. England YC 420-9 dec (M.R. Ramprakash 118, O.C.K. Smith 62, M.W. Alleyne 71, H.R.J. Trump 50*; C. Mendis 4-68) and 208-0 dec (M.R. Ramprakash 120*, M.A. Atherton 84*). Sri Lanka YC 346-6 dec (A.Allirajah 73, C. Mendis 53*, R. Kaluvitharna 119) and 64-2.

One-day Internationals

1 February at Kettarama Stadium, Colombo. SRI LANKA won by 2 wickets. Toss: Sri Lanka. England YC 131-8 (45 overs). Sri Lanka YC 132-8 (43 overs).

14 February at Sinhalese SC, Colombo. ENGLAND won by 88 runs. Toss: Sri Lanka. England YC 229-6 (45 overs) (M.A. Atherton 48, T.R. Ward 41, N. Hussain 61*). Sri Lanka YC 141 (M.W. Alleyne 5-31).

15 February at Tyrone Fernando Stadium, Moratuwa. SRI LANKA won by 2 wickets. Toss: Sri Lanka. England YC 210-7 (45 overs) (M.R. Ramprakash 61, M.A. Atherton 48). Sri Lanka YC 212-8 (44.2 overs) (C. Hathurusinghe 46, S. Ranatunga 52; M.A. Atherton 4-45).

South Africa v Unofficial Australians

South Africa, not having played five-day cricket for 16 seasons, were put to a searching test by Kim Hughes's unofficial Australians in their four-match series, but won 1-0 with a victory in the first match in Johannesburg. This game lasted only four days on a pitch that gave the seamers far more assistance than is usual at this level.

The remaining three 'Tests' were played on good batting pitches and produced disappointing contests. The home side seemed quite happy to sit on their comfortable position, while the Australians, lacking all-rounders, did not have the balance to push for victory with only four front-line bowlers. The series will be remembered mainly for the feats of a handful of batsmen: Steve Smith, Kepler Wessels, John Dyson, and Michael Haysman for the Australians, Peter Kirsten and Ken McEwan for the Springboks. All scored two centuries. Queensland leg-spinner Trevor Hohns was the other big success for the Australians.

In 12 first-class matches, the Australians won two, lost three, and drew seven. They won only two of the eight one-day internationals, losing five, with one abandoned.

Unofficial Tests

24, 26, 27, 28 December at The Wanderers, Johannesburg. SOUTH AFRICAN XI won by 49 runs. Toss: Australian XI. South African XI 254 (C.E.B. Rice 61; R.J. McCurdy 6-76) and 182 (J.N. Maguire 6-61). Australian XI 142 and 245 (K.J. Hughes 54*).

1, 2, 3, 5, 6 January at Newlands, Cape Town. MATCH DRAWN. Toss: Australian XI. South African XI 493 (P.N. Kirsten 173), B.J. Whitfield 77, C.E.B. Rice 72, R.G. Pollock 66) and 257-3 (P.N. Kirsten 105*, K.A. McKenzie 52). Australian XI 496 (J. Dyson 198, M.D. Haysman 153; G.S. Le Roux 5-85).

17, 19, 20, 21, 22 January at Kingsmead, Durban. MATCH DRAWN. Toss: Australian XI. Australian XI 264 (S.B. Smith 137) and 339 (M.D. Haysman 115, J. Dyson 101). South African XI 350 (K.S. McEwan 101, B.J. Whitfield 59; T.V. Hohns 6-98) and 143-7.

30, 31 January, 1, 3, 4 February at St George's Park, Port Elizabeth. MATCH DRAWN. Toss: South African XI. Australian XI 455-9 dec (K.C. Wessels 135, S.B. Smith 77, S.J. Rixon 61, G. Shipperd 53) and 333-4 (S.B. Smith 113, K.C. Wessels 105*, M.D. Haysman 53*). South African XI 533 (R.G. Pollock 144, K.S. McEwan 138*, S.J. Cook 84; R.M. Hogg 5-97).

Cricket in Australia

Justice prevailed in the 85th Sheffield Shield season when Western Australia, unbeaten in their 10 qualifying matches, won Australia's first-class interstate competition by having much the better of a drawn five-day final against Victoria. As the minor premiers, Western Australia enjoyed the advantage of playing the final at home – at Perth's stylishly remodelled WACA Ground – and had only to force a draw to ensure they clinched the Shield for the 10th time, including the ninth time in 20 years (having won it for the first time in 1947-48 – their debut season in which they competed on a restricted basis).

The final lacked some of the drama and excitement of the previous four, but there was no shortage of fine individual performances, highlighted by opening batsman Mike Veletta's obdurate 262 (766 minutes, 550 balls, 34 fours) in Western Australia's first innings total of 654 (off 231 overs in 15 hours, 27 minutes). The previous highest score for Western Australia had been Englishman Colin Milburn's 243 in only two sessions of play against Queensland at Brisbane in 1968-69. Western Australia's previous highest total had been 615-5 declared – in that same Brisbane match.

Veletta, 23, a neat, compact little stylist, is a former Australian under-19 captain who toured India with Allan Border's senior team in 1986 and who was a late replacement for the injured Dean Jones in the Australian team for the Sharjah tournament at the end of the 1986-7 season. Veletta's massive score in the Shield final left him just 29 short of 1,000 for the season (he played in 12 first-class matches) and his average of 74.69 was the best of the Australian season.

Western Australia's immense batting, bowling, and fielding resources, their confident, aggressive attitude, and Graeme Wood's astute captaincy made them clearly the most powerful outfit in the competition, as they proved by winning six of their 10 qualifying matches outright.

The new points system, designed to produce a more positive approach and more outright results, did not gain universal acceptance. An outright win was worth six points, irrespective of the first innings result. Two points were gained for a first-innings lead only if there was not an outright result, and no points were awarded for drawn or abandoned matches, or to the side which led on the first innings and lost outright. Each team had to bowl 96 overs a day (of six hours) and was penalized 0.1 of a point for each under 96; a fate that befell New South Wales and Queensland – and ultimately cost Queensland third position (to South Australia) in the final Shield table. A carefully framed programme allowed each of the six States to have their Test players available for seven of their 10 matches. New South Wales' slide from first the previous season to fifth was the biggest surprise, especially with the talent at their disposal.

Queensland fast bowler Craig McDermott won the Player of the Year award – $A2,000 and a gold tray and four gold goblets. He polled 23 votes (cast by umpires) to win from Tasmania's English import Richard Ellison, of Kent (17) , and two other Test fast bowlers, Victorian Merv Hughes and West Australian Chris Matthews (15 each). South Australian opening batsman Glenn Bishop (14) was next. McDermott was the leading first-class wicket-taker of the Australian season, with 58 at 22.26 apiece, including 44 at 22.57 off 315.1 overs in nine Shield matches.

Cricket history was made in the last qualifying round when South Australia's David Hookes and Wayne Phillips (captain and vice-captain, respectively) figured in a record-shattering, unbeaten partnership of 462 against Tasmania at Adelaide Oval. Their fourth-wicket stand was the highest for any wicket by Australian batsmen anywhere in the world. Hookes made 306 not out, the highest score of his 123-match first-class career, and Phillips' 213 not out was the third-highest score of his 92-match first-class career. Hookes batted for 398 minutes, faced 330 balls, and hit 41 fours and two sixes. He did not give a chance. Phillips batted for 299 minutes, faced 253 balls, and hit 30 fours and one six. He gave only one chance – a regulation catch to wicket-keeper Richard Soule off leg-spinner Steve Milosz when 113. Tasmania fielded one of the weakest attacks ever assembled for a first-class match in Australia, and left-handers Hookes and Phillips collected their runs with controlled, ruthless aggression. The previous highest first-class partnership by Australians was 456, by Victorians Bill Ponsford and Edgar Mayne against Queensland at Melbourne in 1923-24.

A week after South Australia's Shield massacre of Tasmania, by an innings and 146 runs (643 for three declared to 240 and 257), South Australia made a McDonald's Cup record score of 325-6 (off 50 overs) to beat Tasmania (239-9) by 86 runs in the final at Hobart's TCA Ground; the last match to be played there. A new headquarters has been developed at Bellerive. The previous highest score in the eight years of the competition was New South Wales' 310-4 against South Australia at Sydney in 1981-2. The South Australians shared $A17,300 of the $A50,000 available in prize money and awards. Their only other cup final victory had been in 1983-84. They sneaked into the 1986-87 final on a superior run-rate in the qualifying matches, after having tied with Victoria in a semi-final. Western Australia and New South Wales also tied in a qualifying match at Perth.

The most-discussed topic towards the end of the season was the availability in 1987-88 of the 16 'rebel' players who had toured South Africa in 1985-86 and 1986-87. They were eligible to play for their States, but were banned from Test cricket until 1988-89. Several prominent Australian players were among those who did not agree with the South African tourists' being permitted to play, and there was much speculation about the possibility of some States' ignoring their claims for reinclusion. About half of them were expected to resume their first-class careers, the othert either having retired or no longer being considered good enough. A real doubt hung over the future of Kim Hughes, the rebels' captain, who was reputed to be out of favour with West Australian officials because of his costly court action against their State association.

Victoria v Western Australia, 1986-87 Sheffield Shield Final

Match drawn
Played at WACA Ground, Perth, 20, 21, 22, 23, 24 March
Toss: Victoria

Victoria

M.B. Quinn	c Zoehrer b Capes	7	(2)	c Zoehrer b Capes	9
D.F. Whatmore	b Capes	16	(1)	c Marsh b Capes	19
P.A. Hibbert	run out	48		b Marks	34
J.D. Siddons	c Zoehrer b Capes	54		c Marks b Matthews	13
S.P. O'Donnell	c Marsh b Reid	80	(6)	c Capes b Reid	78
P.W. Young	c Veletta b Reid	15	(5)	b Marks	1
A.I.C. Dodemaide	not out	81		not out	13
M.G.G. Dimattina†	c Marsh b Capes	13		not out	26
R.J. Bright*	lbw b Marks	29			
M.G. Hughes	not out	33			
S.P. Davis	did not bat				
Extras	(B4, LB11, NB13)	28		(B5, LB10, NB7)	22
	(8 wkts dec)	**404**		(6 wkts)	**215**

Western Australia

M.R.J. Veletta	c Dodemaide b Davis	262
G.R. Marsh	c Whatmore b Dodemaide	86
T.M. Moody	run out	97
G.M. Wood*	c sub (P.W. Jackson) b Hughes	84
W.S. Andrews	c sub (L.F. Balcam) b Davis	19
K.H. MacLeay	c Dodemaide b Davis	10
T.J. Zoehrer†	st Dimattina b Siddons	53
V.J. Marks	c sub (P.W. Jackson) b O'Donnell	16
C.D. Matthews	c & b O'Donnell	6
P.A. Capes	not out	6
B.A. Reid	b Hughes	4
Extras	(B4, LB3, NB4)	11
		654

W. Australia	O	M	R	W	O	M	R	W
Capes	35	10	90	4	13	4	43	2
MacLeay	20	8	40	0	11	5	32	0
Reid	30	9	106	2	9	2	24	1
Matthews	18	2	84	0	14	3	47	1
Marks	24	4	67	1	31	18	43	2
Moody	1	0	2	0	5	0	11	0
Andrews					1	1	0	0
Zoehrer					1	1	0	0

Victoria	O	M	R	W
Hughes	42	10	113	2
O'Donnell	37	6	134	2
Davis	34	5	127	3
Dodemaide	42	11	111	1
Bright	46	14	85	0
Siddons	14	1	44	1
Hibbert	3	0	9	0
Whatmore	13	7	24	0

Fall of Wickets

	VIC	WA	VIC
Wkt	1st	1st	2nd
1st	12	153	27
2nd	27	316	38
3rd	123	508	61
4th	157	545	62
5th	231	554	106
6th	232	592	170
7th	268	631	–
8th	339	642	–
9th	–	643	–
10th	–	654	–

Sheffield Shield 1986-87

Final Table	P	WO	WI	D	LI	LO	Match Pts	Pen Pts	Total Pts
WESTERN AUSTRALIA	10	6	2	1	1	–	40	–	40
VICTORIA	10	3	1	–	3	3	20	–	20
Queensland	10	2	3	1	3	1	18	–	18
South Australia	10	2	3	–	2	3	18	–	18
New South Wales	10	2	2	1	2	3	16	0.6	15.4
Tasmania	10	–	2	1	2	5	4	–	4

Outright win 6 points, 1st innings win 2 points, 1st innings lead/outright win 6 points, 1st innings win/outright loss 0 points, draw/no result 0 points. Penalty points deducted for failure to bowl 15 overs an hour in a 96-over day.

Leading First-Class Averages

Batting (Qual. 8 innings)	State	M	I	NO	HS	R	Avge	100	50	Ct
M.R.J. Veletta	VIC	12	19	6	262	971	74.69	2	6	15
D.F.G. O'Connor	SA	6	10	3	120	403	57.57	1	2	–
W.S. Andrews	WA	11	12	2	124*	571	57.10	2	4	5
W.B. Phillips	SA	11	18	2	213*	882	55.12	3	2	16
D.W. Hookes	SA	10	16	1	306*	811	54.06	2	4	15
A.R. Border	Q	13	22	2	125	1002	50.10	2	5	15
S.P.O'Donnell	VIC	11	21	3	108	892	49.55	1	9	7
G.R. Marsh	WA	14	26	1	146	1200	48.00	4	4	17
V.J. Marks	WA	11	10	2	66*	370	46.25	–	2	7
B.A. Courtice	Q	12	17	0	94	774	45.52	–	8	7
D.McD. Wellham	NSW	11	19	3	166	715	44.68	2	2	8
T. Moody	WA	12	18	1	111	746	43.88	2	3	7
D.M. Jones	VIC	11	21	1	184*	872	43.60	2	5	9
G.M. Wood	WA	12	17	4	107	560	43.07	2	2	13

Bowling	State	O	M	R	W	Avge	Best	5wI	10wM
P.A. Capes	WA	181	50	458	22	20.81	4-77	–	–
C.J. McDermott	Q	404.3	55	1296	58	22.34	6-89	5	–
A.K. Zesers	SA	499	161	1108	47	23.57	7-67	2	–
B.A. Reid	WA	546.3	127	1443	57	25.31	4-40	–	–
C.D. Matthews	WA	526.4	110	1502	57	26.35	6-46	3	–
R.M. Ellison	TAS	266.5	53	646	23	28.08	6-77	1	–
M.G. Hughes	VIC	571.1	113	1623	57	28.47	5-61	3	1
K.H. MacLeay	WA	484	154	1064	36	29.55	3-32	–	–
M.R. Whitney	NSW	222.1	35	726	24	30.25	5-39	2	–
R.J. Bright	VIC	409.1	123	911	29	31.41	4-62	–	–
V.J. Marks	WA	456.4	153	955	30	31.83	5-55	1	–
P.R. Sleep	SA	383.4	106	961	30	32.03	5-72	1	–
A.I.C. Dodemaide	VIC	372.5	77	1039	32	32.46	4-76	–	–
T.B.A. May	SA	519.5	118	1424	43	33.11	5-60	2	–

McDonald's Cup
Semi-Finals
15 February at Adelaide. SOUTH AUSTRALIA tied with VICTORIA. South Australia 222-7 (50 overs) (J.K. Pyke 57, D.Scott 51*, D.F.G. O'Connor 46; M.G. Hughes 4-34), Victoria 222-6 (50 overs) (P.W. Young 51). South Australia qualified for the final on superior run rate in the preliminary rounds.

15 February at Perth. TASMANIA beat WESTERN AUSTRALIA by 4 wickets. Toss: Tasmania. Western Australia 266-5 (50 overs) (G.M. Wood 96*, M.R.J. Veletta 69, T. Moody 42). Tasmania 271-6 (49.3 overs) (R.D. Woolley 80*, D.C. Boon 80).

Final
15 March at Hobart. SOUTH AUSTRALIA beat TASMANIA by 86 runs. South Australia 325-6 (50 overs) (G.A. Bishop 116, W.B. Phillips 75). Tasmania 239-9 (50 overs) (D.J. Buckingham 56).

Cricket in South Africa

Transvaal, though without Sylvester Clarke for the first time in five seasons, and missing Springbok batsmen Graeme Pollock and Henry Fotheringham for much of the season, re-established themselves as the champions of South African provincial cricket.

Clive Rice's team regained the Castle Currie Cup for the three-day competition from Western Province and, although the Benson & Hedges night series was retained by Western Province and Natal won the Nissan Shield (50 overs), there was no doubt that Transvaal were the best overall side.

They would probably have won the Nissan as well but for the match being shortened by the weather, and they reached the final of the night series.

Eastern Province folded badly in the semi-final at home to Western Province when they had victory within their sights, but Garth Le Roux's final onslaught proved too much on a substandard pitch that had been prepared for the home spinners.

Western Province gave as good as they got in a high-scoring final against Transvaal, but the need to win outright to retain the interprovincial trophy proved to be beyond them.

Highlights of the season included the re-emergence of Eastern Province as a competitive power under the guidance and inspiration of former Australian Test batsman Kepler Wessels and England all-rounder David Capel, and confirmation of the fact that fledgling Free State were capable of holding their own at the highest provincial level.

At an individual level, Free State confirmed that they have two exciting fast-bowling prospects in Corrie van Zyl, who had first made his mark the previous season, and Allan Donald. Both have subsequently been rewarded with county contracts, with Glamorgan and Warwickshire respectively.

The 20-year-old Donald certainly provided the highlight of the domestic season when he ripped through the powerful Transvaal batting order at the Wanderers, returning career-best figures of 8-37. He had to contend without the support of the injured Van Zyl for much of the season, and it was a notable achievement that he should be the leading wicket-taker at the end of the league section of the Currie Cup competition.

South Africa's third outstanding fast bowling prospect, Trevor Packer of Natal, was sidelined virtually throughout the season through injury, and his long-term prospects cannot be very good.

The fast bowlers apart, the past season was not particularly encouraging as far as the younger prospects were concerned. The two Transvaal all-rounders, Brian McMillan and Hugh Page, although both members of the Springbok squad, did not make as much progress as might have been hoped, and the same applied to the Western Province duo of left-arm seamer Brett Matthews and middle-order batsman Daryll Cullinan.

Matthews was actually dropped by Western Province in mid-season, and Cullinan, undoubtedly the most gifted of the younger batsmen, lagged behind the likes of Eastern Province's Mark Rushmere, Transvaal's Louis Vorster, and another young Western Province player, Terence Lazard.

Cullinan showed marked improvement towards the season's end when he was promoted from No. 5 to No. 3, and the approaching season will be an important one for him as he will have to fill the gap left in the Western Province team by the departure of Ken McEwan to Eastern Province.

The old hands, McEwan and opening batsman Lawrence Seeff, both scored three Currie Cup centuries for Western Province – McEwan's coming in four successive innings – while Jimmy Cook and Kevin McKenzie scored two each for Transvaal.

Donald apart, the bowling honours went very much to the seasoned campaigners, with Garth Le Roux spearheading the Western Province efforts and England-qualified seamer Neal Radford and veteran spinner Alan Kourie doing much the same for Transvaal. The lack of good spin bowlers must be a cause for concern. Transvaal's Kevin Kerr will hopefully emerge from the shadows in the wake of Kourie's retirement, and Eastern Province must have delighted traditionalists by playing a trio of leg-spinner, off-spinner, and left-arm spinner on a regular basis. But their success was as a combination rather than as individuals.

No summary of the past season could be complete without reference to Graeme Pollock, who announced his retirement after gracing the South African first-class game for 26 seasons. A model sportsman, he will be remembered forever for his modesty and sportsmanship, in addition to the genius and grace which he brought to the game.

His farewell century for the Springboks against the Australians at St George's Park, his original home ground, ranked with the finest innings he has played. That he was still able to play those thundering cover drives, those savage pulls, and those delicate cuts against international-class fast bowling with the same mastery and control that he first exhibited to the world in his teens speaks volumes for his ageless ability.

For years he maintained the standards of South African cricket almost single-handed, particularly when Garth Le Roux, Clive Rice, Mike Procter, Barry Richards, Eddie Barlow, and Kepler Wessels were away playing for World Series Cricket. And this is probably the greatest contribution he made in the second half of his career from 1970 onwards, when he was denied the opportunity of playing the game on the official international stage.

As the realization dawned on the South African public that they were about to see the great left-hander for the last time, the tail-end of the season became very much an occasion for Pollock nostalgia. South African first-class cricket will not be the same in the seasons ahead.

In retirement, Pollock has taken over from Procter as chairman of the South African Cricket Players' Association.

The player of the season was undoubtedly Garth Le Roux, the model professional. His consistency throughout a long and tiring season, for the Springboks and Western Province, was remarkable. His

Transvaal v Western Province, 1986-87 Currie Cup Final

Match Drawn. (Transvaal win Cup by virtue of topping League.)
Played at the Wanderers, Johannesburg on 13, 14, 15, 16 March
Umpires: K.E. Liebenberg and B.J. Meyer

Western Province

T.N. Lazard	c Jennings b Rice	20	c Rice b Kourie	15
L. Seeff	c Jennings b Rice	16	not out	122
P.N. Kirsten	c Rice b Kourie	54	(4) c Cook b Kourie	30
K.S. McEwan	b Page	4	(5) not out	37
D.J. Cullinan	c and b Page	10	(3) run out	55
A.P. Kuiper*	b Radford	50		
G.S. le Roux	not out	71		
E.O. Simons	b Radford	27		
R.J. Ryall†	not out	1		
B.A. Matthews	did not bat			
M.B. Minnaar	,,			
Extras	(LB14, NB13)	27	(B5, LB10)	15
	(7 wkts dec)	**280**	(3 wkts dec)	**274**

Transvaal

S.J. Cook	b Matthews	110	lbw b Simons	25
H.R. Fotheringham	lbw b Simons	0	not out	72
M. Yachad	c Ryall b Minnaar	12	lbw b le Roux	1
R.G. Pollock	c Cullinan b Matthews	4	not out	63
R.V. Jennings†	lbw b le Roux	99		
C.E.B. Rice*	c Ryall b le Roux	34		
K.A. McKenzie	c le Roux b Simons	11		
A.J. Kourie	not out	31		
H.A. Page	not out	10		
N.V. Radford	did not bat			
J.J. Hooper	,,			
Extras	(B2, LB10, W1, NB16)	29	(B4, LB7, W1, NB3)	15
	(7 wkts dec)	**340**	(2 wkts)	**176**

Transvaal	O	M	R	W	O	M	R	W
Radford	32	10	86	2	16	3	64	0
Page	24	3	72	2	9	0	53	0
Rice	16	5	40	2	7	0	42	0
Hooper	12	2	27	0				
Kourie	16	2	41	1	22	3	100	2

W. Province	O	M	R	W	O	M	R	W
Simons	23	8	89	2	11	0	45	1
Matthews	19	3	50	2	11	2	43	0
Kuiper	12	4	25	0				
Minnaar	23	4	67	1	4	2	7	0
le Roux	14	1	65	2	11	2	44	1
Kirsten	9	1	32	0	4	0	26	0

Fall of Wickets

Wkt	WP 1st	T 1st	WP 2nd	T 2nd
1st	41	5	38	30
2nd	49	35	155	31
3rd	62	53	196	–
4th	84	234	–	–
5th	135	262	–	–
6th	182	276	–	–
7th	267	308	–	–
8th	–	–	–	–
9th	–	–	–	–
10th	–	–	–	–

performances were particularly noteworthy on the unforgiving pitches of Newlands, Kingsmead, and St George's Park. He took five wickets in an innings in the five-day match against the Australians at Newlands, and a match-winning 6-53 in the Currie Cup semi-final. In addition, his big-hitting ability down the order made him one of the top limited-overs cricketers.

Currie Cup Final Table	P	W	L	D	1st Innings points Batting	1st Innings points Bowling	Total points
TRANSVAAL	6	4	0	2	19	28	107
Eastern Province	6	4	2	0	14	24	98
Western Province	6	3	2	1	27	25	97
Northern Transvaal	6	1	4	1	15	23	53
Natal	6	1	0	5	14	22	51
Orange Free State	6	1	3	2	12	17	44
Border	6	0	3	3	8	17	25

Currie Cup Semi-Final

6, 7, 8, 9 March at St George's Park, Port Elizabeth. WESTERN PROVINCE beat EASTERN PROVINCE by 47 runs. W. Province 288-7 (K.S. McEwan 79, T.N. Lazard 62, D.J. Cullinan 51 not out; R.J. McCurdy 5-65) and 256 (D.J. Cullinan 60, P.N. Kirsten 54; R.J. McCurdy 4-61, T.G. Shaw 4-110). E. Province 331-7 (K.C. Wessels 129, M.W. Rushmere 74) and 166 (K.C. Wessels 83; G.S. le Roux 6-53).

Transvaal, as leaders, qualified automatically for the final.

Leading First-Class Averages 1986-87
Batting

(Qual. 500 runs, 40 avge)	M	I	NO	HS	R	Avge	100	50
G.E. McMillan (Trans/TB)	7	10	4	156*	628	104.66	3	3
K. Wessels (EProv/Aus)	12	20	2	137	1160	64.44	5	4
A.J. Moles (Griq.W.)	7	12	1	174	705	64.09	3	2
K.S. McEwan (WProv/SA)	10	17	4	138*	830	63.84	5	2
B.J. Whitfield (Nat/Pres/SA)	10	18	3	129*	845	56.33	2	5
P.N. Kirsten (WProv/SA)	12	21	2	204*	921	48.47	3	4
L.P. Vorster (Trans/TB/SA XI)	9	14	3	74*	516	46.90	–	3
S.J. Cook (Trans/SA)	10	18	2	110	748	46.75	3	2
K.A. McKenzie (Trans/SA)	7	13	2	188	502	45.63	2	1
L. Seeff (WProv)	8	15	3	141	534	44.50	–	–
A.I. Kallicharran (OFS)	7	13	0	110	555	42.69	–	–

Bowling (Qual: 25 wkts, 30 avge)	R	W	Avge	Best	5wI	10wM
J. During (WProv.B)	403	25	16.12	6-53	2	–
J.C. Van Duyker (NTransB)	430	26	16.53	6-70	1	1
G.S. Le Roux	961	49	19.61	6-53	2	–
C.D. Mitchley (NTrans/Pres)	638	31	20.58	5-39	2	–
K.J. Kerr (Trans/TB)	741	35	21.17	6-62	3	–
A.J. Kourie (Trans/SA)	641	30	21.36	6-67	3	–
A.A. Donald (OFS/SAD/SA/Pres)	1116	47	23.74	8-37	2	1
N.V. Radford (Trans)	754	28	26.92	5-61	2	–
T.G. Shaw (EProv)	793	27	29.37	6-49	1	–

Nissan Shield Final

28 February, Johannesburg. NATAL beat TRANSVAAL on faster scoring rate. Natal 236-8 (50 overs) (T. Madsen 70*, N. Daniels 43, R. Bentley 40). Transvaal 201-4 (44.3 overs, rain) (M.Yachad 85*, H. Fotheringham 42).

Cricket in the West Indies

A desperate financial situation, caused mainly by the loss of over US$250,000 on the contentious England tour in 1986, and in spite of sponsorship of US$150,000, forced the West Indies Cricket Board of Control (WICBC) to cut the 1987 Shell Shield tournament in half.

Already the most limited of all the domestic competitions staged by the Test-playing countries, the Shield was reduced from a round-robin league of 15 matches among the six participants to two zones of three matches each, leading to a final. It was a most unsatisfactory arrangement, particularly at a time when the West Indies team was entering an obvious period of transition, but it served to emphasize the fragile nature of cricket in a region of high costs and low returns. Fortunately, the Barbados Cricket Association, through money raised from its very successful lottery, organized two first-class matches on its own outside the Shield, while Lancashire visited Jamaica and Yorkshire toured St Lucia and Barbados as preparation for the English season, playing one first-class match each. Even so, the opportunities for young players eager to press their claims were severely restricted.

Guyana, inspired by the all-round enterprise of captain Roger Harper, clinched the Shield for the first time since 1983, but only by the unconvincing method of first innings lead in their two decisive matches. They qualified for the final by going ahead of Barbados in a rain-spoiled preliminary round match with seven wickets down, and then batted their way to the lead in the drawn final against the Leeward Islands, both played at home on Georgetown's Bourda.

Dropped following the West Indies tour of Australia, Harper returned with a clear mission to reclaim his place immediately. He enjoyed an outstanding pre-Shield match against Barbados in which he took 10 wickets and scored a second innings century in a vain attempt to save his team from defeat. In the Shield proper, he scored another century as Guyana defeated Triniday & Tobago at the Queen's Park Oval for the first time in the competition, and was at the wicket both times as the vital first innings lead was achieved against Barbados and the Leewards, 40 not out in the former, 128, his third century in four matches, in the latter. In addition he bowled his off-spin steadily, fielded brilliantly, and never missed a trick as captain.

Although the tournament was delayed until after the West Indies returned home from Australia, several of the leading players either missed it altogether (such as Desmond Haynes and Larry Gomes) or appeared in only one match (such as Malcolm Marshall, Gordon Greenidge, Vivian Richards, Gus Logie, and Tony Gray).

In his single innings, Greenidge recorded his highest Shield score, 202 against Trinidad and Tobago, adding 306 for the second wicket with the 19-year-old schoolboy Roland Holder, as Barbados completed a heavy innings victory.

Familiar names dominated the bowling. Marshall helped himself to seven wickets in his only match, against Trinidad & Tobago. Off-spinner

Clyde Butts was again a key element in the Guyana team, with 16 wickets in three matches.

Two young batsmen made their marks. Sudesh Dhaniram, a neat, well-organized opener from the same Berbice county that produced Rohan Kanhai and Alvin Kallicharran, batted only twice for Guyana and collected 102 against Barbados and 131 against the Leewards. Keith Arthurton, a fluent left-hander from the small island of Nevis, followed 97 run out for the Leewards against the Windwards with an accomplished 132 against the testing Guyana spinners in the final. With Gomes, like Holding, announcing his retirement from Test cricket, Arthurton seems a ready left-handed replacement in the middle order, particularly since he is a high-class outfielder.

Jamaica, well led by Holding, retained the Geddes Grant/Harrison Line Trophy for the limited-overs tournament, beating Barbados by four wickets in a final that yielded 501 runs from 95 overs for the loss of nine wickets. It was some consolation for their narrow loss to the Leewards in the Shield, when they had been denied victory and entry into the final by a last-wicket stand of 23.

Shell Shield

Zone A	P	W	L	D	1st innings points in draw	Points
Leeward Islands	2	2	–	–	–	32
Jamaica	2	2	1	–	–	16
Windward Islands	2	–	2	–	–	0

Zone B	P	W	L	D	1st innings points in draw	Points
Guyana	2	1	–	1	1	24
Barbados	2	1	–	1	–	20
Trinidad & Tobago	2	–	2	–	–	0

Final
24-27 April, Georgetown. MATCH DRAWN: GUYANA win Shell Shield on first innings. Leeward Islands 317 (L. Lawrence 47, K. Arthurton 132, W. Benjamin 44; C. Butts 3-63, R. Harper 4-93) and 76-0. Guyana 485 (C. Lambert 50, S. Dhaniram 131, R. Harper 128, R. Seeram 50; N. Guishard 3-138).

Leading First-Class Averages

Batting (Qual: Avge 50)	M	I	NO	HS	R	Avge	100	50
S. Dhaniram (Guyana)	2	2	0	131	233	116.50	2	–
R.A. Harper (Guyana)	4	5	1	128	419	104.75	3	–
K.L.T. Arthurton (Leeward Is)	3	5	0	132	281	56.20	1	1
C.A. Davidson (Jamaica)	3	4	0	73	218	54.50	–	3

Batted one innings: C.G. Greenidge (Barbados) 202.

Bowling (Qual: 10 wkts)	O	R	W	Avge	Best	5wI	10wM
V.S. Greene (Barbados)	68.5	186	15	12.40	4-15	–	–
M.A. Holding (Jamaica)	63	169	12	14.08	4-39	–	–
C.A. Walsh (Jamaica)	60.2	212	13	16.30	6-54	1	–
C.G. Butts (Guyana)	161.5	287	16	17.93	5-67	2	–
R.A. Harper (Guyana)	162.4	355	18	19.72	6-63	1	1
W.K.M. Benjamin (Leeward Is)	111.1	294	15	19.40	6.50	1	1

Cricket in New Zealand

In almost every conceivable respect, the 1986-87 cricket season will be remembered for the achievements of Martin Crowe. Not only did this richly gifted batsmwo Test centuries against the West Indies and gain the vice-captaincy of the New Zealand team in Sri Lanka but he totally dominated the Shell Trophy series.

Crowe, leading Central Districts for the first time, steered his side to their first title in the 11 years of the domestic first-class competition, and this after having won only two of their Shell Cup one-day mches.

In the eight rounds, Central won five mches outright to finish a comfortable 14 points clear of defending champions Otago.

Crowe's contribution was immense. He scored 1,348 runs in the Trophy competition, including six centuries, at 103.6. He broke Glenn Turner's domestic record of 1,244, which had stood 10 seasons, and, when he scored a further two hundreds against the West Indies, surpassed Everton Weekes's mark of six centuries in a season, set 31 years ago. He earned the respect of his team in the best possible m, leading from the front.

Other notable contributions for Central came from chunky left-hander Mark Greatbatch, who had easily his best summer, finishing with centuries in the last two mches, and medium-pacers Gary Robertson and Wayne Martin.

The only embarrassing experience for Crowe and Central came at Masterton, when Otago rolled Central over for 145 and 160 on a pitch tailor-made for left-arm spinner Stephen Boock. Crowe made 13 and 8, stumped off Boock both times, and Otago cruised to a 245-run victory. But Otago came unstuck at the end of the competition, losing their last two mches by substantial m. At the same time, Central had handsome victories over Northern Districts and Canterbury.

Internationals Ken Rutherford and Bruce Blair, along with Derek Walker, had their moments with the bat. Boock had a mvellous summer, heading the bowling aggregates and winning a Test recall.

Wellington, who finished third, were not bowled out in an innings in the Trophy. Their batting was strong and had depth, but the bowling – despite the presence of Ewen Chatfield, Paul Allott, and Evan Gray – was not sufficiently penetrative.

Chatfield, along with Boock, passed 500 first-class wickets during the series, and Wellington, who looked one of the most solid if unspectacular teams, ended the season undefeated in their last 24 first-class matches.

Auckland had a disastrous summer. Having won the Shell Cup, they failed to get a point in their first four Trophy m. Disharmony within the team led to captain Peter Webb's resigning, which coincided with a noticeable rise in on-field performance. Danny Morrison developed into a fine new-ball prospect, while Phil Horne capped a splendid summer with the bat by winning Test selection, thus becoming New Zealand's latest double international (his other sport being badminton).

Shell Trophy 1986-87

Final Table	P	W	L	D	1st innings Points	Points
CENTRAL DISTRICTS	8	5	1	2	16	76
Otago	8	4	3	1	14★	62
Wellington	8	2	0	6	26★	50
Auckland	8	2	3	3	16	40
Canterbury	8	1	3	4	20	32
Northern Districts	8	1	5	2	4	16

12 pts for win; 4 pts 1st innings lead. ★ First-innings points shared in one match.

Leading First-Class Averages 1986-87

Batting	M	I	NO	HS	R	Avge	100
M.D. Crowe (Central Districts)	11	21	3	175★	1676	93.11	8
E.B. McSweeney (Wellington)	10	12	4	117★	495	61.87	1
A.H. Jones (Wellington)	10	15	2	163★	710	54.61	2
B.A. Edgar (Wellington)	8	13	2	110	592	53.81	2
J.G. Wright (Canterbury)	11	21	2	192	1019	53.63	3
P.A. Horne (Auckland)	9	17	2	150★	773	51.53	2
M.J. Greatbatch (Central Districts)	9	17	2	135	681	45.40	3
B.R. Blair (Otago)	9	15	1	120	623	44.50	3
D.N. Patel (Auckland)	11	21	2	170★	796	41.89	3
P.S. Briasco (Central Districts)	8	15	5	82★	397	39.70	0
P.N. Webb (Auckland)	9	16	4	82	475	39.58	0
T.D. Ritchie (Wellington)	9	13	1	95	469	39.08	0
T.E. Blain (Central Districts)	7	13	1	161	457	38.08	1
R.H. Vance (Wellington)	10	16	1	94	539	35.93	0
A.J. Hunt (Auckland)	5	7	1	87	200	33.33	0
B.G. Cooper (Northern Districts)	8	16	0	105	532	33.25	2
K.R. Rutherford (Otago)	11	20	0	118	652	32.60	2
D.J. Boyle (Canterbury)	8	15	3	75★	383	31.91	0
D.J. Walker (Otago)	8	13	3	82★	313	31.30	0
J.J. Crowe (Auckland)	11	22	4	110	552	30.66	1
D.J. White (Northern Districts)	8	16	1	109	455	30.33	1
R.T. Latham (Canterbury)	7	12	1	92	326	29.63	0
C.W. Flanagan (Canterbury)	5	6	1	69★	148	29.60	0
J.C. Bracewell (Auckland)	11	17	4	66	379	29.15	0

Qualification: 5 completed innings, average 28.

Bowling	O	M	R	W	Best	Avge
R.J. Hadlee (Canterbury)	407.2	107	935	62	7-49	15.08
S.L. Boock (Otaga)	445	176	920	55	6-62	16.72
E.J. Chatfield (Wellington)	432.5	154	927	48	8-83	19.31
D.A. Stirling (Central Districts)	162	37	498	21	5-59	23.71
J.G. Bracewell (Auckland)	427	138	1,047	44	7-65	23.79
G.K. Robertson (Central Districts)	200	36	627	26	6-47	24.11
M.J. Child (Northern Districts)	110.3	15	372	15	7-59	24.80
K.W. Martin (Central Districts)	207	40	670	27	6-25	24.81
T.J. Wilson (Otago)	246.5	50	811	30	6-73	27.03
M.C. Snedden (Auckland)	309.1	73	894	32	7-67	27.93
D.K. Morrison (Auckland)	313.1	70	1,054	35	7-82	30.11
S.W. Duff (Central Districts)	191.1	54	585	17	4-63	34.41
E.J. Gray (Wellington)	390	136	918	25	7-24	36.72
P.J.W. Allott (Wellington)	226.4	66	604	16	3-52	37.75
V.R. Brown (Canterbury)	307.1	80	942	20	4-106	47.10
D.J. Hartshorn (Canterbury)	232.3	54	773	15	4-45	51.53

Qualification: 15 wickets

Cricket in India

It was a season of so many runs that scorers and statisticians were forced to work overtime. The knock-out phase of the Ranji Trophy Championship, involving just nine matches, saw a record 30 centuries scored (by 23 players) including seven double centuries.

The domestic season, which began with the Duleep Trophy Championship (inter-zone matches) saw the runs flow. In just four matches there were as many as 17 centuries, and all manner of records other than the former, individual and otherwise, created. One batsman, Arun Lal, the opener from Bengal, who figured in the second Test against Pakistan, replacing Sunil Gavaskar, made a total of 501 runs (287 and 214) in two Duleep Trophy innings. The 287 was the new individual best in the tournament. Significantly in the Ranji Trophy knock-out tie against Rajasthan for Bengal, Arun Lal made 287, too. He would surely watch out the next time he gets there.

South Zone won the Duleep Trophy, beating West Zone in the final. Nine centuries were made in the match, a record. South Zone scored the highest ever for a side in the competition, 740.

The Ranji Trophy went to Hyderabad, only their second such success, the first occasion being in 1937-38. Hyderabad, incidentally, played one match that year – the final – gaining walk-overs *en route*.

This was a golden season for Hyderabad. Their batsmen never put a foot wrong. Against Gujarat in the quarter-final they made 605-7 declared. In the semi-final against Bihar they amassed 783-8, the fifth highest score by a team in the Championship. In the final against depleted Delhi (without Maninder Singh, Manoj Prabakhar, and Madan Lal) they displayed the steel to withstand a strong challenge. Three of their front-line batsmen made a double century, while their opener Abdul Azeem, who scored a century in the final, made 303 not out in the Ranji Trophy league game against Tamil Nadu. He became the seventh Indian to score 300 or more.

The only tournament in which a bowler made any sort of impression was the one-match Irani Trophy, which Rest of India won by the handsome margin of an innings and 232 runs. Rest made 637, while Delhi succumbed for 266 and 139, left-arm spinner Azim Khan taking 6-29 in the second innings, after conditions for batting deteriorated.

The number of runs scored did cause a debate about wickets being too heavily loaded in favour of batsmen. Former Test batsman Gundappa Vishwanath, when asked about the phenomenon, said: 'Could be the wickets. But I would say that it is a case of too many bowlers bowling straight and too many batsmen playing straighter.' Whatever it might be, bowlers all over the country had a harrowing time.

For the first time in the Ranji Trophy Championship the quotient rule had to be used. In the quarter-final tie between Delhi and Bengal, the latter, unable to finish their first innings, were eliminated from the tournament because of an inferior run quotient, arrived at by dividing the number of runs scored by the wickets lost of the two sides.

Leading First-Class Averages 1986-87

Batting (Qualification: 600 runs)	I	NO	R	HS	Avge	100
Deepak Sharma (Haryana)	7	2	657	217	131.40	3
Arun Lal (Bengal)	15	2	1388	287	106.76	5
M. Prabhakar (Delhi)	11	3	729	215	91.12	3
B.P. Patel (Karnataka)	10	3	611	151	87.28	2
S. Kalyani (Maharashtra)	11	3	686	200*	85.75	3
K. Bhaskar Pillai (Delhi)	12	2	855	222*	85.50	4
P. Roy (Bengal)	11	2	744	230*	82.66	4
D.B. Vengsarkar (Bombay)	16	4	987	166	82.25	6
A. Ayub (Hyderabad)	11	3	621	206*	77.62	2
M. Azharuddin (Hyderabad)	18	3	1058	199	70.53	4
V. Mohanraj (Hyderabad)	13	2	751	211*	68.27	3
L.S. Rajput (Bombay)	15	2	881	136*	67.76	4
R. Lamba (Delhi)	14	1	873	131	67.15	5
R.J. Shastri (Bombay)	18	4	912	176*	65.14	4
C. Saldanha (Karnataka)	17	1	996	142	62.25	2
A. Azeem (Hyderabad)	14	1	753	303*	57.92	2
S.M. Gavaskar (Bombay)	17	0	897	176	52.76	2
M.R. Srinivasaprasad (Karnataka)	13	0	640	136	49.23	3
K.A. Qayyum (Hyderabad)	15	1	648	203	46.28	3
S. Viswanath (Karnataka)	17	1	715	91	44.68	0
K. Srikkanth (Tamil Nadu)	20	0	742	123	37.10	2
M. Amarnath (Delhi)	21	1	649	131	32.45	1

Bowling (Qualification: 25 wickets)	O	M	R	W	Avge
S. Lahore (Madhya Pradesh)	219.3	49	564	32	17.62
Deepak Sharma (Haryana)	253	54	656	26	25.23
Maninder Singh (Delhi)	670.4	200	1,522	60	25.36
M.V. Narasimha Rao (Hyderabad)	221.5	16	755	28	26.96
S. Talwar (Haryana)	273.5	50	731	27	27.07
P. Sunderam (Rajasthan)	231.4	30	866	31	27.93
A.R. Bhat (Karnataka)	312.3	75	870	26	33.46
W.V. Raman (Tamil Nadu)	332.5	83	935	27	34.62
N.S. Yadav (Hyderabad)	501.5	108	1,299	37	35.10
R. Yadav (Hyderabad)	230.5	25	963	26	37.03
R.J. Shastri (Bombay)	574.3	142	1,385	33	41.96

Ranji Trophy Final

21, 22, 23, 25 March, Delhi. MATCH DRAWN. Hyderabad win Trophy on first innings. Hyderabad 457 (A. Azeem 114, A. Ayub 174) and 480-7 (V. Mohan Raj 211*, Ayub 80; J. Singh 4-132). Delhi 433 (M. Nayyar 64, K.P. Bhaskar 160*, M. Amarnath 85; R. Yadav 5-114, S. Yadav 3-74).

Cricket in Pakistan

In one of the busiest seasons in Pakistan's cricket history, lasting no less than six months, a record number of 126 matches was played in 1986-87. The first first-class tournament of the season, the Patron's Trophy, was won by the National Bank, led by the left-arm Test spinner Iqbal Qasim. The competition, confined to the zonal, city, and divisional teams, was now thrown open to commercial organizations as well. In all, 36 teams contested the championship. The group league was declared non-first-class by the BCCP, but the 12-team final round, which was played on a knock-out basis, was declared first-class. The same 12 teams automatically qualified for Pakistan's premier championship, the Quaid-e-Azam Trophy.

Unlike last year, the players were restricted in 1986-7 to playing the entire season for the same team. Karachi, last year's champions, thus suffered, as their players went back to their commercial organization's team. In the 12-team contest, they slumped to 11th position. Once again National Bank raced to the top, by winning six of their 11 matches, losing none. They also won the Quaid-e-Azam Trophy, and United Bank once again finished second. National Bank's captain, Iqbal Qasim, finished with 62 wickets before being summoned to India to reinforce the Pakistan team. Ameer Akbar of the National Bank became the only batsman in the championship to cross the 1,000 mark, and also topped the overall batting averages (67.45) in the season. Tahir Shah scored three centuries in the championship for the National Bank.

Teams that failed to qualify for the Quaid-e-Azam Trophy were pitched into another first-class tournament, introduced by the BCCP, for the President's Cup. This was played among 17 teams, of which the Railways came out as the winners. The last first-class competition of the season, the PACO Cup, was played among eight teams, the restriction on the five teams only participating in this tournament being waived. Pakistan International Airline beat United Bank to win the championship, United Bank thus finishing second in three tournaments.

Six batsmen passed the 1,000 mark in the season. Ameer Akbar of the National Bank finished top, scoring 1,349 (67.45), while Mansoor Akhtar and Shafiq Ahmed of United Bank made 1,503 (48.48) and 1,498 (51.65), respectively. A new wicket-keeping record was established by Ashraf Ali of United Bank, who had 70 victims (62 ct, 8 st) in 18 matches, thus overtaking Anil Dalpat's 69 in the 1983-84 season. Ashraf Ali also scored 1,026 runs at an average of 51.30.

Fahim Abbasi of Rawalpindi took 30 catches as a close-in fielder, and no fewer than 17 bowlers achieved the 50-wicket target. Raja Sarfraz, captain of the Rawalpindi team, finished with 91 wickets at an average of 17.96. Nadeem Ghauri of Habib Bank took 83 and Iqbal Qasim of National Bank finished with 75. Kazim Mehdi of HBFC, Farrukh-Zaman of MCB, and Pervez Shah of Lahore performed hat-tricks.

The one-day Wills Cup tournament was won by Habib Bank, who regained the trophy by beating the United Bank.

Leading First-Class Averages

Batting	M	I	NO	R	HS	Avge	100
Ameer Akbar (National Bank)	15	27	7	1349	151*	67.45	5
Shafiq Ahmed (United Bank)	19	34	5	1498	124	51.65	3
Ashraf Ali (United Bank)	18	29	9	1026	113	51.30	2
Asif Mohammad (Pakistan Int. Airlines)	9	13	2	535	89*	48.63	–
Mansoor Akhtar (United Bank)	19	34	3	1503	167	48.48	3
Shaukat Mirza (HBFC)	12	21	3	835	125*	46.38	4
Arshad Pervez (Habib Bank)	12	20	1	835	144	43.94	2
Zahid Ahmed (Pakistan Int. Airlines)	18	31	4	1167	127	43.22	1
Raees Ahmed (HBFC)	14	25	3	912	147	41.45	1
Munir-ul-Haq (HBFC)	11	18	2	636	134*	39.75	1
Tahir Shah (National Bank)	15	26	1	993	150	39.72	4
Mazhar Hussain (Lahore City/Lahore)	12	23	3	767	139	38.35	1
Aamer Sohail (Lahore City/Lahore)	12	23	1	839	116	38.13	1
Feroze Mehdi (Pakistan Int. Airlines)	16	29	2	1001	135	37.07	3
Mujahid Hameed (Rawalpindi)	16	28	5	834	90*	36.26	–
Naved Anjum (United Bank)	13	20	1	683	111	35.94	2
Sajid Ali (National Bank)	16	29	2	958	150*	35.48	3
Asad Rauf (National Bank)	15	21	2	672	114	35.36	1
Sajid Khan (Karachi)	10	19	2	577	106*	33.94	1
Saeed Azad (National Bank)	15	26	2	804	121*	33.50	2
Amjad Siddiq (WAPDA)	13	22	3	630	100	33.15	1
Saeed Anwar (Karachi)	12	23	1	711	150	32.31	1
Wasim Ali (Lahore City/Lahore)	14	25	3	696	111*	31.63	1
Zaheer Abbas (Pakistan Int. Airlines)	12	21	3	554	119*	30.77	1
Saadat Ali (HBFC)	15	27	2	766	100	30.64	1
Nasir Shah (Karachi)	12	23	1	673	124	30.59	3
Taslim Arif (National Bank)	15	24	6	550	126	30.55	1
Tanvir Razzaq (WAPDA)	15	26	2	724	131	30.16	1

Qualification: 8 innings, 500 runs, avge 30.00.

Bowling	O	R	W	Avge	Best	5wI
Sajjad Akbar (PNSC)	197.2	473	35	13.51	5-28	2
Amin Lakhani (PNSC)	152.3	339	25	13.56	4-21	–
Zia-ud-Din (Customs)	161.4	425	30	14.16	5-69	1
Iqbal Qasim (National Bank)	566.3	1145	75	15.26	7-77	8
Masood Anwar (PACO)	537.5	1128	67	16.83	6-47	3
Naved Anjum (United Bank)	302.2	1024	60	17.06	7-63	5
Iqbal Sikander (Pakistan Int. Airlines)	489.4	1384	78	17.74	7-52	4
Raja Sarfraz (Rawalpindi)	630.4	1635	91	17.96	8-58	9
Tanvir Ali (Pakistan Int. Airlines)	492.4	1167	64	18.23	8-28	4
Zulfiqar Butt (WAPDA)	643	1484	81	18.32	7-16	6
Ijaz Faqih (Muslim Commercial Bank)	509	1252	68	18.41	7-47	6
Nadeem Ghauri (Habib Bank)	685.3	1566	83	18.86	6-25	8
Shakeel Ahmed (Rawalpindi)	235.2	691	35	19.74	6-86	3
Mohammad Asif (Lahore)	361	776	39	19.89	8-58	2
Sajid Bashir (United Bank)	213	667	33	20.21	5-52	1
Shahid Mahboob (PACO)	452.1	1474	72	20.47	8-65	6
Kazim Mehdi (HBFC)	575.2	1386	66	21.00	7-55	4
Barkatullah (National Bank)	383.1	1386	66	21.00	7-49	2
Pervez Shah (Lahore City/Lahore)	327.4	930	44	21.13	7-68	3
Mian Fayyaz (PACO)	491.3	1131	53	21.33	6-26	3
Raza Khan (Karachi)	336.4	944	44	21.45	7-66	5
Kamal Merchant (United Bank)	307.4	671	31	21.64	5-48	1
Shahid Aziz (United Bank)	257	758	35	21.65	7-56	3
Rashid Khan (Pakistan Int. Airlines)	361.5	1040	48	21.66	6-19	4
Zakaullah Khan (Rawalpindi)	365	957	44	21.75	6-48	4

Qualification: 20 wickets; avge under 22.00.
HBFC – House Building Finance Corporation; PACO – Pakistan Automobile Corporation; PNSC – Pakistan National Shipping Corporation; WAPDA – Water & Power Development Authority.

Cricket in Sri Lanka

Singhalese Sports Club, minus three stalwarts – Sidath Wettimuny (retired), Roy Dias, and Guy de Alwis – were made to fight every inch of the way before retaining their hold on the Lakspray trophy for the 1986-87 season. Joint champions with Nondescript CC last season, SSC took the title outright this time by scoring a narrow 31-run first-innings points victory over a doughty Colombo Colts CC that could boast no big names.

A 95-run ninth-wicket partnership between Senarath Seneviratne and Dashantha Gunawardena saw Colts reach a respectable 305 in the three-day final. Seneviratne, a hard-hitting left-hander, made a top score of 71 in two hours, hitting one six and 9 fours.

SSC found themselves in a similar plight, losing 180 for 6, but once again it was a late rally that swung the fortunes. Duleep Mendis, the Sri Lanka captain, hit a match-winning century (113) off 143 balls, with 14 fours, and shared a seventh-wicket stand of 93 in 96 minutes with wicket-keeper Jeevaka Weerasinghe that turned the tide in SSC's favour.

Mendis with two other hundreds, including the fastest of the season (off 90 balls) against Saracens SC, easily topped the batting averages. Another SSC batsman, the eldest Ranatunga, Dhammika, made the most runs – 911 in 16 innings. Brendon Kuruppu, Sri Lanka's new Test 'find', was second best on aggregate with 779 runs, also off 16 innings. Owen Mottau (Colombo CC) made the highest individual score of the season – 263 against Tamil Union.

The majority of Sri Lankan players missed a good part of the season, being on duty in Sharjah and India. Thus the top six in the bowling averages have unfamiliar names. Only one bowler, Gamini Silva (Police SC), captured over 50 wickets – 54 at 17.72 – while the best return in an innings was 8-31 by Prabath Senanayake for Nomads SC against Moratuwa SC.

Twenty clubs, two more than the previous season, took part in the Lakspray championship.

Lakspray Trophy Final

13, 14, 15 February at Colombo Cricket Club Ground. SINGHALESE SC beat COLOMBO COLTS CC on first innings. Colombo Colts 305 (S.Seneviratne 71) and 115-1 (G.N. Wicknemasinghe 64 not out). Singhalese SC 336 (L.R.D. Mendis 113, A.P. Gurusinha 56; G. Gunesena 4-97).

Leading Lakspray Trophy Averages 1986-87

Batting	M	I	NO	HS	R	Avge	100	50
L.R.D. Mendis (SSC)	6	6	1	151*	466	93.20	3	0
D. Ranatunga (SSC)	14	16	1	241*	911	60.73	3	4
S. Anthonisz (SSC)	13	15	4	110	660	60.00	2	3
D.S.B.P. Kuruppu (Bloomfield)	12	16	3	131	779	59.92	3	3
H.P. Tillakeratne (NCC)	9	12	1	172	658	59.81	3	3
O.S. Mottau (CCC)	12	12	0	263	641	53.41	2	1

Bowling	O	M	R	W	Avge	5wI	10wM
M. Halangoda (SCC)	160	44	380	32	11.87	0	0
L. Sagara (Bloomfield)	188	47	431	34	12.67	2	0
L. Fernando (Saracens)	94.3	31	267	21	12.71	2	0
K. Wijegunawardena (CCC)	162.2	40	508	39	13.02	1	0
G. Gunesena (Colts)	213.4	54	456	34	13.41	2	0
K.N. Amalean (CCC)	93.1	18	302	22	13.72	0	0

Sharjah One-Day Tournaments

Sharjah Champions' Trophy

27 November. INDIA beat SRI LANKA by 7 wickets. Toss: India. Sri Lanka 214-9 (45 overs). India 215-3 (41.3 overs) (K. Srikkanth 92, M. Azharuddin 50*). Award: K. Srikkanth (92).

28 November. WEST INDIES beat PAKISTAN by 9 wickets. Toss: Pakistan. Pakistan 143 (43.4 overs) (Ramiz Raja 49; C.A. Walsh 4-31). West Indies 145-1 (33.2 overs) (C.G. Greenidge 74, D.L. Haynes 59*). Award: A.L. Logie (3ct and 2 run-outs).

30 November. WEST INDIES beat INDIA by 33 runs. Toss: India. West Indies 198-8 (45 overs) (I.V.A. Richards 62, A.L. Logie 58*). India 165-8 (45 overs) (S.M. Gavaskar 63). Award: I.V.A. Richards (62).

2 December. PAKISTAN beat SRI LANKA by 4 wickets. Toss: Pakistan. Sri Lanka 164-7 (45 overs) (A.P. Gurusinha 60). Pakistan 165-6 (44 overs). Award: A.P. Gurusinha (60, 9-0-27-1 and 1ct).

3 December WEST INDIES beat SRI LANKA by 193 runs. Toss: Sri Lanka. West Indies 248-5 (45 overs) (R.B. Richardson 109, C.G. Greenidge 67). Sri Lanka 55 (28.3 overs) (C.A. Walsh 5-1). Award: C.A. Walsh (4.3-3-1-5 and 1ct).

5 December. PAKISTAN beat INDIA by 3 wickets. Toss: Pakistan. India 144 (40.2 overs) (M. Azharuddin 49). Pakistan 145-7 (43.3 overs) (Manzoor Elahi 50*). Award: Manzoor Elahi (50* and 5-0-32-1).

West Indies (3 wins) won Trophy, Pakistan 2nd, India 3rd, Sri Lanka 4th.

Sharjah Cup

2 April. INDIA beat ENGLAND by 3 wickets. Toss: India. England 211-7 (50 overs) (B.C. Broad 57). India 214-7 (48.5 overs) (Kapil Dev 64, K. Srikkanth 56, D.B. Vengsarkar 40). Award: Kapil Dev (8-1-30-1 and 64).

3 April. PAKISTAN beat AUSTRALIA by 6 wickets. Toss: Pakistan. Australia 176-9 (50 overs) (D.C. Boon, 71, S.P. O'Donnell 54). Pakistan 180-4 (46.4 overs) (Javed Miandad 74*, Mudassar Nazar 64). Award: Javed Miandad (74* and 1ct).

5 April. INDIA beat AUSTRALIA by 7 wickets. Toss: India. Australia 176-6 (50 overs) (D.C. Boon 62). India 177-3 (42 overs) (M. Azharuddin 84. S.M. Gavaskar 78*). Award: M. Azharuddin (84).

7 April. ENGLAND beat PAKISTAN by 5 wickets. Toss: England. Pakistan 217-9 (50 overs) (Javed Miandad 60, Imran Khan 46, Ramiz Raja 44). England 220-5 (47.2 overs) (R.T. Robinson 83, B.C. Broad 65, J.J. Whitaker 44*). Award: R.T. Robinson (83).

9 April. ENGLAND beat AUSTRALIA by 11 runs. Toss: Australia. England 230-6 (50 overs) (G.A. Gooch 86, B.C. Broad 44). Australia 219-9 (50 overs) (A.R. Border 84, D.C. Boon 73). Award: G.A. Gooch (86).

10 April. PAKISTAN beat INDIA by 8 wickets. Toss: Pakistan. India 183-8 (50 overs) (D.B. Vengsarkar 95*, Imran Khan 4-27). Pakistan 184-2 (41.4 overs) (Salim Malik 61*, Ramiz Raja 53, Javed Miandad 52*). Award: D.B. Vengsarkar (95*).

England won Cup on run-rate, Pakistan 2nd, India 3rd, Australia 4th.
Player of the Series: D.C. Boon

1987

PAKISTAN
IN ENGLAND

Pakistan in England

Though their performance in the first two rain-ruined Tests was deceptively innocuous, Pakistan's first victory in a series in England was for numerous reasons very far from a surprise. They had recently won a Test match against West Indies and, more recently still, had won in India, no mean feat for any country and one which Pakistan had not achieved before.

They had proved tough opponents in the limited-overs matches England had played against them In Perth, and they had been unlucky to lose in England in 1982, when they had generally looked the better side. Since then, they had beaten England in Pakistan, and their young players of talent had developed well. It was a fair bet, too, that at some stage on English pitches the fast bowling combination of Imran Khan and Wasim Akram would have England in trouble.

In the past, captaincy of Pakistan teams has not always been easy or long-lasting, but in Imran the 1987 team seemed to have an established leader of authority, shrewdness, and vast experience of English cricket.

Against this, England, beaten at home by both India and New Zealand in 1986, had only to offer the less firmly based success of Mike Gatting's team in Australia.

The passage of the Pakistan party round England was somewhat unusual. It had a voluble manager, Haseeb Ahsan, who stirred up controversy with almost every mischievous statement he made. After a time, interviews with him were being sought almost non-stop, so it seemed, and he seldom failed to oblige, least of all in condemnation of the long-standing umpire David Constant. The party was also almost certainly the largest ever to tour England – 20 players took the field at some time or other, and the comings and goings on and off the field during matches provided severe tests of identification for commentators and indeed for umpires.

However, Imran's side won – and won convincingly. They proved a better side than England, with a clear advantage in several departments. They bowled better. England had no one who combined Imran's pace, movement, and accuracy. Admittedly, at 34, he had to use himself sparingly in order to be at his best for Test matches. As captain of a touring side, he was able to do this. A home captain with a similar problem would have had commitments to his county which would have prevented him from turning up fresh for Test matches.

Of the other bowlers, Wasim Akram, already equipped with the late inswing that is the left-arm fast bowler's deadly weapon, was no disappointment. Mohsin Kamal, of whom less had been known, proved an excellent third bowler of pace, steady and lively. Tauseef was an off-spinner with control and variations, and, when the opportunity came at the Oval, Abdul Qadir did all that could have been asked of a leg-spinner, and for hours on end. In any case, even when not taking wickets, he gave the Pakistan bowling variety.

The other decisive strength of the touring side lay not only in the quality of the main batting, but in the depth of the batting. It was hard going for opponents to work through the early batting, with the consistency of Mudassar Nazar, the potential of Ramiz Raja, the prolific run-scoring of Mansoor Akhtar, the near-genius of Javed Miandad, and the obvious class of Salim Malik. But then the bowling side would find that they still had to remove the vigorous Imran, the talented young Ijaz, Salim Yousuf, who was good enough to make a rousing 91 not out at Headingley, and a dangerous hitter of tiring bowling in Wasim Akram. Even numbers 10 and 11 had to be dug out.

This was a very formidable batting side, which could be said to have shown its merit beyond argument at Headingley. There it had the technique to make runs on an indifferent pitch that proved too much for England.

Perhaps Pakistan were lucky that neither the first nor the second Tests could be finished. But in the sort of wet English summer that used to be a nightmare for visiting sides, they came through this period and grew ever stronger. England, of course, were not helped, for the information coming, or not coming, from these two Tests delayed the process of finding the strongest team on current form.

Pakistan had their full share of injuries, such as the one that prevented Imran from bowling at Old Trafford and those that later kept out Ramiz Raja and Tauseef. Not until the last Test did Imran have his strongest side in the field, and before that finished Wasim Akram was in hospital undergoing an appendicitis operation. Yet so capable were the substitutes, notably Shoaib Mohammad, that these misfortunes tended to be overlooked.

The strength of the side at best was not always reflected in its performances against the counties. But usually the counties were not at their best either.

If there was any doubt by the end of July that this had become a strong and successful side, bearing little resemblance to the one that, with Imran off the field, looked disorganized and disheartened at Old Trafford, it could be removed by a look at the fielding. Fortified by success, the Pakistanis held some brilliant catches and were wonderfully nimble about the field. And though not everything that Salim Yousuf did was wholly admirable, and he was acknowledged by his captain to be not a natural wicket-keeper, he missed remarkably little.

First Test: Old Trafford 4, 5, 6, 8, 9 June
Match Drawn.

Not for many years had there been a Test Match in England as thoroughly disrupted by rain as the first Test of 1987 at Old Trafford. Nor would it have escaped the appalling weather if played anywhere else in the country. In the five days, only 207 overs were bowled – and none at all after lunch on the fourth day. At no time was there the prospect of a win – the weather forecast and the sluggishness of the pitch combined to prevent that – and the result was an unreal ill-attended Test match, though one from which England could derive considerable moral advantage. They had bowled and fielded with high efficiency and had made nearly 450 runs in their innings.

Neither side was at full strength. Dilley and Broad were not fit to play for England. Pakistan's leg-spinner Abdul Qadir still had not arrived in England, and when the match started it was soon discovered that Imran Khan was not fit to bowl.

This made his decision to put England in all the harder to justify. Though Wasim Akram was always likely to surprise the batsman and Mohsin Kamal kept going stoutly, there was little menace in the Pakistan attack on a pitch that was soon revealed as holding little for any type of bowler. Early in the match, the England batsmen had to go carefully, but by the time Gatting was out at 133-2 bat was mastering ball. The pillage by the later batsmen was predictable, though the ease and confidence with which the nightwatchman French played was something of a bonus. One end was held for nearly nine hours by Robinson with all the soundness and patience of two years before. His interrupted innings did not end until the second evening.

With Imran off the field, Miandad was left in charge of a Pakistan team that at times looked in grave disarray. Many substitutes came and went, presumably because of minor injuries, and, to the evident frustration of the batsmen, the over-rate was slowed down by these changes, and by lengthy discussions, until only 11 overs were bowled in an hour. This provoked comments from the England manager Micky Stewart, but these were answered next day with some brusqueness by the Pakistan manager Hasib Ahsan, who considered it 'improper' and 'objectionable' that Mr Stewart should publicly accuse Pakistan of spoiling the image of the game. Harmonious relations were restored later.

When bad light stopped an already shortened day's play on Saturday evening, England had taken three wickets for 93, including what seemed the all-important one of Miandad. On Monday morning they took two more, a smart piece of fielding by DeFreitas running out Salim Malik. But no continuity of play was ever foreseeable, and before lunch the action ended for the day and, as it turned out, for the match.

ENGLAND v PAKISTAN FIRST TEST OLD TRAFFORD June 4, 5, 6 1987

ENGLAND 1st INNINGS

No	Batsman	How out	Bowler	Runs	Wkt	Total	6	4	Mins	Balls
1	ATHEY	b	WASIM AKRAM	19	1	50	-	1	106	93
2	ROBINSON	c YOUSUF	MOHSIN KAMAL	166	6	373	-	16	528	365
3	GATTING *	b	MOHSIN KAMAL	42	2	133	-	7	104	84
4	FAIRBROTHER	lbw	MOHSIN KAMAL	0	3	133	-	-	3	4
5	FRENCH †	c IMRAN KHAN	WASIM AKRAM	59	4	246	-	10	154	113
6	GOWER	c YOUSUF	WASIM AKRAM	22	5	284	-	4	48	42
7	BOTHAM	c WASIM AKRAM	TAUSEEF AHMED	48	7	397	1	5	129	69
8	EMBUREY	c SHOAIB	MOHSIN KAMAL	19	9	413	-	4	47	31
9	DeFREITAS	b	WASIM AKRAM	11	8	413	-	2	19	19
10	FOSTER	b	TAUSEEF AHMED	8	10	447	-	-	36	20
11	EDMONDS	not	out	23	-	-	1	2	32	30
	Extras	B 9 LB 15 W 1 NB 5		30						

447

Bowler	O	M	R	W	NB	W
WASIM AKRAM	46	11	111	4	3	
MOHSIN KAMAL	39	4	127	4	2	1
TAUSEEF AHMED	21	4	52	2		
MUDASSAR NAZAR	37	8	133	-	3	

Wkt	Partnership between		Runs	Balls
1	Athey	Robinson	50	181
2	Robinson	Gatting	83	142
3	— · —	Fairbrother	0	4
4	— · —	French	113	231
5	— · —	Gower	38	69
6	— · —	Botham	89	133
7	Botham	Emburey	24	29
8	Emburey	DeFreitas	16	28
9	— · —	Foster	0	3
10	Foster	Edmonds	34	50

Wet square prevented start until 2.45 46
Pakistan won the toss + elected to field
Test debut: N.H. Fairbrother
Tea: 46-0 (25overs) Athey 16* Robinson 24* Imran unable to bowl
Close: 145-3 (59overs) Robinson 62* French 6*
New Ball: 215-3 (85overs) Imran unable to bowl
Lunch: 225-3 (89overs) Robinson 94* French 51*
Umpire Bird injured 3.07 Umpire Birkenshaw took over
Tea: 320-5 (116overs) Robinson 143* Botham 11*
RSP: 5.20 No further play 5/6 402-7 (131.4 overs) Emburey 14* DeFreitas 5*
Wet ground 6/6 - no play until 1.25 (early lunch taken)

143.4 overs + 8 no.balls   10 hours 8 mins
12th men: D.J.Capel + Atif Mujtaba
Umpires: H.D. Bird + B.J. Meyer

Hrs	Balls	Runs	Runs	Balls	Last 50
1	100	32	50	178	-
2	102	30	100	271	93
3	80	44	150	374	103
4	79	43	200	489	115
5	87	40	250	562	73
6	94	39	300	652	90
7	81	55	350	739	87
8	85	44	400	792	53
9	64	59	450		
10			500		
11			550		
12			600		
13			650		

ENGLAND v PAKISTAN   FIRST TEST   OLD TRAFFORD   June 6, 8, 9 (np)

PAKISTAN 1st INNINGS

No	Batsman	How out	Bowler	Runs	Wkt	Total	6	4	Mins	Balls
1	RAMIZ RAJA	c EMBUREY	DeFREITAS	15	2	21	–	1	40	29
2	SHOAIB MOHAMMAD	c FRENCH	FOSTER	0	1	9	–	–	16	7
3	MANSOOR AKHTAR	c FAIRBROTHER	EDMONDS	75	5	139	–	12	199	182
4	JAVED MIANDAD	c FRENCH	BOTHAM	21	3	74	–	2	80	65
5	SALIM MALIK	run out	(DeFreitas/French)	6	4	100	–	–	26	21
6	IMRAN KHAN *	not	out	10	–	–	–	–	71	73
7	MUDASSAR NAZAR	not	out	0	–	–	–	–	4	9
8	SALEEM YOUSUF †									
9	WASIM AKRAM	did not bat								
10	TAUSEEF AHMED									
11	MOHSIN KAMAL									
	Extras	B 9 LB 2 W 1 NB 1		13						

140-5

Bowler	O	M	R	W		NB	W
FOSTER	15	3	34	1			
DeFREITAS	12	4	36	1		2	
BOTHAM	14	7	29	1			1
EMBUREY	16	3	28	–			
EDMONDS	7	5	2	1			

Wkt	Partnership between		Runs	Balls
1	Ramiz	Shoaib	9	25
2	— . —	Mansoor	12	34
3	Mansoor	Javed	53	140
4	— . —	Salim Malik	26	41
5	— . —	Imran Khan	39	135
6	Imran Khan	Mudassar	1*	11
7				
8				
9				
10				

England 447
Tea: 61-2 (24 overs) Mansoor 25* Javed 13*   386 behind
BLSP: 5.13 no further play 6/6
93-3 (38 overs) Mansoor 42* Salim Malik 3*   354 behind
Start delayed until 1130 8/6   7 overs off
RSP: 12.53 no further play 8/6
140-5 (64 overs) Imran 10* Mudassar 0*   307 behind
No play possible 9/6

Match Drawn
Man of the Match: R T Robinson

64 overs + 2 no-balls   3 hours 43 mins

Hrs	Balls	Runs
1	87	29
2	111	45
3	92	48
4		
5		
6		
7		
8		
9		
10		
11		
12		
13		

	Runs	Balls	Last 50
	50	131	–
	100	231	100
	150		
	200		
	250		
	300		
	350		
	400		
	450		
	500		
	550		
	600		
	650		

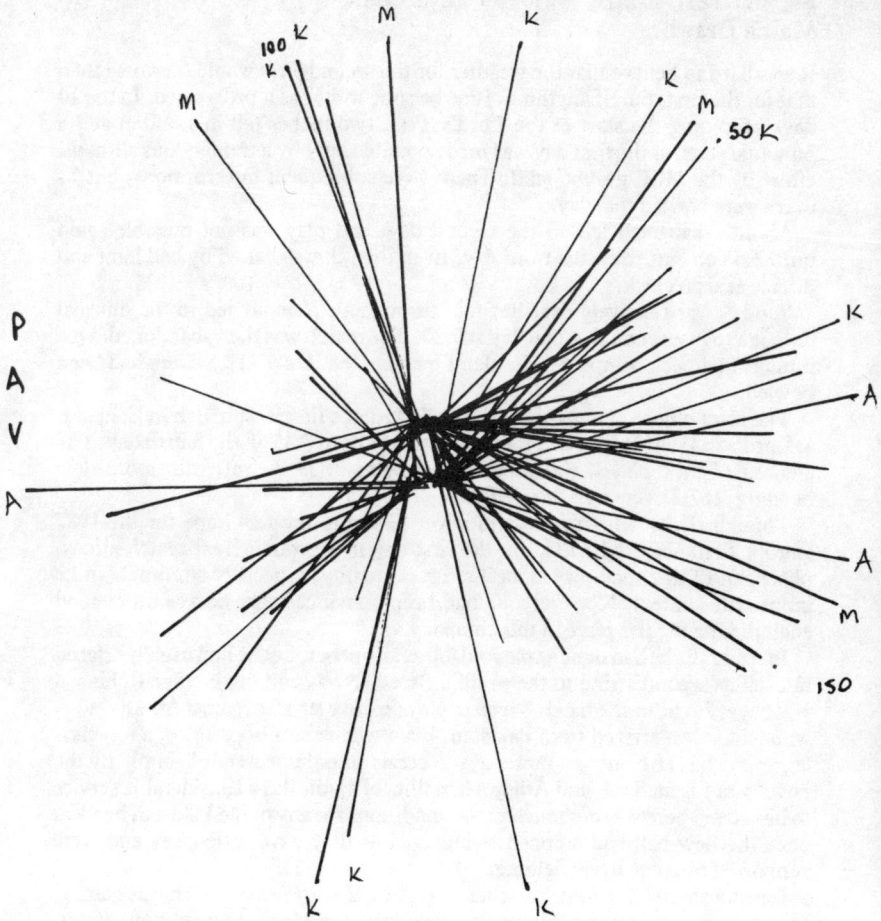

1st Test – Robinson 166

BOWLER		1	2	3	4	6	TOTAL
Wasim Akram	A	10	4	4	3	–	42
Mohsin Kamal	K	7	5	3	9	–	62
Tauseef Ahmed	T	7	1	–	–	–	9
Mudassar Nazar	M	12	5	5	4	–	53
		36	15	12	16	–	166

166 RUNS
365 BALLS
528 MINUTES

Second Test: Lords, 18, 19, 20, 22, 23 June
Match Drawn.

It was hard to believe that the weather for the second Test would be worse than that for the first, but, if anything, June became wetter as it progressed. In the 10 days preceding the start of the Lord's Test, two inches fell in London and a punctual start on the first day was made possible only by a tremendous all-night effort by the MCC ground staff. There were subsequent interruptions, but 73 overs were bowled that day.

Another half-inch fell on the second day, and play was not possible again until 2.45 on Saturday, the third day. Even then, it was halted by bad light and drizzle at six o'clock.

Sunday was relatively dry, but rain throughout Monday led to the unusual decision to inspect on the final day at 9.30. The match was then abandoned. One innings had been completed, England making 368. Only 112.5 overs had been bowled.

The most obvious comparison is with Pakistan's first Test match in England, at Lord's in 1954. Operations then did not start until 3.45 on the fourth day. The amount of time played was much the same as in 1987, but, with more slow bowling, 167.1 overs were bowled.

Though the weather forecasters never held out any real hope for the 1987 Lord's Test, England batted on the first day in a genuine Test match atmosphere, and Bill Athey played an innings of quality, especially admirable in its immediate context. Not everyone had been convinced that he was quite good enough for a regular place in this company.

In Australia he had done a splendid job as an opener, but he had usually effaced himself as second string to the prolific Broad. Now, coming in after Robinson was out at 29, he immediately began to play positive strokes against Abdul Qadir, who had at last arrived from Pakistan. Even when short of practice, a top-class leg-spinner is rare enough nowadays to create initial uncertainty simply by the novelty of his method, and Athey's handling of Qadir did a considerable service to his side. There was not much in the conditions for any of the Pakistan bowlers once the new ball had stopped swinging, but they gave little away and were supported by some lively fielding.

Gatting shared in a fourth-wicket stand of 102 with Athey which was gaining momentum when, with a substantial misjudgement, the captain ran himself out. He had already refused the umpires' offer of the light, and proceedings ended soon afterwards when the light deteriorated further. Athey was 107 not out.

On the Saturday afternoon French played his second confident innings of the series as nightwatchman, revealing a range of reputable strokes. Athey was soon bowled by a good one from Imran with the new ball, but, apart from Botham, who was contained to three scoring strokes in 50 minutes, England batted with purpose. Pakistan played attacking cricket as well, and the 17,700 crowd did at least have a snatch of good entertainment before England's innings ended in the rain. As it proved, the match ended with it.

ENGLAND v PAKISTAN   SECOND TEST   LORD'S   June 18, 19(np), 20

ENGLAND 1st INNINGS

No	Batsman	How out	Bowler	Runs	Wkt	Total	6	4	Mins	Balls
1	BROAD	b	MUDASSAR	55	2	118	-	4	170	120
2	ROBINSON	c YOUSUF	MOHSIN KAMAL	7	1	29	-	-	46	39
3	ATHEY	b	IMRAN KHAN	123	5	272	-	14	315	202
4	GOWER	c YOUSUF	MUDASSAR	8	3	128	-	2	8	9
5	GATTING *	run out	(Malik/Yousuf)	43	4	230	-	7	124	98
6	FRENCH †	b	WASIM AKRAM	42	6	294	-	5	88	69
7	BOTHAM	c JAVED	WASIM AKRAM	6	7	305	-	1	47	32
8	EMBUREY	run out	(Ijaz/Imran)	12	9	340	-	2	60	37
9	FOSTER	b	ABDUL QADIR	21	8	329	-	4	24	22
10	EDMONDS	not out		17	-	-	-	1	47	32
11	DILLEY	c YOUSUF	IMRAN KHAN	17	10	368	-	3	28	24
	Extras	B - LB 12 W 1 NB 4		17						

368

Bowler	O	M	R	W	NB	W
IMRAN KHAN *	34.5	7	90	2	1	1
WASIM AKRAM	28	1	98	2	4	
MOHSIN KAMAL	9	2	42	1		
ABDUL QADIR	25	1	100	1	1	
MUDASSAR NAZAR	16	6	26	2	1	

Also fielded: SHOAIB MOHAMMAD, MANSOOR AKHTAR, JAVED MIANDAD, SALIM MALIK, IJAZ AHMED, & SALEEM YOUSUF †

Wkt	Partnership between		Runs	Balls
1	Broad	Robinson	29	61
2	—.—	Athey	89	179
3	Athey	Gower	10	13
4	—.—	Gatting	102	185
5	—.—	French	42	80
6	French	Botham	22	44
7	Botham	Emburey	11	20
8	Emburey	Foster	24	34
9	—.—	Edmonds	11	27
10	Edmonds	Dilley	28	41

England won the toss & elected to bat
Lunch: 80-1 (28 overs) Broad 29* Athey 39*
Tea: 164-3 (57 overs) Athey 70* Gatting 16*
BLSP until 4.50 12 overs off 21 overs left 18/6
BLSP: 6.01 5 overs left No further play 18/6
Close: 231-4 (73 overs) Athey 107* French 1*
No play possible 19/6/87 1st complete day lost at Lords since 15/6/78
RSP until 2.45 3'5" lost 44 overs to be bowled 20/6
New Ball: 271-4 (85 overs)
Tea: 294-6 (92.5 overs) Botham 5*
No play possible 22/6, 23/6   Match Drawn
Man of the Match: C.W.J. Athey

112.5 overs + 7no-balls   8hours 7mins
12th Men: P.A.J. DeFreitas + Asif Mujtaba
Umpires: D.J. Constant + A.G.T. Whitehead

Hrs	Balls	Runs
1	74	41
2	94	39
3	85	48
4	91	35
5	85	57
6	84	47
7	77	43
8	83	54
9		
10		
11		
12		
13		

Runs	Balls	Last 50
50	94	-
100	197	103
150	305	108
200	406	101
250	500	94
300	571	71
350	653	82
400		
450		
500		
550		
600		
650		

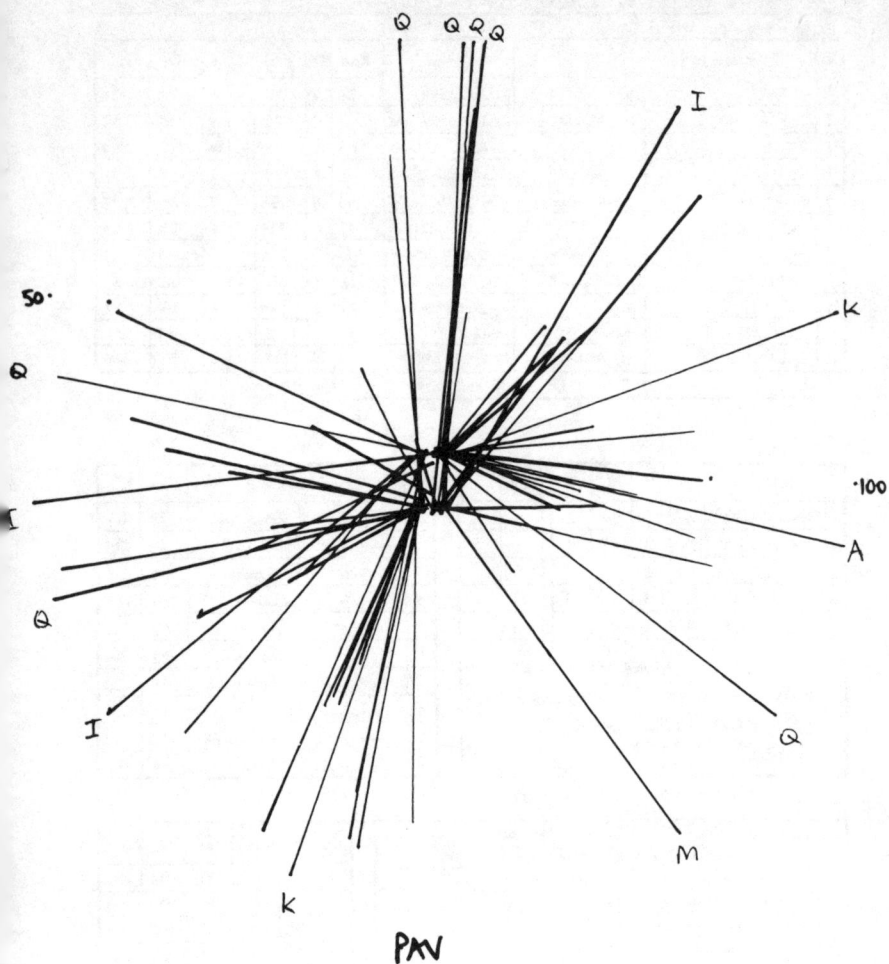

2nd Test – Athey 123

BOWLER		1	2	3	4	6	TOTAL
Abdul Qadir	Q	9	4	2	7	–	51
Mohsin Kamal	K	3	–	–	2	–	11
Wasim Akram	A	4	2	1	1	–	15
Imran Khan	I	4	2	5	3	–	35
Mudassar Nazar	M	4	–	1	1	–	11
		24	8	9	14	–	123

123 RUNS
202 BALLS
315 MINUTES

Third Test: Leeds, 2, 3, 4, 6 July
Pakistan won by an innings and 18 runs.

After two wash-outs with never a hope of victory for either side, the series began in earnest at Headingley in a period of warm and settled weather. With the sunshine came a rude shock for England who, after making the running in such action as was possible at Old Trafford and Lord's, now found themselves completely outplayed.

There must always have been an uneasy feeling in many English minds that sooner or later Imran and Wasim Akram would find conditions to suit them and would sweep aside the England batsmen, whose form and confidence had not been helped by a domestic programme disrupted by weather and limited-overs commitments. At Headingley, Imran, especially, gave a superb exhibition of fast to fast-medium bowling. England had no answer with either bat or ball. The reliance on Foster exposed the limited penetration of the rest of their own bowling. Capel's two dogged innings in his first Test match underlined the vulnerability of their more ambitious stroke-players in awkward conditions.

The first-day problems at Headingley have tended to arise from the amount the ball would swing in certain conditions. On this occasion the clear weather gave no reason to fear excessive swing, and Gatting duly chose to bat, as Imran would apparently have done if the choice had been his.

From the first over England were in trouble on a pitch of uneven bounce and sharp lateral movement, and there was no recovery from the 31-5 to which Imran and Wasim reduced them. A stand of 54 between Botham and Capel delayed Pakistan for a time, but an effective third bowler was on hand in Mohsin Kamal, and in four hours 25 minutes England were out.

By the end of the first day Pakistan were 76-2. Next morning they had their only moments of concern in the match, when Foster in his first over removed Mansur Akhtar and Miandad. The Pakistan reply to that was some solid sensible batting, first by the nightwatchman Salim Yousuf and then, until he was eighth out for 99, by Salim Malik. The ball still darted about extravagantly at times, but only Foster made anything of the conditions. Botham was absent nursing a foot injury. Pakistan made only 204 runs in the day, losing six more wickets, but it was good enough.

Saturday's play began with some robust hitting by Wasim Akram which helped the last two wickets to add 73 in an hour and to take the lead to 217. England's second innings then followed much the same hazardous course as their first. Though Gower made 55, he looked likely to be out almost any ball. Botham batted with a runner and without footwork. Seven wickets were down by Saturday evening, the weather forecast was set fair, and it took only 25 minutes' play on Monday morning to bring Pakistan a most convincing victory.

ENGLAND v PAKISTAN   THIRD TEST   HEADINGLEY   July 2

ENGLAND 1st INNINGS

No	Batsman	How out	Bowler	Runs	Wkt	Total	6	4	Mins	Balls
1	BROAD	c YOUSUF	WASIM AKRAM	8	3	13	-	1	35	25
2	ROBINSON	lbw	IMRAN KHAN	0	1	1	-	-	1	1
3	ATHEY	c YOUSUF	IMRAN KHAN	4	2	13	-	-	27	18
4	GOWER	b	IMRAN KHAN	10	5	31	-	2	29	18
5	GATTING *	lbw	WASIM AKRAM	8	4	31	-	2	18	13
6	BOTHAM	c YOUSUF	MUDASSAR	26	6	85	-	2	115	64
7	CAPEL	c+b	MOHSIN KAMAL	53	8	133	-	6	191	161
8	RICHARDS †	lbw	WASIM AKRAM	6	7	113	-	-	52	29
9	FOSTER	c MALIK	MOHSIN KAMAL	9	10	136	-	-	38	29
10	EDMONDS	c YOUSUF	MOHSIN KAMAL	0	9	133	-	-	1	2
11	DILLEY	not out		1	-	-	-	-	9	7
	Extras	B 1 LB 8 W 1 NB 1		11						

136

Bowler	O	M	R	W	NB	W
IMRAN KHAN	19	3	37	3		
WASIM AKRAM	14	4	36	3		
ABDUL QADIR	5	-	14	-	2	
MUDASSAR NAZAR	14	5	18	1		
MOHSIN KAMAL	8†	2	22	3	1	1

Wkt	Partnership between		Runs	Balls
1	Broad	Robinson	1	3
2	—.—	Athey	12	37
3	—.—	Gower	0	6
4	Gower	Gatting	18	25
5	—.—	Botham	0	5
6	Botham	Capel	54	162
7	Capel	Richards	28	76
8	—.—	Foster	20	39
9	Foster	Edmonds	0	2
10	—.—	Dilley	3	12

England won the toss + elected to bat

Test debut: D.J. Capel

Hrs	Balls	Runs		Runs	Balls	Last 50
1	75	31		50	144	-
2	86	22		100	284	140
3	87	35		150		
4	87	30		200		
5				250		
6				300		
7				350		
8				400		
9				450		
10				500		
11				550		
12				600		
13				650		

60.4 overs + 3 no-balls   4 hours 26 mins

12th Men: J.E. Emburey + Asif Mujtaba

Umpires: K.E. Palmer + D.R. Shepherd

ENGLAND v PAKISTAN   THIRD TEST   HEADINGLEY   July 2, 3, 4

PAKISTAN 1st INNINGS

No	Batsman	How out	Bowler	Runs	Wkt	Total	6	4	Mins	Balls
1	MUDASSAR NAZAR	lbw	FOSTER	24	2	60	-	3	89	60
2	SHOAIB MOHAMMAD	c RICHARDS	FOSTER	16	1	22	-	1	42	39
3	MANSOOR AKHTAR	lbw	FOSTER	29	3	86	-	5	80	72
4	SALEEM YOUSUF †	c ATHEY	FOSTER	37	5	152	-	3	154	132
5	JAVED MIANDAD	c GATTING	FOSTER	0	4	86	-	-	3	4
6	SALIM MALIK	c GOWER	EDMONDS	99	7	280	-	8	331	238
7	IMRAN KHAN *	c RICHARDS	FOSTER	26	6	208	-	2	100	81
8	IJAZ AHMED	c ATHEY	FOSTER	50	8	318	-	9	148	107
9	WASIM AKRAM	c EDMONDS	FOSTER	43	10	353	4	2	61	42
10	ABDUL QADIR	b	DILLEY	2	9	328	-	-	11	9
11	MOHSIN KAMAL	not	out	3	-	-	-	-	12	10
	Extras	B 5 LB 13 W 1 NB 5		24						

353

Bowler	O	M	R	W	NB	W
DILLEY	33	7	89	1	5	
FOSTER	46²	15	107	8		
CAPEL	18	1	64	-		
EDMONDS	25	10	59	1	1	
GATTING	9	3	16	-		1

Wkt	Partnership between		Runs	Balls
1	Mudassar	Shoaib	22	68
2	—.—	Mansoor	38	74
3	Mansoor	Yousuf	26	59
4	Yousuf	Javed	0	4
5	—.—	Malik	66	181
6	Malik	Imran Khan	56	157
7	—.—	Ijaz	72	161
8	Ijaz	Wasim Akram	38	56
9	Wasim Akram	Abdul Qadir	10	15
10	—.—	Mohsin Kamal	25	19

England 136
27 overs remain 2/7
Botham unable to take the field entire innings - injured left foot
Close: 76-2 (27overs) Mansoor 24* Yousuf 4*   60 behind
Lunch: 136-4 (57overs) Yousuf 33* Malik 25*   scores level
Tea: 206-5 (89overs) Malik 61* Imran 26*   70 ahead
New Ball: 208-5 (89.2 overs)
Close: 280-7 (117 overs) Ijaz 33* Wasim Akram 0* 144 ahead

131.2 overs + 6 no.balls   8 hours 44 mins

Hrs	Balls	Runs		Runs	Balls	Last 50
1	92	38		50	117	-
2	100	48		100	246	129
3	85	33		150	366	120
4	98	31		200	521	155
5	92	29		250	610	89
6	94	37		300	750	140
7	80	40		350	789	39
8	92	32		400		
9				450		
10				500		
11				550		
12				600		
13				650		

ENGLAND v PAKISTAN THIRD TEST HEADINGLEY July 4, 6

ENGLAND 2nd INNINGS

No	Batsman	How out	Bowler	Runs	Wkt	Total	6	4	Mins	Balls
1	BROAD	c YOUSUF	IMRAN KHAN	4	1	4	-	1	1	2
2	ROBINSON	c MALIK	IMRAN KHAN	2	2	9	-	-	10	4
3	ATHEY	lbw	IMRAN KHAN	26	3	60	-	2	74	43
4	GOWER	b	IMRAN KHAN	55	5	120	-	6	205	136
5	GATTING *	c JAVED	WASIM AKRAM	9	4	94	-	1	45	35
6	CAPEL	c IJAZ	IMRAN KHAN	28	8	197	-	2	199	134
7	RICHARDS †	c IJAZ	IMRAN KHAN°	2	6	122	-	-	9	8
8	BOTHAM	c MUDASSAR	MOHSIN KAMAL	24	7	160	-	3	57	47
9	FOSTER	b	WASIM AKRAM	22	9	197	-	4	80	57
10	EDMONDS	not	out	0	-	~	-	-	6	1
11	DILLEY	b	IMRAN KHAN	0	10	199	-	-	3	6
	Extras	B5 LB12 W7 NB3		27						

199

Bowler	O	M	R	W		NB	W
IMRAN KHAN	19¹	5	40	7			
WASIM AKRAM	21	5	55	2		3	3
ABDUL QADIR	27	5	60	-			
MOHSIN KAMAL	9	4	19	1		1	1
MUDASSAR NAZAR	2	-	8	-			

Wkt	Partnership between		Runs	Balls
1	Broad	Robinson	4	2
2	Robinson	Athey	5	11
3	Athey	Gower	51	91
4	Gower	Gatting	34	72
5	— .—	Capel	26	83
6	Capel	Richards	2	14
7	— .—	Botham	38	80
8	— .—	Foster	37	111
9	Foster	Edmonds	0	3
10	Edmonds	Dilley	2	6

England 136 Pakistan 353 lead 217

73 overs remains 4/7

Lunch: 44-2 (10 overs) Athey 17* Gower 14* 173 behind

Tea: 114-4 (41 overs) Gower 51* Capel 7* 103 behind

4.20 * Richards = 300 Test wickets Imran Khan

Robinson as runner for Botham

Close: 186-7 (73 overs) Capel 26* Foster 13* 31 behind

24 mins play - 32 balls 6/7

Pakistan won by an innings + 18 runs

Man of the Match: Imran Khan

78.1 overs + 4 no-balls   5 hours 33 mins

Hrs	Balls	Runs		Runs	Balls	Last 50
1	78	49		50	79	-
2	90	44		100	198	119
3	93	27		150	340	142
4	81	30		200		
5	83	35		250		
6				300		
7				350		
8				400		
9				450		
10				500		
11				550		
12				600		
13				650		

Fourth Test: Edgbaston, 23, 24, 25, 27, 28 July
Match Drawn.

For four and a half days the fourth Test pursued a somewhat frustrated course on a slow pitch unhelpful to batsman and bowler alike, but events after lunch on the last day lifted it into the unusual. It was played mostly under cloudy skies – with the morning's play lost on the second day and with two hold-ups for bad light on the last morning, which may have affected the result.

So solidly did Pakistan's batsmen play in making 250-3 on the first day that Mike Gatting's decision to put them in came under immediate fire. In fact, on an overcast morning and with damp in the pitch, he probably did the right thing, and conditions were certainly no worse when England batted.

England's bowlers, Foster excepted, were not at their best on the first day. Catches were missed, and Mudassar Nazar batted carefully through a day of 105 overs for 102 not out. A better spell by Dilley and Botham brought a temporary decline to 317-7 next morning, but the last three Pakistan wickets added 122 under the uncomplicated Saleem Yousuf, with vigorous support from Wasim Akram. That evening there was time for only seven overs, which Broad and Robinson negotiated safely.

They advanced steadily to 119 on the third day, and though Robinson was third out at 157, Gower and Gatting played well together until, near the end, Gower and nightwatchman French were both out, leaving a score of 273-5 and plenty still to do.

It was done after the week-end mainly by Gatting in making his eighth Test hundred, and with the help of Emburey and others England earned a first innings lead of 82. When Mudassar and Shoaib reduced this by 38 without mishap that evening, a draw seemed a certainty.

It seemed a bigger certainty when, after an interrupted morning and the loss of 52 minutes through bad light, Pakistan were 73-1. But after lunch Foster, in a splendid spell, took three for 10 in 18 balls and Botham found a new fire.

Three overs were lost to bad light, but at tea Pakistan had slipped to 156-7, only 74 ahead. Akram was out at 165, but Qadir survived a hazardous start and helped Imran to add 39 vital runs before the innings ended, leaving England to make 124 in 18 overs.

Under the proper Laws of Cricket – not the rules devised for one-day cricket – this was clearly a huge task against Imran and Akram, whose bowling was predictably high, wide, and fast. However, Broad gave England such a start, 30 out of 37 in five overs, that victory was really in their sights.

While Gower and Gatting were together, the required rate of seven an over was maintained. But the going was never easy, and hopes faded when, with Athey his partner, Gatting was run out. Later Emburey did hit Imran for 14 in an over, but 24 were still needed off the last two overs and that was well beyond the remaining batsmen.

ENGLAND v PAKISTAN   FOURTH TEST   EDGBASTON   July 23 24
PAKISTAN 1st INNINGS

No	Batsman	How out	Bowler	Runs	Wkt	Total	6	4	Mins	Balls
1	MUDASSAR NAZAR	lbw	DILLEY	124	4	284	-	16	416	362
2	SHOAIB MOHAMMAD	c FOSTER	EDMONDS	18	1	44	-	2	64	49
3	MANSOOR AKHTAR	b	FOSTER	26	2	83	-	4	87	86
4	JAVED MIANDAD	lbw	DILLEY	75	3	218	1	8	153	145
5	SALIM MALIK	c FRENCH	DILLEY	24	5	289	-	3	127	95
6	IJAZ AHMED	b	BOTHAM	20	7	317	-	4	50	35
7	IMRAN KHAN *	c EMBUREY	DILLEY	0	6	289	-	-	1	1
8	SALEEM YOUSUF†	not	out	91	-	-	-	14	181	151
9	WASIM AKRAM	c BOTHAM	FOSTER	26	8	360	1	4	52	44
10	ABDUL QADIR	c EDMONDS	DILLEY	6	9	384	-	-	36	30
11	MOHSIN KAMAL	run out	(Dilley)	10	10	439	-	1	61	47
	Extras	B 4 LB 11 W 1 NB 3		19						

439

Bowler	O	M	R	W	NB	W
DILLEY	35	6	92	5	4	
FOSTER	37	8	107	2		
EMBUREY	26	7	48	-		
EDMONDS	24³	12	50	1		
BOTHAM	48	13	121	1		1
GATTING	3	-	6	-		

Wkt	Partnership between		Runs	Balls
1	Mudassar	Shoaib	44	112
2	—.—	Mansoor	39	178
3	—.—	Javed	135	264
4	—.—	Malik	66	169
5	Malik	Ijaz	5	32
6	Ijaz	Imran Khan	0	1
7	—.—	Yousuf	28	42
8	Yousuf	Wasim Akram	43	82
9	—.—	Abdul Qadir	24	55
10	—.—	Mohsin Kamal	55	110

England won the toss + elected to field
Lunch : 70-1 (38 overs) Mudassar 32* Mansoor 15*
Tea : 153-2 (73 overs) Mudassar 64* Javed 35*
New Ball : 198-2 (86.2 overs)
Close : 250-3 (105 overs) Mudassar 102* Malik 13*
No play morning 24/7 Lunch 12.45-1.25   26 overs off
BLSP: 2-31 - 2-49 5 overs off
Tea: (4.10) 346-7 (142 overs) Yousuf 20* Akram 21*

173.3 overs + 4 no-balls   10 hours 23 mins
12th Men: N.V. Radford + Asif Mujtaba
Umpires: B.J. Meyer + A.G.T. Whitehead

Hrs	Balls	Runs		Runs	Balls	Last 50
1	103	41		50	138	-
2	126	29		100	328	190
3	102	31		150	433	105
4	109	52		200	525	92
5	102	54		250	633	108
6	90	39		300	772	139
7	94	38		350	857	85
8	88	39		400	950	93
9	90	43		450		
10	90	59		500		
11				550		
12				600		
13				650		

ENGLAND v PAKISTAN   FOURTH TEST   EDGBASTON   July 24, 25, 27

ENGLAND 1st INNINGS

No	Batsman	How out	Bowler	Runs	Wkt	Total	6	4	Mins	Balls
1	BROAD	c YOUSUF	IMRAN KHAN	54	1	119	-	5	208	148
2	ROBINSON	c YOUSUF	WASIM AKRAM	80	3	157	-	11	272	208
3	ATHEY	b	IMRAN KHAN	0	2	132	-	-	27	17
4	GOWER	c YOUSUF	IMRAN KHAN	61	4	251	-	10	158	105
5	GATTING *	c AKRAM	IMRAN KHAN	124	8	484	-	16	400	281
6	FRENCH †	b	IMRAN KHAN	0	5	251	-	-	2	2
7	BOTHAM	c +b	WASIM AKRAM	37	6	300	-	6	59	39
8	EMBUREY	lbw	WASIM AKRAM	58	7	443	1	8	179	141
9	FOSTER	run out	(Ijaz)	29	9	512	-	3	78	63
10	EDMONDS	not	out	24	-	-	-	3	36	27
11	DILLEY	b	IMRAN KHAN	2	10	521	-	-	8	8
	Extras	B1 LB24 W11 NB6		52						

521

Bowler	O	M	R	W		NB	W
IMRAN KHAN	41.5	8	129	6		2	1
WASIM AKRAM	43	12	83	3		6	2
ABDUL QADIR	21	4	65	-		3	
MUDASSAR NAZAR	35	7	97	-		9	3
MOHSIN KAMAL	29	2	122	-			1

Wkt	Partnership between		Runs	Balls
1	Broad	Robinson	119	303
2	Robinson	Athey	13	40
3	— . —	Gower	25	47
4	Gower	Gatting	94	166
5	Gatting	French	0	2
6	— . —	Botham	49	85
7	— . —	Emburey	143	267
8	— . —	Foster	41	77
9	Foster	Edmonds	28	39
10	Edmonds	Dilley	9	13

Pakistan 439   7 overs remain 24/7

Close : 18-0 (7 overs) Broad 14* Robinson 2*   421 behind
Lunch : 72-0 (34 overs) Broad 39* Robinson 26*   367 behind
Tea : 155-2 (63 overs) Robinson 80* Gower 10*   284 behind
New Ball : 233-3 (86 overs) Follow-on saved 88-2 overs
Close : 273-5 (97 overs) Gatting 35* Botham 16*   166 behind
Lunch : 364-6 (127 overs) Gatting 88* Emburey 11*   75 behind
Tea : 456-7 (155 overs) Gatting 113* Foster 5*   17 ahead

169.5 overs + 20 no-balls   11 hours 52 mins

Hrs	Balls	Runs		Runs	Balls	Last 50
1	90	34		50	137	-
2	79	25		100	264	127
3	93	40		150	373	109
4	83	37		200	457	84
5	86	37		250	555	98
6	98	60		300	640	85
7	84	50		350	746	106
8	90	39		400	839	93
9	90	49		450	928	89
10	85	54		500	1007	79
11	88	40		550		
12				600		
13				650		

ENGLAND v PAKISTAN FOURTH TEST EDGBASTON July 27, 28

PAKISTAN 2nd INNINGS

No	Batsman	How out	Bowler	Runs	Wkt	Total	6	4	Mins	Balls
1	MUDASSAR NAZAR	b	DILLEY	10	1	47	-	1	67	48
2	SHOAIB MOHAMMAD	lbw	FOSTER	50	5	104	-	7	151	135
3	MANSOOR AKHTAR	lbw	FOSTER	17	2	80	-	2	56	34
4	JAVED MIANDAD	c EMBUREY	FOSTER	4	3	85	-	1	8	8
5	SALIM MALIK	c † b	BOTHAM	17	4	104	-	4	10	14
6	IJAZ AHMED	b	BOTHAM	11	6	116	-	1	13	18
7	IMRAN KHAN *	lbw	FOSTER	37	9	204	-	5	127	94
8	SALEEM YOUSUF †	c GATTING	EDMONDS	17	7	156	-	1	51	44
9	WASIM AKRAM	c EDMONDS	DILLEY	6	8	165	-	1	14	18
10	ABDUL QADIR	run out	(Foster/French)	20	10	205	-	2	45	26
11	MOHSIN KAMAL	not	out	0	-	-	-	-	4	4
	Extras	B - LB 13 W 1 NB 2		16						

205

Bowler	O	M	R	W		NB	W
FOSTER	27	7	59	4		1	1
DILLEY	18	3	53	2			
EMBUREY	4	1	3	-			
BOTHAM	20³	3	66	2		1	
EDMONDS	4	1	11	1			

Wkt	Partnership between		Runs	Balls
1	Mudassar	Shoaib	47	115
2	Shoaib	Mansoor	33	92
3	— . —	Javed	5	14
4	— . —	Malik	19	17
5	— . —	Ijaz	0	4
6	Ijaz	Imran	12	33
7	Imran	Yousuf	40	84
8	— . —	Wasim Akram	9	21
9	— . —	Abdul Qadir	39	56
10	Abdul Qadir	Mohsin Kamal	1	7

Pakistan 439 England 521 Lead 82
15 overs left 27/7
Close: 38-0 (15 overs) Mudassar 6* Shoaib 32* 44 behind
B.SP: 11.54 73-1 (28.2 overs) Resume 12.20 6 overs off
Lunch: 79-1 (32 overs) Shoaib 49* Mansoor 16* 3 behind
B.SP: 2.47 125-6 (48.5 overs) Resume 2.58 3 overs off
Tea: 156-7 (59.3 overs) Imran Khan 21* 74 ahead

Hrs	Balls	Runs		Runs	Balls	Last 50
1	105	43		50	124	-
2	91	36		100	236	112
3	90	40		150	343	107
4	94	46		200	430	87
5				250		
6				300		
7				350		
8				400		
9				450		
10				500		
11				550		
12				600		
13				650		

73.3 overs + 2 no-balls 4 hours 46 minutes

ENGLAND v PAKISTAN FOURTH TEST EDGBASTON July 28

ENGLAND 2nd INNINGS

No	Batsman	How out	Bowler	Runs	Wkt	Total	6	4	Mins	Balls
1	BROAD	c MUDASSAR	IMRAN KHAN	30	1	37	-	5	25	23
2	ROBINSON	c IMRAN	WASIM AKRAM	4	2	39	-	-	29	10
3	GOWER	b	IMRAN KHAN	18	4	72	-	2	27	15
4	BOTHAM	c KAMAL	WASIM AKRAM	6	3	53	-	1	6	7
5	GATTING *	run out	(Ijaz)	8	5	73	-	1	19	10
6	ATHEY	not	out	14	-	-	-	1	35	20
7	EMBUREY	run out	(Mansoor/Yousuf)	20	6	108	1	2	27	18
8	EDMONDS	run out	(Wasim Akram)	0	7	108	-	-	2	2
9	FRENCH †	not	out	1	-	-	-	-	1	1
10	FOSTER	} did not bat								
11	DILLEY									
	Extras	B - LB 7 W 1 NB -		8						

109-7

Bowler	O	M	R	W	NB	W
IMRAN KHAN	9	-	61	2		1
WASIM AKRAM	8⁴	-	41	2		

Wkt	Partnership between		Runs	Balls
1	Broad	Robinson	37	30
2	Robinson	Gower	2	4
3	Gower	Botham	14	11
4	— · —	Gatting	19	19
5	Gatting	Athey	1	3
6	Athey	Emburey	35	36
7	— · —	Edmonds	0	2
8	— · —	French	1*	1
9				
10				

Pakistan 439 + 205 England 521
England need 124 to win off remaining 18 overs @ 6.88 p.o.

Match Drawn
Man of the Match: M.W. Gatting

17.4 overs   1 hour 31 mins

Hrs	Balls	Runs		Runs	Balls	Last 50
1	67	73		50	42	-
2				100	94	52
3				150		
4				200		
5				250		
6				300		
7				350		
8				400		
9				450		
10				500		
11				550		
12				600		
13				650		

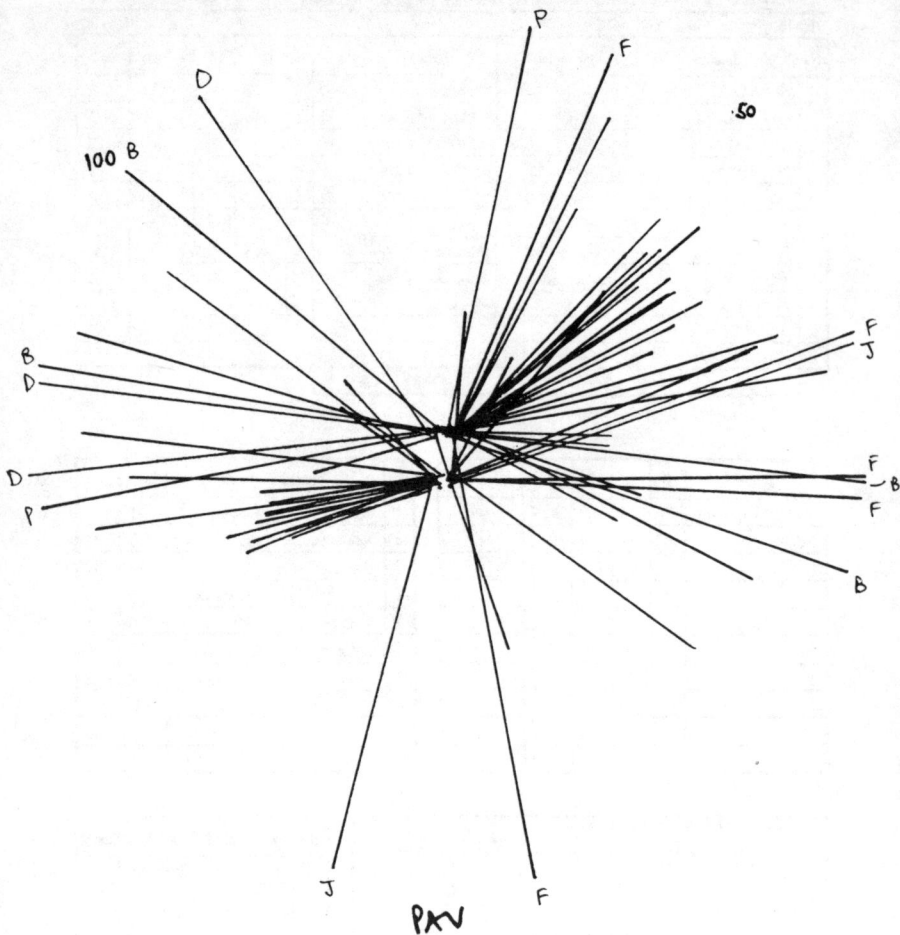

4th Test – Mudassar 124

BOWLER		1	2	3	4	6	TOTAL
Dilley	D	7	–	1	3	–	22
Foster	F	9	2	2	5	–	39
Emburey	J	6	1	–	2	–	16
Edmonds	P	5	–	–	2	–	13
Botham	B	7	2	1	4	–	30
Gatting	G	1	–	1	–	–	4
		35	5	5	16	–	124

124 RUNS
362 BALLS
416 MINUTES

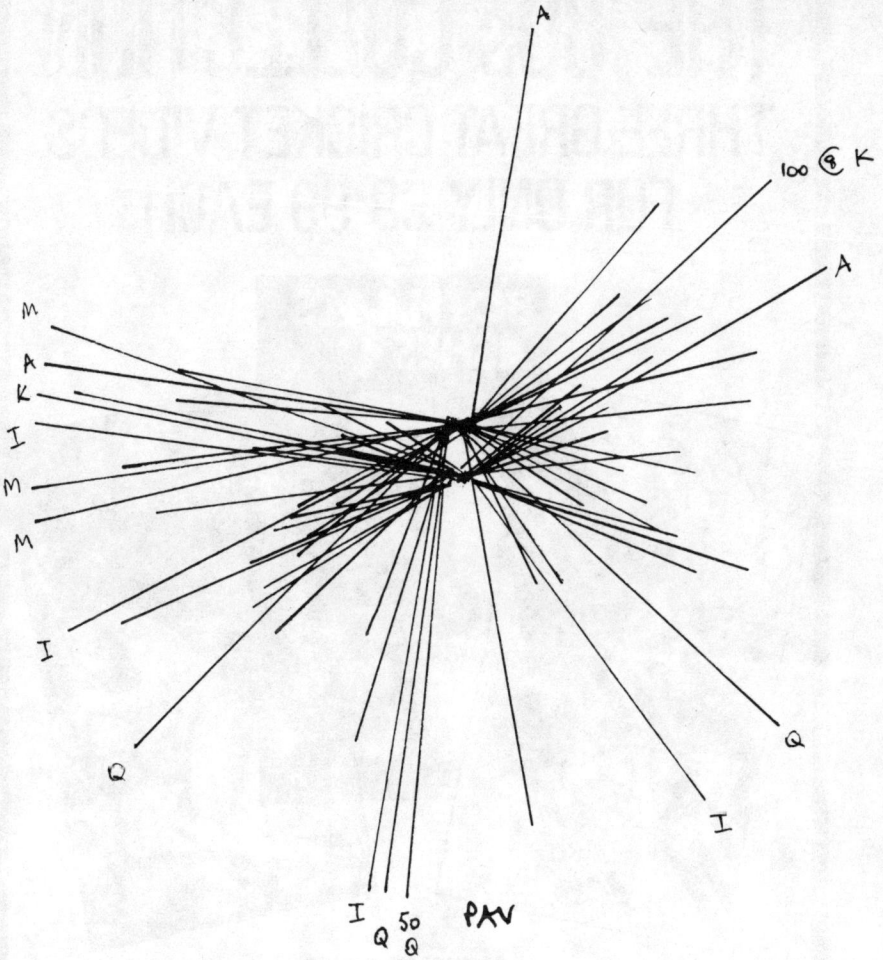

4th Test – Gatting 124

BOWLER		1	2	3	4	6	TOTAL
Mohsin Kamal	K	12	2	–	2	–	24
Wasim Akram	A	9	1	–	3	–	23
Mudassar Nazar	M	9	2	–	3	–	25
Abdul Qadir	Q	8	1	–	4	–	26
Imran Khan	I	8	1	–	4	–	26
		46	7	–	16	–	124

124 RUNS
281 BALLS
400 MINUTES

Fifth Test: The Oval, 6, 7, 8, 10, 11 August
Match Drawn.

The toss proved of high importance, for the pitch, mild and true, was a superb one for batting on the first two days, and only posed problems later when the spinners pitched in the rough. Pakistan took their chance impressively with their score of 708. If England had batted first, they would doubtless have made a big score, too, but it is hard to envisage their enforcing the follow-on, as Pakistan did.

From the first over, the bowlers knew their fate, and it was a surprise when Pakistan lost two wickets for 45 to Botham and Dilley. When nine, Miandad might have followed, but a mishook off Botham fell just short of long-leg.

That was almost the last time that Miandad looked vulnerable in an innings lasting until late on the second day. Mudassar was out at 148, but the first day ended with the score 297-3, Miandad 131.

Salim Malik, playing soundly in support, had already helped Miandad to add 149, and they extended it next day to 234. With Imran equally confident, Miandad passed his fourth Test 200 and shared in a fifth-wicket stand of 191.

England's attack had been weakened early on when Foster, after bowling 12 overs, retired with a strained side. Dilley damaged an ankle in pulling up sharply when a pigeon crossed his path, and for hours England toiled with little effect.

Miandad's magnificent exhibition ended when least expected. Dilley, limping, seemed to be having difficulty in finishing an over, and, after consultation with Gatting, bowled a slower ball off a shortened run. An equally weary Miandad gave him a return catch which he juggled and held.

Imran's fine innings ended when he was thrown out by Botham, and Pakistan finished at 616-6. Next morning Dilley often beat the bat and eventually took the last four wickets, but not before Pakistan had passed 700.

England, left with 10 minutes before lunch, lost Broad to the fourth ball, a good one from Imran. Their main trial, however, was to come from Abdul Qadir, who for once found some of the answers to a leg-spinner's prayers, a pitch with bounce, worn patches, and a wealth of runs behind him. Gatting, with Botham in support, was not going to suffer dictation from either Qadir or the off-spinner Tauseef, and from 78-4 they reached 144 before bad light intervened 50 minutes early.

Attempts to dominate failed on Monday, and by mid-afternoon England were following on 476 behind. Broad batted through the final three hours' play, but at 95-3 a draw seemed a distant hope.

Yet Gatting, five overnight, survived a chance to first slip off Imran from his first ball next morning and batted stoutly through the final day against an attack now lacking Wasim Akram. Only Broad was lost, and for the last four and a quarter hours Botham, correct and self-disciplined, helped Gatting to restore some of England's reputation.

ENGLAND v PAKISTAN   FIFTH TEST   OVAL   August 6, 7, 8

PAKISTAN 1st INNINGS

No	Batsman	How out	Bowler	Runs	Wkt	Total	6	4	Mins	Balls
1	MUDASSAR NAZAR	c MOXON	BOTHAM	73	3	148	-	8	174	142
2	RAMIZ RAJA	b	BOTHAM	14	1	40	-	2	40	25
3	MANSOOR AKHTAR	c FRENCH	DILLEY	5	2	45	-	1	10	10
4	JAVED MIANDAD	c +b	DILLEY	260	5	573	1	28	617	521
5	SALIM MALIK	c GOWER	BOTHAM	102	4	382	-	6	267	237
6	IMRAN KHAN*	run out	(Radford/Botham)	118	6	601	1	11	256	201
7	IJAZ AHMED	c MOXON	DILLEY	69	8	707	-	9	188	97
8	SALEEM YOUSUF†	c +b	DILLEY	42	7	690	-	4	94	68
9	WASIM AKRAM	c BOTHAM	DILLEY	5	10	708	-	-	25	15
10	ABDUL QADIR	c MOXON	DILLEY	0	9	707	-	-	2	4
11	TAUSEEF AHMED	not	out	0	-	-	-	-	6	3
	Extras	B2 LB18 W - NB -		20						

708

Bowler	O	M	R	W		NB	W
DILLEY	47³	10	154	6			
FOSTER	12	3	32	-			
BOTHAM	52	7	217	3			
EMBUREY	61	10	143	-			
EDMONDS	32	8	97	-			
GATTING	10	2	18	-			
MOXON	6	2	27	-			

Wkt	Partnership between		Runs	Balls	
1	Mudassar	Ramiz	40	57	
2	— . —	Mansoor	5	17	
3	— . —	Javed	103	207	
4	Javed	Malik	234	452	Ⓡ
5	— . —	Imran Khan	191	376	
6	Imran Khan	Ijaz	28	42	
7	Ijaz	Yousuf	89	139	Ⓡ
8	— . —	Wasim Akram	17	20	
9	Wasim Akram	Abdul Qadir	0	4	
10	— . —	Tauseef	1	9	

Ⓡ Record Pakistan v England

Pakistan won the toss + elected to bat

Lunch: 95 - 2 (32 overs) Mudassar 45* Javed 25*

Tea: 206 - 3 (67 overs) Javed 82* Malik 23*

Foster strained side + left field end 52nd over + took no further part in the innings

New Ball: 253 - 3 (86.2 overs)

Close: 297 - 3 (101 overs) Javed 131* Malik 64*

Lunch: 406 - 4 (133 overs) Javed 189* Imran 12*

Tea: 500 - 4 (168 overs) Javed 243* Imran 51*

New Ball: 525-4 (174.2 overs)

Close: 616 - 6 (197 overs) Ijaz 22* Yousuf 6* HS Pakistan v England

Pakistan HS in Test
(prev. 674.6 v India (Faisalabad) 1984.85)

220.3 overs   13 hours 44 mins

12th Men: N.V. Radford + Asif Mujtaba

Umpires: D.J. Constant + K.E. Palmer

Hrs	Balls	Runs	Runs	Balls	Last 50
1	99	47	50	93	-
2	108	48	100	204	111
3	94	56	150	283	79
4	112	54	200	392	109
5	123	50	250	518	126
6	83	41	300	612	94
7	88	58	350	689	77
8	104	52	400	770	81
9	97	33	450	925	155
10	113	61	500	996	71
11	84	66	550	1077	81
12	90	50	600	1151	74
13	86	70	650	1216	65
			700	1303	87

ENGLAND v PAKISTAN   FIFTH   TEST   OVAL   August 8, 10

ENGLAND 1st INNINGS

No	Batsman	How out		Bowler	Runs	Wkt	Total	6	4	Mins	Balls
1	BROAD	c YOUSUF	IMRAN KHAN		0	1	0	-	-	2	4
2	MOXON	c JAVED	ABDUL QADIR		8	2	32	-	-	59	45
3	ROBINSON	b	ABDUL QADIR		30	3	54	-	5	78	62
4	GOWER	b	TAUSEEF AHMED		28	4	78	-	4	62	39
5	GATTING *	c IMRAN	ABDUL QADIR		61	6	166	-	10	164	136
6	BOTHAM	b	ABDUL QADIR		34	5	165	-	3	114	82
7	EMBUREY	c MALIK	ABDUL QADIR		53	10	232	1	6	128	116
8	FRENCH †	c MALIK	ABDUL QADIR		1	7	184	-	-	35	29
9	FOSTER	c IJAZ	TAUSEEF AHMED		4	8	198	-	-	43	51
10	EDMONDS	lbw	ABDUL QADIR		2	9	223	-	-	24	26
11	DILLEY	not	out		0	-	—	-	-	12	11
	Extras	B4 LB3 W1 NB3			11						

232

Bowler	O	M	R	W		NB	W
IMRAN KHAN	18	2	39	1			
WASIM AKRAM	14	2	37	-		1	1
ABDUL QADIR	44+	15	96	7		2	
TAUSEEF AHMED	23	9	53	2			

Wkt	Partnership between		Runs	Balls
1	Broad	Moxon	0	4
2	Moxon	Robinson	32	87
3	Robinson	Gower	22	32
4	Gower	Gatting	24	57
5	Gatting	Botham	87	181
6	—·—	Emburey	1	9
7	Emburey	French	18	63
8	—·—	Foster	14	91
9	—·—	Edmonds	25	54
10	——	Dilley	9	23

Pakistan 708
64 overs remain 8/8
Lunch: 0-1 (2 overs) Moxon 0* Robinson 0*
Tea: 81-4 (31 overs) Gatting 11* Botham 1*   627 behind
BLSP: 5-11 No further play 8/8 144-4 (50 overs) Gatting 50* Botham 23*   564 behind
+ Close
Lunch: 193-7 (84 overs) Emburey 29* Foster 1*   515 behind
Innings closed 2.29 - 476 behind - follow-on enforced

99. 4 overs + 3 no-balls   6 hours 9 mins

Hrs	Balls	Runs		Runs	Balls	Last 50
1	91	32		50	118	-
2	84	46		100	207	89
3	94	53		150	312	105
4	92	34		200	539	227
5	97	27		250		
6	125	31		300		
7				350		
8				400		
9				450		
10				500		
11				550		
12				600		
13				650		

ENGLAND v PAKISTAN   FIFTH TEST   OVAL   August 10, 11

ENGLAND 2nd INNINGS

No	Batsman	How out	Bowler	Runs	Wkt	Total	6	4	Mins	Balls
1	BROAD	c IJAZ	ABDUL QADIR	42	4	139	–	3	253	206
2	MOXON	c YOUSUF	TAUSEEF AHMED	15	1	22	–	1	69	57
3	ROBINSON	c AKRAM	ABDUL QADIR	10	2	40	–	1	26	24
4	GOWER	c MUDASSAR	ABDUL QADIR	34	3	89	–	3	60	58
5	GATTING *	not	out	150	–	–	–	21	346	302
6	BOTHAM	not	out	51	–	–	–	9	252	209
7	EMBUREY									
8	FRENCH †		did not bat							
9	FOSTER									
10	EDMONDS									
11	DILLEY									
	Extras	B4 LB5 W1 NB3		13						

315 - 4

Bowler	O	M	R	W	NB	W
IMRAN KHAN	26³	9	59	–		
WASIM AKRAM	6	3	3	–		
ABDUL QADIR	53	21	115	3	1	
TAUSEEF AHMED	46³	15	98	1	1	
MUDASSAR	6	–	21	–		1
JAVED MIANDAD	4	2	10	–	2	

Wkt	Partnership between		Runs	Balls
1	Broad	Moxon	22	105
2	—.—	Robinson	18	53
3	—.—	Gower	49	114
4	—.—	Gatting	50	152
5	Gatting	Botham	176*	432
6				
7				
8				
9				
10				

Pakistan 708 England 232 Follow-on enforced- 476 to avoid was defeat
38 overs remain 10/8
Tea: 17-0 (15 overs) Broad 5* Moxon 10*   459 behind
Close: 95-3 (50 overs) Broad 26* Gatting 5*   381 behind
11/8 Wasim Akram to hospital with suspected appendicitis
Lunch: 170-4 (86 overs) Gatting 61* Botham 1*   306 behind
New Ball: 175-4 (89 overs)
Ijaz hit on head (Gatting off Imran) 2.19 → hospital X-rays
Tea: 257- 4 (120 overs) Gatting 121* Botham 25*   219 behind
Last 20 overs: 293-4 (135 overs) Gatting 139* Botham 41*
Play called off 5.28 – 13 overs remain of last 20
Match Drawn   Pakistan win series 1-0
Man of the Match: Javed Miandad
Men of the Series: M.W. Gatting + Imran Khan

142 overs + 4 no-balls   8 hours 27 mins

Hrs	Balls	Runs	Runs	Balls	Last 50
1	92	17	50	188	–
2	113	40	100	338	150
3	99	38	150	456	118
4	100	29	200	570	114
5	116	50	250	690	120
6	88	36	300	827	137
7	116	47	350		
8	88	36	400		
9			450		
10			500		
11			550		
12			600		
13			650		

Chris Broad, Player of the Series, acknowledges the reception at Adelaide of his third hundred in successive Tests, the springboard from which England won the Ashes.

LEFT: Allan Lamb
during the World
Series, in which he won
a vital match for
England by making 18
off the last over in
Sydney.

BELOW: Mike Gatting
with the second of
England's three
trophies won in
Australia, the Perth
Challenge.

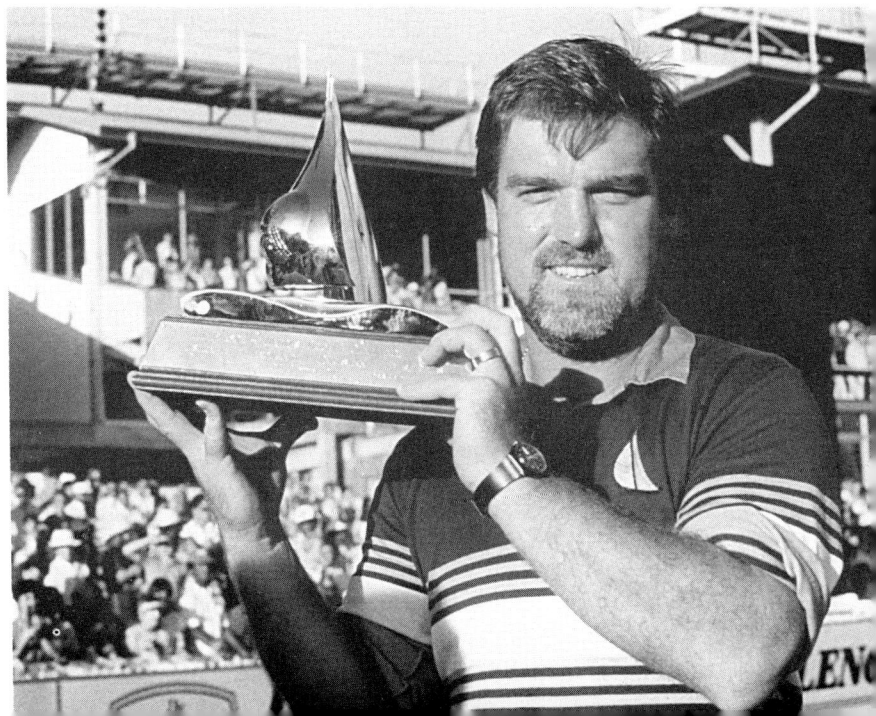

ABOVE: A moment of elation on the first day of the fourth Test in Melbourne, after Botham has had Border caught at the wicket by Richards.

BELOW: Melbourne, December 1986. After victory in the fourth Test, by an innings in three days, and with the series won, the celebrations begin.

ABOVE: The MCC team at Lord's in the Bicentenary Match, August 1987. *Standing:* French, Broad, Shastri, Edmonds, Emburey, Richards. *Seated:* Hadlee, Rice, Marshall, Gatting (captain), Stewart (manager), Gower, Gooch, Greenidge.

BELOW: Two eminent 'drinks waiters' at Lord's, Dean Jones (left) and Phil Edmonds.

ABOVE: The Rest of the World Team at Lord's. *Standing:* Clive Lloyd (manager), Maninder Singh, Ratnayeke, Harper, Walsh, Reid, Bracewell, Jones, Imran Khan, Jim Danks (scorer). *Seated:* Dujon, Vengsarkar, Abdul Qadir, Gavaskar, Border (captain), Kapil Dev, Javed Miandad, Haynes.

RIGHT: Graham Gooch, who made a sudden and welcome return to form in the Bicentenary Match, during his fine innings of 117. He followed it with 70 in the second innings.

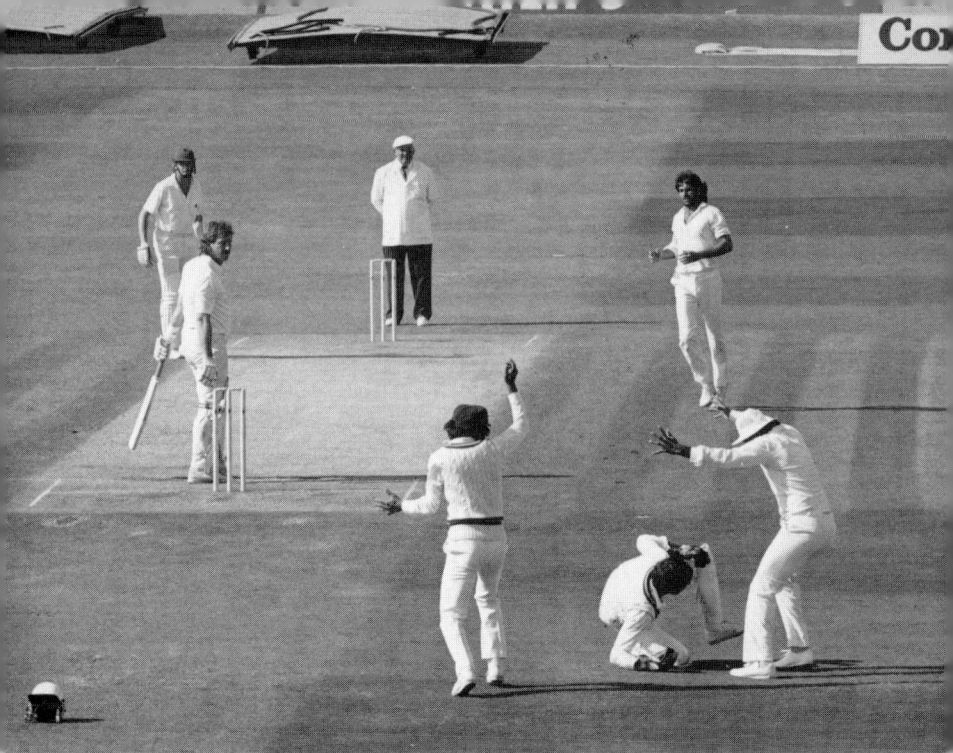

ABOVE: A controversial incident in the 3rd England-Pakistan Test. Salim Yousef, after seeming to lose the ball, recovers it and prepares to claim the catch.

LEFT: The batsman, Ian Botham, is somewhat critical of Yousef's appeal. He was supported by almost everyone else including the umpire, David Shepherd.

RIGHT: Javed Miandad in aggressive mood during the fourth Test at Edgbaston. England were let off with 75 here, but his magnificent 260 was to follow at The Oval.

BELOW: Mike Gatting hooks Imran at Edgbaston during his innings of 124, which almost led England to victory in the fourth Test.

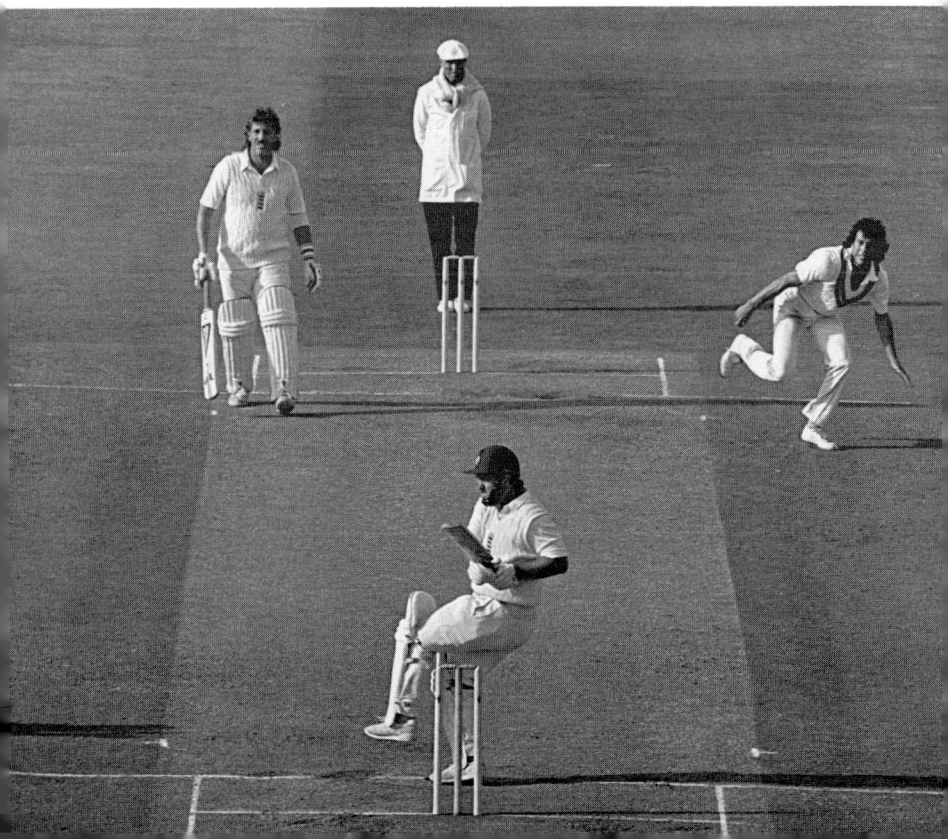

ABOVE: Nottinghamshire 1987, winners of two – and very nearly three – major trophies. *Back Row:* P. Pollard, R.J. Evans, C.D. Fraser-Darling, K.P. Evans, J.A. Afford, M. Newell. *Middle Row:* D.J.R. Martindale, C.W. Scott, R.A. Pick, K. Saxelby, D. Millns, K.E. Cooper, P. Johnson. *Seated:* B.N. French, E.E. Hemmings, D.W. Randall, R.T. Robinson, K.A. Taylor (manager), C.E.B. Rice (capt), B.C. Broad, J.D. Birch, M.K. Bore. *Inset:* R. Hadlee.

BELOW: Three reasons for Nottinghamshire's success: Clive Rice, Richard Hadlee, and Bruce French.

RIGHT: Richard Hadlee in his moment of triumph at Lord's in the NatWest Trophy final.

BELOW: Nottinghamshire's last match of the season, against Glamorgan at Trent Bridge. Paul Johnson, one of their hopes for the future, dives to pick up a close catch. Notts' victory virtually clinched the Championship, as Lancs failed to take maximum points from their final match.

ABOVE: Worcestershire, 1987
Sunday League champions.
Standing: L.K. Smith, D.A.
Leatherdale, S.R. Lampitt,
J.P. Wright, I.T. Botham,
G.R. Dilley, S.M. McEwan,
P. Bent, G.J. Lord, C.M.
Tolley. *Seated:* B.L.
D'Oliveira (coach), M.J.
Weston, G.A. Hick, N.V.
Radford, T.S. Curtis, P.A.
Neale (capt), A.P. Pridgeon,
D.B. D'Oliveira, P.J.
Newport, S.J. Rhodes, R.K.
Illingworth.

RIGHT: Graeme Hick of
Zimbabwe and
Worcestershire. Many hope
that his 10-year period of
qualification for England will
be shortened.

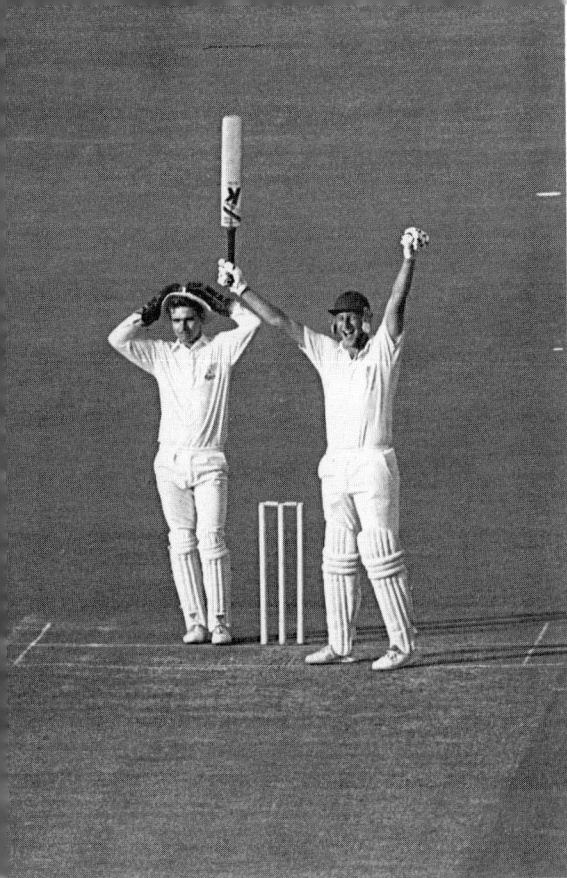

LEFT: Jim Love in a moment of jubilation near the end of his innings which took Yorkshire home in the Benson & Hedges against the luckless Northants. He remained unbeaten in the whole of the competition, and won the Gold Award in the final.

BELOW: Phil Carrick, in his first year as the Yorkshire captain, holds the Benson & Hedges Cup aloft.

1

2

3

4

8
▶

5
◀

6
◀

7
◀

The Daily Telegraph Cricketers of the Year
(see pages 19-20):
1 Roger Harper (West Indies)
2 Mike Gatting (England)
3 Dean Jones (Australia)
4 Garth Le Roux (South Africa)
5 Imran Khan (Pakistan)
6 Dilip Vengsarkar (India)
7 Brendan Kuruppu (Sri Lanka)
8 Martin Crowe (New Zealand)

Retired after the 1987 season: Derek
Underwood (LEFT), who first played for
Kent aged 17 in 1963 and subsequently took
297 wickets in 86 Test matches. Dennis
Amiss (ABOVE), the most recent batsman to
reach 100 first-class hundreds, 11 of which
were in Tests. He first played for
Warwickshire in 1960.

BELOW: Bill Bowes, who died on 5
September 1987, seen here in the days when
he was a successful bowler for Yorkshire and
England. Later he became an equally
respected cricket writer.

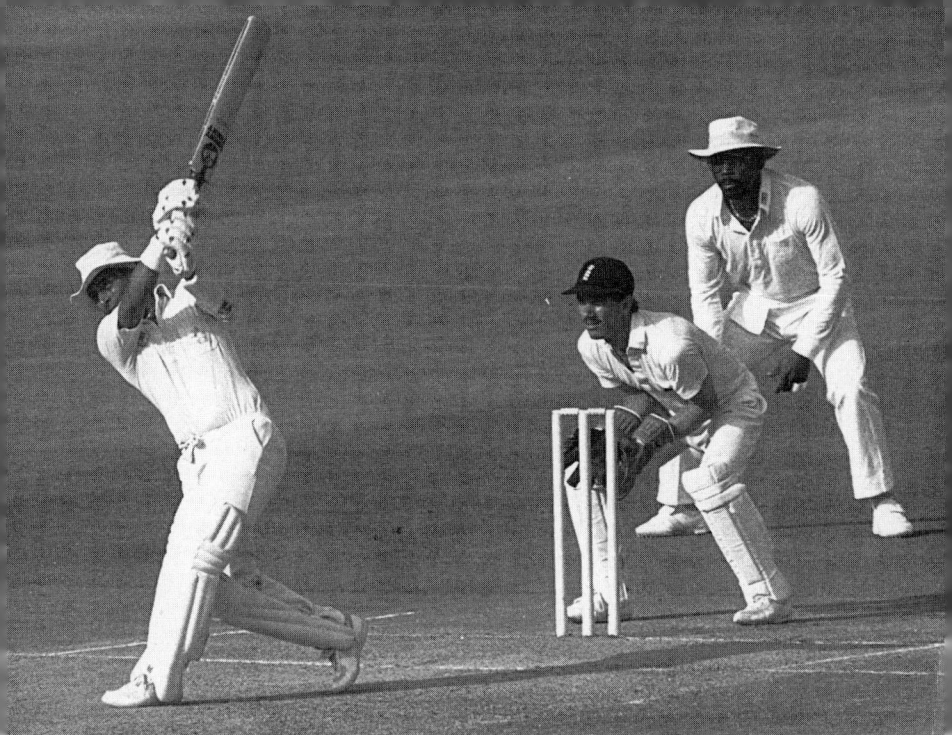

ABOVE: Sunil Gavaskar
making his brilliant 188 in
the Bicentenary Match,
probably his last first-class
match. Remarkably this
was his first hundred at
Lord's.

RIGHT: Graeme Pollock's
retirement from first-class
cricket in South Africa,
aged 43, was a reminder of
what crowds elsewhere had
missed.

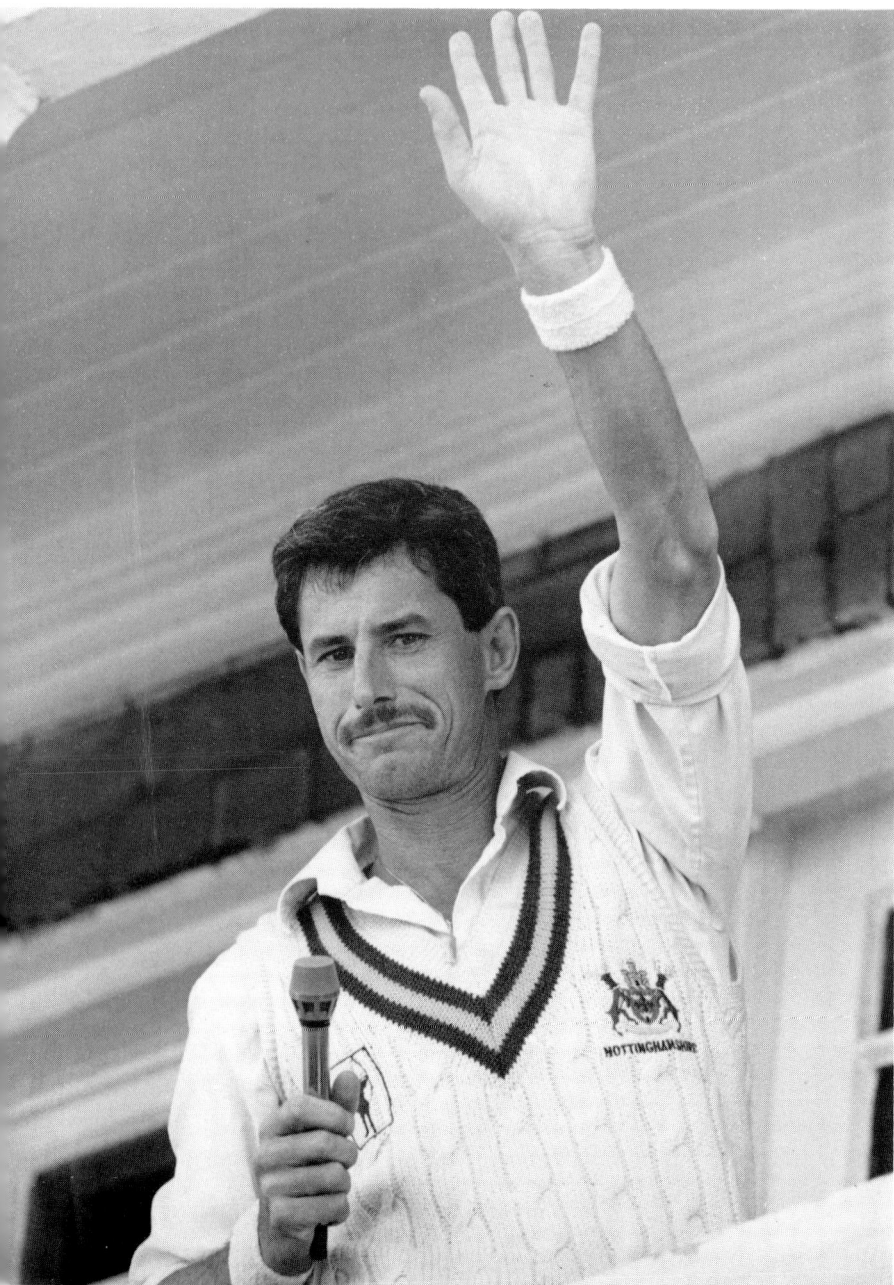

A great cricketer's farewell to the county game in England. Richard Hadlee says good-bye from the balcony at Trent Bridge.

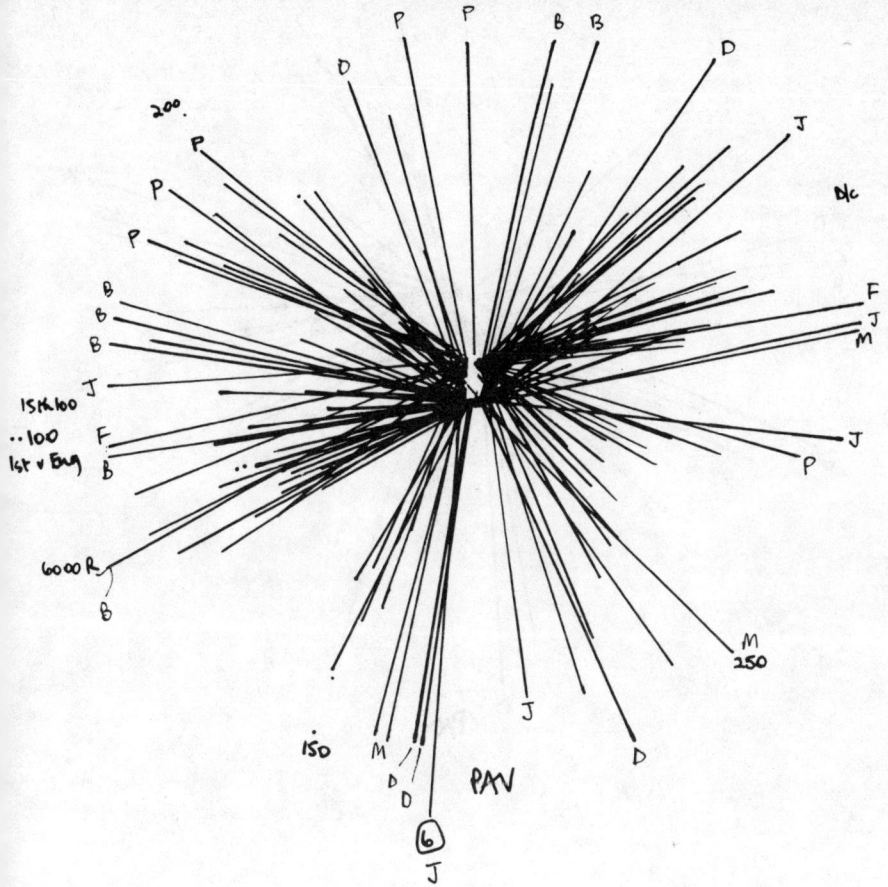

5th Test – Javed 260

BOWLER		1	2	3	4	6	TOTAL	
Botham	B	17	4	1	7	–	56	
Dilley	D	7	4	1	5	–	38	
Foster	F	3	–	1	2	–	14	260 RUNS
Emburey	J	29	3	–	5	1	61	521 BALLS
Edmonds	P	19	5	5	6	–	68	617 MINUTES
Gatting	G	3	1	–	–	–	5	
Moxon	M	2	2	–	3	–	18	
		80	19	8	28	1	260	

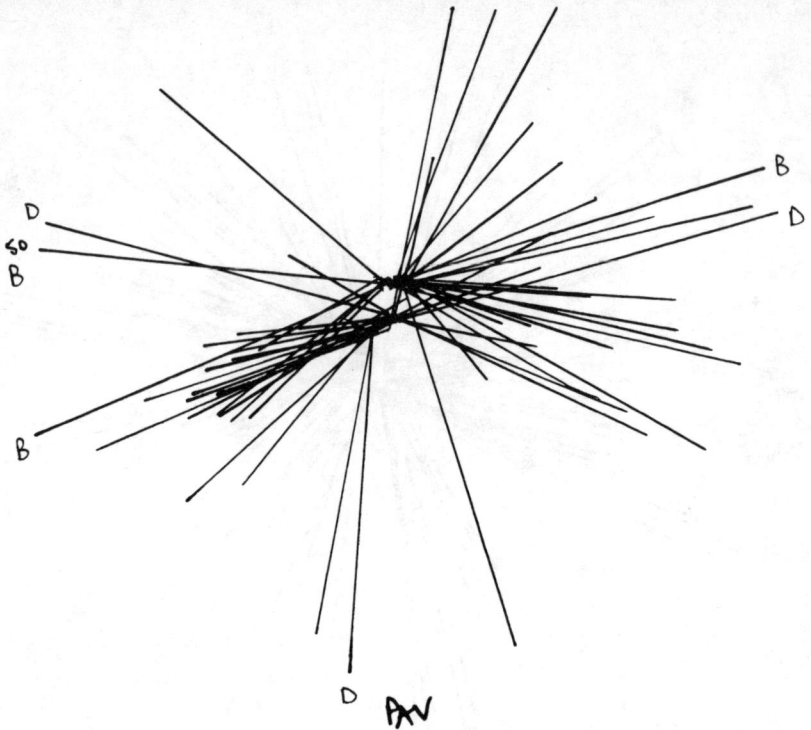

5th Test – Salim Malik 102

BOWLER		1	2	3	4	6	TOTAL
Foster	F	–	–	1	–	–	3
Botham	B	11	4	2	3	–	37
Edmonds	P	7	2	4	–	–	23
Emburey	J	8	2	1	–	–	15
Dilley	D	4	1	1	3	–	21
Gatting	G	3	–	–	–	–	3
		33	9	9	6	–	102

102 RUNS
237 BALLS
267 MINUTES

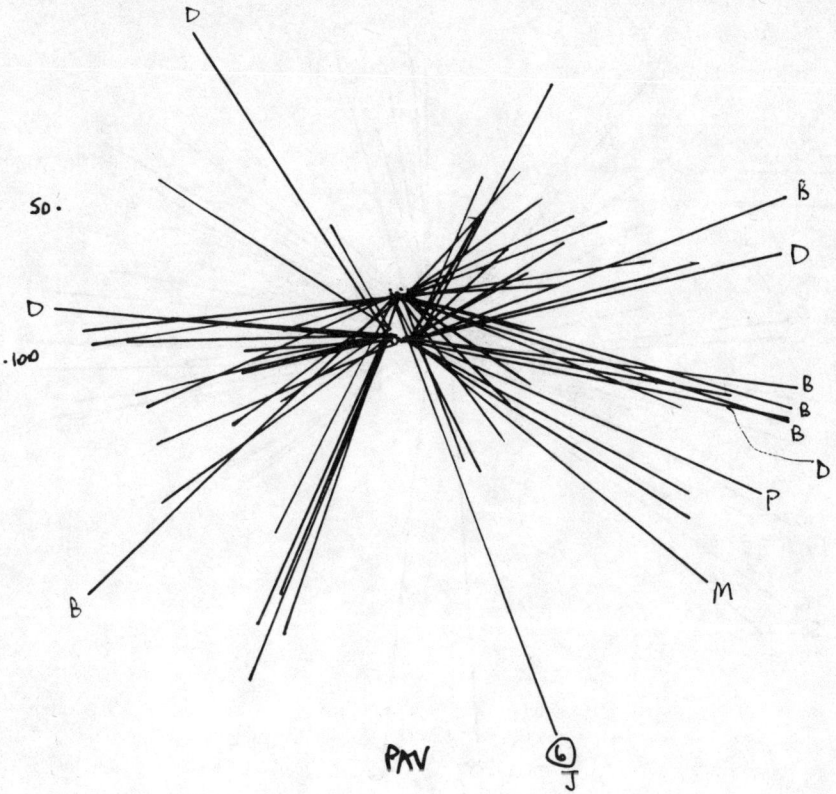

5th Test – Imran 118

BOWLER		1	2	3	4	6	TOTAL	
Botham	B	6	2	4	5	–	42	
Emburey	J	11	2	1	–	1	24	118 RUNS
Dilley	D	5	3	2	4	–	33	201 BALLS
Edmonds	P	2	–	–	1	–	6	256 MINUTES
Moxon	M	3	1	–	1	–	9	
Gatting	G	4	–	–	–	–	4	
		31	8	7	11	1	118	

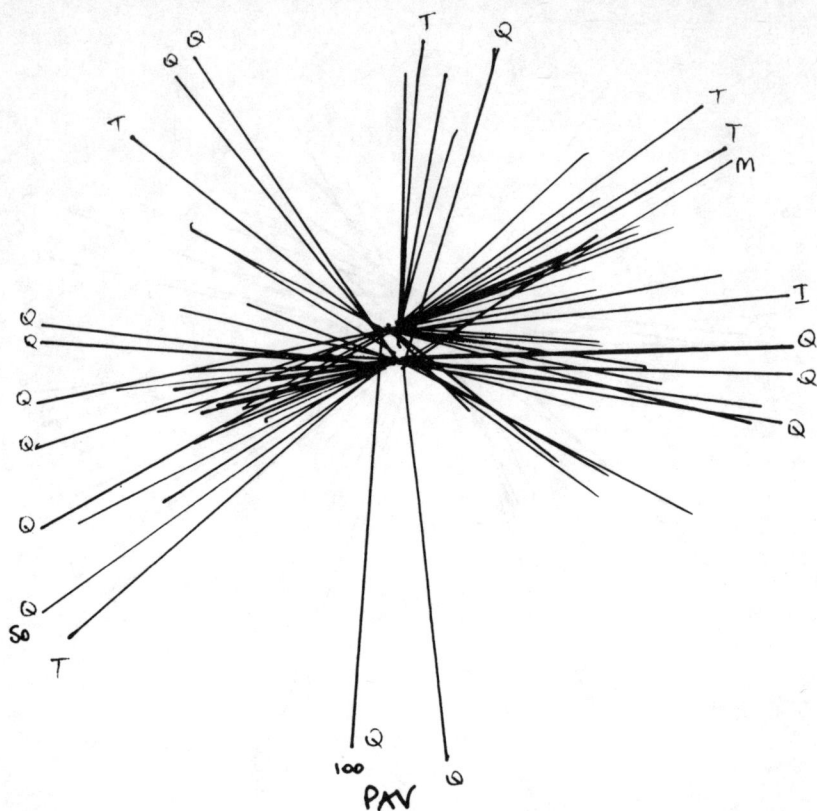

5th Test – Gatting 150*

BOWLER		1	2	3	4	6	TOTAL
Abdul Qadir	Q	13	5	–	14	–	79
Imran Khan	I	7	2	–	1	–	15
Tauseef Ahmed	T	14	6	–	5	–	46
Mudassar Nazar	M	3	–	–	1	–	7
Javed Miandad	J	3	–	–	–	–	3
		40	13	–	21	–	150

150 RUNS
209 BALLS
252 MINUTES

Cornhill

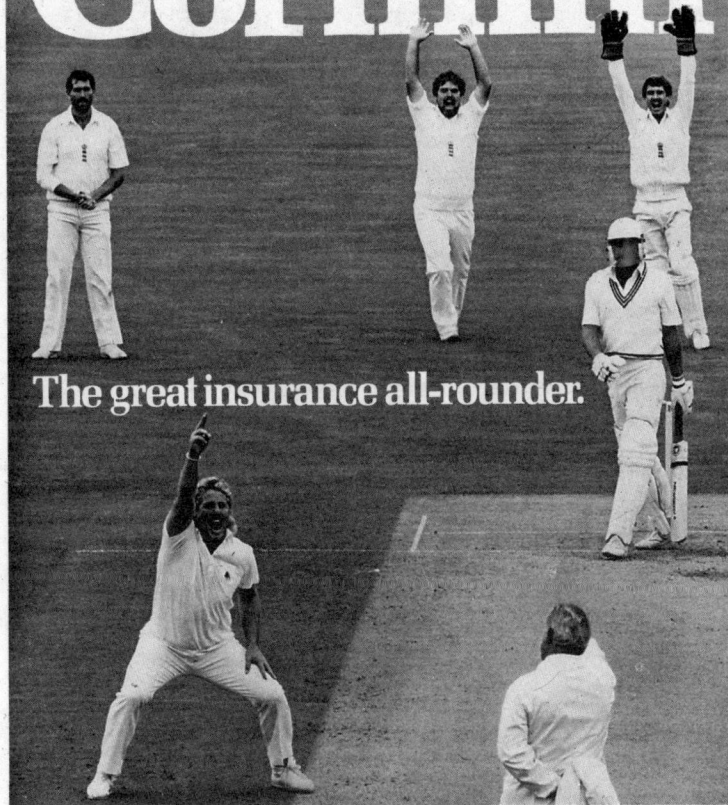

The great insurance all-rounder.

Behind this magic moment you'll find the name of the great insurance all-rounder – Cornhill Insurance, the sponsor of Test cricket in England.

Whether it's insurance for your car, home, life or business you'll find us equally competitive. Ask your broker about Cornhill Insurance today.

Cornhill
INSURANCE
Test Series

Cornhill Insurance, 32 Cornhill, London EC3V 3LJ.

Test Match Averages: England v Pakistan 1987

England

Batting and Fielding	M	I	NO	HS	R	Avge	100	50	Ct/St
M.W. Gatting	5	8	1	150*	445	63.57	2	1	2
R.T. Robinson	5	8	0	166	299	37.37	1	1	–
C.W.J. Athey	4	6	1	123	186	37.20	1	–	2
I.T. Botham	5	8	1	51*	232	33.14	–	1	3
J.E. Emburey	4	5	0	58	162	32.40	–	2	3
D.I. Gower	5	8	0	61	236	29.50	–	2	2
B.C. Broad	4	7	0	55	193	27.57	–	2	–
B.N. French	4	5	1	59	103	25.75	–	1	4
P.H. Edmonds	5	7	4	24*	66	22.00	–	–	3
N.A. Foster	5	6	0	29	93	15.50	–	–	1
G.R. Dilley	4	5	2	17	20	6.66	–	–	2

Also batted: D.J. Capel (1 match) 53, 28; P.A.J. DeFreitas (1 match) 11; N.H. Fairbrother (1 match) 0; 1ct; M.D. Moxon (1 match) 8, 15, 3ct; C.J. Richards (1 match) 6, 2, 2ct.

Bowling	O	M	R	W	Avge	Best	5wI	10wM
N.A. Foster	137.2	36	339	15	22.60	8-107	1	–
G.R. Dilley	133.3	26	388	14	27.71	6-154	2	–
I.T. Botham	134.3	30	433	7	61.85	3-217	–	–

Also bowled: D.J. Capel 18-1-64-0; P.A.J. DeFreitas 12-4-36-1; P.H. Edmonds 92.3-36-219-4; J.E. Emburey 107-21-222-0; M.W. Gatting 22-5-40-0; M.D. Moxon 6-2-27-0.

Pakistan

Batting and Fielding	M	I	NO	HS	R	Avge	100	50	Ct/St
Javed Miandad	5	5	0	260	360	72.00	1	1	3
Saleem Yousuf	5	4	1	91*	187	62.33	–	1	15
Mudassar Nazar	5	5	1	124	231	57.75	1	1	3
Salim Malik	5	5	0	102	248	49.60	1	1	4
Imran Khan	5	5	1	118	191	47.75	1	1	3
Ijaz Ahmed	4	4	0	69	150	37.50	–	2	4
Mansoor Akhtar	5	5	0	75	152	30.40	–	1	–
Shoaib Mohammad	4	4	0	50	84	21.00	–	1	1
Wasim Akram	5	4	0	43	80	20.00	–	–	4
Abdul Qadir	4	4	0	20	28	7.00	–	–	–

Also batted: Mohsin Kamal (4 matches) 3*, 10, 0*, 2ct; Ramiz Raja (2 matches) 15, 14; Tauseef Ahmed (2 matches) 0*.

Bowling	O	M	R	W	Avge	Best	5wI	10wM
Imran Khan	168.2	33	455	21	21.66	7-40	2	1
Wasim Akram	180.4	38	464	16	29.00	4-111	–	–
Mohsin Kamal	94.4	14	332	9	36.88	4-127	–	–
Tauseef Ahmed	91.1	28	203	5	40.60	2-52	–	–
Abdul Qadir	175.4	46	450	11	40.90	7-96	1	1

Also bowled: Javed Miandad 4-2-10-0; Mudassar Nazar 110-26-303-3.

Statistical Highlights of the Tests

1st Test, Old Trafford. Botham bowled his 20,000th ball in Tests (only Underwood with 21,862 has bowled more) and conceded his 9,988th run, the most by any bowler. Robinson's 166 was his 4th Test 100 and the first between England and Pakistan at Old Trafford. Wasim Akram took his 50th wicket in his 16th Test. Almost 16 hours' playing time was lost.

2nd Test, Lord's. Three full days' play lost at Lord's for 2nd time against Pakistan (cf 1954). Athey made his first 100 in his 15th Test. Monte Lynch (Surrey) was selected as 12th man for last two days (no play), but was replaced by team-mate David Ward when it was realized that Lynch was still under a 3-year ban from international cricket following his tour to South Africa with rebel West Indian team in 1983-84. Pakistan had objected to selection of umpire Constant, but had been overruled by TCCB.

3rd Test, Headingley. Pakistan won their 1st Test at Headingley (6th attempt) after just 24 minutes' play on the 4th morning, recording only their 4th win over England and the 1st by an innings. Imran took his 300th wicket in his 68th Test, the 8th player and the 1st from Pakistan to reach 300. His 7-40 was best Pakistan bowling in England, his 20th 5-wicket haul and 5th 10 wickets in match (10-77). Foster's 8-107 was his best first-class analysis, the best bowling for England against Pakistan at Headingley, and his 4th 5-wicket haul in Tests. Pakistan's 353 was their highest Test score at Headingley, and Salim Malik's 99 the highest individual Pakistan score there, beating Sadiq's 97 in 1978.

4th Test, Edgbaston. Mudassar made his 9th Test 100, his 2nd against England. Dilley chalked up his 2nd 5-wicket haul, his first in England. Foster took his 50th wicket in his 18th Test. Botham, in his 93rd Test, became the 1st bowler to concede 10,000 runs. Gatting made his 8th Test 100, his 1st against Pakistan and his 3rd in successive Tests at Edgbaston (100 v Australia 1985, 183 v India 1986). Gower passed Tom Graveney's aggregate of 943 runs against Pakistan. Imran played his 100th Test innings (2nd innings).

5th Test, Oval. Pakistan's 708 was their highest Test innings (beating 674-6 v India, 1984-85) and 6th highest in Test history. Javed Miandad's 260 was his 15th Test 100, his 1st against England, and the highest score for Pakistan against England at the Oval. He became the 17th player to reach 6,000 runs in Tests, the 1st for Pakistan in his 86th Test. Salim Malik made his 6th Test 100 (2nd v England), Imran his 4th (1st v England). Miandad/Malik 234 stand was a record for the 4th wicket for Pakistan against England, as was Ijaz Ahmed/Yousef 89 for 7th wicket. Dilley's 6-154 was his best Test analysis and his 3rd 5 wickets. Botham (3-217) was the 11th bowler to concede 200 runs in a Test innings, only the 2nd for England, but exceeds Ian Peebles' 204 conceded against Australia (Oval 1930). Abdul Qadir's 7-96 was his best Test bowling, the best for Pakistan at the Oval, and his 11th 5-wicket haul. He reached 50 wickets against England. Gatting's 150 not out was his 9th Test 100 in his 100th Test innings, Botham's 2nd innings was his 150th. Emburey reached 1,000 runs in his 46th Test, the 5th England player to do so without scoring a 100. Pakistan recorded their 1st series win in 8 series in England. England have now played 11 Tests at home since their last win (v Australia at the Oval in 1985). Imran's 21 wickets equals his own series record (1982) for Pakistan in England.

Texaco Trophy

England won the Texaco Trophy 2-1 after the series, marvellously unmolested in the unsettled weather of the Spring Bank Holiday week-end, had finished in an extraordinary climax. They beat Pakistan in the third match by one wicket with three balls to spare.

England had won the first match at The Oval comfortably by seven wickets on the most straightforward of the three pitches, all of which gave greater assistance to the side bowling first. The side winning the toss won all three matches. At the Oval, a masterly innings of 113 by Miandad, supported by Mudassar in a third-wicket stand of 110, did not quite repair the damage done by the loss of two early wickets. Ramiz Raja had been run out in the first over without receiving a ball. England bowled and fielded well and subsequently Broad batted with authority for his 99. Lamb was also in fine form and England had 11 balls to spare.

At Trent Bridge, two days later, the positions were reversed. England lost two wickets cheaply, but it was the failure of the middle batting, lacking the injured Gatting, that led to the inadequate total of 157. Miandad again batted supremely well, England bowled less tidily than at The Oval, and, though Pakistan were 81-4, Imran joined Miandad in a stand that took them home by six wickets with three overs to spare.

This cleared the way for what proved a remarkable match at Edgbaston – from the first ball. Thomas, deputizing for the injured Dilley, had Mudassar lbw with the first ball of the match and Mansoor Akhtar well caught at the wicket off the fourth. As the new ball quickly lost its venom, he was played with ease by Miandad who, first with Ramiz Raja and then with the vigorous Salim Malik, took the score to 168-3.

With 12 overs to go Pakistan were handsomely placed, but at this point Miandad was brilliantly caught at short mid-wicket by Gower. In 18 balls, five wickets fell for two runs to Foster and Emburey. The ninth fell at 178, but Imran was able to bat out the 55 overs and conjure up 35 precious runs with Mohsin Kamal. Before long it was looking as if these had won the match.

England's innings until the last few minutes never promised to be a winning one. Gatting for a time looked capable of rallying it, but when he was out at 105-5, there was still much to do. Botham, pinned down by the off-spin of Tauseef, directed as far as was legally possible down the leg-side, could not sustain the required rate, and at 167-8 with less than six overs left, England seemed almost finished.

Salvation and a memorable win came with some clean hitting by DeFreitas, who made 33 off 22 balls. After he had dragged the first ball of the penultimate over onto his stumps, Foster and Thomas, despite some nerve-racking running between the wickets, were able to find the five runs still needed.

England v Pakistan 1st Texaco Trophy International

England won by 7 wickets
Played at Kennington Oval, London, 21 May
Toss: England. Umpires: D.R. Shepherd and A.G.T. Whitehead
Man of the Match: B.C. Broad (Adjudicator P.I. Pocock)

Pakistan		Runs	Mins	Balls	6	4
Mudassar Nazar	c DeFreitas b Foster	45	154	132	–	3
Ramiz Raja	run out (Foster/Richards)	0	2	0	–	–
Mansoor Akhtar	c Gatting b Dilley	12	28	17	–	1
Javed Miandad	c Lamb b Dilley	113	197	142	–	10
Imran Khan*	c Broad b Foster	7	22	18	–	–
Wasim Akram	b Emburey	12	24	11	1	–
Manzoor Elahi	not out	18	16	11	–	1
Salim Malik	not out	8	10	6	–	–
Tauseef Ahmed	,,					
Saleem Yousuf†	,,					
Ijaz Ahmed	did not bat					
Extras	(B1, LB8, W4, NB4)	17				
	(55 overs; 209 minutes)	**232-6**				

England		Runs	Mins	Balls	6	4
B.C. Broad	c sub (Asif Mujtaba) b Akram	99	201	168	–	4
C.W.J. Athey	c Malik b Mudassar	33	96	61	–	3
M.W. Gatting*	retired hurt (83-1)	2	6	3	–	–
A.J. Lamb	c sub (Asif Mujtaba) b Tauseef	61	85	71	1	3
D.I. Gower	not out	15	21	15	–	1
I.T. Botham	not out	6	10	10	–	1
C.J. Richards†	did not bat					
J.E. Emburey	,,					
P.A.J. DeFreitas	,,					
G.R. Dilley	,,					
N.A. Foster	,,					
Extras	(LB9, W2, NB6)	17				
	(53.1 overs; 212 minutes)	**233-3**				

England	O	M	R	W
Dilley	11	1	63	2
DeFreitas	11	3	50	0
Botham	11	2	38	0
Foster	11	0	36	2
Emburey	11	1	36	1

Pakistan	O	M	R	W
Imran Khan	8	0	30	0
Manzoor Elahi	11	1	31	0
Wasim Akram	11	0	60	1
Mudassar Nazar	11	1	41	1
Tauseef Ahmed	10.1	0	47	1
Mansoor Akhtar	2	0	15	0

Fall of Wickets

Wkt	P	E
1st	0	76
2nd	18	199
3rd	128	218
4th	169	–
5th	206	–
6th	208	–
7th	–	–
8th	–	–
9th	–	–
10th	–	–

England v Pakistan 2nd Texaco Trophy International

Pakistan won by 6 wickets
Played at Trent Bridge, Nottingham, 23 May
Toss: Pakistan. Umpires: D.J. Constant and B.J. Meyer
Man of the Match: Javed Miandad (Ajudicator R.W. Taylor)

England		Runs	Mins	Balls	6	4
B.C. Broad	c Yousuf b Akram	52	105	84	–	3
C.W.J. Athey	lbw b Imran	1	7	9	–	–
G.A. Gooch	lbw b Kamal	9	38	31	–	1
A.J. Lamb	c Yousuf b Tauseef	26	86	57	–	–
D.I. Gower	b Mudassar	24	48	43	–	1
I.T. Botham	c Kamal b Tauseef	0	8	8	–	–
C.J. Richards†	c Elahi b Kamal	0	17	9	–	–
J.E. Emburey*	b Akram	25	47	46	–	3
P.A.J. DeFreitas	c Elahi b Imran	3	17	9	–	–
N.A. Foster	run out (Imran)	5	14	11	–	–
G.R. Dilley	not out	0	1	0	–	–
Extras	(LB8, W4)	12				
	(51.1 overs; 209 minutes)	**157**				

Pakistan		Runs	Mins	Balls	6	4
Mudassar Nazar	lbw b Foster	12	64	39	–	1
Ramiz Raja	c Gooch b DeFreitas	13	40	30	–	1
Mansoor Akhtar	b Foster	21	61	52	–	3
Javed Miandad	not out	71	125	128	–	3
Salim Malik	run out (Foster)	9	16	18	–	1
Imran Khan*	not out	21	69	46	1	–
Mohsin Kamal	did not bat					
Manzoor Elahi	,,					
Wasim Akram	,,					
Tauseef Ahmed	,,					
Saleem Yousuf†	,,					
Extras	(LB8, W2, NB1)	11				
	(52 overs; 191 minutes)	**158-4**				

Pakistan	O	M	R	W
Imran Khan	9	1	31	2
Mohsin Kamal	11	1	31	2
Wasim Akram	9.1	1	18	2
Mudassar Nazar	11	1	36	1
Tauseef Ahmed	11	1	33	2

England	O	M	R	W
Dilley	9	4	16	0
DeFreitas	11	2	30	1
Foster	11	1	25	2
Botham	7	0	34	0
Emburey	11	2	33	0
Gooch	3	0	12	0

Fall of Wickets

Wkt	E	P
1st	15	23
2nd	45	29
3rd	75	64
4th	117	81
5th	117	–
6th	117	–
7th	121	–
8th	144	–
9th	157	–
10th	157	–

England v Pakistan 3rd Texaco Trophy International

England won by 1 wicket
Played at Edgbaston, Birmingham, 25 May
Toss: England. Umpires: H.D. Bird and K.E. Palmer
Man of the Match: P.A.J. DeFreitas (Adjudicator: M.J.K. Smith)

Pakistan		Runs	Mins	Balls	6	4
Mudassar Nazar	lbw b Thomas	0	1	1	–	–
Ramiz Raja	run out (Gatting)	46	88	72	–	6
Mansoor Akhtar	c Richards b Thomas	0	2	3	–	–
Javed Miandad	c Gower b Foster	68	152	128	–	3
Salim Malik	b Emburey	45	72	61	–	3
Imran Khan*	not out	24	51	42	2	–
Manzoor Elahi	b Emburey	0	1	2	–	–
Saleem Yousuf†	run out (Gower)	0	3	3	–	–
Wasim Akram	c Richards b Foster	0	2	5	–	–
Tauseef Ahmed	b Foster	0	7	4	–	–
Mohsin Kamal	not out	11	28	12	–	2
Extras	(B2, LB13, W1, NB3)	19				
	(55 overs; 210 minutes)	**213-9**				

England		Runs	Mins	Balls	6	4
B.C. Broad	c Miandad b Kamal	15	53	38	–	–
C.W.J. Athey	c Yousuf b Imran	5	37	26	–	–
D.I. Gower	b Mudassar	11	29	20	–	–
A.J. Lamb	c Akhtar b Mudassar	14	62	48	–	–
M.W. Gatting*	c Miandad b Kamal	41	72	56	–	6
I.T. Botham	c sub (Asif Mujtaba) b Tauseef	24	64	40	–	2
C.J. Richards†	run out (Malik)	16	62	36	–	–
J.E. Emburey	run out (Malik)	16	34	19	1	–
N.A. Foster	not out	14	39	21	–	1
P.A.J. DeFreitas	b Imran	33	19	22	1	3
J.G. Thomas	not out	1	8	3	–	–
Extras	(LB14, W12, NB1)	27				
	(54.3 overs; 246 minutes)	**217-9**				

England	O	M	R	W
Thomas	11	0	59	2
DeFreitas	11	1	30	0
Botham	11	1	31	0
Foster	11	1	29	3
Emburey	11	1	49	2

Pakistan	O	M	R	W
Imran Khan	11	0	43	2
Mohsin Kamal	11	0	47	2
Wasim Akram	10.3	2	34	0
Mudassar Nazar	11	2	17	2
Tauseef Ahmed	11	0	62	1

Fall of Wickets

Wkt	P	E
1st	0	18
2nd	0	31
3rd	73	34
4th	168	75
5th	170	105
6th	170	140
7th	170	155
8th	170	167
9th	178	209
10th	–	–

Pakistan Tour of England 1987

First-Class Matches: Played 18; Won 2, Lost 1, Drawn 14, No Result 1
All Matches: Played 28; Won 6, Lost 4, Drawn 16, No Result 2

First Class Averages

Batting and Fielding	M	I	NO	HS	R	Avge	100	50	Ct/St
Javed Miandad	11	14	1	260	822	63.23	2	3	5
Mansoor Akhtar	16	24	3	169*	1156	55.04	4	5	5
Salim Malik	17	22	4	102	901	50.05	1	7	8
Mudassar Nazar	13	16	2	124	588	42.00	2	4	5
Shoaib Mohammad	16	23	5	121*	727	40.38	2	4	4
Imran Khan	12	13	3	118	349	34.90	1	–	5
Saleem Yousuf	16	14	4	91*	347	34.70	–	1	37/2
Ramiz Raja	11	15	–	150	501	33.40	1	3	1
Ijaz Ahmed	11	13	1	69	382	31.83	–	4	9
Manzoor Elahi	4	6	0	74	182	30.33	–	1	4
Wasim Akram	14	11	2	59*	245	27.22	–	1	7
Mohsin Kamal	12	11	7	28	76	19.00	–	–	5
Tauseef Ahmed	8	6	3	16*	47	15.66	–	–	4
Abdul Qadir	10	7	0	24	70	10.00	–	–	2
Asif Mujtaba	4	5	0	5	11	2.20	–	–	7

Also batted: Zakir Khan (8 matches) 0, 9*, 17, 22* (4 ct); Zulqarnain (1 match) 0*.
Azeem Hafeez, Iqbal Qasim and Saleem Jaffer played in one match but did not bat.

Bowling	O	M	R	W	Avge	Best	5wI	10wM
Imran Khan	300.4	67	768	36	21.33	7-40	3	1
Wasim Akram	394	82	1095	39	28.07	6-34	2	–
Mohsin Kamal	288.4	47	1046	36	29.05	6-100	1	–
Mudassar Nazar	212	51	545	15	36.33	5-28	1	–
Tauseef Ahmed	212.2	66	477	13	36.69	4-51	–	–
Zakir Khan	165	32	554	14	39.57	4-27	–	–
Abdul Qadir	299.5	66	845	19	44.47	7-96	1	1

Also bowled: Asif Mujtaba 1-0-2-0; Azeem Hafeez 15-2-84-2; Ijaz Ahmed 4-0-21-0; Iqbal Qasim 18-6-41-1; Javed Miandad 5-2-11-0; Mansoor Akhtar 5-0-10-2; Manzoor Elahi 31.3-5-106-2; Saleem Jaffer 18-10-17-3; Salim Malik 29-6-71-2; Shoaib Mohammad 18.3-3-69-2.

1987

ENGLISH SEASON

Britannic Assurance Championship

The Britannic Assurance Championship of 1987 had to negotiate one of the worst of English summers, but it had an intriguing climax before Nottinghamshire emerged worthy winners. Their triumph was a wholly satisfying end to the county careers of two very fine cricketers in Clive Rice and Richard Hadlee. Notts succeeded despite losing Broad, Robinson, and French on numerous occasions to the England selectors, and despite having to play two crucial matches in August without Rice, Hadlee, Broad, and French, all required for the MCC Bicentenary Match.

In late May they had been plumb bottom (with Leicestershire, who eventually finished third, lying 16th), but they had played only two matches against the five of the early leaders Lancashire. At the end of June, Yorkshire and Lancashire led from Northants, with Notts 11th and Leicestershire still 16th. By the end of July Yorkshire still led, but were only a point ahead of Northants, who had played four fewer matches. Leicestershire were up to eighth, Lancashire fourth. Warwickshire, Middlesex, and Sussex had settled at the bottom.

Notts were then third and moving up fast in what looked certain to be a winning run until Lancashire produced five wins in a row. When the Bicentenary Match claimed their four players, Notts led the fading Northants by 32 points and were 62 ahead of Lancashire, who were fifth. When it ended, their lead over Lancashire was down to 30 points, though their reserves had done them well.

For once, Lancashire in 1987 had not been one of the worst hit by the weather. In fact, when they were winning their fifth successive victory, on September 11th at Old Trafford, other counties were being defeated by rain when within sight of victory.

This narrowly gained win, after Surrey's declaration, cut short celebrations at Trent Bridge, where Notts had finished their programme early in the day, and gave Lancashire, only 15th in 1986, a distinct chance of becoming champions. If they drew level with Notts by taking the full 24 points against Essex at Chelmsford, they would win the Championship through having won more matches. The snag, of course, was the weather. It would be a great help to Lancashire if they had three full days' play and if the Chelmsford pitch would allow a side to make 300, which had not often been the case in 1987.

Nothing quite worked out on the Saturday, for they lost the toss, were put in, which promised to make their task more difficult, and were deprived of half the first day's play by rain. At 155-5, they were still in with a chance of earning full batting points, but, though Monday was fine, they were bowled out for 220 and Notts were champions. Lancashire, however, won the match to make it six in a row.

It was certainly to Notts' advantage, especially towards the end, that they played on pitches at Trent Bridge that made a result likely. But they had the bowlers to make good use of them. They had their share of injuries. Here again they made their own luck, for when Randall was absent in August, they had Newell, full of runs, to replace him.

It may also be forgotten that in 1984 they suffered one of the nearest of all near-misses. If a low-trajectory drive at Taunton, the last stroke of the season, had been just wide of long-off instead of being caught, they would have been champions instead of Essex.

While the revival of Yorkshire, with a promising young side, led by Phil Carrick, gave widespread pleasure, so did that of Lancashire, also with a seasoned left-arm spinner as their new captain in David Hughes. With much the same resources as Yorkshire and with none of Yorkshire's stern resolve to field only players born in the county, Lancashire have not won the Championship outright since 1934. In modern times, perhaps, they may have been diverted by their success at the limited-overs game.

Now, however, they progressed with a young side of high promise, and were not afraid to blood the 19-year-old Michael Atherton at No. 3 after the Cambridge term. The improved form and fitness of Patterson, in an attack which had variety, served them well, and if they were robbed of Neil Fairbrother in the last weeks through injury, they had John Abrahams on hand as a successful deputy.

Northants did well until the last month, with prolific batting and much improved bowling, and as they faded, Leicestershire came up to third place with a formidable hand of fast and fast-medium bowling in Ferris, DeFreitas, and Agnew. The presence of Surrey, Hampshire, and Derbyshire in the first six was not unconnected with the fact that each had a top-class West Indian fast bowler, Clarke, Marshall, and Holding, respectively. Surrey, indeed, had two, being able to choose between Clarke and Gray.

The significance of this is corroborated when one looks at the other end of the table and finds there are four counties not so formidably equipped in Kent, Warwickshire, Middlesex, and Sussex.

Kent sadly were without Ellison, but until Cowans returned no one had more trouble in bowling sides out than Middlesex. As champions in 1985, they may have come down in the world, but no more abruptly than Essex, champions in 1986 and 13th now. Middlesex could also consider this a season of transition, in which the improvement of several young batsmen, notably John Carr, was most heartening. They were also on the verge of winning five or six matches when rain or the opposition's late-order batsmen frustrated them.

There have been fine dry summers when a side would win the Championship by making a lot of runs quickly and giving its relatively modest bowling extra time in which to operate. But the summer of 1987 was definitely not one of them, and what counted was the ability of bowlers to make quick use of favourable conditions.

Britannic Assurance County Championship 1987

Final Table	P	W	L	D	1st Innings Points Batting	Bowling	Total Points
1 NOTTINGHAMSHIRE (4)	23★	9	1	13	68	80	292
2 Lancashire (15)	24	10	4	10	55	73	288
3 Leicestershire (7)	24	8	3	13	57	75	260
4 Surrey (3)	24	7	4	13	65	73	250
5 Hampshire (6)	24	7	3	14	59	73	244
6 Derbyshire (11)	24	6	5	12	51	70	225‡
7 Northamptonshire (9)	24	7	4	13	48	68	224§
8 Yorkshire (9)	23★	7	3	13	52	58	222
9 Worcestershire (10)	24	5	4	15	58	68	206
10 Gloucestershire (2)	24	5	8	10	62	50	200‡
11 Somerset (16)	24	2	3	19	61	70	163
12 Essex (1)	24	2	4	18	45	77	162†
13 Glamorgan (17)	24	3	9	12	40	70	158
14 Kent (8)	24	2	7	15	53	66	151
15 Warwickshire (12)	24	2	7	15	48	67	147
16 Middlesex (12)	23★	2	8	13	47	60	139
17 Sussex (14)	23★	1	8	14	47	56	119

1986 positions are shown in brackets. ★ No play possible in one match. †includes 8 points for drawn match in which scores finished level. ‡ includes 8 points for tied match. § includes 12 points for win in one-innings match.

Points

For a win: 16 points, plus any first innings points. For winning a match reduced to a single innings because it started with less than eight hours' playing time remaining: 12 points. First innings points are awarded during the first 100 overs of each first innings:

Batting		Bowling	
150 to 199 runs	1	3 or 4 wickets	1
200 to 249 runs	2	5 or 6 wickets	2
250 to 299 runs	3	7 or 8 wickets	3
300 runs and over	4	9 or 10 wickets	4

Final Positions 1890-1987

	D	E	Gm	Gs	H	K	La	Le	M	Nh	Nt	Sm	Sy	Sx	Wa	Wo	Y
1890	—	—	—	6	—	3	2	—	7	—	5	—	1	8	—	—	3
1891	—	—	—	9	—	5	2	—	3	—	4	5	1	7	—	—	8
1892	—	—	—	7	—	7	4	—	5	—	2	3	1	9	—	—	6
1893	—	—	—	9	—	4	2	—	3	—	6	8	5	7	—	—	1
1894	—	—	—	9	—	4	4	—	3	—	7	6	1	8	—	—	2
1895	5	9	—	4	10	14	2	12	6	—	12	8	1	11	6	—	3
1896	7	5	—	10	8	9	2	13	3	—	6	11	4	14	12	—	1
1897	14	3	—	5	9	12	1	13	8	—	10	11	2	6	7	—	4
1898	9	5	—	3	12	7	6	13	2	—	8	13	4	9	9	—	1
1899	15	6	—	9	10	8	4	13	2	—	10	13	1	5	7	12	3
1900	13	10	—	7	15	3	2	14	7	—	5	11	7	3	6	12	1
1901	15	10	—	14	7	7	3	12	2	—	9	12	6	4	5	11	1
1902	10	13	—	14	15	7	5	11	12	—	3	7	4	2	6	9	1
1903	12	8	—	13	14	8	4	14	1	—	5	10	11	2	7	6	3
1904	10	14	—	9	15	3	1	7	4	—	5	12	11	6	7	13	2
1905	14	12	—	8	16	6	2	5	11	13	10	11	4	3	7	8	1
1906	16	7	—	9	8	1	4	15	11	11	5	11	3	10	6	14	2
1907	16	7	—	10	12	8	6	11	5	15	1	14	4	13	9	2	2
1908	14	11	—	10	9	2	7	13	4	15	8	16	3	5	12	6	1
1909	15	14	—	16	8	1	2	13	6	7	10	11	5	4	12	8	3
1910	15	11	—	12	6	1	4	10	3	9	5	16	2	7	14	13	8
1911	14	6	—	12	11	2	4	15	3	10	8	16	5	13	1	9	7
1912	12	15	—	11	6	3	4	13	5	2	8	14	7	10	9	16	1
1913	13	15	—	9	10	1	8	14	6	4	5	16	3	7	11	12	2
1914	12	8	—	16	5	3	11	13	2	9	10	15	1	6	7	14	4

	D	E	Gm	Gs	H	K	La	Le	M	Nh	Nt	Sm	Sy	Sx	Wa	Wo	Y
1919	9	14	—	8	7	2	5	9	13	12	3	5	4	11	15	—	1
1920	16	9	—	8	11	5	2	13	1	14	7	10	3	6	12	15	4
1921	12	15	17	7	6	4	5	11	1	13	8	10	2	9	16	14	3
1922	11	8	16	13	6	4	5	14	7	15	2	10	3	9	12	17	1
1923	10	13	16	11	7	5	3	14	8	17	2	9	4	6	12	15	1
1924	17	15	13	6	12	5	4	11	2	16	6	8	3	10	9	14	1
1925	14	7	17	10	9	5	3	12	6	11	4	15	2	13	8	16	1
1926	11	9	8	15	7	3	1	13	6	16	4	14	5	10	12	17	2
1927	5	8	15	12	13	4	1	7	9	16	2	14	6	10	11	17	3
1928	10	16	15	5	12	2	1	9	8	13	3	14	6	7	11	17	4
1929	7	12	17	4	11	8	2	9	6	13	1	15	10	4	14	16	2
1930	9	6	11	2	13	5	1	12	16	17	4	13	8	7	15	10	3
1931	7	10	15	2	12	3	6	16	11	17	5	13	8	4	9	14	1
1932	10	14	15	13	8	3	6	12	10	16	4	7	5	2	9	17	1
1933	6	4	16	10	14	3	5	17	12	13	8	11	9	2	7	15	1
1934	3	8	13	7	14	5	1	12	10	17	9	15	11	2	4	16	5
1935	2	9	13	15	16	10	4	6	3	17	5	14	11	7	8	12	1
1936	1	9	16	4	10	8	11	15	2	17	5	7	6	14	13	12	3
1937	3	6	7	4	14	12	9	16	2	17	10	13	8	5	11	15	1
1938	5	6	16	10	14	9	4	15	2	17	12	7	3	8	13	11	1
1939	9	4	13	3	15	5	6	17	2	16	12	14	8	10	11	7	1
1946	15	8	6	5	10	6	3	11	2	16	13	4	11	17	14	8	1
1947	5	11	9	2	16	4	3	14	1	17	11	11	6	9	15	7	7
1948	6	13	1	8	9	15	5	11	3	17	14	12	2	16	7	10	4
1949	15	9	8	7	16	13	11	17	1	6	11	9	5	13	4	3	1
1950	5	17	11	7	12	9	1	16	14	10	15	7	1	13	4	6	3
1951	11	8	5	12	9	16	3	15	7	13	17	14	6	10	1	4	2
1952	4	10	7	9	12	15	3	6	5	8	16	17	1	13	10	14	2
1953	6	12	10	6	14	16	3	3	5	11	8	17	1	2	9	15	12
1954	3	15	4	13	14	11	10	16	7	7	5	17	1	9	6	11	2
1955	8	14	16	12	3	13	9	6	5	7	11	17	1	4	9	15	2
1956	12	11	13	3	6	16	2	17	5	4	8	15	1	9	14	9	7
1957	4	5	9	12	13	14	6	17	7	2	15	8	1	9	11	16	3
1958	5	6	15	14	2	8	7	12	10	4	17	3	1	13	16	9	11
1959	7	9	6	2	8	13	5	16	10	11	17	12	3	15	4	14	1
1960	5	6	11	8	12	10	2	17	3	9	16	14	7	4	15	13	1
1961	7	6	14	5	1	11	13	9	3	16	17	10	15	8	12	4	2
1962	7	9	14	4	10	11	16	17	13	8	15	6	5	12	3	2	1
1963	17.	12	2	8	10	13	15	16	6	7	9	3	11	4	4	14	1
1964	12	10	11	17	12	7	14	16	6	3	15	8	4	9	2	1	5
1965	9	15	3	10	12	5	13	14	6	2	17	7	8	16	11	1	4
1966	9	16	14	15	11	4	12	8	12	5	17	3	7	10	6	2	1
1967	6	15	14	17	12	2	11	3	7	9	16	8	4	13	10	5	1
1968	8	14	3	16	5	2	6	9	10	13	4	12	15	17	11	7	1
1969	16	6	1	2	5	10	15	14	11	9	8	17	3	7	4	12	13
1970	7	12	2	17	10	1	3	15	16	14	11	13	5	9	7	6	4
1971	17	10	16	8	9	4	3	5	6	14	12	7	1	11	2	15	13
1972	17	5	13	3	9	2	15	6	8	4	14	11	12	16	1	7	10
1973	16	8	11	5	1	4	12	9	13	3	17	10	2	15	7	6	14
1974	17	12	16	14	2	10	8	4	6	3	15	5	7	13	9	1	11
1975	15	7	9	16	3	5	4	1	11	8	13	12	6	17	14	10	2
1976	15	6	17	3	12	14	16	4	1	2	13	7	9	10	5	11	8
1977	7	6	14	3	11	1	16	5	1	9	17	4	14	8	10	13	12
1978	14	2	13	10	8	1	12	6	3	17	7	5	16	9	11	15	4
1979	16	1	17	10	12	5	13	6	14	11	9	8	3	4	15	2	7
1980	9	8	13	7	17	16	15	9	1	12	3	5	2	4	14	11	6
1981	12	5	14	13	7	9	16	8	4	15	1	3	6	2	17	11	10
1982	11	7	16	15	3	13	12	2	1	9	4	6	5	8	17	14	10
1983	9	1	15	12	3	7	12	4	2	6	14	10	8	11	5	16	17
1984	12	1	13	17	15	5	16	4	3	11	2	7	8	6	9	10	14
1985	13	4	12	3	2	9	14	16	1	10	7	17	6	7	15	5	11
1986	11	1	17	2	6	8	15	7	12	9	4	16	3	14	13	5	10
1987	6	12	13	10	5	14	2	3	16	7	1	11	4	17	15	9	8

Derbyshire

Not even Derbyshire's most loyal and optimistic supporter could wholly suppress queasy doubts about prospects when no less than seven players rejected offers to join the county before the 1987 season began. But the summer nonetheless turned into one of commendable progress.

There were still occasional days of spectacular collapse and some obvious limitations in the playing staff, the lack of an experienced spinner and a fluent middle-order batsman the foremost among them, but sixth in the Championship was their best position since 1967 and an improvement of five places on the previous season.

A tendency to freeze under pressure undermined them in the NatWest Trophy and Benson & Hedges Cup, but they still had a chance to win the Refuge Assurance League right up to the final Sunday of the season, when defeat by Somerset cost them a share of the prize money.

The form of Bruce Roberts was the major advance in the batting department. The sketchiness and evident disaffection of the previous summer was put firmly behind him, and he ended with more than 1,600 runs to make him the fourth-highest run-maker in the national averages. He signalled new confidence and maturity with a career-best 184 against Sussex in the first Championship game of the season, and went on to score three more first-class hundreds as well as two in limited-overs matches.

Kim Barnett and John Morris, who both found consistency elusive early on, bloomed late to confirm rich talent, while Bernie Maher responded emphatically to doubts about his future. A county cap was no less than he deserved for a season that saw him add 834 runs to his first place in the wicket-keepers' table with 76 victims.

Iain Anderson's failure to take his chance in the middle-order gap led to his release, and meant that Reg Sharma and Roger Finney were forced to bat higher than their pedigree indicated. But both made substantial contributions. They offered solid and sensible discretion when catastrophe beckoned, and proved able to hit the ball hard and often when quick runs were needed.

Finney's physical problems forced him to give up his place in the seam department, but there was evidence of promising slow-bowling talent in his new guise as a left-arm spinner. Michael Holding began and ended the season in potent form, though overwork blunted his effectiveness in mid-summer when injuries tested resources.

Mortensen, refusing to allow a deep-seated knee injury to depress him, performed splendidly throughout to claim seventh place in the national averages, and Derbyshire could reasonably have hoped for greater success in both the NatWest Trophy and the Sunday competition had not both Paul Newman and Allan Warner fallen prey to back problems. Two Refuge League matches and a NatWest quarter-final were lost during their absence.

Martin Jean-Jacques and Devon Malcolm found first-class cricket

Britannic Assurance County Championship: 6th; Won 6, Tied 1, Lost 5, Drawn 12
All First-Class Matches: Won 7, Tied 1, Lost 5, Drawn 12
NatWest Bank Trophy: Lost to Nottinghamshire in quarter-final
Benson & Hedges Cup: Failed to qualify for quarter-final (3rd in Group A)
Refuge Assurance League: 5th; Won 8, Lost 4, Tied 1, No Result 3

Championship Averages

Batting and Fielding	M	I	NO	HS	R	Avge	100	50	Ct/St
B. Roberts	24	40	3	184	1554	41.72	4	7	22
J.G. Wright	10	17	2	118	558	37.20	1	3	6
K.J. Barnett	24	39	1	130	1370	36.05	3	6	10
J.E. Morris	24	37	1	162	1294	35.94	3	6	13
R. Sharma	17	27	4	111	596	25.91	1	3	19
R.J. Finney	22	34	4	77	683	22.76	–	3	11
I.S. Anderson	14	20	2	87*	363	20.16	–	3	5
P.G. Newman	16	22	5	42	332	19.52	–	–	4
A.E. Warner	17	27	4	72	444	19.30	–	1	4
B.J.M. Maher	24	39	1	105	716	18.84	1	2	70/4
M.A. Holding	13	18	2	63*	278	17.37	–	1	10
O.H. Mortensen	19	24	10	74*	168	12.00	–	1	5
M. Jean-Jacques	15	18	2	47	183	11.43	–	–	6
M. Beardshall	8	8	3	25	47	9.40	–	–	1
T.J.E. O'Gorman	2	4	1	11	19	6.33	–	–	2
D.E. Malcolm	13	16	4	9*	43	3.58	–	–	5

Also batted: C.F.B.P. Rudd (2 matches 9, 3*, 0 (1ct).

Hundreds (13)

4 **B. Roberts:** 184 v Sussex, Chesterfield; 137* v Leics, Leicester; 106 v Hants, Heanor; 128 v Kent, Canterbury.
3 **K.J. Barnett:** 125 v Warwicks, Derby; 110 v Glos, Bristol; 130 v Notts, Trent Bridge.
  J.E. Morris: 162 v Notts, Derby; 106 v Notts, Trent Bridge; 113* v Somerset, Taunton.
1 **B.J.M. Maher:** 105 v Surrey, Chesterfield.
  R. Sharma: 111 v Yorks, Chesterfield.
  J.G. Wright: 118 v Somerset, Taunton.

Bowling	O	M	R	W	Avge	Best	5wI	10wM
O.H. Mortensen	432.5	111	1084	55	19.70	5-57	2	–
K.J. Barnett	68.2	19	194	9	21.55	4-43	–	–
B. Roberts	64.2	14	189	8	23.62	3-45	–	–
M.A. Holding	391.2	72	1194	49	24.36	5-41	2	–
P.G. Newman	341	65	1059	42	25.21	5-46	1	–
R.J. Finney	254.2	55	779	26	29.96	3-39	–	–
A.E. Warner	304.5	59	986	32	30.81	4-12	–	–
D.E. Malcolm	255	45	898	26	34.53	3-47	–	–
R. Sharma	206	46	640	15	42.66	6-80	1	–
M. Jean-Jacques	312	52	1051	24	43.79	4-39	–	–
M. Beardshall	158.2	21	572	12	47.66	4-68	–	–

Also bowled: I.S. Anderson 10-0-42-1; J.E. Morris 5.3-0-61-1; C.F.B.P. Rudd 29-6-126-1.

tougher than they might have supposed from brief acquaintance in 1986, but Mark Beardshall showed promise, and victory in the Bain-Dawes Second Eleven competition under Alan Hill's guidance suggested that there is fresh talent in the pipeline.

Above all 1987 underlined Barnett's great qualities as a leader and motivator. High morale and commitment not infrequently overcame teams which appeared, on paper, better equipped.

Essex

During the past decade, Essex have been County Champions on four occasions, Sunday League champions on three, and have won both the NatWest Trophy and the Benson & Hedges Cup, so that until last summer they could claim with some justification to be the strongest all-round county. Although dramatic, and a big disappointment to their many supporters, the sudden decline of the championship holders and runners-up in the Sunday League was entirely logical, and largely the result of three major factors. First, they lost the services of their most accomplished batsman, Border. Then, their other international-class batsman, Gooch, after a century in the opening game, experienced a patch of catastrophic proportions. Finally, their third most accomplished batsman, the talented Prichard, missed most of the season through injury.

In other words, for much of the season, the club had to make do without not only a third of their runs, but also those quality runs that so often win limited-overs games and provide the attack with the opportunity to dismiss the opposition twice in a three-day match.

Although both Hardie and Fletcher, especially the former, who had an excellent season, did their best to camouflage this run deficiency and the 'tail' wagged with commendable vigour and frequency, the middle order was most disappointing, collapsing with depressing regularity. To make matters worse, neither of the newcomers, Miller and Page, was able to make the impact that had been anticipated.

For the first time for many years, the team found themselves struggling and losing matches, which inevitably led to a loss of confidence and was reflected in several ways. First, most of the players had never experienced being a member of a weak team, which could explain why the promising youngsters, and the not so young youngsters, when given the opportunity, usually failed to provide the runs in the quantities required. Second, the Essex fielding, which has been such an outstanding feature, appeared to have lost some of its sparkle and snap, while too many chances were put down for comfort. Third, there was a tendency to abandon a chase earlier than in the past, while, unless Gooch could provide a major innings, they were unlikely to be able to get or to set a large total in a one-day game.

The attack certainly was not responsible for the decline, and it is worth noting that Essex gained one more bowling point than when winning the Championship. As usual, the seam section was powerful and, though Lever had naturally lost some of his pace, Foster, off his short run, enjoyed an outstanding season for England and Essex, while Pringle turned in some very tidy performances which gained him a place in the World Cup party. Topley was probably the club's most improved player, and at the end Pont showed that he was a useful support bowler. Although Childs could not repeat his success of 1986, he suffered from lack of opportunity, with Miller often preferred to him.

If Essex are to make a come-back in 1988, more runs will be required.

Britannic Assurance County Championship: 12th; Won 2, Lost 4, Drawn 18
All First-Class Matches: Won 2, Lost 5, Drawn 20
NatWest Bank Trophy: Lost to Northamptonshire in quarter-final
Benson & Hedges Cup: Failed to qualify for quarter-final (3rd in Group C)
Refuge Assurance League: 14th; Won 4, Lost 8, No Result 4

Championship Averages

Batting and Fielding	M	I	NO	HS	R	Avge	100	50	Ct/St
G.A. Gooch	20	34	6	171	1100	39.28	2	5	16
P.J. Prichard	9	12	2	72	335	33.50	–	3	3
A.W. Lilley	19	27	4	102	759	33.00	1	3	11
K.W.R. Fletcher	22	31	3	121	865	30.89	1	5	10
B.R. Hardie	24	38	4	111	1008	29.64	2	6	20
D.R. Pringle	21	31	8	84*	655	28.47	–	4	14
J.P. Stephenson	13	22	3	67*	515	27.10	–	2	7
N.A. Foster	14	15	2	49*	305	23.46	–	–	5
T.D. Topley	11	13	4	66	201	22.33	–	1	2
C. Gladwin	7	12	2	76	202	20.20	–	1	3
I.L. Pont	6	7	2	39	86	17.20	–	–	1
H.A.Page	12	16	4	42*	201	16.75	–	–	4
D.E. East	24	26	1	73	394	15.76	–	1	49/4
G. Miller	20	25	4	33*	290	13.80	–	–	26
J.H. Childs	19	19	10	26	109	12.11	–	–	5
J.K. Lever	13	7	2	18	60	12.00	–	–	2
I.R. Redpath	7	12	1	46	128	11.63	–	–	2

Also batted: M.G. Field-Buss (1 match) 6, 34*; N. Hussain (2 matches) 12, 18, 2 (2ct).   :ches)

Hundreds (6)

2 G.A. Gooch: 171 v Glos, Bristol; 159 v Northants, Ilford.
 B.R. Hardie: 111 v Leics, Leicester; 111 v Sussex, Eastbourne.
1 K.W.R. Fletcher: 121 v Middlesex, Lord's.
 A.W. Lilley: 102 v Middlesex, Chelmsford.

Bowling	O	M	R	W	Avge	Best	5wI	10wM
N.A. Foster	470.3	93	1397	61	22.90	7-33	4	1
D.R. Pringle	562.4	149	1365	54	25.27	5-70	1	–
T.D. Topley	256.2	55	713	26	27.42	4-75	–	–
G. Miller	349.3	74	923	29	31.82	7-59	1	1
G.A. Gooch	212.3	55	584	18	32.44	4-42	–	–
J.H. Childs	424	126	1100	33	33.33	5-40	2	1
H.A. Page	240.2	34	839	25	33.56	4-36	–	–
J.K. Lever	324	77	906	26	34.84	5-59	2	–
I.L. Pont	183	19	671	19	35.31	5-73	1	–

Also bowled: D.E. East 1-0-5-0; K.W.R. Fletcher 2-0-9-0; B.R. Hardie 13-1-65-0;
A.W. Lilley 12-1-77-0; J.P. Stephenson 25.1-3-94-1.

Glamorgan

Glamorgan might have looked unarguably weak at times — no team suffered more than their nine defeats — but there was still decided encouragement to be gained in their rise from the bottom of the table to 13th place. Likewise, they scored fewer bonus batting points than any other county and yet could proudly boast one of the most exciting young batsmen in their 21-year-old Matthew Maynard.

On his debut in 1985, Maynard, from Anglesey, scored a memorable hundred against Yorkshire (three successive sixes to pass the mark) and this season he was Glamorgan's leading run scorer. Promoted to No. 4, he was awarded his county cap after completing his highest score, 160 against Somerset at Weston-super-Mare, in early August.

Maynard also excelled in the field. A slip specialist, but also a true athlete in the deep, he led the fielding statistics with 30 catches.

Glamorgan also awarded county caps to Butcher, who scored more than 1,000 runs and topped their Championship averages, their leading wicket-taker Barwick, and the excellent wicket-keeping recruit Metson, previously captain of Middlesex 2nd XI.

The signing of Butcher, from Surrey, was an undoubted success. In six matches late in the season, he scored three hundreds, emphasizing the loss suffered in 11 matches, after he tore a calf muscle while batting against Yorkshire in May.

Barwick clearly profited from his winter in South Africa, and, although his 47 wickets cost 38.27 apiece, he had returned with improved fitness and confidence to take the new ball. He bore the brunt of the bowling on many frustratingly slow home pitches.

It was the dull pace of those pitches that decided the inclusion of Glamorgan's overseas player, with Indian all-rounder Shastri invariably playing at home and Van Zyl, from South Africa, in away matches. Shastri scored 755 runs in only 12 games, but, with MCC's Bicentenary Match and then a recall to India in preparation for the World Cup, he missed the last six championship matches. This was a further handicap for Glamorgan, as Van Zyl had suffered a stress fracture of the foot and had returned home with nine matches still remaining.

The attack often proved expensive, and Thomas, persistently under medical care, took only 27 championship wickets. His season ended in some distress and embarrassment all-round when he was suspended — after the last match — for undergoing a leg operation without first seeking the club's permission.

One unexpected bowling success was the medium-paced Base, who, until the Worcestershire game at Neath on 22 August, had captured just six wickets in 1987. He then took 22 wickets in the next three matches.

The captain, Hugh Morris, hit three hundreds in his 1,304 runs overall. At 23, he is the second youngest fully appointed county captain since the war — S.J. Syminton being only 22 years old when he led Leicestershire for one season in 1949.

Britannic Assurance County Championship: 13th; Won 3, Lost 9, Drawn 12
All First-Class Matches: Won 3, Lost 9, Drawn 14
NatWest Bank Trophy: Lost to Yorkshire in 2nd round
Benson & Hedges Cup: Failed to qualify for quarter-final (4th in Group D)
Refuge Assurance League:15th; Won 5, Lost 9, No Result 2

Championship Averages

Batting and Fielding	M	I	NO	HS	R	Avge	100	50	Ct/St
A. R. Butcher	14	26	2	135*	1007	41.95	3	4	6
R.J. Shastri	12	21	2	103	755	39.73	1	6	7
M.P.Maynard	24	43	4	160	1508	38.66	2	10	29
H.Morris	24	46	2	115	1161	26.38	2	4	15
G.C. Holmes	23	41	6	95	912	26.05	–	5	9
R.C. Ontong	14	24	5	100	487	25.63	1	–	11
J. Derrick	16	26	6	57	380	19.00	–	1	6
C.J.P.G. Van Zyl	6	5	0	35	85	17.00	–	–	–
P.A. Todd	13	23	0	135	380	16.52	1	1	12
C.P. Metson	24	37	7	81	493	16.43	–	1	45/6
P.A. Cottey	6	9	1	42*	130	16.25	–	–	2
J.A. Hopkins	14	25	2	39*	369	16.04	–	–	12
I. Smith	16	23	5	45	288	16.00	–	–	6
J.G. Thomas	9	15	2	48	200	15.38	–	–	3
S.P. James	6	11	1	43*	137	13.70	–	–	4
S.J. Base	8	14	4	38	127	12.70	–	–	1
S.R. Barwick	23	30	10	21*	150	7.50	–	–	1
P.D. North	5	7	1	15	39	6.50	–	–	2
S. Monkhouse	5	8	3	15	23	4.60	–	–	1

Also batted: M.J. Cann (2 matches) 16*, 8*.

Hundreds (10)

3 A.R. Butcher: 135 v Leics, Abergavenny; 135* v Worcs, Neath; 113* v Derbys, Cardiff.

2 M.P. Maynard: 160 v Somerset, Weston-super-Mare; 119 v Derbys, Cardiff.

  H. Morris: 115 & 105 v Warwicks, Edgbaston.

1 R.C. Ontong: 100 v Lancs, Swansea.

  R.J. Shastri: 103 v Northants, Swansea.

  P.A. Todd: 135 v Worcs, Worcester.

Bowling	O	M	R	W	Avge	Best	5wI	10wM
S.J. Base	203.1	38	660	28	23.57	5-67	2	–
J.G. Thomas	215.3	40	756	27	28.00	6-109	2	–
R.J. Shastri	419.1	96	1051	34	30.91	5-100	1	–
J. Derrick	291.3	61	1015	31	32.74	5-50	1	–
S. Monkhouse	70	4	305	9	33.88	2-34	–	–
R.C. Ontong	461.4	87	1395	41	34.02	6-91	2	–
P.D. North	103.3	27	242	7	34.57	4-43	–	–
S.R. Barwick	603.1	122	1799	47	38.27	4-60	–	–
C.J.P.G Van Zyl	138	25	439	11	39.90	3-35	–	–
I. Smith	195.3	38	692	17	40.70	3-65	–	–

Also bowled: A.R. Butcher 21–1–52–3; M.J. Cann 23.5-3-110-1; G.C. Holmes 95-16-340-2; M.P. Maynard 20-3-68-1; H. Morris 5-1-20-0.

Gloucestershire

Gloucestershire, having previously finished third and second in the Championship table, dropped to 10th place, with an undoubted failure on the bowling front. In fact, they achieved fewer bowling points than any other county – even fewer than bottom team Sussex. Their batsmen, in contrast, were surpassed on bonus points by only the champions Nottinghamshire and fourth-placed Surrey.

There was admirable depth to Gloucestershire's batting order, with five players reaching 1,000 runs and the beneficiary Stovold failing by only 12 runs to join the quintet. Lloyds, with rewarding consistency, was the leading batsman, with over 1,200 first-class runs, followed by Curran, Romaines, Athey, and Wright.

The success of Romaines was especially welcome, following disappointments of the previous years with aggregates of only 423 and 429. Athey played a notable innings of 160 against Nottinghamshire on their renowned Trent Bridge wicket, and in the last match of the season opener Wright anticipated the award of his county cap the following day with a career top score of 161 against Glamorgan at Bristol.

Gloucestershire finished in style with a comfortable victory there by 114 runs, but they had enjoyed a far from happy start to the season. They lost their first match to Essex by 10 wickets and then suffered two defeats by an innings before finally recording their first win, on 7 July, against those favourite opponents Glamorgan, at Swansea.

Walsh was once again a most effective bowler, with 59 wickets, but, alas, there was nothing approaching those 1986 glories of 118 wickets. His absence was dearly felt in August when on duty for MCC's Bicentenary celebrations, and he will be sadly missed in 1988 when touring with the West Indies. For his replacement, Gloucestershire have signed up for one year Craig McDermott, the fast bowler who headed the Australian averages, with 51 wickets, on their 1985 England Tour – including 8-141 in the Old Trafford Test Match.

The Barbadian pace bowler Greene was Walsh's overseas deputy last season and gained one telling return of 7-96 against Nottinghamshire at Trent Bridge. But Gloucestershire's attack was far too often a failure, with Lawrence, who suffered from a rib injury, taking only 38 wickets at 37 apiece, Lloyds 36 at over 40 and the captain Graveney collecting just 25 Championship wickets.

The wicket-keeping prowess of Russell continued as a feature for Gloucestershire in the field, while his batting yet again improved to record the highest aggregate of his seven-year career, with 798 runs.

Tomlins (formerly of Middlesex), who scored a hundred against Oxford in The Parks, and Sainsbury, previously with Essex, both left the staff at the end of the season. There was also a sad departure for Gloucestershire in the retirement of their 70-year-old scorer Bert Avery, who joined the 2nd XI in 1965 and then spent 18 years with the county team. His willing assistance and rhythmic italic handwriting will be sorely missed in the box.

Britannic Assurance County Championship: 10th; Won 5, Tied 1, Lost 8, Drawn 10
All First-Class Matches: Won 5, Tied 1, Lost 8, Drawn 12
NatWest Bank Trophy: Lost to Nottinghamshire in semi-final
Benson & Hedges Cup: Lost to Kent in quarter-final
Refuge Assurance League: 3rd; Won 9, Lost 4, Tied 1, No Result 2

Championship Averages

Batting and Fielding	M	I	NO	HS	R	Avge	100	50	Ct/St
C.W.J. Athey	16	26	4	160	1069	48.59	5	2	11
J.W. Lloyds	22	30	4	130	1159	44.57	2	9	16
K.M. Curran	20	31	6	119	1067	42.68	3	3	11
P. Bainbridge	16	23	6	151	628	36.94	2	3	9
R.C. Russell	24	34	7	57*	779	28.85	–	4	49/8
A.J. Wright	22	36	2	161	975	28.67	1	6	19
P.W. Romaines	23	39	1	115	1004	26.42	1	5	5
M.W. Alleyne	18	26	7	82	499	26.26	–	4	6
A.W. Stovold	24	40	2	88	897	23.60	–	5	2
V.S. Greene	6	8	2	62*	141	23.50	–	1	2
K.B. Ibadulla	4	6	1	46*	113	22.60	–	–	1
K.P. Tomlins	6	8	1	34	107	15.28	–	–	1
D.A. Graveney	17	16	3	30	121	9.30	–	–	8
D.V. Lawrence	17	19	4	65*	138	9.20	–	1	2
C.A. Walsh	17	21	1	27	166	8.30	–	–	9
G.E. Sainsbury	11	14	7	5	15	2.14	–	–	4

Also batted: J.N. Shepherd (1 match) 5, 1 (2ct).

Hundreds (14)

5 C.W.J. Athey: 115 & 114* v Warwicks, Edgbaston; 160 v Notts, Trent Bridge; 101* v Yorks, Headingley; 101* v Glamorgan, Bristol.
3 K.M. Curran: 114* v Essex, Bristol; 102* v Glamorgan, Swansea; 119 v Kent, Cheltenham.
2 P. Bainbridge: 134* v Sussex, Hove; 151 v Leics, Leicester.
 J.W. Lloyds: 130 v Glamorgan, Swansea; 105 v Surrey, Cheltenham.
1 P.W. Romaines: 115 v Somerset, Bristol.
 A.J. Wright: 161 v Glamorgan, Bristol.

Bowling	O	M	R	W	Avge	Best	5wI	10wM
C.A. Walsh	471.3	95	1433	59	24.28	5-38	2	–
P. Bainbridge	271.4	59	885	30	29.50	5-70	1	–
V.S. Greene	167.5	18	625	20	31.25	7-96	1	–
D.A. Graveney	324.2	97	812	25	32.48	5-37	1	–
D.V. Lawrence	350.1	44	1411	38	37.13	6-63	1	–
J.W. Lloyds	364.4	58	1315	32	41.09	6-57	2	–
G.E. Sainsbury	298.2	71	798	17	46.94	3-48	–	–
M.W. Alleyne	149.4	32	577	9	64.11	4-128	–	–

Also bowled: C.W.J. Athey 37.4-3-136-2; K.M. Curran 48-5-203-2; K.B. Ibadulla 43-8-112-4; R.C. Russell 0.1-0-0-0; J.N. Shepherd 28-9-92-2.

Hampshire

Although it was not until their ninth match, in late June, that Hampshire registered their first Championship win, they were within two rungs and 19 points of the leaders at the beginning of September, and participated in the hectic tussle for places in the frame. They fell just outside it, finishing fifth, up a place from their 1986 position, with the same number of wins – seven. However, the token advance would have provided little consolation, more so as there was little promise of better things in 1988, when Greenidge and Marshall will be touring with the West Indies.

Reasons for Hampshire's failure to realize their full potential would seem to be the absence of Greenidge from 11 matches and Robin Smith's from seven. Then there was the weather, which not only deprived Hampshire of three possible wins but, on other occasions, of bonus points, which had to be sacrificed when declaring to keep rain-affected matches alive.

To suggest that Greenidge, whose knee required an operation in mid-season and whose back troubled him later, was not missed would be ridiculous. But the irony was that six of Hampshire's wins were gained without him and, what is more curious, two without Marshall. The weather was indeed unkind to them, but, then, in a particularly wretched summer, no county was spared.

More pertinently, Hampshire's main batsmen were an unconscionable time getting into stride. Terry passed 50 only twice in the first eight matches and did not get a hundred until the tenth. Chris Smith, who with 1,382 was the county's highest scorer for the season, did not pass 38 in his first 11 innings, after which he scored 102 not out, 69 not out, 5, 132 not out, and 217 in his next five.

Robin Smith was out for many weeks with a broken thumb, and it was mid-July before he made his presence felt with a spectacularly volatile 209 against Essex, at Southend. Apart from two centuries, one in early June and another a month later, Nicholas struggled desperately for runs until the tide turned as late as the second week of August.

If in the weeks of shortage Hampshire did not flounder, it was because the veteran Turner invariably came to the rescue. At 38, the little left-hander aggregated more runs than anyone in the side save Chris Smith. All-rounder Kevan James, too, played three significant innings during these lean days.

As for the bowling, Marshall (72 wickets) was less damaging than in previous years. Not that there was any suggestion of declining pace or hostility. The shortfall was made up by Tremlett who, after a poor season in 1986, turned in some noteworthy performances, as did Maru. Judging by the number of wickets he took on either side of his long absence, indicative of rising promise, the injury to Andrew severely handicapped Hampshire. James, left-arm, was prominent on a couple of occasions, and the Dutchman, Bakker, indicated with a match-winning 7-31 against Kent that Hampshire's bowling resources may have greater

Britannic Assurance County Championship: 5th; Won 7, Lost 3, Drawn 14
All First-Class Matches: Won 7, Lost 3, Drawn 16
NatWest Bank Trophy: Lost to Leicestershire in 2nd round
Benson & Hedges Cup: Lost to Yorkshire in quarter-final
Refuge Assurance League: 7th; Won 6, Lost 6, Tied 2, No Result 2

Championship Averages

Batting and Fielding	M	I	NO	HS	R	Avge	100	50	Ct/St
K.D. James	16	15	5	142*	517	51.70	1	2	5
R.A. Smith	17	24	7	209*	852	50.11	1	4	15
D.R. Turner	23	33	8	184*	1240	49.60	2	8	8
C.G. Greenidge	11	16	0	163	725	45.31	2	5	21
C.L. Smith	24	38	7	217	1382	44.58	4	4	22
M.C.J. Nicholas	23	34	7	147	1115	41.29	4	4	11
V.P. Terry	21	34	4	122	1172	39.06	1	9	28
M.D. Marshall	21	22	5	99	610	35.88	–	3	6
R.J. Parks	23	19	8	62*	370	33.63	–	2	53/4
T.M. Tremlett	22	16	4	42	157	13.08	–	–	7
N.G. Cowley	8	10	1	30	89	9.88	–	–	4
R.J. Maru	24	14	3	15	92	8.36	–	–	24
C.A. Connor	13	9	5	11*	31	7.75	–	–	5

Also batted: S.J.W. Andrew (13 matches) 3, 4* (1ct); A.N. Aymes (1 match) 58 (1ct); P.J. Bakker (2 matches) 0; I.J. Chivers (1 match) 20*; T.C. Middleton (1 match) 7 (1ct).

Hundreds (15)

4 M.C.J. Nicholas: 147 v Sussex, Horsham; 103* v Derbys, Heanor. 133 v Kent, Bournemouth; 110* v Worcs, Worcester.
  C.L. Smith: 102* c Surrey, Oval; 132* v Middlesex, Southampton; 217 v Warwicks, Edgbaston; 118* Worcs, Worcester.
2 C.G. Greenidge: 106 v Glos, Southampton; 163 v Glos, Gloucester.
  D.R. Turner: 184* v Glos, Gloucester; 104* v Derbys, Heanor.
1 K.D. James: 142* v Notts, Bournemouth.
  R.A. Smith: 209* v Essex, Southend.
  V.P. Terry: 122 v Warwicks, Edgbaston.

Bowling	O	M	R	W	Avge	Best	5wI	10wM
P.J. Bakker	56.5	18	146	10	14.60	7-31	1	–
T.M. Tremlett	503.4	146	1251	66	18.95	6-53	3	–
M.D. Marshall	571.4	149	1445	72	20.06	5-49	1	–
S.J.W. Andrew	302.1	56	996	46	21.65	7-92	2	–
R.J. Maru	751.4	218	1937	66	29.34	5-45	3	–
C.A. Connor	350	74	943	28	33.67	4-26	–	–
N.G. Cowley	205.1	51	521	14	37.21	4-77	–	–
K.D. James	192.1	33	728	19	38.31	5-62	1	–

Also bowled: I.J. Chivers 3-1-4-1; M.C.J. Nicholas 6.5-0-31-0; R.J. Parks 8-0-56-0; C.L. Smith 25-5-75-1; R.A. Smith 12-0-88-2.

depth next season.

While Greenidge will be offered a fresh contract in 1989, there seems little prospect of his acceptance. Uncertainty also surrounds the return of Marshall. As his immediate replacement, Hampshire have signed Australian Bruce Reid.

In 1986, Hampshire's disappointments were mitigated by their winning the Sunday League. No such consolation was available this time. They finished seventh, and were early casualties in the two other one-day competitions.

Kent

As was inevitable from the onset, Kent's championship season foundered on the glaring deficiency of top-class bowling that followed the departure of Graham Dilley and the retirement of Terry Alderman. Yet the loss of two bowlers who, in 1986, claimed 142 wickets at around 23 runs each, did not unduly concern the Board of Admirals at Canterbury, who expressed confidence in the ability of the ratings to rally round Eldine Baptiste, Kevin Jarvis, and Richard Ellison.

Instead, Ellison, stricken with back and leg problems, failed to appear all season, Jarvis's early injuries were exacerbated by his being called back into action too quickly, and the second-string were pressed into bowling more overs than their experience and/or their stamina could cope with.

By mid-June Kent were finally obliged to recognize the gravity of the situation, but their hasty recruitment of Roy Pienaar did little more than take some physical strain from the incumbent bowlers. Indeed, after the South African had taken only five wickets for 201 in his first three matches, it became apparent that Kent had hauled aboard another batsman rather than an incisive strike bowler.

With Mark Benson, Neil Taylor, and Chris Tavaré already in the top half of the national batting averages, this was a particular irony, and one with which Chris Cowdrey, the captain, was destined to wrestle for the remainder of the season. Apart from the loss of brother Graham, whose jaw was broken by Holding, at Derby, Cowdrey enjoyed considerable — and generally consistent — batting resources, not least from Benson, who comfortably exceeded 1,500 runs.

In that same match against Derbyshire, Derek Aslett scored a century, as did Pienaar. Richard Hinks and the occasionally over-ambitious Baptiste had their day, and Steve Marsh invariably could be relied upon for a workmanlike innings. So, too, could his wicket-keeping deputy Paul Farbrace — an excellent prospect.

Unfortunately, the seam bowling seldom rose above average, and Derek Underwood's gleeful anticipation of uncovered pitches for his last summer was sadly frustrated — not by lack of rain but by the fact that, in the substance of their preparation, wet wickets no longer behave as they once did.

By the end of the season, Chris Cowdrey was willing to concede that the disappointments of the campaign had arisen in Kent's lack of experienced bowlers. 'We talked about it a lot,' he admitted, 'but did nothing about it. Next season we will have to come up with a solution. There is no guarantee that Ellison will be available. Underwood has retired. There seems no alternative but to sign at least one quality bowler . . . but from where?'

That question undoubtedly will echo and re-echo around the St Lawrence ground this winter.

Britannic Assurance County Championship: 14th; Won 2, Lost 7, Drawn 15
All First-Class Matches: Won 3, Lost 7, Drawn 16
NatWest Bank Trophy: Lost to Derbyshire in 2nd round
Benson & Hedges Cup: Lost to Northamptonshire in semi-final
Refuge Assurance League: 6th; Won 8, Lost 5, No Result 3

Championship Averages

Batting and Fielding	M	I	NO	HS	R	Avge	100	50	Ct/St
M.R. Benson	23	38	0	131	1619	42.60	4	10	17
R.F. Pienaar	7	8	0	153	327	40.87	1	1	2
N.R. Taylor	22	36	3	142*	1224	37.09	3	5	11
G.R. Cowdrey	4	7	1	68	198	33.00	–	3	3
C.J. Tavaré	24	40	7	152	1035	31.36	1	5	22
P. Farbrace	4	6	2	75*	121	30.25	–	1	7/–
D.G. Aslett	23	37	7	101*	895	29.83	1	4	11
S.G. Hinks	19	31	1	112	818	27.26	1	2	16
E.A.E. Baptiste	15	22	3	95	510	26.84	–	3	5
C.S. Cowdrey	23	35	5	135	783	26.10	2	2	18
S.A. Marsh	20	26	5	72*	387	18.42	–	2	38/1
D.L. Underwood	21	20	9	29*	168	15.27	–	–	3
S.C. Goldsmith	2	4	0	25	49	12.25	–	–	1
C. Penn	15	16	1	37	175	11.66	–	–	4
K.B.S. Jarvis	10	8	7	4*	11	11.00	–	–	–
R.P. Davis	7	9	4	21*	43	8.60	–	–	5
D.J.M. Kelleher	12	12	1	20	81	7.36	–	–	1
A.P. Igglesden	12	13	2	30	69	6.27	–	–	3

Also batted: T.R. Ward (1 match) 6, 13*.

Hundreds (13)

4 M.R. Benson: 122 v Worcs, Worcester; 113 v Northants, Northampton; 114 v Sussex, Hove; 131 v Surrey, Oval.

3 N.R. Taylor: 113 v Glamorgan, Canterbury; 142* v Essex, Ilford; 123* v Notts, Canterbury.

2 C.S. Cowdrey: 100* v Glamorgan, Canterbury; 135 v Hants, Bournemouth.

1 D.G. Aslett: 101* v Derbys, Derby.
  S.G. Hinks: 112 v Middlesex, Lord's.
  R.F. Pienaar: 153 v Derbys, Derby.
  C.J. Tavaré: 152 v Worcs, Worcester.

Bowling	O	M	R	W	Avge	Best	5wI	10wM
D.J.M. Kelleher	301	72	878	34	25.82	6-109	2	–
E.A.E. Baptiste	490.3	110	1409	51	27.62	8-76	2	1
R.F. Pienaar	135.4	27	427	15	28.46	4-66	–	–
A.P. Igglesden	332	48	1189	39	30.48	5-45	2	–
C. Penn	387.1	66	1313	43	30.53	5-52	2	–
D.L. Underwood	562.3	192	1201	38	31.60	5-43	1	–
K.B.S. Jarvis	224.2	32	827	26	31.80	5-48	1	–
R.P. Davis	153	35	473	10	47.30	3-68	–	–
C.S. Cowdrey	259.1	58	817	17	48.05	2-30	–	–

Also bowled: D.G. Aslett 63.1-6-288-2; M.R. Benson 2-0-8-0; G.R. Cowdrey 8-2-43-0; S.C. Goldsmith 6-0-37-1; S.G. Hinks 9-0-51-0; C.J. Tavaré 29.1-5-124-1; N.R. Taylor 2-0-15-0.

Lancashire

Lancashire, comparatively ineffective in the one-day competitions which have for so long been their strength, finished a praiseworthy second to Nottinghamshire in the County Championship in the tightest of finishes. This, their highest position in English cricket's most prestigious competition for 27 years was doubly welcome after a run of 11 seasons in which their best final placing had been 12th, and showed that the Red Rose county was once more a power in the land.

The new Captain, David Hughes, in his 40th year, generated confidence and self-belief in his players, as was amply demonstrated during the county's Championship run-in when all showed nerves of steel as the last six matches were won. Hughes and his men benefited greatly from the 'glasnost' that percolated through the club from chairman Bob Bennett downwards, and made Old Trafford a friendly and welcoming place once more.

In terms of individual performances, the experienced players did all that was expected of them. Fowler, who had easily his most prolific year, was the ideal opener, at once consistent and aggressive, and Mendis, his partner, was an ideal lieutenant. Allott used the new ball skilfully and batted most usefully, Simmons was the highest-placed spinner in the National averages apart from Derbyshire's Barnett, who bowled little, and Patterson, experimenting successfully with a shorter run-up, at last repaid some of Lancashire's investment in him.

It was, however, the younger players who took the eye. Fairbrother's classy left-handed batting brought him a Test cap, and there are surely many more to follow. Watkinson produced match-winning performances both with his medium-paced bowling and with his positive middle-order batting. Folley, who had many destructive spells with his slow left-arm, was the leading wicket-taker. The Cambridge Blue Atherton and wicket-keeper Hegg, both only 19, looked thoroughly at home under pressure and have great futures.

Atherton, who scored nearly 1,200 runs at an average of 38 in his debut year, was for many judges the find of the season. The strict orthodoxy of his batting does not preclude a wide variety of stroke which will give bowlers some grief when he fills out a little and gains in power. He hits the ball firmly off either foot and on both sides of the wicket, and concentrates fiercely whether attacking or defending.

Folley must have a bright future in a field in which English cricket is not particularly rich. When he converted from medium pace three years ago, he soon demonstrated genuine powers of spin, but, because he bowled too many bad balls, did not get a great amount of work. Last season Hughes placed responsibility on him, requiring him to bowl long spells even on good pitches. Folley responded to this, and his growing accuracy can be measured by the fact that he conceded runs at less than 2½ per over. With young men like these fully blooded, and more, it is rumoured, in the pipe-line, Lancashire's future should be assured.

Britannic Assurance County Championship: 2nd; Won 10, Lost 4, Drawn 10
All First-Class Matches: Won 10, Lost 4, Drawn 11
NatWest Bank Trophy: Lost to Gloucestershire in 1st round
Benson & Hedges Cup: Failed to qualify for quarter-final (3rd in Group B)
Refuge Assurance League: 9th; Won 5, Lost 6, No Result 5

Championship Averages

Batting and Fielding	M	I	NO	HS	R	Avge	100	50	Ct/St
G. Fowler	23	41	5	169*	1689	46.91	3	10	12
N.H. Fairbrother	19	27	5	109*	963	43.77	3	3	17
G.D. Mendis	23	40	6	203*	1384	40.70	3	7	6
J. Abrahams	8	14	1	140*	515	39.61	1	3	5
M.A. Atherton	11	19	2	76	602	35.41	–	3	1
M. Watkinson	19	27	4	91	776	33.73	–	6	18
P.J.W. Allott	21	26	4	88	612	27.81	–	4	22
D.W. Varey	7	10	1	59	220	24.44	–	2	1
S.J. O'Shaughnessy	8	14	3	61*	243	22.09	–	1	14
W.K. Hegg	13	20	4	130	350	21.87	1	–	24/11
K.W. McLeod	6	6	0	31	92	15.33	–	–	1
D.P. Hughes	24	34	6	43*	422	15.07	–	–	19
I. Folley	23	29	6	38	341	14.82	–	–	18
A.N. Hayhurst	4	4	1	30*	37	12.33	–	–	1
J. Simmons	21	23	5	43*	188	10.44	–	–	16
B.P. Patterson	17	16	8	29	65	8.12	–	–	1
J. Stanworth	11	9	3	14*	39	6.50	–	–	19/3

Also batted: I.D. Austin (2 matches) 37; M.R. Chadwick (2 matches) 11, 4, 38 (1ct);
D. Fitton (1 match) 3; A.J. Murphy (1 match) 5 (1ct).

Hundreds (11)

3 N.H. Fairbrother: 100 v Somerset, Taunton; 101 v Leics, Leicester; 109* v Notts, Old Trafford.
  G. Fowler: 169* v Kent, Liverpool; 121 v Essex, Old Trafford; 100 v Kent, Maidstone.
  G.D. Mendis: 203* v Middlesex, Old Trafford; 155 v Yorks, Old Trafford; 100* v Yorks, Headingley.
1 J. Abrahams: 140* v Surrey, Old Trafford.
  W.K. Hegg: 130 v Northants, Northampton.

Bowling	O	M	R	W	Avge	Best	5wI	10wM
P.J.W. Allott	504.3	151	1188	56	21.21	7-42	1	–
J. Simmons	613.3	178	1397	63	22.17	6-20	4	1
M. Watkinson	318	66	986	42	23.47	7-25	4	–
K.W. McLeod	126.4	24	409	17	24.05	5-8	2	–
I. Folley	678.3	212	1668	68	24.52	7-15	5	1
B.P. Patterson	419.1	61	1359	52	26.13	6-40	4	–
A.N. Hayhurst	92.4	20	299	8	37.37	4-27	–	–

Also bowled: J. Abrahams 23-6-66-2; M.A. Atherton 51-6-187-4; I.D. Austin
33.5-7-64-3; N.H. Fairbrother 22-2-111-2; D. Fitton 7-0-23-1; G. Fowler
13.3-3-43-3; D.P. Hughes 22-4-87-2; G.D. Mendis 10-1-33-0; A.J. Murphy
36-5-133-4; S.J. O'Shaughnessy 96-18-289-4.

Leicestershire

In the early part of the 1987 season it seemed likely that Leicestershire's main claim to distinction might well be succeeding Yorkshire as the most fractious and publicly disputatious county in the Championship. The reek of cordite and rumble of internecine strife were frequently evident as Leicestershire lurched into July in 16th place in the Championship, all of which rendered their eventual third place one of the season's most remarkable achievements.

Secretary/manager Mike Turner maintained throughout that the 'personality clashes' featuring captain Peter Willey, Phil DeFreitas, Paddy Clift, Jon Agnew, and Winston Benjamin were somewhat distorted by the media's spy-glass, and stemmed from having more talent than available places, especially in the seam department. There could be little doubt, however, that Willey's assertive brand of captaincy did not suit all tastes. But common sense and professionalism overcame lingering animosities, and Leicestershire launched themselves upwards with a stirring sequence of five Championship wins in eight games, carrying them to fourth place by August.

Nobody personified the new purpose of the side more than Agnew, shortening his run and relying less on sheer pace to outstrip by far anything achieved when he was touted as England's white hope. He claimed five or more wickets nine times in first-class matches to end with 101 victims, and formed, with Ferris, who dislodged Benjamin from the overseas berth, a new-ball partnership as potent as any in the Championship.

After two disappointing years, Ferris re-emerged to claim 30 wickets from his first 170 overs, and Clift, as ever, staged an object lesson in 'line and length' bowling as well as making a commendable contribution of more than 600 runs.

DeFreitas, who took 89 wickets and scored 630 runs in Championship cricket in 1986, was the player apparently most affected by the dressing-room upheavals, suffering a worrying loss of output amid rumours of a desire to move elsewhere.

Peter Such proved a valuable acquisition for a county that claimed only 16 wickets from spin the previous summer. The batting was enriched by having David Gower more often available and by Nigel Briers' rediscovery of form and fitness. Briers, whose six innings in 1986 yielded 220 runs, this time scored two 100s and nine 50s to lead the run-scorers, while Gower made his first Championship centuries since 1985 to become one of five Leicestershire players to pass 1,000 first-class runs.

Boon, another of them, reached 50 eleven times, and Whitaker overcame inconsistent form early in the year to contribute two hundreds and 10 half-centuries. Willey scored over 230 runs more than in 1986, but at an average significantly reduced, and Russ Cobb, Ian Butcher, and Laurie Potter were only fitfully effective. Whitticase failed to make the expected progress as a batsman, perhaps because of a persistent knee problem, but maintained his standards with the gloves to finish third in

Britannic Assurance County Championship: 3rd; Won 8, Lost 3, Drawn 14
All First-Class Matches: Won 9, Lost 3, Drawn 14
NatWest Bank Trophy: Lost to Northamptonshire in semi-final
Benson & Hedges Cup: Failed to qualify for quarter-final (5th in Group A)
Refuge Assurance League: 12th; Won 3, Drawn 6, No Result 7

Championship Averages

Batting and Fielding	M	I	NO	HS	R	Avge	100	50	Ct/St
D.I. Gower	12	19	4	125	840	56.00	2	4	2
N.E. Briers	20	31	4	104	1244	46.07	2	9	9
T.J. Boon	18	24	2	94	858	39.00	–	9	13
J.J. Whitaker	24	35	5	105	1020	34.00	1	9	16
P. Willey	24	38	2	122	1153	32.02	2	6	9
P.B. Clift	16	21	3	88	576	32.00	–	4	8
I.P. Butcher	7	11	0	88	320	29.09	–	3	3
R.A. Cobb	16	25	5	88	540	27.00	–	2	8
L. Potter	13	19	4	47*	333	22.20	–	–	21
P.A.J. DeFreitas	15	20	2	74	369	20.50	–	2	9
J.P. Agnew	24	27	4	90	387	16.82	–	1	1
P.J. Whitticase	24	29	5	59	336	14.00	–	1	65/1
C.C. Lewis	4	4	0	42	53	13.25	–	–	1
G.J.F. Ferris	13	13	4	25	93	10.33	–	–	–
L.B. Taylor	8	9	3	16	66	11.00	–	–	–
W.K.M. Benjamin	7	8	1	30	57	8.14	–	–	4
P.M. Such	19	16	8	12	28	3.50	–	–	7

Hundreds (7)

2 N.E. Briers: 104 v Yorks, Scarborough; 102* v Glos, Leicester.

  D.I. Gower: 105* v Glos, Cheltenham; 125 v Derbys, Derby.

  P. Willey: 113 v Somerset, Leicester; 122 v Derbys, Leicester.

1 J.J. Whitaker: 105 v Yorks, Scarborough.

Bowling	O	M	R	W	Avge	Best	5wI	10wM
G.J.F. Ferris	359.1	69	1143	52	21.98	6-42	4	–
P.B. Clift	376.1	106	829	36	23.02	6-64	2	–
J.P. Agnew	750	132	2409	99	24.33	7-46	9	2
P.A.J. DeFreitas	398.2	92	1187	44	26.97	7-85	2	–
L.B. Taylor	143.4	19	524	18	29.11	6-47	2	–
W.K.M. Benjamin	187.2	46	470	15	31.33	5-50	1	–
C.C. Lewis	63	9	167	5	33.40	2-26	–	–
P.M. Such	420.3	117	1099	31	35.45	3-50	–	–
P. Willey	173.2	33	524	12	43.66	2-36	–	–

Also bowled: N.E. Briers 3-1-8-0; I.P.Butcher 2-0-4-0; L. Potter 40-6-163-4.

the national list with 69 victims.

Clift, who left the county at the end of the season, will be hard to replace, but Leicestershire's sustained challenge for the Championship after so unpromising a start will undoubtedly convince them that the squad remains equipped to compete effectively for honours in future.

Middlesex

The rumble of internal politics involving senior players did not enhance Middlesex's hopes of success during a season in which they finally achieved virtually nothing except, perhaps, the realization of their belief that John Carr would emerge as an opening batsman of high quality.

The long-standing conflict of personalities between Phil Edmonds and Mike Gatting, the club captain, was publicly manifest in an incident during the Championship match at Bath, while John Emburey made no secret of his interest in joining another county in the role of captain. None of this can have helped the general morale of a club already shaken by its dramatic decline of status since winning the Championship in 1985.

Accordingly, Middlesex failed to find the corporate form or spirit to do more than occasionally suggest a resurgence, though, in achieving a Championship victory in May.(at Hove), they improved considerably on the previous season's first win, in August.

The success against Sussex, by three wickets, was due largely to Roland Butcher, who dominated the decisive run-chase with a century off 73 balls — the fastest of the season — but, at this point, Middlesex were still having a problem with the opening partnership — one that had persisted since the retirement of Graham Barlow.

Wilf Slack and Andrew Miller began promisingly enough with opening stands of 159, 7, 68, and 79, but thereafter the decline set in and, in June, Carr was promoted to open against the Pakistan tourists.

Carr, who made his debut in 1983 as an off-break bowler and a batsman with curiously cramped, knock-kneed stance, now began to emerge as a fluent stroke-player of excellent temperament. He opened again against Essex, at Lord's, hitting 23 fours in a splendid 156. And so he went on: 123 not out against Surrey, at the Oval, 100 before lunch against Surrey, at Lord's, and into September with a marvellous 92, at Uxbridge, to set up the second Championship win of the season.

Meanwhile, however, Middlesex had made little impression, either in the Championship or the limited-overs arena, where they failed even to reach the knock-out rounds in defence of their Benson & Hedges trophy.

Certainly, during the international matches, they missed the runs of Gatting and the wickets of Edmonds and Emburey, though vice-captain Downton deserved the highest praise for his resolute batting — particularly his unbeaten century against Surrey. But, as so often happened, having scored 337-8 in the first innings and 272-1 in the second, Middlesex lost at the Oval — albeit off the last ball — because the bowling was below par.

Most of the bowlers had their day, but it was significant that, as the season drew to its close, only Norman Cowans appeared in the national averages. Next season Edmonds will be gone and several of the other senior professionals will be looking towards retirement, rather than revitalization.

Britannic Assurance County Championship: 16th; Won 2, Lost 8, Drawn 13, No Play 1
All First-Class Matches: Won 2, Lost 8, Drawn 15, No Play 1
NatWest Bank Trophy: Lost to Nottinghamshire in 2nd round
Benson & Hedges Cup: Failed to qualify for quarter-final (4th in Group C)
Refuge Assurance League: 10th; Won 5, Lost 7, No Result 4

Championship Averages

Batting and Fielding	M	I	NO	HS	R	Avge	100	50	Ct/St
M.W. Gatting	11	18	1	196	892	52.47	2	4	10
J.D. Carr	22	37	3	156	1385	40.73	3	5	10
W.N. Slack	23	39	0	173	1419	36.38	2	7	12
J.E. Emburey	12	19	4	74	541	36.06	–	5	6
P.R. Downton	23	34	6	103*	995	35.53	1	8	47/5
A.J.T. Miller	8	13	1	97	354	29.50	–	3	1
M.R. Ramprakash	8	14	3	71	321	29.18	–	2	6
K.R. Brown	15	24	3	70	579	27.57	–	5	15
R.O. Butcher	14	18	1	118	466	27.41	1	2	13
C.T. Radley	7	10	2	45*	182	22.75	–	–	2
M.A. Roseberry	9	13	2	52	248	22.54	–	1	4
A. Needham	9	11	2	33	161	17.88	–	–	3
P.H. Edmonds	9	10	2	32	142	17.75	–	–	3
N.F. Williams	8	8	4	18*	64	16.00	–	–	1
S.P. Hughes	16	19	6	26*	174	13.38	–	–	6
A.R.C. Fraser	21	21	5	38	173	10.81	–	–	4
W.W. Daniel	15	12	8	9*	31	7.75	–	–	5
N.G. Cowans	12	14	3	24	77	7.00	–	–	3
P.C.R. Tufnell	8	8	4	12*	21	5.25	–	–	5

Also batted: J.F. Sykes (3 matches) 8, 10, 3* (2ct).

Hundreds (9)

3 J.D. Carr: 156 v Essex, Lord's; 123* v Surrey, Oval; 133 v Surrey, Lord's.

2 M.W. Gatting: 196 v Somerset, Bath; 132 v Essex, Chelmsford.

  W.N. Slack: 116 v Lancs, Old Trafford; 173 v Glamorgan, Lord's.

1 R.O. Butcher: 118 v Sussex, Hove.

  P.R. Downton: 103* v Surrey, Oval.

Bowling	O	M	R	W	Avge	Best	5wI	10wM
N.G. Cowans	281.3	63	781	44	17.75	5-43	2	–
J.F. Sykes	50	16	115	6	19.16	4-49	–	–
M.W. Gatting	41	10	137	5	27.40	3-40	–	–
P.H. Edmonds	335.1	114	733	26	28.19	4-34	–	–
J.E. Emburey	397.3	117	908	32	28.37	5-60	1	–
P.C.R. Tufnell	316.2	56	939	31	30.29	6-60	1	–
A.R.C. Fraser	533.1	128	1420	44	32.27	4-50	–	–
N.F. Williams	148.4	28	420	11	38.18	3-55	–	–
S.P. Hughes	303.1	48	955	24	39.79	3-74	–	–
W.W. Daniel	333	46	1246	29	42.96	4-69	–	–
A. Needham	155	24	508	9	56.44	4-96	–	–

Also bowled: K.R. Brown 13-1-54-3; R.O. Butcher 2.3-1-9-0; J.D. Carr 15-3-54-2; A.J.T. Miller 1-0-4-0; M.R. Ramprakash 1-0-1-0; M.A. Roseberry 5-0-25-0; W.N.Slack 25-7-69-1.

Fortunately, among their successors are several potentially exciting talents – not least the elegant Mark Ramprakash, Philip Tufnell, and the Fraser brothers, Angus and Alastair. Above all, however, Middlesex need stability, self-belief – and a little more luck than they enjoyed in 1987.

Northamptonshire

For Northants players and supporters, 1987 will always be remembered as the nearly, but not quite, summer, when the team promised so much and came so close, but finished without a title. They reached the final of the Benson & Hedges Cup and of the NatWest Trophy, yet lost both by the narrowest of margins in the last over. Despite the disadvantage of a docile pitch at Northampton and a somewhat limited attack, the club were for a period well placed to capture the County Championship for the first time in their history, only to be let down by their batting, their strongest feature. Too many 'no result' matches effectively killed off their interest in the Refuge Assurance League.

Northants were generally considered to be the best limited-overs side in the country, especially adept at chasing a big total. In Larkins, Lamb, and Bailey, they possessed three players who were all capable of producing that big, high-calibre innings that so frequently decides the outcome of a one-day game. In addition, Geoff Cook was a good and experienced opener, the much improved Capel showed the value of an excellent technique and a good temperament, Williams rediscovered his best form with bat and ball, Wild played several valuable innings, and the lower order could usually provide extra runs when required.

There can be few finer strokemakers in England than Larkins, so that it is hard to understand why he has played in only six Tests and why he was not included in the World Cup squad. Lamb, dropped from the England team, did not score as many runs for his county as hoped, but he has the ability and the determination to rectify this in the future. Although Bailey clearly favours the front foot, there have been several great players with the same preference, and he remains an excellent international prospect.

Unlike most counties, Northants, who were captained quietly and efficiently by Geoff Cook, employed with success two slow bowlers, Nick Cook and Williams, in one-day cricket. The former was close to establishing himself in the England XI as a left-hand spinner, while the latter was a much better bowler than is sometimes realized.

The main weakness lay in the seam support for the formidable Davis, which did not have sufficient penetration for three-day matches, nor the accuracy required for one-day, making the choice of Capel for England as an all-rounder rather a surprise. The club was handicapped by not having acquired in recent years the honours that their ability warranted. As a result, they did not always possess sufficient belief in themselves, which showed at Lords against Notts, when their fielding and bowling cracked under the pressure of the occasion.

Because regulations did not allow the inclusion of both their West Indians, Northants had, in Harper, the best 12th man in the world. Although this may seem hard, especially when one considers the contribution of Hadlee and Rice to Notts, it did give England-born Williams the opportunity to play.

Britannic Assurance County Championship: 7th; Won 7, Lost 4, Drawn 13
All First-Class Matches: Won 7, Lost 4, Drawn 15
NatWest Bank Trophy: Lost to Nottinghamshire in final
Benson & Hedges Cup: Lost to Yorkshire in final
Refuge Assurance League: 11th; Won 4, Lost 6, No Result 6

Championship Averages

Batting and Fielding	M	I	NO	HS	R	Avge	100	50	Ct/St
R.A. Harper	5	5	3	127*	165	82.50	1	–	6
R.G. Williams	20	24	6	104	775	43.05	1	4	5
W. Larkins	24	41	4	120	1363	36.83	3	6	17
R.J. Bailey	24	38	7	158	1099	35.45	3	2	17
A.J. Lamb	23	34	4	101*	982	32.73	1	5	20
G. Cook	24	40	9	111*	957	30.87	1	6	13
D.J. Wild	20	19	5	102*	406	29.00	1	2	14
D. Ripley	23	21	4	125*	439	25.82	1	1	37/8
S.J. Brown	3	4	3	20	24	24.00	–	–	1
D.J. Capel	19	25	3	91*	503	22.86	–	2	9
R.J. Boyd-Moss	6	10⁻	1	60	203	22.55	–	1	2
A. Walker	17	9	5	41*	78	19.50	–	–	5
N.G.B. Cook	24	22	5	64	268	15.76	–	2	10
W.W. Davis	19	18	5	25*	186	14.30	–	–	7
G. Smith	5	5	1	29*	47	11.75	–	–	1
M.A. Robinson	7	6	2	2	4	1.00	–	–	1

Also batted: S.N.V. Waterton (1 match) 4, 50*.

Hundreds (12)

3 R.J. Bailey: 152* v Yorks, Northampton; 158 v Lancs, Northampton; 137* v Sussex, Hove.
  W. Larkins: 120 v Hants, Southampton; 101* v Yorks, Northampton; 115 v Worcs, Northampton.
1 G. Cook: 111* v Worcs, Northampton.
  R.A. Harper: 127* v Worcs, Worcester.
  A.J. Lamb: 101* v Kent, Northampton.
  D. Ripley: 125* v Lancs, Old Trafford.
  D.J. Wild: 102* v Worcs, Worcester.
  R.G. Williams: 104 v Notts, Trent Bridge.

Bowling	O	M	R	W	Avge	Best	5wI	10wM
A. Walker	373.5	97	989	44	22.47	4-39	–	–
R.G. Williams	225.4	59	612	26	23.53	5-81	1	–
R.A. Harper	172	46	378	16	23.62	5-28	2	–
G. Smith	81	9	308	13	23.69	6-72	1	–
D.J. Capel	416.5	78	1266	50	25.32	7-46	4	–
W.W. Davis	591.1	104	1906	70	27.22	6-57	5	2
N.G.B. Cook	659.2	216	1478	52	28.42	6-77	1	–
M.A. Robinson	150	25	501	13	38.53	3-45	–	–
D.J. Wild	186.3	53	510	7	72.85	2-26	–	–

Also bowled: R.J. Bailey 14-5-33-1; R.J. Boyd-Moss 25-6-79-1; S.J. Brown 42-11-106-4; G. Cook 10.1-2-71-0; A.J. Lamb 2-0-18-1; W. Larkins 16.2-4-51-0; D.Ripley 9-0-89-2.

Nottinghamshire

For all the dark mutterings about 'pitch-doctoring' at Trent Bridge, few could begrudge the double of the Championship title and the NatWest Trophy as a retirement bonus for Nottinghamshire's distinguished overseas partnership of Richard Hadlee and Clive Rice. Both were persuaded to postpone their departure from county cricket for one last attempt to add further honours to the Championship success of 1981, and the result was a summer of glorious achievement for them and for the county.

Worcestershire denied them a unique hat-trick of honours by forcing them into second place in the Refuge Assurance Sunday League. But it remained doubtful whether any county had previously dominated a season as completely as Notts dominated this one.

Hadlee, arguably the greatest cricketer of his generation, ended only three wickets short of repeating the double of 1,000 runs and 100 victims he achieved in 1984. His 6-36 against Glamorgan in the final Championship game was his ninth return of five or more wickets, and set up Notts for a victory which ensured that Lancashire's remarkable late surge could not overtake them.

Hadlee's 10 years at Trent Bridge bore a rich harvest: 5,854 runs and 612 wickets at about 14 apiece. Rice topped 1,000 runs in each of his 13 seasons with Notts, accumulating 17,115 runs and taking 476 wickets. Which pair of overseas players has ever served any county with greater distinction? Rice's century in that crucial win over Glamorgan was his 37th for the county. Hadlee took five or more wickets in an innings for them 38 times. For the second successive season, he topped both batting and bowling averages for the county.

No less vital a component in Notts' *tour de force* was the off-spin and sheer capacity for toil of Eddie Hemmings, the summer's most successful slow-bowler by a distance. His 872 overs constituted the heaviest workload in the Championship, and his 88 victims offered eloquent rebuke to those who found the fuller figure a source of ribaldry. More shark than whale, perhaps, especially when pitches showed early signs of wear, as did so many at Trent Bridge.

Kevin Saxelby was a renewed force at a reduced pace, and, with Andy Pick as competitive as ever, the prolonged absence of Kevin Cooper through injury did not unduly incommode the side.

Tim Robinson was 'blooded' in the captaincy in three-day cricket, until mounting tensions compelled that the reins be handed back; with increased responsibility, there had been a slight decrease in output with the bat.

Chris Broad found 'commuting' between county and international cricket a test of form, but the continued development of Paul Johnson, the reliability of John Birch, and the startling return of Mike Newell ensured that the middle order rarely lacked substance.

Newell took over in mid-July when Randall broke a hand, immediately scored 203 not out against Derbyshire and added two more

Britannic Assurance County Championship: 1st; Won 9, Lost 1, Drawn 13, No Play 1
All First-Class Matches: Won 10, Lost 1, Drawn 14, No Play 1
NatWest Bank Trophy: Winners
Benson & Hedges Cup: Failed to qualify for quarter-final (4th in Group A)
Refuge Assurance League: 2nd; Won 9, Lost 3, No Result 4

Championship Averages

Batting and Fielding	M	I	NO	HS	R	Avge	100	50	Ct/St
R.J. Hadlee	20	27	7	133*	1075	53.75	2	6	16
C.E.B. Rice	21	30	6	138	1040	43.33	3	5	24
R.T. Robinson	13	23	4	137	808	42.52	2	2	9
B.C. Broad	10	17	4	80	503	38.69	–	4	15
P. Johnson	23	36	4	125	1232	38.50	3	5	18
M. Newell	19	33	7	203*	1001	38.50	3	3	15
D.W. Randall	11	17	1	133	601	37.56	1	3	17
J.D. Birch	21	29	2	82	774	28.66	–	7	8
E.E. Hemmings	23	25	6	75	377	19.84	–	3	4
P. Pollard	5	7	0	59	132	18.85	–	1	4
C.W. Scott	12	15	1	45	250	17.85	–	–	27/2
D.J.R. Martindale	9	13	2	103	192	17.45	1	–	3
R.A. Pick	16	15	5	42*	154	15.40	–	–	1
B.N. French	11	12	1	29	161	14.63	–	–	37/3
J.A. Afford	9	9	6	16	23	7.66	–	–	1
K. Saxelby	17	14	6	14	60	7.50	–	–	2
K.E. Cooper	6	6	1	17	22	4.40	–	–	1
M.K. Bore	6	5	1	7	13	3.25	–	–	1

Also batted: C.D. Fraser-Darling (1 match) 16.

Hundreds (15)

3 P. Johnson: 108 v Kent, Canterbury; 125 v Leics, Trent Bridge; 106 v Derbys, Trent Bridge.
  M. Newell: 203* v Derbys, Derby; 116 v Lancs, Old Trafford; 133* v Essex, Chelmsford.
  C.E.B. Rice: 115 v Yorks, Trent Bridge; 138 v Leics, Leicester; 104* v Glamorgan, Trent Bridge.
2 R.J. Hadlee: 133* v Somerset, Taunton; 101 v Somerset, Trent Bridge.
  R.T. Robinson: 102 v Northants, Trent Bridge; 137 v Essex, Chelmsford.
1 D.J.R. Martindale: 103 v Warwicks, Worksop.
  D.W. Randall: 133 v Warwicks, Edgbaston.

Bowling	O	M	R	W	Avge	Best	5wI	10wM
R.J. Hadlee	568	186	1154	97	11.89	6-20	9	2
E.E. Hemmings	816.4	267	2004	82	24.43	6-62	7	1
K.E. Cooper	158.3	50	387	15	25.80	3-38	–	–
C.E.B. Rice	296.3	89	737	28	26.32	4-42	–	–
M.K. Bore	148.2	58	344	13	26.46	4-52	–	–
K. Saxelby	393.1	101	1140	38	30.00	6-49	1	–
J.A. Afford	251.4	76	675	21	32.14	5-79	1	–
R.A. Pick	344.4	67	1185	36	32.91	4-75	–	–

Also bowled: J.D. Birch 16.2-3-55-1; C.D. Fraser-Darling 17-4-69-0; P. Johnson 6-0-64-0; M.Newell 8.3-0-45-2.

centuries to top 1,000 runs. Duncan Martindale again hinted at genuine class, and Paul Pollard also created a favourable impression when injuries and MCC Bicentenary calls strained resources.

Having both overseas players available together – and both of them gifted all-rounders – was perhaps Notts' greatest advantage. But there was enough quality evident elsewhere in the side to suggest that the loss of Hadlee and Rice need not usher the county back among the also-rans.

Somerset

Those Somerset supporters who viewed the 1987 season with trepidation after the upheavals that eventually saw Ian Botham leave Taunton in the wake of other world stars in Vivian Richards and Joel Garner will surely have been gratified by their County's performances during the summer.

Measured against 1986, as they inevitably must be, they show gratifying improvement in all competitions except the NatWest, where there was an ignominious first-round defeat at the hands of Buckinghamshire. Against that Somerset climbed five places in the Britannic Assurance County Championship, from 16th to 11th, rose from 6th to 4th in the Refuge Assurance Sunday League, and reached the quarter-finals in the Benson & Hedges Cup.

Such heartening results reflect credit on the county's management, which, having grasped an awkward nettle to the general satisfaction of its members, recruited shrewdly, and also on the thoughtful leadership of Peter Roebuck, who received the whole-hearted support of his players. Nevertheless, there remain weaknesses that must be rectified if Somerset are to challenge for the major prizes.

Firstly, the batting relied too much on Martin Crowe and Roebuck. Crowe, despite missing matches with a broken thumb, scored nearly 3,000 runs in all competitions, and his fluent strokeplay, based on the soundest of techniques, was a joy to watch. Roebuck, also handicapped by a broken finger, incurred while making a very fine hundred on a spiteful Headingley pitch in May, scored heavily. He now hits the ball much harder on the off-side, while sacrificing none of his defensive skill, and is a most formidable opener.

That said, neither Felton nor Hardy, though making useful contributions, progressed as hoped, and Harden disappointed. This put pressure on the lower order, and here Burns, secured from Essex, batted valuably in addition to keeping wicket promisingly. Rose, the young former Middlesex all-rounder, also shaped well with the bat, and Marks chipped in regularly.

A glance at the averages reveals that the bowling tended to be expensive. Jones's pace earned respect and his strength and stamina were undeniable, but he was too frequently wild on helpful pitches. Mallender bowled steadily and had some prosperous days, but was not always fit, and the fast-medium Rose also tended to break down, which was a pity as he always looked likely to take wickets. The spin bowling remained almost exclusively in Marks's charge, and he responded cheerfully. He bowled most overs and took most wickets, but would surely have benefited from capable slow-bowling support.

These criticisms apart, Somerset certainly looked to be on the right path again. Their new men, Jones, Mallender, and Burns, all did more than enough to justify their signings and were capped late in the season along with Hardy. The county can approach next season with anticipation rather than apprehension.

Britannic Assurance County Championship: 11th; Won 2, Lost 3, Drawn 19
All First-Class Matches: Won 2, Lost 3, Drawn 19
NatWest Bank Trophy: Lost to Buckinghamshire in 1st round
Benson & Hedges Cup: Lost to Northamptonshire in quarter-final
Refuge Assurance League: 4th; Won 8, Lost 4, No Result 4

Championship Averages

Batting and Fielding	M	I	NO	HS	R	Avge	100	50	Ct/St
S.R. Waugh	4	6	3	137*	340	113.33	2	1	4
M.D. Crowe	18	29	5	206*	1627	67.79	6	6	15
P.M. Roebuck	16	29	5	165*	1199	49.95	5	4	15
J.J.E. Hardy	24	40	2	119	1089	28.65	1	7	8
N.A. Felton	24	41	0	110	1094	26.68	1	5	18
N.D. Burns	24	35	7	100*	729	26.03	1	4	44/6
V.J. Marks	22	31	6	63*	635	25.40	–	2	8
G.D. Rose	18	23	4	95	470	24.73	–	1	10
R.J. Harden	19	30	6	59	568	23.66	–	2	9
J.G. Wyatt	8	13	2	58*	250	22.72	–	1	2
N.J. Pringle	11	18	1	79	347	20.41	–	2	1
G.V. Palmer	14	16	4	68	234	19.50	–	1	4
N.A. Mallender	15	17	9	20*	131	16.37	–	–	6
M.D. Harman	6	8	2	41	94	15.66	–	–	7
B.C. Rose	3	4	0	31	60	15.00	–	–	1
A.N. Jones	23	21	8	15	114	8.76	–	–	8
M.R. Davis	8	8	1	23*	57	8.14	–	–	4

Also batted: R.J. Bartlett (1 match) 0; D.J. Foster (5 matches) 9, 0*, 16 (3ct); R.G. Woolston (1 match) 0.

Hundreds (16)

6 **M.D. Crowe:** 148 v Surrey, Taunton; 102* v Middlesex, Bath; 100 v Essex, Chelmsford; 206* v Warwicks, Edgbaston; 105, v Worcs, Worcester; 148 v Glamorgan, Weston-super-Mare.

5 **P.M. Roebuck:** 103* v Surrey, Taunton; 102 v Yorks, Headingley; 135* v Worcs, Worcester; 122 v Glamorgan, Weston-super-Mare; 165* v Hants, Weston-super-Mare.

2 **S.R. Waugh:** 111* v Surrey, Oval; 137* v Glos, Bristol.

1 **N.D. Burns:** 100* v Essex, Chelmsford.

N.A. Felton: 110 v Worcs, Worcester.

J.J.E. Hardy: 119 v Glos, Taunton.

Bowling	O	M	R	W	Avge	Best	5wI	10wM
N.A. Mallender	351	61	1129	46	24.54	7-61	1	–
G.D. Rose	314.4	56	976	38	25.68	5-24	1	–
A.N. Jones	517.1	85	1800	63	28.57	7-85	3	1
V.J. Marks	778.5	203	2155	70	30.78	5-35	3	–
S.R. Waugh	112	18	348	11	31.63	3-48	–	–
D.J. Foster	111.5	10	490	13	37.69	4-56	–	–
G.V. Palmer	316	54	1162	29	40.06	4-63	–	–
M.R. Davis	153.5	25	505	11	45.90	3-43	–	–
M.D. Harman	131	35	369	7	52.71	2-38	–	–

Also bowled: M.D. Crowe 33-8-100-0; R.J. Harden 2-0-8-0; N.J. Pringle 93-14-341-4; P.M. Roebuck 13-1-54-0; R.G. Woolston 43-10-107-2.

Surrey

Surrey's overall performances in the 1987 season were those of a highly competent, sometimes brilliant, side who nevertheless failed quite to reach the highest class. That said, it is several years since the Oval emanated such spirit, unity, and cheerful optimism.

Basically it was a matter of psychological chemistry, in which the prime catalyst was Ian Greig, hastily — some thought incredibly — summoned from semi-retirement in Australia to assume the captaincy. Coincidentally, Greig's appointment followed the departure of former manager Micky Stewart, whose shrewd and disciplined method, not universally appreciated at the Oval, was mutually rewarding in his appointment as England 'supremo'.

In the event, David Smith — formerly banished to Worcester — returned to Surrey and, in common with the rest of the playing staff, immediately found rapport with the enthusiastic new captain. So much so that, despite a recurring back injury, Smith — as he demonstrated with an undefeated 110 against Worcestershire in the Benson & Hedges quarter-finals — became a substantial asset to Surrey's batting line-up.

Greig, meanwhile, established that the responsibilities of leadership had not inhibited his all-round ability with bat and ball. Nor did he allow a broken finger to impede his leadership-by-example. This was typified by a fine performance at the Oval, when he claimed four wickets for 47 runs, held two stinging catches, and would surely have doomed Yorkshire to defeat had not rain intervened.

That match also produced a magnificent century from Alec Stewart and an imperious partnership with Monte Lynch (87), and, against Middlesex at the Oval, the same pair put on 208 in 42 overs. This was familiar stuff from Lynch, who also hit a century before lunch at Cheltenham, with 17 fours and two sixes.

But Stewart surpassed them all against Somerset, again at the Oval, when, after taking five superb catches as stand-in wicket-keeper, he hit his third century of the season in the first innings and 93 in the second.

Martin Bicknell also made a big impression in the same game, snapping up six for 63 in the first innings. Brother Darren, meanwhile, was having a mixed season. Generally out of touch as an up-and-coming opening bat, he hit his maiden hundred against Hampshire (Marshall *et al*) and was out for one in his next match . . . at Fenners. All part of a professional player's moral training.

Surrey's younger players, in general, continued to mature well under the influence of Greig and Jesty — another whose example has been thoroughly professional. Chris Bullen, Nick Falkner, Keith Medlycott, Mark Feltham . . . all have played their part in Surrey's renewed drive.

Above all, however, Surrey owed their stinging power to Tony Gray and Sylvester Clarke, neck and neck at the summit of the bowling averages throughout a season highlighted, perhaps, by Clarke's hat-trick against Essex, at Colchester.

Britannic Assurance County Championship: 4th; Won 7, Lost 4, Drawn 13
All First-Class Matches: Won 7, Lost 4, Drawn 15
NatWest Bank Trophy: Lost to Northamptonshire in 2nd round
Benson & Hedges Cup: Lost to Yorkshire in semi-final
Refuge Assurance League: 8th, Won 6, Lost 6, No Result 2

Championship Averages

Batting and Fielding	M	I	NO	HS	R	Avge	100	50	Ct/St
A.J. Stewart	21	33	2	132	1217	39.25	3	8	20
D.M. Smith	16	26	4	121*	847	38.50	1	7	10
C.J. Richards	18	22	4	172*	683	37.94	1	4	57/7
D.J. Bicknell	11	19	3	105	599	37.43	1	4	5
T.E. Jesty	23	35	5	124*	1074	35.80	1	5	7
M.A. Lynch	24	37	5	128*	1057	33.03	2	5	23
G.S. Clinton	17	28	2	93	825	31.73	–	7	5
K.T. Medlycott	23	28	5	153	719	31.26	1	5	14
I.A. Greig	24	33	5	88	778	27.78	–	5	16
G.E. Brown	4	5	4	8*	26	26.00	–	–	6/–
C.K. Bullen	9	11	3	57	172	21.50	–	1	12
D.J. Thomas	16	16	4	49	220	18.33	–	–	5
D.M. Ward	5	9	0	44	141	15.66	–	–	7/–
M.P. Bicknell	14	14	7	18	108	15.42	–	–	5
A.H. Gray	9	7	3	35	54	13.50	–	–	4
N.J. Falkner	3	4	0	29	47	11.75	–	–	–
M.A. Feltham	10	11	3	18	90	11.25	–	–	5
S.T. Clarke	14	15	1	44	131	9.35	–	–	8

Also batted: R.J. Doughty (1 match) 0, 5 (2ct); C.S. Mays (2 matches) 5*, 2 (1ct).

Hundreds (10)

3 A.J. Stewart: 127 v Middlesex, Oval; 132 v Yorks, Oval; 105 v Somerset, Oval.
2 M.A. Lynch: 128* v Somerset, Taunton; 114 v Glos, Cheltenham.
1 D.J. Bicknell: 105 v Hants, Oval.
  T.E. Jesty: 124* v Lancs, Old Trafford.
  K.T. Medlycott: 153 v Kent, Oval.
  C.J. Richards: 172* v Kent, Oval.
  D.M. Smith: 121* v Worcs, Oval.

Bowling	O	M	R	W	Avge	Best	5wI	10wM
A.H. Gray	261.1	56	667	44	15.15	5-46	2	–
S.T. Clarke	440.4	111	1123	66	17.01	8-62	6	2
T.E. Jesty	72.4	11	212	10	21.20	6-81	1	–
M.P. Bicknell	363.2	94	997	42	23.73	6-63	2	–
C.K. Bullen	190.4	57	504	19	26.52	6-119	1	–
M.A. Feltham	377.5	91	1108	35	31.65	4-24	–	–
I.A. Greig	397.4	82	1220	35	34.85	4-47	–	–
K.T. Medlycott	485.4	134	1469	38	38.65	5-103	1	–
D.J. Thomas	348	58	1205	31	38.87	5-73	1	–

Also bowled: R.J. Doughty 26-3-76-0; M.A. Lynch 51.3-8-184-2; C.S. Mays 56-7-201-2.

Sussex

Starting it against the background of a palace revolution in which their coach, Stuart Storie, was brought down, Sussex endured their worst season in living memory. It was by no means the first time they finished in the cellar, but not even on the three previous occasions since the war when they held up the table were they confined to just one win. Moreover, Sussex were the only county that Middlesex, who finished 16th, were able to beat – twice! Also, they failed to make a mark in any of the limited overs competitions.

It is not unusual for counties to be discomfited by their overseas star being on tour, and, no doubt, Sussex's prospects were dimmed by Imran Khan's absence. But even in past seasons, they had had to make do without him for a large part of their fixture list. There were, however, other problems.

Adrian Jones, so promising a pace bowler, transferred his allegiance to Somerset during the winter.˙It is said that others on the staff had packed their bags, but stayed after Storie was asked to go. No replacement as a coach could be found, and, in a difficult season, the county had to make do with part-timers in John Snow and Jim Parks.

Sussex's sole Championship win of the season came quite early. In only their third match, following a trouncing by Derbyshire and a narrow shave against Gloucestershire, they beat Worcestershire away. This victory was in no small measure due to Ian Gould, who, at the end of the season, was left with no other course but to lay down the captaincy – only a year after his day of glory at Lord's when he held aloft the NatWest Trophy.

Problems began to pile up in the wake of the win at Worcester. A little over a fortnight afterwards, Sussex played Middlesex, and Wayne Daniel, as he has done on many visits to Hove, left behind a trail of broken bones. This time, they belonged to Parker, Sussex's main run-getter in 1986, and Lenham who, on the evidence of his maiden first-class hundred against Pakistan shortly before, was in prime form.

Parker missed four games in June and never afterwards discovered his best form. Lenham returned after 10 weeks, only to be struck devastatingly on the foot by a full toss from Yorkshire's Dennis during his very first innings back. There ended the youngster's season – on August 10.

It was not only Sussex's batting that was often below strength. During a season in which their bowling resources were already short of experience, they had to make do for long stretches without Pigott and Le Roux. Pigott was suspended for a month for a misdemeanour outside the ground and out of playing hours, while Le Roux, in his last season with the county, went in the back with 10 matches remaining.

Happily, Sussex's distress brought out the best in their all-rounder, Colin Wells, who topped their batting aggregates and averages and, delivering most overs, was also their main wicket-taker, the only one to claim over 50. He was unlucky not to get recognition from the England selectors for any of the winter tours. The only other Sussex batsman to

Britannic Assurance County Championship: 17th; Won 1, Lost 8, Drawn 14, No Play 1
All First-Class Matches: Won 1, Lost 8, Drawn 15, No Play 1
NatWest Bank Trophy: Lost to Gloucestershire in 2nd round
Benson & Hedges Cup: Failed to qualify for quarter-final (5th in Group D)
Refuge Assurance League: 16th; Won 4, Lost 8, No Result 4

Championship Averages

Batting and Fielding	M	I	NO	HS	R	Avge	100	50	Ct/St
C.M. Wells	23	38	7	148*	1411	45.51	5	6	15
D.A. Reeve	16	22	8	87*	576	41.14	–	6	14
G.S. Le Roux	13	15	5	73	375	37.50	–	2	3
I.J. Gould	21	29	5	111	792	33.00	1	4	23/–
A.P. Wells	22	36	4	161*	1003	31.34	3	3	11
S.J.S. Kimber	7	8	2	54	155	25.83	–	1	1
A.M. Green	20	36	2	115	821	24.14	1	3	9
R.I. Alikhan	18	33	3	78	663	22.10	–	3	9
N.J. Lenham	3	4	3	12*	22	22.00	–	–	2
P.W.G. Parker	18	31	4	85	548	20.29	–	2	15
A.C.S. Pigott	19	27	4	62	456	19.82	–	2	12
P. Moores	17	23	2	55	380	18.09	–	2	19/–
D.K. Standing	16	28	3	56	438	17.52	–	2	5
P.A.W. Heseltine	17	18	3	26	172	11.46	–	–	3
K. Greenfield	2	4	0	18	34	8.50	–	–	2
A.N. Babington	14	15	8	16	58	8.28	–	–	3

Also batted: S.D. Myles (2 matches) 0, 1, 18* (1ct); C.I.O. Ricketts (3 matches) 29 (1ct); I.C. Waring (2 matches) 0*, 0*, 0 (1ct).

Hundreds (10)

5 C.M. Wells: 106 v Derbys, Chesterfield; 140* v Kent, Hove; 148* v Essex, Eastbourne; 118 v Warwicks, Hove; 105* v Somerset, Hove;
3 A.P. Wells: 119 v Middlesex, Hove; 161* v Kent, Hove; 119 v Warwicks, Nuneaton.
1 I.J. Gould: 111 v Northants, Hove.
  A.M. Green: 115 v Worcs, Worcester.

Bowling	O	M	R	W	Avge	Best	5wI	10wM
G.S. Le Roux	266.5	54	768	32	24.00	5-64	1	–
D.A. Reeve	427	103	1145	41	27.92	7-37	1	–
C.M. Wells	527.1	97	1483	52	28.51	6-34	2	–
A.C.S. Pigott	455.2	86	1443	45	32.06	5-32	3	–
P.A.W. Heseltine	295.2	71	869	21	41.38	3-33	–	–
A.N. Babington	248.1	44	898	21	42.76	3-44	–	–
S.J.S. Kimber	136	19	550	12	45.83	2-13	–	–
C.I.O. Ricketts	71.4	8	253	5	50.60	2-40	–	–

Also bowled: R.I. Alikhan 0.1-0-4-0; I.J. Gould 1-0-1-0; A.M. Green 38-7-130-4; S.D. Myles 4-0-28-0; P.W.G. Parker 2.2-0-15-0; D.K. Standing 30.2-6-147-2; I.C. Waring 50-9-172-2; A.P. Wells 22-1-119-3.

pass the thousand mark, although he did not do himself full justice, was the younger Wells brother, Alan.

To add to Sussex's agony, Ian Greig, whom they had dispensed with two seasons before, was making a success of captaining Surrey, who, for their part, paid off Trevor Jesty at the end of the season. Sussex were not long in announcing that they had plans to recruit Jesty as captain for 1988, although they showed no interest in Edmonds, who parted from Middlesex.

Warwickshire

At the last count before the winter recess, Warwickshire had vacancies for a cricket committee chairman, a captain, and a commercial manager. In order, the gaps were created by the resignation of Bob Willis, the planned retirement of Norman Gifford (though his decision was not necessarily irrevocable after the failure to entice John Emburey to Edgbaston), and the departure of Jim Cumbes to Lancashire.

Willis spent only seven weeks at the head of an important policy-making committee. The obvious political undertones of his hasty exit – not least because of a clash with the general secretary, David Heath – inevitably fuelled the mood of revolt among the membership. Within a week of the season ending, there was a successful call for a special general meeting for the second time in two years.

All this tended to distract from the more regular cause of irritation – the poor playing record. Warwickshire finished 15th in the County Championship and were bottom of the Sunday League (their third wooden spoon since winning the title in 1980). The two knock-out competitions brought nothing better, and in all cricket, they achieved only five wins in 44 attempts against first-class counties.

The eagerly anticipated restructuring of the new-ball attack was a success in that Tony Merrick and Allan Donald, who alternated in the overseas position, took 94 wickets between them, but overall a disappointment because Gladstone Small played in only half of the Championship programme because of a strained side.

The supporting pace bowlers, Gordon Parsons and Tim Munton, were also affected by injuries – though not before Parsons was awarded a county cap – and Gifford's contribution understandably declined in a summer when Edgbaston pitches invariably suited the seamers.

Yet the bowling was not the meat of the problem. Warwickshire managed only 48 batting bonus points and were flattered that five batsmen reached 1,000 runs. Dennis Amiss, who retired as the most prolific batsman of all-time for his county, Andy Lloyd, and Geoff Humpage were heavier scorers in previous seasons, while Andy Moles and Asif Din relied on a late rush of form for their respectable figures. Too often, the batting broke down under pressure. Paul Smith suffered badly from injuries and his shuttling up and down the order, and the non-registration of Alvin Kallicharran – a sacrifice made to get in the two overseas bowlers – left a massive hole at No.3. This situation is unlikely to change unless the West Indian wins his protracted struggle to be reclassified as an English-qualified player.

The end-of-season advance by Asif Din, who won his county cap on moving into the problem first-wicket position, and Moles, who scored three centuries in four innings, was something at least for the harassed county to cling to as the political storm gathered in the wake of the summer's rain clouds.

The road to recovery will be a long one. Any immediate improvement will depend on their winter shopping for senior players, and in the longer

Britannic Assurance County Championship: 15th; Won 2, Lost 7, Drawn 15
All First-Class Matches: Won 2, Lost 7, Drawn 16
NatWest Bank Trophy: Lost to Gloucesterhire in quarter-final
Benson & Hedges Cup: Failed to qualify for quarter-final (4th in Group B)
Refuge Assurance League: 17th; Won 3, Lost 9, No Result 4

Championship Averages

Batting and Fielding	M	I	NO	HS	R	Avge	100	50	Ct/St
G.W. Humpage	23	40	8	99*	1315	41.09	–	13	31/2
Asif Din	22	36	4	115*	1056	33.00	2	5	10
A.J. Moles	24	45	3	151	1355	32.26	4	3	24
T.A. Lloyd	24	45	2	162	1353	31.46	2	5	11
D.L. Amiss	24	44	1	123	1276	29.67	2	6	8
G.J. Parsons	15	19	2	67*	422	24.82	–	3	6
A.C. Storie	15	25	8	66*	391	23.00	–	1	14
P.A. Smith	17	31	5	89	506	19.46	–	2	1
N.M.K. Smith	2	4	1	23	56	18.66	–	–	1
E.T. Milburn	3	4	2	24	37	18.50	–	–	2
G.C. Small	12	20	4	42	257	16.06	–	–	4
A.A. Donald	10	10	3	37*	111	15.85	–	–	1
A.T. Merrick	14	19	5	74*	220	15.71	–	1	6
G.A. Tedstone	10	14	1	51	180	13.84	–	1	13/2
T.A. Munton	15	16	5	38	116	10.54	–	–	3
N. Gifford	24	25	12	36	131	10.07	–	–	1
D.A. Thorne	9	14	1	43	116	8.92	–	–	10

Also batted: A.R.K. Pierson (1 match) 0 (2ct).

Hundreds (10)

4 A.J. Moles: 145* v Somerset, Edgbaston; 137 v Worcs, Edgbaston; 151 v Kent, Edgbaston; 101 v Yorks, Scarborough.
2 D.L. Amiss: 123 v Worcs, Worcester; 120 v Leics, Hinckley.
  Asif Din: 110 v Sussex, Hove; 115* v Glos, Edgbaston.
  T.A. Lloyd: 151* v Glamorgan, Edgbaston; 162 v Sussex, Hove.

Bowling	O	M	R	W	Avge	Best	5wI	10wM
A.T. Merrick	433.3	71	1439	57	25.24	7-45	4	1
T.A. Munton	336.1	70	982	38	25.84	6-69	2	–
A.A. Donald	281.4	35	968	37	26.16	6-74	2	–
N. Gifford	447	134	1116	36	31.00	5-71	2	–
G.C. Small	350	70	1067	34	31.38	4-80	–	–
G.J. Parsons	391.5	73	1178	33	35.69	5-80	1	–
P.A. Smith	177.5	21	783	17	46.05	3-31	–	–
Asif Din	52	9	233	5	46.60	3-86	–	–
A.J. Moles	173.4	47	492	9	54.66	3-50	–	–

Also bowled: G.W. Humpage 2-0-8-0; T.A. Lloyd 1-0-1-0; E.T. Milburn 36-6-128-2; A.R.K. Pierson 26-7-102-3; N.M.K. Smith 42-6-152-4; D.A. Thorne 13-2-45-0.

term they must hope to bring through more youngsters with a made-at-Edgbaston pedigree. Their record in this respect has been a matter for concern in recent years.

Worcestershire

There was no more deserving captain than Phil Neale – nor more deserving county than Worcestershire – when he held aloft the Refuge Assurance League trophy on the last Sunday of the season. It was the fulfilment of a lengthy rebuilding programme, organized with great purpose by front-of-house administrators Duncan Fearnley and Mike Jones, and carried out faithfully by Neale in his six years in charge on the field.

There were times when success seemed to be on a distant horizon. Worcestershire were 16th in the Championship in 1983 and your correspondent recalls Neale's concern in that difficult summer. Worried that his fledgling players were being affected by the coldness of statistics in print, he asked: 'Do you really need to mention we haven't won for so long?'

Neale was able to smile when reminded of that incident on the morning after New Road was awash with champagne last September. Worcestershire worked hard to snatch the title by winning their last five games, and celebrated even harder. It was their first major trophy since 1974. And, of course, it was the year of Ian Botham and, to a lesser extent, the injury-hounded Graham Dilley.

Worcestershire signed the two England players with the idea that they would be the finishing touch to a bright, enthusiastic side who had finished fifth in the championship and reached the two knock-out semi-finals in 1986. What they did not realize at the time was that they would lose the services of David Smith and Dipak Patel. In the event, the part-time contributions of Botham and Dilley did not easily compensate for the full-time output of the two players whom they effectively replaced.

For a long time, it seemed that Worcestershire's ambition would be served only by an increase of 2,000 in their membership. They failed to make an impact in the two knock-out tournaments, dropped four places in the Championship, but suddenly got the chemistry right in the Refuge League. Botham's performances in this competition were immense. Like Tim Curtis and Graeme Hick, he scored more than 500 runs, and in his Sunday role as an opener he enjoyed four consecutive century partnerships with Curtis – a League record. Curtis played so consistently that more and more people wonder for how much longer he can be ignored by England, and Hick again showed what England are denied by the qualification rules by scoring 2,970 in all cricket.

England did take note of Neal Radford, the highest wicket-taker in the Championship for the second time in three seasons. His willingness to bowl long spells, coupled with his old-fashioned attacking instincts, brought him 109 first-class victims, but Worcestershire did not provide as much support as was envisaged at the start of the season. Dilley played in only six Championship matches, Botham bowled in only seven three-day games, and Phil Newport's effectiveness declined, partly because he had fewer opportunities in favourable conditions when the England bowlers were in the side.

Britannic Assurance County Championship: 9th; Won 5, Lost 4, Drawn 15
All First-Class Matches: Won 5, Lost 4, Drawn 16
NatWest Bank Trophy: Lost to Essex in 2nd round
Benson & Hedges Cup: Lost to Surrey in quarter-final
Refuge Assurance League: 1st; Won 11, Lost 4, No Result 1

Championship Averages

Batting and Fielding	M	I	NO	HS	R	Avge	100	50	Ct/St
R.K. Illingworth	19	19	11	120*	448	56.00	1	1	9
G.A. Hick	24	37	2	173	1868	53.37	8	6	13
T.S. Curtis	24	39	6	138*	1566	47.45	4	5	10
P.J. Newport	24	25	12	64*	534	41.07	–	3	8
P.A. Neale	24	33	6	103*	925	34.25	2	4	9
D.B. D'Oliveira	24	36	3	121*	975	29.54	1	5	24
I.T. Botham	11	14	1	126*	366	28.15	1	1	7
S.J. Rhodes	24	31	7	80	544	22.66	–	3	51/6
M.J. Weston	14	21	2	54	426	22.42	–	3	5
G.J. Lord	11	18	2	66	347	21.68	–	2	3
G.R. Dilley	6	4	1	29	40	13.33	–	–	–
N.V. Radford	23	21	4	31	197	11.58	–	–	14
S.R. Lampitt	13	14	3	24	111	10.09	–	–	6
L.K. Smith	2	4	1	20*	30	10.00	–	–	1
A.P. Pridgeon	16	10	2	19	57	7.12	–	–	7

Also batted: S.M. McEwan (5 matches) 1.

Hundreds (17)

8 G.A. Hick: 107 v Sussex, Worcester; 138 v Glos, Gloucester; 132 v Somerset, Worcester; 173 v Middlesex, Lord's; 107 v Northants, Northampton; 126 v Warwicks, Edgbaston; 156 v Essex, Colchester; 140* v Northants, Worcester
4 T.S. Curtis: 106* v Sussex, Worcester; 138* v Notts, Trent Bridge; 110 v Notts, Kidderminster; 129 v Middlesex, Lord's.
2 P.A. Neale: 103* v Somerset, Worcester; 100* v Essex, Colchester.
1 I.T. Botham: 126* v Somerset, Taunton.
  D.B. D'Oliveira: 121* v Derbys, Worcester.
  R.K. Illingworth: 120* v Warwicks, Worcester.

Bowling	O	M	R	W	Avge	Best	5wI	10wM
G.R. Dilley	124	25	387	21	18.42	6-42	2	–
N.V. Radford	741.5	123	2269	109	20.81	8-55	8	1
A.P. Pridgeon	334	77	891	28	31.82	7-44	1	–
I.T. Botham	125.3	17	450	14	32.14	3-51	–	–
S.M. McEwan	87.4	12	298	9	33.11	3-29	–	–
G.A. Hick	301.2	59	980	25	39.20	4-31	–	–
R.K. Illingworth	466.2	115	1331	33	40.33	4-28	–	–
P.J. Newport	498.4	79	1803	42	42.92	4-28	–	–
M.J. Weston	96	18	326	7	46.57	2-37	–	–

Also bowled: T.S. Curtis 19-2-94-2; D.B. D'Oliveira 31.2-5-147-3; S.R. Lampitt 79.2-11-273-3; G.J. Lord 2-0-24-0; P.A. Neale 3.1-0-12-0; L.K. Smith 7-2-20-1.

Spin bowling was a problem. Richard Illingworth, who had a good season with the bat, had his best spells in one-day cricket, and Hick was used more and more with his previously untried off-breaks.

The absence of a regular partner for Curtis was the only serious flaw in the batting, once Neale had recovered from his worst start to a season. Newport and Steve Rhodes, who ended on a high note with his wicket-keeping, chipped in with more than 500 runs each from numbers seven and eight.

Yorkshire

Yorkshire will look back on 1987 with mixed feelings. Before the season started there were dire prophecies concerning the effect on their batting of entering a season Boycott-less for the first time since 1962, and there was also concern over the general quality of their bowling and reservations about Phil Carrick's ability, after 17 years in the ranks, to take on the role of commissioned officer.

During the early part of the campaign such fears seemed groundless. The county were at or near the top of the Championship table, they met with success in the Sunday League, and their triumphant progress through the Benson & Hedges competition culminated when they beat Northants in a pulsating final at Lord's to carry off the Cup for the first time.

Thereafter, however, the wheels undeniably fell off. Yorkshire lost their NatWest quarter-final to Leicestershire, and failed to win a Sunday League match after July 12th. Indeed, of their last 21 games in all competitions, only two were won, Leicestershire and Gloucestershire both being defeated in the County Championship. Eighth position in the Championship, though a marginal improvement over the previous year, was disappointing after so spectacular a start. So sudden and complete a loss of form indicates that much remains to be done in the areas of application and intestinal fortitude.

Individually, gratifying advances were made by Richard Blakey and Paul Jarvis. Blakey, at 20, was the side's heaviest scorer. His unbeaten 204 against Gloucestershire made him the county's youngest double centurion. As impressive as Blakey's scoring feats were his technique and temperament. A sound, watchful player, he displayed many handsome strokes, particularly on the off-side, and should go far in the game.

Jarvis, 21 at the start of the season, was the highest wicket-taker with 81 in first-class matches. His pace was at times genuinely fast, and his stamina remarkable. On his best days he bowled an attacking length at off-stump and sorely troubled even the best players. His selection for England's winter tours was well deserved.

Of other batsmen, Moxon again looked a class player and averaged over 40. Only the infrequency with which he truly dominates opposing attacks is preventing him from forcing himself into the England side. Metcalfe, who plundered one-day bowling, will be a little disappointed with his three-day batting, but he is too gifted not to regain his rich scoring touch of 1986. Bairstow played a number of belligerent innings but Love, despite some excellent performances in the Benson & Hedges Cup, and Sharp disappointed. Robinson, whose refreshingly direct approach brought him success more than once, would benefit from greater opportunity.

The bowling, Jarvis apart, was moderate. Sidebottom, not always fit, was a little expensive, as were Fletcher and Peter Hartley. Carrick bowled his slow left-arm steadily, but was rarely penetrative even on helpful pitches. The lack of variety in Yorkshire's attack might be

Britannic Assurance County Championship: 8th; Won 7, Lost 3, Drawn 13, No Play 1
All First-Class Matches: Won 7, Lost 4, Drawn 13, No Play 1
NatWest Bank Trophy: Lost to Leicestershire in quarter-final
Benson & Hedges Cup: Winners
Refuge Assurance League: 13th; Won 5, Lost 8, No Result 3

Championship Averages

Batting and Fielding	M	I	NO	HS	R	Avge	100	50	Ct/St
R.J. Blakey	23	36	5	204*	1343	43.32	4	6	26
M.D. Moxon	21	35	4	130	1298	41.87	2	10	23
P.E. Robinson	6	11	2	95	330	36.66	–	2	7
D.L. Bairstow	19	22	1	128	695	33.09	2	2	30/4
A.A. Metcalfe	22	38	4	113	1010	29.70	1	6	8
K. Sharp	20	32	4	81*	751	26.82	–	6	6
J.D. Love	20	28	6	79*	590	26.81	–	4	7
C. Shaw	6	5	4	22*	24	24.00	–	–	–
I.G. Swallow	4	7	2	55	107	21.40	–	1	2
S.N. Hartley	9	16	1	63	284	18.93	–	2	3
P.J. Hartley	21	25	7	49	332	18.44	–	–	7
P. Carrick	23	28	2	61	450	17.30	–	2	8
P.W. Jarvis	22	24	11	32	212	16.30	–	–	5
A. Sidebottom	17	21	5	33	260	16.25	–	–	5
S.D. Fletcher	15	12	6	15	61	10.16	–	–	3

Also batted: S.J. Dennis (2 matches) 4, 1. R. Berry (2ct) played in three matches but did not bat.

Hundreds (9)

4 R.J. Blakey: 101* v Glamorgan, Cardiff; 124* v Lancs, Old Trafford; 108 v Northants, Northampton; 204* v Glos, Headingley.
2 D.L. Bairstow: 104 v Derbys, Harrogate; 128 v Leics, Scarborough.
  M.D. Moxon: 130 v Derbys, Harrogate; 104 v Essex, Headingley.
1 A.A. Metcalfe: 113 v Sussex, Sheffield.

Bowling	O	M	R	W	Avge	Best	5wI	10wM
P.W. Jarvis	596.2	137	1831	75	24.41	7-82	2	–
P. Carrick	534.4	189	1199	48	24.97	5-42	1	–
I.G. Swallow	84	19	267	10	26.70	7-95	1	–
A. Sidebottom	425.1	80	1182	42	28.14	4-46	–	–
S.D. Fletcher	276.3	54	903	32	28.21	4-22	–	–
C. Shaw	95.2	21	268	9	29.77	6-64	1	–
P.J. Hartley	485	86	1641	46	35.67	4-52	–	–

Also bowled: D.L. Bairstow 5-0-29-0; P.J. Berry 14-3-55-1; S.J. Dennis 47-8-168-2; S.N. Hartley 12-2-50-2; J.D. Love 99.2-13-345-4; A.A. Metcalfe 12.2-1-62-3; M.D. Moxon 29-7-78-1; K. Sharp 37.1-6-189-1.

alleviated if more chances are given to the young off-spinners Swallow and Berry.

Oxford and Cambridge

The 143rd University Match ended in a discontented draw after Oxford, having surprisingly held authority for the first two days, failed to threaten Cambridge in the second innings. It was, at least, a match distinguished by a maiden hundred from the Oxford freshman Crawley (140) and some firm strokeplay by both Hooper (89) and Bail (90), which comfortably saved the game for Cambridge.

On the first morning Cambridge were soon in trouble against Oxford's opening bowlers, Firth and Henderson, losing three wickets for 18 runs. Price, in his second year of captaincy, staged some recovery, with top score of 46, but Cambridge were all out for 207. However, Oxford started in equal distress, losing their first three wickets for 11 runs to good fast bowling by Scott and Perry.

Some positive batting in the last hour by Kilborn and Sardesai revived Oxford, and these two continued next morning for an important third-wicket partnership of 80. Then entered Mark Crawley to play his invaluable innings of 140.

Crawley, who won the 1986 Daily Telegraph Schools Award for batsmen (under-19) while at Manchester Grammar School, had played no innings of note in The Parks prior to Lord's. Yet he joined M.J.K. Smith and the Nawab of Pataudi as only the third Oxford freshman to score a hundred in the University Match since World War II.

It was a sixth-wicket partnership by Crawley and Weale that gave Oxford dominance at 326-6. Weale's tenacity, with much glancing and cutting, brought him a career best score of 76, while Crawley profited with many perfectly timed straight drives. Oxford declared with a first-innings lead of 140.

Oxford's hopes were further inspired that evening when Firth once again had Cambridge's prime batsman Atherton lbw early in the innings, this time for 0.

Atherton, a contemporary of Crawley's at Manchester GS, may not have flourished at Lord's, but his batting prowess at Fenners certainly gave a much required boost to University cricket morale against the counties. Indeed his timing and composure had perhaps provided the most striking spectacle for Cambridge since Majid Khan in 1970-72. Next season, in only his second year, he will be captain.

Oxford started the final day full of optimism. But Hooper, from Latymer Upper, and Tremellem, of Bradfield, batted forcefully from the start and made 122 in 100 minutes. Bail then took over the attacking role and by lunch Cambridge were clearly in command.

Hooper, in only his third match, made an excellent 89 before his departure first ball afterwards. However, runs still flowed handsomely off Bail's bat, including three sixes, and thoughts even arose of a Cambridge declaration. Bail, who made 174 in the 1986 University Match, came to Lord's this time with a top score of only 49. Recovering his form of old, he reached 90 before he was caught at deep mid-on, an event which finally killed any hopes of a finish.

Cambridge University v Oxford University

Match drawn
Played at Lord's, 1, 2, 3, July
Toss: Cambridge. Umpires: J.H. Harris and J.A. Jameson

Cambridge

P.A.C. Bail	lbw b Henderson	5	(4)	c Kilborn b Weale	90
M.A. Atherton	lbw b Firth	7		lbw b Firth	0
A.M. Hooper	b Edwards	15	(1)	c Tooley b Edwards	89
D.J. Fell†	c Kilborn b Henderson	0	(5)	not out	67
D.G. Price*	b Firth	46	(6)	c Kilborn b Tooley	57
S.R. Gorman	c Cope b Crawley	26			
J.M. Tremellem	b Edwards	28	(3)	b Edwards	39
G.A. Pointer	lbw b Firth	33			
J.N. Perry	b Weale	10			
A.M.G. Scott	not out	11			
M.R. Middleton	b Crawley	6			
Extras	(B1, LB6, W3, NB10)	20		(B2, LB8, W2, NB13)	25
		207		(5 wkts dec)	**367**

Oxford

R.E. Morris	lbw b Scott	0	(2)	not out	13
A.R. Beech	c Fell b Perry	1	(1)	c Fell b Pointer	6
M.J. Kilborn	c & b Scott	59		not out	6
C.D.M. Tooley*	lbw b Scott	5			
R.D. Sardesai	lbw b Atherton	40			
M.A. Crawley	b Scott	140			
S.D. Weale	b Scott	76			
I.M. Henderson	not out	4			
J.E.B. Cope†	did not bat				
P.G. Edwards	"				
T. Firth	"				
Extras	(B7, LB7, W2, NB6)	22		(LB2, NB2)	4
	(7 wkts dec)	**347**		(1 wkt)	**29**

Oxford	O	M	R	W	O	M	R	W
Firth	21	4	64	3	26	6	101	1
Henderson	9	0	29	2	12	1	75	0
Edwards	22	7	50	2	22	9	63	2
Weale	13	4	27	1	11	2	25	1
Crawley	7.1	1	30	2	17	6	38	0
Kilborn					3	0	23	0
Tooley					5.3	1	21	1
Morris					2	0	11	0

Cambridge	O	M	R	W	O	M	R	W
Scott	33.3	7	97	5				
Perry	19	3	50	1	3	0	14	0
Pointer	23	2	61	0	5	1	9	1
Middleton	15	1	47	0				
Atherton	22	0	66	1	1	0	4	0
Tremellem	2	0	12	0				

Fall of Wickets

Wkt	CU 1st	OU 1st	CU 2nd	OU 2nd
1st	16	0	1	13
2nd	16	5	123	–
3rd	18	11	183	–
4th	54	91	261	–
5th	104	135	367	–
6th	122	326	–	–
7th	158	347	–	–
8th	177	–	–	–
9th	190	–	–	–
10th	207	–	–	–

Cambridge University

Results: Played 8; Lost 3, Drawn 5

First-Class Averages

Batting	M	I	NO	HS	R	Avge
M.A. Atherton†	8	13	2	109*	411	37.36
J.M. Tremellem†	4	6	2	39	131	32.75
A.M. Hooper†	3	4	0	89	112	28.00
D.J. Fell†	8	13	1	67*	252	21.00
D.G. Price†	7	11	0	57	228	20.72
P.A.C. Bail†	8	13	0	90	257	19.76
R. Bate	3	4	0	36	65	16.25
R. Clitheroe	3	4	0	36	63	15.75
G.A. Pointer†	7	10	3	33	101	14.42
S.R. Gorman	7	11	1	39	117	11.70
S.D. Heath	4	7	1	26	54	9.00
M.S. Ahluwahlia	4	7	0	17	53	7.57
R.J. Hart	6	9	1	12	46	5.75
A.M.G. Scott†	7	10	4	11*	17	5.66
J.E. Davidson	2	4	0	5	11	2.75

Also batted: M.R. Middleton† (2 matches) 6;
S. Palmer (1 match) 18; J.N. Perry† (3 matches)
0, 10; T.M. Verghese (1 match) 2.

Hundreds (1)

1 M.A. Atherton: 109* v Derbyshire, Cambridge

Bowling	O	M	R	W	Avge	Best
Perry	66.5	12	193	8	24.15	3-56
Scott	250.3	50	744	18	41.33	5-97
Davidson	79	10	274	6	45.66	3-101
Hart	166.2	40	477	9	53.00	2-19
Pointer	171	25	543	10	54.30	3-52
Atherton	100.5	8	320	5	64.00	1-14

Also bowled: Middleton 36-5-119-1;
Palmer 16-3-57-1; Price 5-1-24-1;
Tremellem 35-4-179-1; Verghese 22.2-1-110-1.

Fielding

7 Clitheroe (5ct, 2st); 6 Atherton; 5 Fell;
4 Gorman; 3 Scott; 1 Ahluwahlia, Bail, Bate,
Davidson, Hart, Perry, Pointer, Tremellem.

Oxford University

Results: Played 7; Drawn 7

First-Class Averages

Batting	M	I	NO	HS	R	Avge
R.D. Sardesai†	6	8	1	63*	220	31.42
M.J. Kilborn†	7	11	2	59	266	29.55
M.A. Crawley†	7	10	1	140	263	29.22
C.D.M. Tooley†	7	9	1	61*	178	22.25
S.D. Weale†	7	8	0	76	165	20.62
R.E. Morris†	6	9	2	34	98	14.00
D.A. Hagan	3	4	0	37	52	13.00
P.G. Edwards†	7	7	4	8	23	7.66
A.R. Beech†	4	7	0	33	49	7.00
I.M. Henderson†	6	7	1	14	33	5.50
T. Firth†	6	6	0	10	32	5.33
J.E.B. Cope†	7	7	3	4	17	4.25

Also batted: A.A.G. Mee (1 match) 6;
J.D. Nuttall (1 match) 3; R.A. Rydon
(1 match) 8; N.V. Salvi (1 match) 5.

Hundreds (1)

1 M.A. Crawley: 140 v Cambridge University, Lord's

Bowling	O	M	R	W	Avge	Best
Edwards	172.4	42	500	14	35.71	4-93
Firth	203.3	29	663	13	51.00	4-129
Henderson	111	13	437	7	62.42	3-48
Crawley	161.1	32	516	6	86.00	2-30
Weale	185	44	523	6	87.16	2-87

Also bowled: Kilborn 3-0-23-0; Morris 2-0-11-0;
Nuttall 19-5-48-1; Rydon 13-3-47-1;
Tooley 7.3-1-37-2.

Fielding

8 Cope (7ct, 1st), Kilborn; 4 Tooley; 3 Edwards,
Hagan; 2 Crawley, Henderson; 1 Beech, Firth,
Morris, Rydon, Salvi, Sardesai.

* not out † Blue 1987

First-Class Averages 1987

Batting	M	I	NO	HS	Runs	Avge	100s	50s
M.D. Crowe	18	29	5	206*	1627	67.79	6	6
Javed Miandad	12	14	1	260	822	63.23	2	3
K.D. James	17	16	6	142*	620	62.00	2	2
M.W. Gatting	19	29	2	196	1646	60.96	6	5
R.K. Illingworth	20	19	11	120*	448	56.00	1	1
Mansoor Akhtar	16	24	3	169*	1156	55.04	4	5
R.J. Hadlee	21	28	7	133*	1111	52.90	2	6
G.A. Hick	25	38	2	173	1879	52.19	8	6
Salim Malik	17	22	4	102	901	50.05	1	7
P.M. Roebuck	16	29	5	165*	1199	49.95	5	4
C.G. Greenidge	12	18	0	163	899	49.94	3	6
D.R. Turner	25	35	8	184*	1328	49.18	2	9
R.A. Smith	18	25	7	209*	869	48.27	1	4
R.A. Harper	7	9	5	127*	193	48.25	1	–
G. Fowler	24	43	5	169*	1800	47.36	3	11
T.S. Curtis	25	40	6	138*	1601	47.08	4	5
C.L. Smith	26	42	9	217	1519	46.03	4	5
C.E.B. Rice	22	32	8	138	1103	45.95	3	6
C.M. Wells	24	39	7	148*	1456	45.50	5	6
R.G. Williams	22	27	7	104	898	44.90	1	5
N.E. Briers	21	32	4	104	1257	44.89	2	9
C.W.J. Athey	21	34	5	160	1295	44.65	6	2
D.I. Gower	20	31	4	125	1197	44.33	2	6
M.R. Benson	24	39	0	131	1725	44.23	5	10
J.W. Lloyds	23	32	4	130	1213	43.32	2	9
B. Roberts	25	41	3	184	1643	43.23	4	8
V.P. Terry	23	37	5	122	1382	43.18	2	10
K.M. Curran	21	33	6	119	1142	42.29	3	4
N.H. Fairbrother	21	30	6	109*	1011	42.25	3	3
T.J. Boon	20	26	2	94	1009	42.04	–	11
Mudassar Nazar	13	16	2	124	588	42.00	2	4
J.D. Carr	24	41	4	156	1541	41.64	3	7
R.J. Blakey	24	38	5	204*	1361	41.24	4	6
G.W. Humpage	24	41	9	99*	1318	41.18	–	13
P.J. Newport	25	25	12	64*	534	41.07	–	3
R.F. Pienaar	7	8	0	153	327	40.87	1	1
M.C.J. Nicholas	25	38	9	147	1183	40.79	4	4
M.P. Maynard	26	45	5	160	1626	40.65	2	12
D.A. Reeve	17	23	8	87*	606	40.40	–	6
Shoaib Mohammad	16	23	5	121*	727	40.38	2	4
A.R. Butcher	15	27	2	135*	1009	40.36	3	4
R.J. Shastri	13	22	3	103	765	40.26	1	6
M.D. Moxon	22	37	4	130	1321	40.03	2	10
Imran Khan	13	14	3	118	431	39.18	1	1
R.T. Robinson	21	36	4	166	1250	39.06	3	3
M. Newell	20	34	7	203*	1054	39.03	3	4
W.N. Slack	25	42	0	173	1636	38.95	3	7
G.A. Gooch	24	41	6	171	1361	38.88	3	7
G.R. Mendis	24	42	6	203*	1390	38.61	3	7
M.A. Atherton	21	35	4	110	1193	38.48	2	4
P.E. Robinson	7	13	2	95	421	38.27	–	3
A.J. Stewart	22	34	2	132	1219	38.09	3	8

Batting (contd)	M	I	NO	HS	Runs	Avge	100s	50s
D.M. Smith	17	27	4	121*	873	37.95	1	7
G.S. LeRoux	13	15	5	73	375	37.50	–	2
J. Abrahams	9	15	1	140*	525	37.50	1	3
R.J. Bailey	26	42	8	158	1274	37.47	3	4
P.R. Downton	26	39	9	103*	1120	37.33	1	9
C.T. Radley	9	13	3	72	373	37.30	–	3
J.G. Wright	10	17	2	118	558	37.20	1	3
N.R. Taylor	24	38	3	142*	1300	37.14	3	6
C.J. Richards	20	26	6	172*	738	36.90	1	4
P.A. Neale	25	34	7	103*	994	36.81	2	5
K.J. Barnett	25	40	1	130	1429	36.64	3	7
J.J. Whitaker	27	39	5	126	1245	36.61	2	10
P. Johnson	25	39	4	125	1257	35.91	3	5
M.D. Marshall	22	22	5	99	610	35.88	–	3
I.G. Swallow	5	9	2	114	249	35.57	1	1
D.J. Bicknell	12	20	3	105	600	35.29	1	4
P. Bainbridge	17	25	6	151	668	35.15	2	3
B.R. Hardie	27	43	4	143	1370	35.12	3	8
D.W. Randall	13	20	1	133	665	35.00	1	3
W. Larkins	25	43	4	120	1364	34.97	3	6
T.A. Lloyd	25	46	3	162	1503	34.95	3	5
Saleem Yousuf	16	14	4	91*	347	34.70	–	1
T.E. Jesty	24	36	5	124*	1074	34.64	1	5
J.E. Morris	26	40	1	162	1343	34.43	3	6
P. Willey	26	40	3	122	1256	33.94	2	7
I.P. Butcher	8	12	0	88	407	33.91	–	4
M. Watkinson	19	27	4	91	776	33.73	–	6
R.J. Parks	25	19	8	62*	370	33.63	–	2
D.B. D'Oliveira	25	37	4	131*	1106	33.51	2	5
D.L. Bairstow	20	23	1	128	736	33.45	2	2
Ramiz Raja	11	15	0	150	501	33.40	1	3
P.J. Prichard	11	16	3	72	434	33.38	–	4
A.J. Moles	25	46	3	151	1431	33.27	4	4
M.A. Lynch	26	39	5	128*	1127	33.14	2	6
C.J. Tavaré	26	42	7	152	1157	33.05	1	6
Asif Din	23	36	4	115*	1056	33.00	2	5
I.J. Gould	21	29	5	111	792	33.00	1	4
A.J. Lamb	23	34	4	101*	982	32.73	1	5
J.E. Emburey	18	26	4	74	710	32.27	–	7
B.C. Broad	15	26	4	80	708	32.18	–	6
A.P. Wells	23	37	4	161*	1058	32.06	3	4
S.G. Hinks	21	33	2	112	992	32.00	2	3
P.B. Clift	17	22	3	88	608	32.00	–	4
Ijaz Ahmed	11	13	1	69	382	31.83	–	4
R.C. Ontong	16	27	8	100	600	31.57	1	1
J.D. Birch	23	32	3	82	914	31.51	–	8
A.W. Lilley	20	29	4	102	783	31.32	1	3
G.R. Cowdrey	5	8	1	68	219	31.28	–	3
A.A. Metcalfe	24	42	4	152	1178	31.00	2	6
C.S. Cowdrey	25	37	6	135	958	30.90	3	3
I.A. Greig	26	35	6	104*	887	30.58	1	5
G. Cook	25	41	9	111*	969	30.28	1	6
D.G. Aslett	25	40	8	101*	969	30.28	1	4
G.S. Clinton	19	30	2	93	848	30.28	–	7
D.L. Amiss	25	46	3	123	1300	30.23	2	6
I.T. Botham	16	22	2	126*	598	29.90	1	2

Batting (contd)	M	I	NO	HS	Runs	Avge	100s	50s
A.J.T. Miller	10	15	2	97	387	29.76	–	3
D.J. Wild	22	23	6	102*	501	29.47	1	3
M.J. Kilborn	8	12	2	59	294	29.40	–	1
D.W. Pringle	22	33	9	84*	705	29.37	–	4
K.T. Medlycott	25	30	5	153	734	29.36	1	5
M.A. Crawley	7	10	1	140	263	29.22	1	1
M.R. Ramprakash	8	14	3	71	321	29.18	–	2
R.A. Cobb	17	26	5	88	612	29.14	–	3
K.W.R. Fletcher	24	35	3	121	925	28.90	1	5
J.J.E. Hardy	24	40	2	119	1089	28.65	1	7
P.W. Romaines	25	42	2	119	1144	28.60	2	5
A.J. Wright	23	38	2	161	1022	28.38	1	6
H. Morris	26	48	2	143	1304	28.34	3	4
P.J.W. Allott	22	27	4	88	641	27.86	–	4
J.D. Love	21	30	7	79*	639	27.78	–	4
R.D. Sardesai	7	9	1	63*	222	27.75	–	1
R.O. Butcher	17	22	1	118	580	27.61	1	2
K.R. Brown	15	24	3	70	579	27.57	–	5
R.C. Russell	26	38	9	57*	798	27.51	–	4
M.W. Alleyne	20	30	7	82	628	27.30	–	5
Wasim Akram	14	11	2	59*	245	27.22	–	1
J.P. Stephenson	13	22	3	67*	515	27.10	–	2
S.J.S. Kimber	8	9	3	54	161	26.83	–	1
K. Sharp	20	32	4	81*	751	26.82	–	6
R.J. Boyd-Moss	8	13	1	77	321	26.75	–	2
N.A. Felton	24	41	0	110	1094	26.68	1	5
V.S. Greene	8	11	4	62*	186	26.57	–	1
N.D. Burns	24	35	7	100*	729	26.03	1	4
R.Sharma	17	27	4	111	596	25.91	1	3
C.K. Bullen	11	13	3	65	259	25.90	–	2
K.P.Tomlins	7	9	1	100	207	25.87	1	–
E.A.E. Baptiste	16	23	3	95	517	25.85	–	3
V.J. Marks	22	31	6	63*	635	25.40	–	2
D.G. Price	8	12	1	57	279	25.36	–	2
L. Potter	14	20	4	68	401	25.06	–	1
D. Ripley	25	24	5	125*	474	24.94	1	1
G.C. Holmes	25	43	6	95	922	24.91	–	5
G.J. Parsons	16	19	2	67*	422	24.82	–	3
G.D. Rose	18	23	4	95	470	24.73	–	1
M.A. Roseberry	10	14	3	52	270	24.54	–	1
R.J. Finney	23	36	5	77	760	24.51	–	4
D.W. Varey	7	10	1	59	220	24.44	–	2
A.M. Green	20	36	2	115	821	24.14	1	3
A.W. Stovold	26	43	2	88	988	24.09	–	5
D.J. Capel	22	30	3	91*	639	23.66	–	3
R.J. Harden	19	30	6	59	568	23.66	–	2
S.J. O'Shaughnessy	9	16	4	61*	275	22.91	–	1
A.C. Storie	16	26	8	66*	410	22.77	–	1
J.G. Wyatt	8	13	2	58*	250	22.72	–	1
S.J. Rhodes	25	31	7	80	544	22.66	–	3
C. Gladwin	10	17	2	77	339	22.60	–	2
M.J. Weston	14	21	2	54	426	22.42	–	3
W.K. Hegg	13	20	4	130	350	21.87	1	–
R.I. Alikhan	19	34	3	78	666	21.48	–	3
I.S. Anderson	15	21	2	87*	407	21.42	–	3
B.J.M. Maher	25	41	2	105	834	21.38	2	2

Batting (contd)	M	I	NO	HS	Runs	Avge	100s	50s
S.D. Weale	8	9	0	76	192	21.33	–	2
T.D. Topley	12	15	4	66	231	21.00	–	1
C.D.M. Tooley	8	10	1	61*	189	21.00	–	1
G.J. Lord	12	19	2	66	353	20.76	–	2
K.B.K. Ibadulla	5	8	1	46*	145	20.71	–	–
S.P. James	8	13	1	106	246	20.50	1	–
E.E. Hemmings	25	27	8	75	389	20.47	–	3
N.J. Pringle	11	18	1	79	347	20.41	–	2
B.N. French	18	20	2	70	365	20.27	–	2
P.W.G. Parker	19	32	4	85	565	20.17	–	2
N.A. Foster	21	23	2	49*	419	19.95	–	–
J. Derrick	18	27	7	57	398	19.90	–	1
A.C.S. Pigott	19	27	4	62	456	19.82	–	2
N.G. Cowley	10	12	2	96	197	19.70	–	1
P.A.J. DeFreitas	18	23	2	74	412	19.61	–	2
P.A. Todd	14	24	0	135	470	19.58	1	2
D.J. Fell	9	14	1	67*	254	19.53	–	1
G.V. Palmer	14	16	4	68	234	19.50	–	1
P.A. Smith	17	31	5	89	506	19.46	–	2
D.J. Thomas	17	17	4	49	243	18.69	–	–
S.A. Marsh	21	27	5	72*	411	18.68	–	2
S.N. Hartley	10	18	2	63	298	18.62	–	2
A.E. Warner	18	28	4	72	444	18.50	–	1
P.A.C. Bail	9	14	0	90	257	18.35	–	1
P.J. Hartley	22	26	7	49	347	18.26	–	–
A. Needham	10	12	3	33	164	18.22	–	–
P.G. Newman	17	24	5	42	341	17.94	–	–
P.A. Cottey	7	10	1	42*	161	17.88	–	–
C.W. Scott	12	15	1	45	250	17.85	–	–
D.M. Ward	6	10	0	44	178	17.80	–	–
P. Moores	18	24	2	55	385	17.50	–	2
D.J.R. Martindale	9	13	2	103	192	17.45	1	–
P. Carrick	24	29	2	61	471	17.44	–	2
M.A. Holding	13	18	2	63*	278	17.37	–	1
D.P. Hughes	25	35	6	81	503	17.34	–	1
P.H. Edmonds	16	18	6	32	208	17.33	–	–
D.K. Standing	17	29	3	56	443	17.03	–	2
J.P. Agnew	25	27	4	90	387	16.82	–	1
H.A. Page	15	20	4	60	266	16.62	–	1
N.G.B. Cook	26	25	7	64	299	16.61	–	2
C.P. Metson	25	37	7	81	493	16.43	–	1
N.A. Mallender	15	17	9	20*	131	16.37	–	–
A. Sidebottom	18	22	6	33	261	16.31	–	–
P.W. Jarvis	24	24	11	32	212	16.30	–	–
G.C. Small	12	20	4	42	257	16.06	–	–
I. Smith	18	23	5	45	288	16.00	–	–
A.A. Donald	11	10	3	37*	111	15.85	–	–
T.A. Merrick	14	19	5	74*	220	15.71	–	1
M.D. Harman	6	8	2	41	94	15.66	–	–
A. Walker	18	10	5	41*	78	15.60	–	–
D.E. East	27	32	3	73	449	15.48	–	1
J.A. Hopkins	15	26	2	39*	371	15.45	–	–
M.P. Bicknell	14	14	7	18*	108	15.42	–	–
R.A. Pick	17	15	5	42*	154	15.40	–	–
J.G. Thomas	10	15	2	48	200	15.38	–	–
D.L. Underwood	23	20	9	29*	168	15.27	–	–

Batting (contd)	M	I	NO	HS	Runs	Avge	100s	50s
G. Miller	23	30	5	33*	371	14.84	–	–
C. Penn	17	18	2	53	237	14.81	–	1
I. Folley	25	31	7	38	355	14.79	–	–
M.A. Feltham	11	12	3	39	129	14.33	–	–
W.W. Davis	19	18	5	25*	186	14.30	–	–
P.J.J. Whitticase	26	31	6	59	351	14.04	–	1
S.P. Hughes	18	20	7	26*	182	14.00	–	–
R.E. Morris	6	9	2	34	98	14.00	–	–
G.A. Tedstone	10	14	1	51	180	13.84	–	1
Mohsin Kamal	12	11	6	28	69	13.80	–	–
T.M. Tremlett	24	17	5	42	161	13.41	–	–
A.H. Gray	10	8	3	35	67	13.40	–	–
J. Simmons	22	24	5	64	252	13.26	–	1
G.A. Pointer	8	11	3	33	104	13.00	–	–
N.F. Williams	10	9	4	18*	64	12.80	–	–
S.J. Base	8	14	4	38	127	12.70	–	–
J.H. Childs	22	22	13	26	113	12.55	–	–
O.H. Mortensen	19	24	10	74*	168	12.00	–	1
M. Jean-Jacques	16	20	4	47	192	12.00	–	–
A.R.C. Fraser	22	22	5	38	202	11.88	–	–
S.R. Gorman	7	11	1	39	117	11.70	–	–
I.R. Redpath	7	12	1	46	128	11.63	–	–
N.V. Radford	23	21	4	31	197	11.58	–	–
P.A.W. Heseltine	18	18	3	26	172	11.46	–	–
K.B.S. Jarvis	11	8	7	4*	11	11.00	–	–
L.B. Taylor	9	9	3	16	66	11.00	–	–
T.A. Munton	16	16	5	38	116	10.54	–	–
G.J.F. Ferris	13	13	4	25	93	10.33	–	–
S.D. Fletcher	15	12	6	15	61	10.16	–	–
S.R. Lampitt	13	14	3	24	111	10.09	–	–
N. Gifford	25	25	12	36	131	10.07	–	–
G.R. Dilley	11	9	3	29	60	10.00	–	–

Bowling	O	M	R	W	Avge	Best	5wI	10wM
R.J. Hadlee	591	189	1227	97	12.64	6-20	9	2
A.H. Gray	291.1	59	748	48	15.58	5-46	2	–
K.J. Barnett	88.2	27	225	13	17.30	4-31	–	–
S.T. Clarke	456.4	114	1160	67	17.31	8-62	6	2
N.G. Cowans	341.3	77	958	51	18.78	5-43	2	–
T.M. Tremlett	547	153	1407	72	19.54	6-53	3	–
O.H. Mortensen	432.5	111	1084	55	19.70	5-57	2	–
M.D. Marshall	594.1	152	1508	76	19.84	5-49	1	–
P.J.W. Allott	535.2	166	1222	59	20.71	7-42	1	–
N.V. Radford	741.5	123	2269	109	20.81	8-55	8	1
A. Walker	390.2	104	1011	48	21.06	4-22	–	–
T.E. Jesty	72.4	11	212	10	21.20	6-81	1	–
J. Simmons	640.3	196	1425	67	21.26	6-20	4	1
S.J.W. Andrew	316.1	61	1022	48	21.29	7-92	2	–
G.J.F. Ferris	359.1	69	1143	52	21.98	6-42	4	–
N.A. Foster	672.5	147	1892	86	22.00	8-107	5	1
G.R. Dilley	265.3	52	817	35	23.34	6-43	4	–
M. Watkinson	318	66	986	42	23.47	7-25	4	4
S.J. Base	203.1	38	660	28	23.57	5-67	2	–
Imran Khan	338.4	77	898	38	23.63	7-40	3	1

Bowling (contd)	O	M	R	W	Avge	Best	5wI	10wM
M.P. Bicknell	363.2	94	997	42	23.73	6-63	2	–
G.S. LeRoux	266.5	54	768	32	24.00	5-64	1	–
K.W. McLeod	126.4	24	409	17	24.05	5-8	2	–
E.E. Hemmings	872.4	295	2119	88	24.07	6-62	7	1
J.P. Agnew	777	144	2451	101	24.26	7-46	9	2
P.G. Newman	364	75	1093	45	24.28	5-46	1	–
P.B. Clift	405.1	114	900	37	24.32	6-64	2	–
M.A. Holding	391.2	72	1194	49	24.36	5-41	2	–
N.A. Mallender	351	61	1129	46	24.54	7-61	1	–
P.W. Jarvis	644.1	149	1991	81	24.58	7-82	2	–
I. Folley	753.1	240	1865	74	25.20	7-15	5	1
T.A. Merrick	433.3	71	1439	57	25.24	7-45	4	1
T.A. Munton	341.1	72	992	39	25.43	6-69	2	–
C.A. Walsh	524.4	108	1609	63	25.53	5-38	2	–
R.G. Williams	241.4	61	67	26	25.65	5-81	1	–
G.D. Rose	314.4	56	976	38	25.68	5-24	1	–
K.E. Cooper	158.3	50	387	15	25.80	3-38	–	–
D.J.M. Kelleher	301	72	878	34	25.82	6-109	2	–
P.A.J. DeFreitas	477.2	107	1450	56	25.89	7-85	3	–
L.B. Taylor	154.4	20	545	21	25.95	6-47	2	–
P. Carrick	575.4	198	1323	51	25.94	7-42	1	–
A.A. Donald	301.4	36	1012	39	25.94	6-74	2	–
A.P. Igglesden	382.3	54	1351	52	25.98	5-45	3	–
B.P. Patterson	419.1	61	1359	52	26.13	6-40	4	–
D.J. Capel	464.5	87	1396	53	26.33	7-46	4	–
D.W. Pringle	599.4	155	1457	55	26.49	5-70	1	–
E.A.E. Baptiste	519.3	117	1495	56	26.69	8-76	2	1
C.K. Bullen	225.4	71	564	21	26.85	6-119	1	–
K. Saxelby	452.1	121	1278	47	27.19	6-49	1	–
W.W. Davis	591.1	104	1906	70	27.22	6-57	5	2
T.D. Topley	300.2	66	840	30	28.00	4-75	–	–
J.A. Afford	276.4	86	729	26	28.03	5-79	1	–
Wasim Akram	394	82	1095	39	28.07	6-34	2	–
P. Bainbridge	288.4	62	927	33	28.09	5-70	1	–
S.D. Fletcher	276.3	54	903	32	28.21	4-22	–	–
V.S. Greene	236.5	32	819	29	28.24	7-96	1	–
A.N. Jones	517.1	85	1800	63	28.57	7-85	3	1
C.E.B. Rice	308.3	90	800	28	28.57	4-42	–	–
D.L. Underwood	611.3	211	1295	45	28.77	5-43	1	–
R.J. Maru	802.4	229	2061	71	29.02	5-45	3	–
Mohsin Kamal	288.4	47	1046	36	29.05	6-100	1	–
N.G.B. Cook	705.2	227	1574	54	29.14	6-77	1	–
J.G. Thomas	245.3	48	875	30	29.16	6-109	2	–
A.E. Warner	328.5	67	1026	35	29.31	4-12	–	–
A. Sidebottom	446.5	83	1261	43	29.32	4-46	–	–
C.M. Wells	546.1	99	1531	52	29.44	6-34	2	–
D.A. Reeve	450	108	1240	42	29.52	7-37	1	–
P.C.R. Tufnell	335.2	65	984	33	29.81	6-60	1	–
M.A. Feltham	412.1	101	1202	40	30.05	5-66	1	–
D.A. Graveney	356.1	112	848	28	30.28	5-37	1	–
C. Penn	439.1	78	1469	48	30.60	5-52	2	–
P.M. Such	490.1	142	1256	41	30.63	4-14	–	–
V.J. Marks	778.5	203	2155	70	30.78	5-35	3	–
R.A. Pick	361.4	74	1206	39	30.92	4-75	–	–
R.J. Finney	275.2	57	839	27	31.07	3-39	–	–
G. Miller	379.3	84	995	32	31.09	7-59	1	1

Bowling (contd)	O	M	R	W	Avge	Best	5wI	10wM
N. Gifford	453	136	1121	36	31.13	5-71	2	–
J. Derrick	321.3	70	1064	34	31.29	5-50	1	–
G.C. Small	350	70	1067	34	31.38	4-80	–	–
R.A. Harper	256	56	662	21	31.52	5-28	2	–
K.B.S. Jarvis	251.2	38	884	28	31.57	5-48	1	–
J.K. Lever	396	99	1079	34	31.73	5-59	2	–
R.J. Shastri	461.1	100	1181	37	31.91	5-100	1	–
A.C.S. Pigott	455.2	86	1443	45	32.06	5-32	3	–
G.A. Gooch	250.3	64	687	21	32.71	4-42	–	–
A.P. Pridgeon	344	80	920	28	32.85	7-44	1	–
C.A. Connor	397	87	1061	32	33.15	4-26	–	–
J.H. Childs	479.3	143	1228	37	33.18	5-40	2	1
H.A. Page	340.2	52	1172	35	33.48	5-26	1	–
P. Willey	219.2	46	614	18	34.11	4-32	–	–
P.H. Edmonds	481.5	160	1094	32	34.18	4-34	–	–
A.R.C. Fraser	569.1	143	1506	44	34.22	4-50	–	–
R.C. Ontong	469.4	89	1410	41	34.39	6-91	2	–
N.G. Cowley	250.1	57	689	20	34.45	4-35	–	–
D.E. Malcolm	255	45	898	26	34.53	3-47	–	–
W.K.M. Benjamin	207.2	54	525	15	35.00	5-50	1	–
I.L. Pont	183	19	671	19	35.31	5-73	1	–
P.G. Edwards	172.4	42	500	14	35.71	4-93	–	–
I.A. Greig	413.4	86	1257	35	35.91	4-47	–	–
G.J. Parsons	418.5	81	1229	34	36.14	5-80	1	–
Mudassar Nazar	212	51	545	15	36.33	5-28	1	–
Tauseef Ahmed	212.2	66	477	13	36.69	4-51	–	–
P.J. Hartley	501	89	1726	47	36.72	4-52	–	–
D.V. Lawrence	350.1	44	1411	38	37.13	6-63	1	–
D.J. Thomas	357	61	1230	33	37.27	5-73	1	–
J.E. Emburey	570.3	153	1311	35	37.45	5-60	1	–
D.J. Foster	111.5	10	490	13	37.69	4-56	–	–
S.R. Barwick	603.1	122	1799	47	38.27	4-60	–	–
M.A. Robinson	150	25	501	13	38.53	3-45	–	–
K.T. Medlycott	546.4	148	1640	42	39.04	5-103	1	–
M. Jean-Jacques	325	59	1068	27	39.55	4-39	–	–
Zakir Khan	165	32	554	14	39.57	4-27	–	–
W.W. Daniel	348.1	50	1275	32	39.84	4-69	–	–
I. Smith	211.3	40	757	19	39.84	3-65	–	–
K.D. James	206.1	36	757	19	39.84	5-62	1	–
G.V. Palmer	316	54	1162	29	40.06	4-63	–	–
S.P. Hughes	358	55	1167	29	40.24	3-74	–	–
J.W. Lloyds	403.2	63	1466	36	40.72	6-57	2	–
A.M.G. Scott	250.3	50	744	18	41.33	5-97	1	–
G.A. Hick	310.2	59	1042	25	41.68	4-31	–	–
I.T. Botham	260	47	883	21	42.04	3-51	–	–
R. Illingworth	478.2	117	1391	33	42.15	4-289	–	–
R. Sharma	206	46	640	15	42.66	6-80	1	–
A.J. Moles	182.3	47	513	12	42.75	3-21	–	–
A.M. Babington	248.1	44	898	21	42.76	3-44	–	–
P.J. Newport	506.4	79	1839	42	43.78	4-28	–	–
N.F. Williams	189.4	32	575	13	44.23	3-55	–	–
Abdul Qadir	352.1	82	987	22	44.86	7-96	1	1
A. Needham	179	34	545	12	45.41	4-96	–	–
P.A.W. Heseltine	316.2	75	963	21	45.85	3-33	–	–
C.S. Cowdrey	278.1	64	871	19	45.84	2-30	–	–
M.R. Davis	153.5	25	505	11	45.90	3-43	–	–

Bowling (contd)	O	M	R	W	Avge	Best	5wI	10wM
P.A. Smith	177.5	21	783	17	46.05	3-31	–	–
R.P. Davis	153	35	473	10	47.30	3-68	–	–
M. Beardshall	158.2	21	572	12	47.66	4-68	–	–
D.J. Wild	214.4	68	531	11	48.27	2-11	–	–
G.E. Sainsbury	344.2	79	922	19	48.52	3-48	–	–
T. Firth	209.3	29	682	14	48.71	4-129	–	–
S.J.S. Kimber	152	21	639	12	53.25	2-13	–	–
G.A. Pointer	176	25	568	10	56.80	3-52	–	–
M.W. Alleyne	172.4	35	709	11	64.45	4-128	–	–

The following bowlers took 10 wickets but bowled in fewer than 10 innings:

	O	M	R	W	Avge	Best	5wI	10wM
P.J. Bakker	92.5	23	249	12	20.75	7-31	1	–
G. Smith	81	9	308	13	23.69	6-72	1	–
M.K. Bore	148.2	58	344	13	26.46	4-52	–	–
R.F. Pienaar	135.4	27	427	15	28.46	4-66	–	–
S. Monkhouse	82	7	326	11	29.63	2-21	–	–
S.R. Waugh	112	18	348	11	31.63	3-48	–	–
I.G. Swallow	111	25	349	11	31.72	7-95	1	–
C.J.P.G. Van Zyl	172	37	511	14	36.50	3-35	–	–

Fielding Statistics (Qualification: 20 dismissals)

76 B.J.M. Maher (72c, 4s)
74 C.J. Richards (67c, 7s)
69 P.J. Whitticase (67c, 2s)
65 P.R. Downton (57c, 8s)
64 R.C. Russell (54c, 10s)
61 D.E. East (57c, 4s)
61 R.J. Parks (56c, 5s)
57 S.J. Rhodes (51c, 6s)
53 C.P. Metson (47c, 6s)
50 N.D. Burns (44c, 6s)
49 B.N. French (45c, 4s)
48 D. Ripley (39c, 9s)
41 S.A. Marsh (39c, 2s)
39 Saleem Yousuf (37c, 2s)
36 D.L. Bairstow (31c, 5s)
35 G.W. Humpage (32c, 3s)
35 W.K. Hegg (24c, 11s)
30 M.P. Maynard
29 C.W. Scott (27c, 2s)
29 C.J. Tavaré
29 V.P. Terry

28 R.J. Blakey
28 G. Miller
27 C.L. Smith
26 M.D. Moxon
26 C.E.B. Rice
25 D.B. D'Oliveira
25 J. Stanworth (21c, 4s)
24 P.J.W. Allott
24 M.A. Lynch
24 R.J. Maru
24 A.J. Moles
23 I.J. Gould (23c, 0s)
22 B.R. Hardie
22 L. Potter
22 B. Roberts
21 C.S. Cowdrey
21 C.G. Greenidge
20 G.A. Gooch
20 P. Johnson
20 A.J. Lamb
20 A.J. Stewart

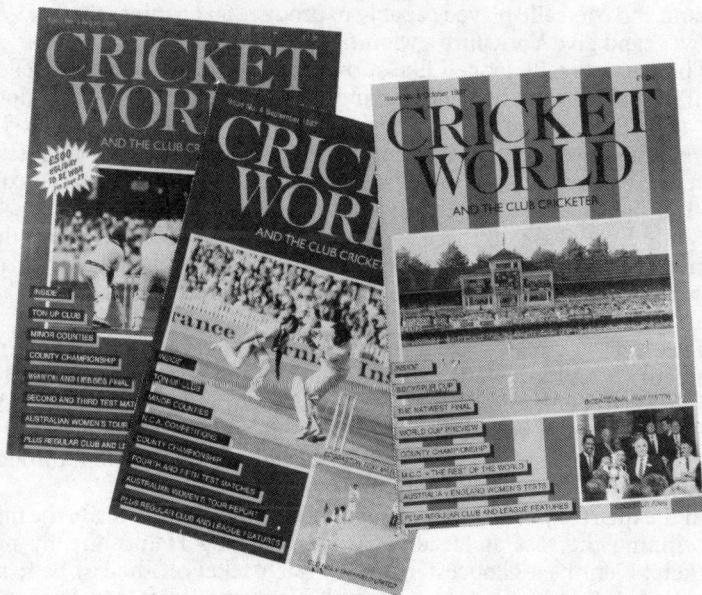

Benson & Hedges Cup

Yorkshire won the Benson & Hedges Cup for the first time in a final that ended with the scores level but with Northants having lost one wicket more.

They had put Northants in and, with greater help from the pitch than was available later, had reduced them to 48-3. Yet so well did Capel play in making 97 off 109 balls and so active was his support from Lamb and Williams, that Northants finished with 244-7, a score that would have been quite enough to win most limited-overs matches at Lord's.

What was required was early bowling of the quality provided for Yorkshire by Jarvis. That, unfortunately for Northants, was not forthcoming. The tall Winston Davis was not easily scored off, but Walker was less accurate and Capel began by conceding 33 runs off six overs. Moxon and Metcalfe played capably to produce an opening stand of 97 in 24 overs and give Yorkshire a winning platform.

They never really looked like surrendering this, though an excellent spell of spin bowling by Williams and Cook not only slowed them down but took four wickets. The decisive innings was then played by Jim Love, who never seemed likely to be out and with sensible aggression kept the required rate at around seven an over, helped by Capel's second spell, which was even more wayward than his first.

While Love was still there and Yorkshire had wickets in hand, they seemed certain to win, however narrowly, and eventually, with the scores level, Love had only to keep out Davis's last ball to win the Cup. With it, for him, came the Gold Award.

The final was played on a superb summer's day and generally the competition had a better deal than usual from the weather. Only two matches had been unfinished in the preliminary rounds, which ended with the giants of recent years, Essex and Middlesex, both failing to qualify from Group C, in which Somerset and Hampshire went through. Yorkshire and Surrey were unbeaten.

In the quarter-finals, all completed in a day, Yorkshire made the most of winning the toss at Headingley, demolishing Hampshire by nine wickets; Kent beat Gloucestershire by one wicket off the last ball; and Capel's bowling had much to do with Northants' defeat of Somerset. Surrey beat Worcestershire with an unbroken fourth-wicket stand of 159 between David Smith and Trevor Jesty.

The abysmal June weather had started by the time the semi-finals were played, though Northants were only briefly interrupted at Canterbury, where they made 279-6 to beat Kent, Lamb 126 not out. Yorkshire needed three days to finish at Headingley, but batted well to make 238-7 and reduced Surrey to 41-3 in 17 overs by the first evening.

Victory was clinched two days later, and Yorkshire and Northants, already lying first and second in the Britannic Assurance Championship, had endorsed current form by reaching the B & H final.

Zonal Results

Group A	P	W	L	NR	Pts
GLOUCESTERSHIRE	4	3	1	–	6
NORTHAMPTONSHIRE	4	2	2	–	4
Derbyshire	4	2	2	–	4
Nottinghamshire	4	2	2	–	4
Leicestershire	4	1	3	–	2

Group C	P	W	L	NR	Pts
SOMERSET	4	3	1	–	6
HAMPSHIRE	4	3	1	–	6
Essex	4	2	2	–	4
Middlesex	4	1	2	1	3
Combined Universities	4	–	3	1	1

Group B	P	W	L	NR	Pts
YORKSHIRE	4	4	–	–	8
WORCESTERSHIRE	4	3	1	–	6
Lancashire	4	1	2	1	3
Warwickshire	4	1	2	1	3
Scotland	4	–	4	–	0

Group D	P	W	L	NR	Pts
SURREY	4	4	–	–	8
KENT	4	3	1	–	6
Minor Counties	4	1	3	–	2
Glamorgan	4	1	3	–	2
Sussex	4	1	3	–	2

Note: Where two or more teams in a group have equal points, their positions are determined by faster run-rate (balls faced divided by runs scored) in all zonal matches.

Final Rounds

Quarter-Finals 27 May	Semi-Finals 10, 11, 12 June	Final 12 July
Northamptonshire, Somerset† (£2,375)	Northamptonshire	Northamptonshire (£10,000)
Gloucestershire† (£2,375), Kent	Kent† (£4,750)	
Surrey† Worcestershire (£2,375)	Surrey (£4,750)	Yorkshire
Yorkshire† Hampshire (£2,375)	Yorkshire†	YORKSHIRE (£20,000)

† Home team.
  Prize money in brackets.

Benson & Hedges Cup Winners

1972	Leicestershire	1978	Kent	1984	Lancashire
1973	Kent	1979	Essex	1985	Leicestershire
1974	Surrey	1980	Northamptonshire	1986	Middlesex
1975	Leicestershire	1981	Somerset	1987	Yorkshire
1976	Kent	1982	Somerset		
1977	Gloucestershire	1983	Middlesex		

Northamptonshire v Yorkshire, 1987 Benson & Hedges Cup Final

Yorkshire won by losing fewer wickets
Played at Lord's, 11 July
Toss: Yorkshire. Umpires: H.D. Bird and K.E. Palmer
Man of the Match: J. D. Love (Adjudicator: M.W. Gatting)

Northamptonshire		Runs	Mins	Balls	6	4
G. Cook*	c Blakey b Jarvis	1	8	11	–	–
W. Larkins	c Carrick b Hartley	15	46	37	–	3
R.J. Bailey	c Moxon b Fletcher	26	50	38	–	5
A.J. Lamb	c Bairstow b Jarvis	28	47	36	–	3
D.J. Capel	b Hartley	97	138	109	–	11
R.G. Williams	c Bairstow b Jarvis	44	89	91	–	4
D.J. Wild	b Jarvis	6	6	4	–	1
W.W. Davis	not out	10	9	7	–	1
D.J. Ripley†	not out	6	4	4	–	1
N.G.B. Cook	did not bat					
A. Walker	,,					
Extras	(B2, LB3, W2, NB4)	11				
	(55 overs; 206 minutes)	**244-7**				

Yorkshire		Runs	Mins	Balls	6	4
M.D. Moxon	b N.G.B. Cook	45	86	71	–	6
A.A. Metcalfe	c Davis b Williams	47	93	85	1	6
R.J. Blakey	c Davis b Williams	1	14	15	–	–
K. Sharp	b Williams	24	62	42	–	–
J.D. Love	not out	75	112	93	–	5
D.L. Bairstow†	run out (G. Cook/Ripley)	24	41	25	–	2
P. Carrick*	run out (Bailey/G. Cook)	10	5	6	–	2
A. Sidebottom	not out	2	9	3	–	–
P.J. Hartley	did not bat					
P.W. Jarvis	,,					
S.D. Fletcher	,,					
Extras	(B1, LB4, W4, NB7)	16				
	(55 overs; 215 minutes)	**244-6**				

Yorkshire	O	M	R	W
Jarvis	11	2	43	4
Sidebottom	11	1	40	0
Fletcher	11	1	60	1
Hartley	11	0	66	2
Carrick	11	2	30	0

Northamptonshire	O	M	R	W
Davis	11	1	37	0
Walker	11	0	62	0
Capel	11	0	66	0
Cook, N.G.B.	11	1	42	1
Williams	11	0	32	3

Fall of Wickets

Wkt	N	Y
1st	3	97
2nd	31	101
3rd	48	103
4th	92	160
5th	212	223
6th	226	235
7th	232	–
8th	–	–
9th	–	–
10th	–	–

THE KINGSWOOD PRESS
Christmas XXXX Christmas
Essential Cricket Presents List

Key

G – Grandad/Grandma	CC – Cricket Connoisseur
D – Dad	FS – Favoured Son
M – Mum	SD – Special Daughter
Y – Yuppie	

Cricket XXXX Cricket by Frances Edmonds   £9.95

The Contessa of iconoclastic wit's account of her experiences in Australia.
Cricket book of the year.
G D M Y

Ashes to Ashes: The England Tour to Australia 1986-87 by Peter Roebuck £9.95

Reprinted within two week's of publication. Outstanding assessment by an outstanding author.
CC FS SD

The MCC Cricket Coaching Book   £9.95

Revised and updated to coincide with MCC bi-centenary. Fifth edition.
G D CC FS

Masterstokes by Allen Synge and Derek Anns   £14.95

Lavishly illustrated whimsical review of cricket's time-less batting lessons drawn from the game's literature over the last 150 years.
G D CC FS

Cricket Impressions by Adrian Murrell   £12.95

The leading cricket photographer's decade of brilliant evocative and unusual photographs.
G D M Y CC FS SD

The Demon and the Lobster by Anthony Meredith   £12.95

An outstanding first book by Stowe historian Anthony Meredith; he traces the lives of Kortright, demon fast-bowler and Jephson, the last of the great underarm lob bowlers and questions if there was a Golden Age in the late nineteenth century.
G D Y CC FS

Essex County Cricket Club: The Official History by David Lemmon and Mike Marshall   £15.95

Essentially two books in one – a history of cricket in Essex and a history of Essex CCC. 93 b+w and 7 colour photographs.
G D M CC FS SD

NatWest Bank Trophy

Richard Hadlee said at one stage of the season that the force motivating more strongly than any other during his farewell summer at Trent Bridge was the vision of Nottinghamshire landing their first-ever one-day title. The redoubtable New Zealander realized this dream for himself, playing a memorable innings of 70 not out in the final against Northamptonshire, who looked certain winners until Hadlee, making his final Lord's appearance, came on stage.

Although it was reduced to 50 overs a-side because of a delayed start, the final, further interfered with by rain, was spread over two days – for only the second time in the 25 years of the competition. Notts were favourites not just on the basis of their all-round strength and high form but also because Northants, at the time, seemed to have run out of luck as well as inspiration and were plagued by injuries to key players. They only just managed to put out a full side.

The one favour Northants had from luck was to be put in by Rice, for when the time came in the evening for Notts to start their innings, sighting the ball was difficult because of its passage from bright light into heavy shadow. This hazard played some considerable part, as Notts, replying to a handsome score, were reduced to 57-4 when play ended on Saturday. Earlier, every Northants batsman who got to the wicket made a worthwhile contribution, but the cornerstone of their daunting score was a brilliant 84 by Larkins, who had figured prominently in their victories in the two previous rounds.

Northants continued to tighten their grip when play resumed on Monday. Rice, who made 63 without being able to capture the freedom required to meet the steadily mounting asking rate, was sixth out at 146, and Notts now needed 83 from eight overs. Only a storybook performance could keep them in the hunt, and the remarkable Hadlee provided it, hitting two sixes and four fours in an innings of 61 balls.

The impetus came in a dramatic 44th over, the last from Williams, who bowled magnificently and dismissed Rice. Hadlee, who had already had one escape in the previous over, from Wild, could have been caught off each of its first three balls, although every one was a most difficult chance in the deep. Off the last ball, French survived a stumping chance. To add to Northants' agony, this bizarre over unfairly cost 15 runs. Nevertheless, Notts needed 51 off the last five overs and got them, with three balls to spare – to win by three wickets.

Notts had had a fairly easy ride into the final. Nor, for that matter, were Northants desperately stretched. While the new ball combination of Davis and Capel was one of their main strengths, Northants used 36 overs of spin to advantage in beating Surrey in the second round.

The big sensation of the competition was Buckinghamshire's defeat of Somerset in the first round, in which another Minor County, Devon, was at the receiving end of the highest score in a limited-overs match in England – 404-3 by Worcestershire. The holders, Sussex, bowed out in the second round. At the same stage, Glamorgan were bowled out by

Gillette Cup Winners

1963	Sussex	1969	Yorkshire	1975	Lancashire
1964	Sussex	1970	Lancashire	1976	Northamptonshire
1965	Yorkshire	1971	Lancashire	1977	Middlesex
1966	Warwickshire	1972	Lancashire	1978	Sussex
1967	Kent	1973	Gloucestershire	1979	Somerset
1968	Warwickshire	1974	Kent	1980	Middlesex

NatWest Bank Trophy Winners

1981 Derbyshire   1982 Surrey   1983 Somerset   1984 Middlesex   1985 Essex
1986 Sussex   1987 Notts

1987 Tournament

1st Round 24 June	2nd Round 8 July	Q-Finals 29, 30 July	S-Finals 12, 13 Aug	Final (Lord's) 5 Sept
Northants† / Ireland	Northants†	Northants	Northants	Northants (£10,000)
Herts / Surrey†	Surrey			
Essex / N'berland†	Essex†	Essex† (£2,375)		
Devon / Worcs†	Worcs			
Leics† / Oxon	Leics†	Leics	Leics† (£4,750)	
Dorset / Hants†	Hants			
Cheshire / Glamorgan†	Glamorgan	Yorks† (£2,375)		
Wilts† / Yorks	Yorks†			
Glos / Lancs†	Glos	Glos†	Glos† (£4,750)	Notts
Cumbria / Sussex†	Sussex†			
Bucks† / Somerset	Bucks	Warwicks (£2,375)		
Staffs† / Warwicks	Warwicks†			
Cambs† / Derbys	Derbys	Derbys† (£2,375)	Notts	
Kent / Scotland†	Kent†			
Durham† / Middlesex	Middlesex†	Notts		
Notts† / Suffolk	Notts			

NOTTS (£20,000)

†Home team.
Amounts in brackets show prize-money won by that county.

Yorkshire for 83, earning the Headingley pitch one of its several black marks of the season.

Northamptonshire v Nottinghamshire, 1987 NatWest Bank Trophy Final

Nottinghamshire won by 3 wickets
Played at Lord's, 5, 7 September
Toss: Nottinghamshire. Umpires: D.J. Shepherd and A.G.T. Whitehead
Man of the Match: R.J. Hadlee (Adjudicator: M.J. Stewart)

Northamptonshire		Runs	Mins	Balls	6	4
G. Cook*	c French b Saxelby	26	63	52	–	2
W. Larkins	lbw b Pick	87	140	124	–	12
A.J. Lamb	b Rice	41	96	65	–	3
R.J. Bailey	not out	39	49	40	–	2
D.J. Capel	not out	29	30	24	1	2
R.G. Williams	did not bat					
D.J. Wild	,,					
D. Ripley†	,,					
N.G.B. Cook	,,					
W.W. Davis	,,					
A. Walker	,,					
Extras	(B1, LB2, NB3)	6				
	(50 overs; 191 minutes)	**228-3**				

Nottinghamshire		Runs	Mins	Balls	6	4
B.C. Broad	lbw b Davis	3	20	16	–	–
R.T. Robinson	c Ripley b Davis	2	11	11	–	–
D.W. Randall	b N.G.B. Cook	10	35	25	–	–
C.E.B. Rice*	c G. Cook b Williams	63	129	96	–	3
P. Johnson	lbw b Walker	1	9	8	–	–
J.D. Birch	b Walker	21	40	53	–	1
R.J. Hadlee	not out	70	92	61	2	4
B.N. French†	run out (Capel)	35	39	27	–	4
E.E. Hemmings	not out	0	1	0	–	–
R.A. Pick	did not bat					
K. Saxelby	,,					
Extras	(LB18, W8)	26				
	(49.3 overs; 195 minutes)	**231-7**				

Nottinghamshire	O	M	R	W
Hadlee	10	1	29	0
Pick	10	1	36	1
Rice	10	0	45	1
Saxelby	10	0	63	1
Hemmings	10	0	52	0

Northamptonshire	O	M	R	W
Davis	10	1	45	2
Capel	6.3	1	31	0
Walker	10	0	38	2
Cook, N.G.B.	10	2	30	1
Williams	10	0	48	1
Wild	3	0	21	0

Fall of Wickets

Wkt	Nh	Nt
1st	61	11
2nd	152	12
3rd	169	31
4th	–	38
5th	–	84
6th	–	146
7th	–	221
8th	–	–
9th	–	–
10th	–	–

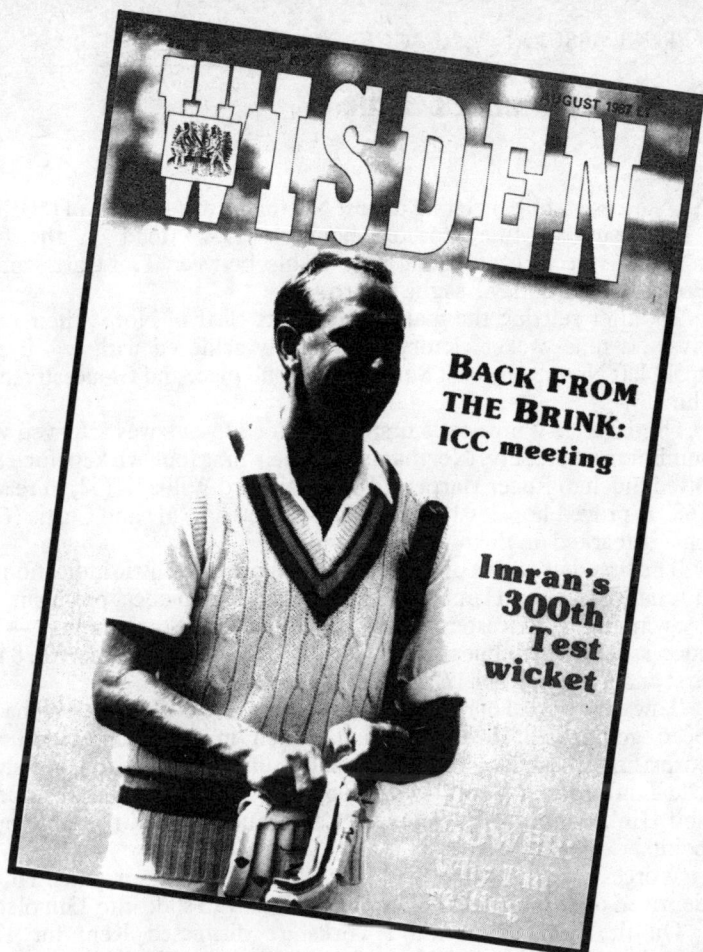

Refuge Assurance League

Worcestershire, needing to beat Northants to be certain of the Refuge Assurance title, coasted home at New Road on the fourth consecutive century opening partnership between Tim Curtis and Ian Botham — a Sunday League record.

So, after starting the match two points clear of Notts, their nearest rivals, a nine-wicket victory comfortably achieved with two overs to spare left Notts, who beat Surrey, in second place and Gloucestershire in third.

On the day, Worcester's first trophy for 13 years was achieved with a minimum of anxiety. Northants lost their first four wickets for 28 and owed much to Roger Harper (55) and Richard Williams (53) in reaching 168. It proved hopelessly inadequate as Botham (61) and Curtis (69 not out) embarked on their decisive stand.

The first four weeks of the competition provided little indication of its ultimate outcome. Hampshire the title-holders, made a promising start by winning at Leicester and against Surrey, at Southampton — both successes heavily influenced by Gordon Greenidge, who scored 78 in the first and a magnificent 172 not out in the second.

Towards the end of the first month, however, Yorkshire, who had also been going well, lost their first match in any competition when surprisingly beaten by Glamorgan at Cardiff. Hants lost to Lancashire at Old Trafford, and Kent — with an opening stand of 123 between Benson and Hinks — beat Middlesex, at Canterbury, to lead the table by two points.

Worcester, meanwhile, had given little hint of their potential, and, deprived of Botham and Dilley, lost at Derby to slide into 13th place.

On the last day of May, Yorkshire dismissed Kent for 175 at Middlesbrough (Jarvis 4-19), and, with Sharp and Metcalfe in excellent form, won by nine wickets, to join Kent, together with Hampshire and Derbyshire, at the top with 12 points each.

On the same day, Worcester, inspired by a brilliant 125 not out by Botham, beat Essex by nine wickets to start a winning sequence that vanquished Leicestershire and Middlesex and put them joint second with Kent, behind Derbyshire.

Kent's success was reinforced by an emphatic win against Lancashire at Liverpool, when Benson (92) and Tavaré (90) powered them to a remarkable 290-4. As Worcester were beaten by Notts at Trent Bridge (Randall and Rice in the 80s), Kent kept the pressure on Derbyshire, who stayed clear by beating Gloucestershire at Ilkeston (Holding 4-34).

On 28 June, Botham's Sunday-best 5-27 was of no avail as Worcester's match at Gloucester was abandoned. And, as Kent stumbled at Canterbury, dismissed by Somerset for only 91, Notts seized their chance to chase Derby by beating Sussex at Hove.

They kept up the pressure the following week when Randall hit a superb 123 at Trent Bridge, to crush Yorks and effectively end their title hopes. Though Derby still shared top place with 24 points, Notts had one game in hand, and two over Hants, now lying third with 22.

At last a pattern was beginning to emerge – and one of strong Midlands substance. For several weeks Notts remained the favourites, with Derbyshire only fractionally behind. On 20 July, however, play was possible in only one match, and while the rest received two points each, Gloucestershire beat Yorkshire on a faster run-rate to move into fourth.

The order, the following week, when Worcs were beaten by Somerset was: Notts, Derby, Gloucestershire, Hants, and Worcs.

On 2 August, Worcester clawed their way into second place with a faster-scoring-rate win at Eastbourne, and Derbyshire – who earlier in the season had achieved a run of five wins and a tie – now suffered their second successive defeat (against Kent).

The jockeying continued until, on 30 August, Derbyshire beat Notts by seven wickets at Derby, and Worcestershire, with a contemptuous nine-wicket victory against Surrey (Botham 80), took the lead for the first time.

Seven days later Notts' game in hand fell foul of the weather and the stage was set for the last, decisive tilt.

Final Table	P	W	L	T	NR	Pts	6s	4w
1 WORCESTERSHIRE (16)	16	11	4	0	1	46	32	3
2 Nottinghamshire (3)	16	9	3	0	4	44	8	3
3 Gloucestershire (17)	16	9	4	1	2	42	17	4
4 Somerset (6)	16	8	4	0	4	40	27	3
5 Derbyshire (9)	16	8	4	1	3	40	29	2
6 Kent (6)	16	8	5	0	3	38	37	4
7 Hampshire (1)	16	6	6	2	2	32	32	1
8 Surrey (12)	16	6	6	0	4	32	33	1
9 Lancashire (12)	16	5	6	0	5	30	21	0
10 Middlesex (9)	16	5	7	0	4	28	13	2
11 Northamptonshire (5)	16	4	6	0	6	28	31	2
12 Leicestershire (15)	16	3	6	0	7	26	13	0
13 Yorkshire (8)	16	5	8	0	3	26	45	3
14 Essex (2)	16	4	8	0	4	24	15	2
15 Glamorgan (12)	16	5	9	0	2	24	18	4
16 Sussex (4)	16	4	8	0	4	24	37	3
17 Warwickshire (9)	16	3	9	0	4	20	12	0

For the first four places only, the final positions for teams finishing with equal points are decided by the most wins. 1986 final positions are shown in brackets.

Sunday League Winners

1969	Lancashire	1976	Kent	1983	Yorkshire
1970	Lancashire	1977	Leicestershire	1984	Essex
1971	Worcestershire	1978	Hampshire	1985	Essex
1972	Kent	1979	Somerset	1986	Hampshire
1973	Kent	1980	Warwickshire	1987	Worcestershire
1974	Leicestershire	1981	Essex		
1975	Hampshire	1982	Sussex		

1987 Awards

£20,000 and League Trophy to champions WORCESTERSHIRE; £10,000 to runners-up Nottinghamshire; £4,500 to third-placing Gloucestershire; £2,625 to fourth-placing Somerset; £275 to winner of each match (shared in the event of 'no results' and ties). £400 to the batsman hitting most sixes in the season: C.S. Cowdrey (Kent) 18; £400 to the bowler taking four or more wickets most times in the season: 10 bowlers took four wickets twice (shared); £250 to the batsman scoring the fastest 50 in a match televised on BBC2: M.P. Maynard (Glamorgan) – 34 balls v Somerset at Weston-super-Mare on 2 August.

MCC Bicentenary Match

L ike many other matches in the dismal summer of 1987, the one
between teams representing MCC and the Rest of the World was not
spared by the weather. But it began with two superb days which helped
to create a most felicitous atmosphere. The players entered into the spirit
of the occasion, playing hard and competitively with just the right
amount of relaxation. The big crowds, captivated by the grace and
quality of cricket far removed from the hectic limited-overs bludgeoning
and defensiveness, excelled themselves. There was a generous appreciation of the finer points, there was no stampede, no buffeting of players
and umpires, no mindless chanting.

When the players had to give way to rain on Saturday evening, they
were roundly applauded, not only for their effort in staying out so long,
but for that of the ground staff in providing play as early as 11.30 after a
night's rain.

Lord's had also provided a supremely good pitch, inevitably slow in a
sunless summer but allowing batsmen to play their strokes and challenging bowlers to try their hardest.

Each day had its batting hero. On the first it was Gooch, unexpectedly,
for only the previous week-end he had still been in a run of wretched
form, making 1 and 1 against Middlesex at Chelmsford.

On the second day it was Gatting. Having worked hard for 68 overnight, he made 90 before lunch and when he was out soon afterwards, his
fifth-wicket stand of 201 with Clive Rice had produced enough runs for
him to declare.

The pugnacity of Gatting was followed by the correctness of Gavaskar,
with his head resolutely over the ball and his footwork as the textbook
advises. He was 80 that night and next day, having just announced his
retirement from first-class cricket, he passed his first 100 at Lord's on his
way to 188. Imran was a vigorous partner against some high-class
bowling, notably by Marshall.

The weather closed in again after tea, but, when Saturday's play
ended, the Rest were only 34 runs behind and the match was on course
for a good finish.

Unfortunately, this never seemed likely on Monday, for though an
almost full day's play was possible and the match was kept on schedule,
the weather forecast left no doubt that Tuesday would be hopeless.

After Border's declaration on Monday morning, Greenidge made the
fourth 100 of the match, showing unusual respect for bowling which had
Abdul Qadir restored after a finger injury suffered on the first day. Gooch
outscored Greenidge in his second excellent innings, Gower made some
elegant runs, and with a batting order adjusted to accommodate some
who had not previously batted, Gatting declared, leaving the Rest to
make 353 in 104 overs. Before the light faded in the seventh of the final
eight overs that night, Marshall bowled Gavaskar.

That proved to be all, save for the batting, bowling and fielding awards
next day to Gavaskar, Marshall, and Rice.

MCC v Rest of World XI

Match Drawn
Played at Lord's, 20, 21, 22, 24, 25 (np) August
Toss: MCC. Umpires: H.D. Bird and D.R. Shepherd

MCC

C.G. Greenidge	c Harper b Abdul Qadir	52		b Abdul Qadir	122
B.C. Broad	lbw b Imran Khan	10		c Dujon b Kapil Dev	2
G.A. Gooch	run out (Harper)	117		b Harper	70
D.I. Gower	c Dujon b Harper	8		c Border b Imran Khan	40
M.W. Gatting*	b Walsh	179			
C.E.B. Rice	not out	59	(8)	not out	4
R.J. Shastri	did not bat		(6)	not out	10
R.J. Hadlee	,,		(5)	c Imran Khan b Walsh	36
M.D. Marshall	,,				
J.E. Emburey	,,		(7)	c Haynes b Abdul Kadir	7
B.N. French†	,,				
Extras	(B11, LB15, W1, NB3)	30		(B16, LB10, NB1)	27
	(5 wkts dec)	**455**		(6 wkts dec)	**318**

Rest of World

S.M. Gavaskar	c & b Shastri	188		b Marshall	0
D.L. Haynes	c Rice b Marshall	23		not out	3
D.B. Vengsarkar	c Gooch b Marshall	22			
A.R. Border*	c Rice b Shastri	26			
P.J.L. Dujon†	c Gooch b Marshall	9			
Imran Khan	b Shastri	82			
Kapil Dev	c Marshall b Emburey	13			
R.A. Harper	not out	17	(3)	not out	9
C.A. Walsh	not out	21			
Abdul Qadir	did not bat				
Javed Miandad	,,				
Extras	(B3, LB8, W4, NB5)	20		(LB1)	1
	(7 wkts dec)	**421**		(1 wkt)	**13**

Rest of World	O	M	R	W	O	M	R	W
Imran Khan	25	6	97	1	13	4	33	1
Walsh	28.1	6	102	1	12	3	54	1
Kapil Dev	24	8	54	0	7	0	21	1
Abdul Qadir	16.2	7	30	1	36	9	112	2
Harper	34	5	125	1	20	2	72	1
Javed Miandad	5.4	0	21	0				

MCC	O	M	R	W	O	M	R	W
Marshall	20	3	53	3	2.3	0	10	1
Hadlee	21	2	71	0	2	1	2	0
Rice	12	1	63	0				
Shastri	42	4	130	3				
Emburey	29	7	93	1				

Fall of Wickets

Wkt	M 1st	R 1st	M 2nd	R 2nd
1st	21	46	11	2
2nd	96	93	146	–
3rd	151	148	231	–
4th	254	173	289	–
5th	455	353	293	–
6th	–	372	308	–
7th	–	389	–	–
8th	–	–	–	–
9th	–	–	–	–
10th	–	–	–	–

Second XI Competition

A nail-biting finish saw the Second XI Championship shared for the first time. Kent and Yorkshire, having played the same number of matches, met at Canterbury for their final fixture with the visitors one point ahead. Kent made up the deficit by bowling Yorkshire out for 151 after compiling 229 in their own first innings. Kent's second innings total of 258-8, thanks largely to a fine 124 by R.F. Pienaar, was too much for Yorkshire, who nevertheless held out for 191-8 to earn a share of the title, with the same average points and the same number of wins as Kent.

Notable individual performances during the season, in which no fewer than 10 matches were abandoned without a ball being bowled, included T.R. Ward's 212 not out for Kent against Hants, the only double century, and bowling figures of 8-33 by G.J.F. Ferris of Leicestershire. The latter county's bowlers suffered, however, against Middlesex, when A.J.T. Miller (163) and J.F. Sykes (125) put on 304 for the first wicket. And Middlesex, who finished way down the table with only two wins, could take additional solace from other fine individual performances, a 193 not out by J.D. Carr and bowling of 8-56 by A.G.J. Fraser, who also recorded a hat trick.

Second XI Championship Final Table

	P	W	L	D	Bonus Pts Bat	Bonus Pts Bowl	Total Pts	Avge
1 KENT (13)	15	5	1	9*	35	40	163	10.87
YORKSHIRE (5)	15	5	2	8	35	48	163	10.87
3 Lancashire (1)	17	5	1	11*	38	53	179	10.53
4 Sussex (15)	10	3	4	3	24	29	101	10.10
5 Hampshire (14)	12	3	2	7	27	43	118	9.83
6 Warwickshire (2)	16	4	7	5	32	52	148	9.25
7 Glamorgan (17)	17	4	4	9	42	49	155	9.12
8 Surrey (10)	15	3	5	7	42	45	135	9.00
9 Somerset (7)	11	3	4	4	18	33	99	9.00
10 Leicestershire (6)	15	4	1	10	29	40	133	8.87
11 Essex (3)	13	3	3	7	23	36	107	8.23
12 Worcestershire (8)	10	2	2	6	23	27	82	8.20
13 Northamptonshire (12)	13	2	3	8	27	43	102	7.85
14 Middlesex (4)	13	2	0	11	23	32	87	6.69
15 Nottinghamshire (11)	16	2†	5	9	21	44	93	5.81
16 Gloucestershire (16)	13	1	4	8	23	30	69	5.31
17 Derbyshire (9)	13	0	3	10	23	37	60	4.62

* Includes tied match (8 pts). † Includes win in one-innings match (12 pts).

Warwick Under-25 Competition

Zonal Group A	P	W	L	NR	Pts
YORKSHIRE	3	3	0	0	12
Derbyshire	3	1	1	1	6
Lancashire	3	0	1	2	4
Nottinghamshire	3	0	2	1	2

Zonal Group C	P	W	L	NR	Pts
SURREY	3	2	0	1	10
Kent	3	2	1	0	8
Hampshire	3	1	1	1	6
Sussex	3	0	3	0	0

Zonal Group B	P	W	L	NR	Pts
MIDDLESEX	3	2	0	1	10
Northamptonshire	3	0	0	3	6
Essex	3	0	1	2	4
Leicestershire	3	0	1	2	4

Zonal Group D	P	W	L	NR	Pts
WORCESTERSHIRE	4	4	0	0	16
Glamorgan	4	2	1	1	10
Warwickshire	4	1	2	1	6
Somerset	4	1	2	1	6
Gloucestershire	4	0	3	1	2

Semi-Finals
YORKSHIRE beat Surrey by 4 wickets
WORCESTERSHIRE beat Middlesex by 5 wickets

Final
YORKSHIRE beat Worcestershire by 8 wickets

Bain Dawes Trophy

North Zone	P	W	L	NR	Pts
DERBYSHIRE	10	5	2	3	13
Leicestershire	10	5	3	2	12
Lancashire	10	4	3	3	11
Northamptonshire	10	2	4	4	8
Yorkshire	10	2	4	4	8
Nottinghamshire	10	3	5	2	8

South-East Zone	P	W	L	NR	Pts
HAMPSHIRE*	10	6	2	2	14
Surrey	10	6	2	2	14
Middlesex	10	4	3	3	11
Essex	10	3	5	2	8
Kent	10	3	6	1	7
Sussex	10	2	6	2	6

*Hampshire qualify on faster run rate.

South-West Zone	P	W	L	NR	Pts
WARWICKSHIRE	8	4	0	4	12
Somerset	8	3	2	3	9
Worcestershire	8	3	2	3	9
Gloucestershire	8	2	4	2	6
Glamorgan	8	1	5	2	4

Round Robin
Hampshire beat Warwickshire by 65 runs
Derbyshire beat Hampshire by 50 runs
Warwickshire v Derbyshire abandoned

Final
Derbyshire beat Hampshire by 7 wickets

Minor Counties

A season whose weather was once again memorable only for the wrong reasons was, nonetheless, marked by some cricket of a high order.

Pride of place must go to Buckinghamshire, who not only enjoyed a thrilling victory over Somerset in the NatWest Trophy but won the Championship by virtue of having lost fewer wickets in a tied play-off with Cambridgeshire. The latter, the first county to figure in both finals in the same season, had the mortification of losing on each occasion.

The knock-out was won comfortably by Cheshire, their success in this competition being some consolation for suffering the most cruelly of all from the weather. It says much for the quality of their cricket that, despite the loss of no less than six of their eight days' Championship cricket at home to the elements, they took third place in the Western Division. In the East, Staffordshire equalled the points tally of Cambridgeshire, but had an inferior strike rate; thus, for the fourth year in succession they just missed qualifying for the Worcester final.

The Representative XI showed much improved form, beating Glamorgan in the Benson & Hedges Cup early in the season (Paul Todd for the second time in three matches taking the Gold Award) and playing well against Pakistan.

Minor Counties Championship

E. Division	P	W	L	U	T	B	NR	Pts	W. Division	P	W	L	U	T	B	NR	Pts
1 Cambs*	9	5	0	2	0	1	1	59†	1 Bucks*	9	4	1¹	2	0	2	0	51
2 Staffs*	9	5	0	2	0	1	1	59	2 Berks*	9	3	0	4	0	2	0	44
3 Durham*	9	4	1¹	3	0	0	1	54	3 Cheshire*	9	2	1¹	2	0	1	3	36
4 C'berland*	9	4	4	1	0	0	0	43	4 Wilts*	9	2	1	2	0	3	1	31
5 Herts*	9	2	5³	1	0	0	1	34	5 Devon*	9	2	0	1	0	5	1	30
6 Lincs*	9	2	3¹	2	0	2	0	31	6 Somerset II	9	1	0	5	0	1	2	30
7 Suffolk*	9	2	3¹	0	0	4	0	27	7 Shrops*	9	2	3	1	0	3	0	26
8 Beds	9	1	2	2	0	4	0	20	8 Oxon	9	1	3	2	0	3	0	19
9 N'berland	9	0	2¹	1	0	4	2	14	9 Dorset	9	0	4¹	4	0	1	0	16
10 Norfolk	9	0	5	2	0	0	2	10	10 Cornwall	9	0	4¹	1	0	3	1	11

Points: 10 for win; 2 for no result (NR); 1st innings points – U = up (3 pts), T = tied (2), B = Behind (1); 3 for 1st innings lead in match lost – superior figure in lost (L) column indicates number of times points gained in matches lost. *Qualified for 1988 NatWest Bank Trophy. †Cambridgeshire win section on basis of better nett batting averages than Staffs.

Leading Averages

Batting	I	NO	HS	Runs	Avge	Bowling	O	M	R	W	Avge
R. Baigent	13	5	150*	713	89.13	S.Turner	210.3	53	484	39	12.41
P.R. Oliver	9	5	78*	246	61.50	P.J. Kippax	144.4	50	376	24	15.67
M.D. Nurton	13	3	103*	597	59.70	J.H. Jones	212	57	497	31	16.03
J.G. Wyatt	9	1	129	444	55.50	D.A. Toseland	150.5	51	362	22	16.45
G.J. Blackburn	10	7	51*	161	53.67	D. Halliwell	168.4	38	462	28	16.50
P. Burn	13	4	109*	476	52.89	R.J. Hailey	143	33	367	22	16.68
I.S. Lawrence	12	4	100*	423	52.88	J.F.M. O'Brien	203	54	540	31	17.42
I.J. Tansley	11	1	131*	519	51.90	R. Woolston	192	48	576	32	18.00
N.A. Folland	11	2	98*	461	51.22	G. Monkhouse	154.5	38	414	22	18.82
M.A. Fell	16	3	117	643	49.46	B.J. Griffiths	261.5	67	701	37	18.95

Knock-out Competition

Final: At Christ Church, Oxford, 26 July. CHESHIRE beat CAMBRIDGESHIRE by 8 wickets (55 overs). Cambridgeshire 131 (49.5 overs) (J.D.R. Benson 33; G.J. Blackburn 4-11, N.T. O'Brien 4-32). Cheshire 132-2 (47.4 overs) (I.J. Tansley 54, S.T. Crawley 30).

Buckinghamshire v Cambridgeshire, Minor Counties Championship Play-off

Buckinghamshire won by virtue of having lost fewer wickets
Played at the County Ground, Worcester, 10 September 1987 (55 overs)
Match sponsored by the Carphone Group
Toss: Cambridgeshire. Umpires: P.J. Eele and D.J. Halfyard

Buckinghamshire

A.R. Harwood	b Stephenson	20
M.J. Roberts	not out	132
D.E. Smith	c Garnham b Wing	12
S. Burrow	c Turner b Lethbridge	35
*N.G. Hames	b Turner	2
G.R. Black	c Turner b Lethbridge	4
T.J.A. Scriven	did not bat	
S.J. Edwards	,,	
S.J. Tungate	,,	
A.W. Lyon	,,	
C.D. Booden	,,	
Extras		30
	(5 wkts, 55 overs)	**235**

Cambridgeshire

*N.T. Gadsby	b Edwards	3
I.S. Lawrence	c Tungate b Edwards	33
†M.A. Garnham	c Tungate b Edwards	9
J.D.R. Benson	c Tungate b Burrow	121
S. Turner	run out	2
C. Lethbridge	lbw b Lyon	11
A.D. Cuthill	c & b Scriven	0
C. Thornely	c Smith b Burrow	27
D.C. Collard	not out	12
M.G. Stephenson	b Burrow	0
D.C. Wing	not out	5
Extras		22
	(9 wkts, 55 overs)	**235**

Buckinghamshire	O	M	R	W
Turner	11	3	34	1
Lethbridge	11	0	61	2
Collard	11	2	28	0
Wing	11	1	51	1
Stephenson	11	2	38	1

Cambridgeshire	O	M	R	W
Booden	11	1	35	0
Edwards	11	4	20	3
Lyon	11	1	44	1
Black	10	0	52	0
Scriven	6	0	26	1
Burrow	6	1	39	3

Fall of Wickets

Wkt	B	C
1st	67	7
2nd	100	30
3rd	204	41
4th	220	43
5th	235	93
6th	–	108
7th	–	178
8th	–	216
9th	–	216
10th	–	–

Village and Club Cricket

The 'grass roots' finals at Lord's enjoyed some of the summer's best weather, in late August, and produced two worthy winners in Old Hill, the club champions of 1984 and 1985, and Longparish, a thoroughly genuine village side.

The Cockspur Cup (45 overs). Lord's, 28 August. Teddington won toss.
Teddington 185-5 (G. Morgan 52, D.C. Holliday 30, D.J. Malan 27, S. Munday 21; D. Headley 2-32, Mushtaq Mohammad 1-29). Old Hill 188-5 (44.3 overs) (Mushtaq Mohammad 64, C. Hemsley 57, R.J. Lanchbury 31; G. Harris 4-21). **Old Hill won by 5 wickets.**

For the fifth successive year the senior club championship was won by a Birmingham League side, Old Hill beating Teddington in the final to become the first winners under the new sponsorship. This was a good match, watched by a sizeable crowd, which saw Mushtaq Mohammad in fine form.

Teddington, hoping to become the first southern club to win since Southgate in 1977, chose to bat first, according to their custom. Morgan of Suffolk made 52 before being bowled round his legs by Mushtaq. Dean Headley, son of Ron and grandson of the great George Headley, bowled fast and accurately to take two good wickets and Teddington were kept to 185-5.

Old Hill soon lost Oliver, once of Warwickshire, but Hemsley and Mushtaq put on 109, and Wilkinson, Old Hill's captain in their previous victories at Lord's, made the winning hit with nine balls to spare. Old Hill received the Cockspur Cup and £1,250; Teddington took £750.

National Village Championship (40 overs). Lord's, 31 August. Longparish won toss. Longparish 166 (39.5 overs) (J.D. Heagren 63, R.D. Sturt 22; M. Thorpe 3-6). Treeton Welfare 90 (37.1 overs) (J.N. Jacobs 21; R.D. Sturt 3-14, B.Smith 3-36, K. Sutcliffe 2-20). **Longparish won by 76 runs.**

The Hampshire village of Longparish, near Andover, became the first southern side to win the village competition since Linton Park of Kent in 1978. It was not the most exciting final, but Longparish were very popular winners. They lost the 1980 final to Marchwiel of Clwyd when Denis Heagren, local head gamekeeper, was captain. In 1987, the second winners of the competition since Norsk Hydro Fertilizer of Suffolk became the sponsors, were led by John Heagren, underkeeper to his father.

Heagren went in first and made a stylish 63, featuring perfectly timed cover driving. He was out towards the end of his side's innings, having steered them up from 35-3.

Treeton Welfare, a mining community from near Rotherham and Sheffield, never came on terms with their target and, despite vociferous supporters' encouragement, they lost wickets with alarming rapidity. Sturt, tall and fast, took the first three wickets and finished with figures of 8-2-14-3.

Jacobs and his captain Allsopp lifted the score above the previous lowest in a final, ironically Longparish's 82-9 in 1980, and the Bank Holiday crowd of some 4,000 saw Hubert Doggart, deputizing for the convalescent President of MCC, present Longparish with their prize of £600 and Treeton with £350.

Schools and Youth Cricket

Post-term festivals are very much the vogue, and in 1987 there were some 20 hosts, Winchester, Charterhouse, Merchant Taylors', Sherborne, Mill Hill, Repton, and Shrewsbury among them. There was also the MCC Schools Festival at Oxford, where independent and state schools combine, and in 1987, for the first time, the Sir Garfield Sobers International Schools Tournament in Barbados, to which six English schools travelled and did well. In 1988 this event will expand.

The English school cricket term was generally cold and wet, but some good players emerged or confirmed earlier promise. Jon Longley of Tonbridge was probably the outstanding schoolboy cricketer and one with a firm commitment to higher things in the game. Longley, Knight (Felsted), Forward (Canford), Kardoni (Sherborne), Khan and Winchester (Rugby), Hall and C. Wall (Repton), Hodgson (Wellington), Zagni and Shahid (Ipswich), and Meadows and Bailey (Clifton) all took the eye. In Nadheem Shahid, Ipswich have an all-rounder of the greatest potential, already playing at Minor County level, a sound opening or early-order batsman and a leg-spinner of much skill and infinite variety.

The MCC Schools Festival at Oxford is now a valued July fixture. On the neighbouring grounds of Keble College and St Edward's School, the first two days were devoted to separate English Schools Cricket Association and Headmasters' Conference Schools trials. The week-end weather was not of the kindest, but mostly play was possible, and on the Monday the 44 best players, regardless of educational background, formed four sides from whom the sides for a final one-day trial on the fine Christ Church ground were chosen.

Rain caused the abandonment of this halfway through, but the trial selectors named the following 12 for the two one-day matches at Lord's:

H.R.J. Trump (capt) (Millfield), A.L. Penberthy (Camborne), D.A. Graham (Chipping Camden), G. Thorpe (Farnham College), B.J. Rendall (Avon), N. Shahid (Ipswich), M.R. Newton (Hants), W.M.I. Bailey (Clifton), I.J. Houseman (Harrogate GS), C.J. Adams (Repton), P.J. Martin (Danum Doncaster), and N.A. Derbyshire (Ampleforth).

The weather was again foul and there was no play on either day.

There was some relenting by the next day, plus much dedicated work by the Lord's ground staff, and the National Cricket Association Young Cricketers started their annual match against the Combined Services. It was another which was soon abandoned. The NCAYC team was:

M.P. Speight (capt) (Sussex), T. Orrell (Lancs), M. Pooley, O.C.K. Smith, D.A. Graham (Gloucs), M.R. Newton (Hants), H.R.J. Trump (Somerset), Nadheem Shahid (Suffolk), A.M. Smith, I.J. Houseman, N.A. Derbyshire (Yorks).

Altogether a disappointingly wet season, but young cricketers are not easily discouraged, and boys from six English schools, Uppingham, Emanuel, Repton, Ipswich, Greshams, and Clifton, raised the necessary funds and set out for Barbados in early August to compete in the inaugural Sir Garfield Sobers Schools Tournament. Teams from eight other schools took part. The schools played warm-up round-robin matches (of 40 overs a side) in two sections. League I comprised Appleby College (Canada), St Mary's (Trinidad & Tobago), Coleridge-Parry (Barbados), Harrison College (Barbados), Clifton, Emanuel, and Uppingham. In League II were: Combermere (Barbados), Queens Royal and Fatima College (Trinidad & Tobago), Upper Canada, Greshams, Ipswich, and Repton.

By August 20, the *Barbados Advocate* was tipping strongly as future Test players Roland Holder of Combermere, Brian Lara (Fatima), Nadheem Shahid (Ipswich), and John Meadows (Clifton), with Repton's Charlie Wall 'an Ian Botham of the future'.

The tournament was lavishly sponsored, the Barbados Board of Tourism aiming to increase visitors to the island by enhancing its sporting image. Wesley Hall, the great fast bowler, is now Minister responsible for sport, and no tournament could be in better hands.

Unfortunately, August in Barbados proved not dissimilar to August 1987 in England. Rain certainly had its effect on the final, which was played on the Test ground of Kensington Oval, and which Combermere won by defeating Repton on faster run rate. Needing 206 to win, Repton had reached 105-4 after 25 overs when rain ended play, and though Combermere's run rate was 5.12 against 4.24, Dominic Hall and Steve Hall were engaged in a fifth-wicket partnership so far worth 66. According to a local reporter, they were 'dominating the game' when the premature end came.

The Lords Taverners *Cricketer* Colts Trophy was won by Rugby School, who received it from the President of MCC, Colin Cowdrey, after beating Wellington College in the final at Trent Bridge by 83 runs.

Esso Youth Sport sponsored for the second year the NAYC under-19 county festivals at Oxford and Cambridge in August. Matches were played on a round-robin basis, 54 overs a side, Yorkshire, winners of the Cambridge section, travelling to Oxford to play Hampshire in the final on the Christ Church ground. On a brilliantly sunny Saturday, Yorkshire won a fairly straightforward victory by 49 runs. Of the 108 overs bowled, 83 came from spinners, I. Turner, left-arm, from the Hambledon club, taking 5-67 in 21 overs, while Yorkshire made 217-8 (S. Kellett 63, S. Foster 60). Hampshire found runs hard to come by when acceleration was needed. Esso will again sponsor this most worthwhile competition in 1988.

Women's Cricket

The tour of England by the Australian Women's Cricket team was an undoubted triumph for the visitors, but left areas of concern for the England Women's Cricket Association. England lost their first home Test series in 50 years and they also lost the one-day series on a slower run rate.

Australia, captained by Lyn Larsen, won the Tests 1-0 with two drawn, but were on top in all departments; they were also unbeaten in their county games.

The opening one-day international at Lord's started late owing to monsoon-like conditions – and the historic game (only the second ever women's international to be played at cricket's headquarters) was covered by Channel Four Television. The game was reduced to 37 overs, but Australia held the upper hand throughout, and England's performance was decidedly second rate. Lindsay Reeler, Australia's opener, hit an attractive 69 to guide Australia to a win by 70 runs.

The second game, at Guildford, was washed out. In the final contest, at Canterbury, England's brightest performance in a rather dismal summer produced a six-wicket win, thanks to a marvellous 36 runs off 22 deliveries by newcomer 18-year-old Jo Chamberlain from Leicestershire.

Australia's confidence was on a high by the time the first Test started at Worcester. They sensed that, with their superior pace and spin attack, excellent team spirit, and skilled captaincy, they were the better side – and they were right. England lost by an innings and 21 runs on the third of the four days, and the team were kept behind 'after school' for a stern practice in an attempt to set matters right.

Wendy Watson, another East Midlander, scored a half-century in this Test, on her debut, one of the few bright spots for the home side. But they were dismissed for 134. Belinda Haggett's 126, her maiden century, helped Australia to a first innings lead of 159. England's Gill McConway took 6-71 – a marathon bowling effort by this skilled left-arm spinner. England crumbled to 138 all out, with Carole Hodges, England's beleagured captain, scoring a determined 55. It signalled the beginning of the end for England's hopes in the series.

The second Test was at the small Yorkshire club ground of Collingham, where 7½ hours of rain enabled England to escape with a draw. The highlight of the game was a brilliant world record 193 by Denise Annetts, the diminutive New South Wales batsman, who was cruelly run out before she could complete her double century. She combined with Reeler in a staggering third-wicket partnership of 309. Australia finished on 346-3 declared in reply to England's first knock total of 201, which included half-centuries from Janette Brittin, struggling to find her real form, and Wendy Watson. Annetts' innings was her maiden Test century, and the slowest in women's cricket history, taking 7½ hours.

England produced one milestone in this match – Jan Brittin passed 1,000 runs in Test cricket to join Myrtle McLagan, Enid Bakewell, and Rachael Flint in the record books.

England's hopes of squaring the series at Hove in the third Test were dashed fairly rapidly. They won the toss and put Australia in, a decision made to look rather strange by Australia's score of 366-7. England were all but slipping into a follow-on, on the third day at 108-6, but then an exhilarating world record seventh wicket stand of 110 by teenagers Jo Chamberlain and Karen Hicken, also from the East Midlands, took England through to 265-8 at the end of the day. England declared at that overnight score, but Australia understandably did not throw back a generous declaration – they were in England to win the series and this they did handsomely.

Australia were superior to England in all aspects, and their coach Peter Bakker, who accompanied them, presented a well drilled side who displayed a level of professionalism that was a credit to the game. In pace bowlers Karen Brown and Sally Griffiths they have two of the fastest, most penetrative bowlers seen in women's cricket for many years. And their spinner Jenny Owens wove spells on some of the less experienced English batsmen.

England's encouragement came from the three East Midlanders – Hicken, Chamberlain, and Watson – although they must fear for their prospects in the 1988 World Cup in Australia, with so many of their senior players failing to live up to their potential.

First Test, Worcester. AUSTRALIA won by an innings and 21 runs. England 134 (W. Watson 50; K. Brown 3-17) and 138 (C. Hodges 55; J. Owens 4-18). Australia 293 (B. Haggett 126, L.Fullston 41*; G. McConway 6-71).

Second Test, Collingham. MATCH DRAWN. England 201 (J. Brittin 56, W. Watson 69; J. Owens 5-55) and 116-4 (J. Brittin 70*). Australia 346-3 dec (D. Annetts 193, L. Reeler 110*).

Third Test, Hove. MATCH DRAWN. Australia 366-7 dec (R. Buckstein 83, L. Reeler 53, D. Annetts 51, L. Larsen 70*; K. Hicken 3-63) and 262-8 (L. Reeler 75, D. Annetts 74). England 265-8 dec (K. Hicken 64, J. Chamberlain 59, C. Hodges 46; K. Brown 5-32).

Australia won series 1-0.

One-Day Internationals

Lord's. AUSTRALIA won by 70 runs. Australia 174-3 (31 overs) (Reeler 69, Annetts 36*). England 104-5 (31 overs) (Court 35; Fullston 4-12).

Guildford. MATCH ABANDONED.

Canterbury. ENGLAND won by 6 wickets. Australia 177-7 (53 overs) (Reeler 60, Annetts 50; Potter 3-41). England 178-4 (49.3 overs) (Brittin 38, Hodges 54, Court 42*, Chamberlain 36*).

Australia won series on superior run-rate.

EXTRAS

Test Career Records

The following individual career averages include all official Test matches to the end of the 1987 English season.

England

Batting / Fielding	M	I	NO	HS	R	Avge	100	50	Ct/St
C.W.J. Athey	17	30	1	123	722	24.89	1	4	10
I.T. Botham	94	150	5	208	5057	34.87	14	22	109
B.C. Broad	14	25	2	162	961	41.78	3	4	6
D.J. Capel	1	2	0	53	81	40.50	–	1	–
P.A.J.DeFreitas	5	6	1	40	88	17.60	–	–	1
G.R. Dilley	30	42	13	56	391	13.48	–	2	9
P.H. Edmonds	51	65	15	64	875	17.50	–	2	42
J.E. Emburey	46	68	14	75	1027	19.01	–	5	28
N.A. Foster	19	27	3	29	220	9.16	–	–	4
B.N. French	9	12	3	59	158	17.55	–	1	16/-
M.W. Gatting	58	100	13	207	3563	40.95	9	17	49
G.A. Gooch	59	105	4	196	3746	37.08	7	21	57
D.I. Gower	96	164	12	215	6789	44.66	14	34	66
A.J. Lamb	51	88	7	137★	2644	32.64	7	10	52
M.D. Moxon	3	6	0	74	134	22.33	–	1	4
C.J. Richards	6	9	0	133	272	30.22	1	–	17/1
R.T. Robinson	21	36	3	175	1351	40.99	4	4	6
G.C. Small	4	5	2	21★	49	16.33	–	–	1
J.J. Whitaker	1	1	0	11	11	11.00	–	–	1

Bowling	Balls	R	W	Avge	Best	5wI	10wM
I.T. Botham	20801	10392	373	27.86	8-34	27	4
D.J. Capel	108	64	0	–	–	–	–
P.A.J. DeFreitas	922	482	10	48.20	3-62	–	–
G.R. Dilley	5917	2972	99	30.02	6-154	3	–
P.H. Edmonds	12028	4273	125	34.18	7-66	2	–
J.E. Emburey	10868	3855	115	33.52	7-78	6	–
N.A. Foster	3847	1819	54	33.68	8-107	4	1
M.W. Gatting	614	256	2	128.00	1-14	–	–
G.A. Gooch	1419	546	13	42.00	2-12	–	–
D.I. Gower	36	20	1	20.00	1-1	–	–
A.J. Lamb	30	23	1	23.00	1-6	–	–
M.D. Moxon	36	27	0	–	–	–	–
R.T. Robinson	6	0	0	–	–	–	–
G.C. Small	856	314	16	19.62	5-48	2	–

Australia

Batting / Fielding	M	I	NO	HS	R	Avge	100	50	Ct/St
D.C. Boon	23	42	2	131	1399	34.97	4	7	12
A.R. Border	89	157	26	196	6917	52.80	21	33	94
R.J. Bright	25	39	8	33	445	14.35	–	–	13
G.C. Dyer	1	0	0	0	0	–	–	–	2/–
D.R. Gilbert	9	12	4	15	57	7.12	–	–	–
M.G. Hughes	5	7	0	16	31	4.42	–	–	3
D.M. Jones	10	19	2	210	947	55.70	2	4	4
G.F. Lawson	37	60	10	57*	756	15.12	–	3	8
C.J. McDermott	17	23	1	36	189	8.59	–	–	5
G.R. Marsh	14	26	1	118	974	38.96	3	3	8
C.D. Matthews	2	3	0	11	21	7.00	–	–	1
G.R.J. Matthews	21	34	6	130	1031	36.82	3	4	13
S.P.O'Donnell	6	10	3	48	206	29.42	–	–	4
B.A. Reid	13	16	8	13	45	5.62	–	–	1
G.M. Ritchie	30	53	5	146	1690	35.20	3	7	14
P.R. Sleep	7	12	0	64	149	12.41	–	1	1
P.L. Taylor	1	2	0	42	53	26.50	–	–	–
S.R. Waugh	13	21	4	79*	482	28.35	–	4	12
D.McD. Wellham	6	11	0	103	257	23.36	1	–	5
T.J. Zoehrer	10	14	2	52*	246	20.50	–	1	18/1

Bowling	Balls	R	W	Avge	Best	5wI	10wM
D.C. Boon	12	5	0	–	–	–	–
A.R. Border	1781	699	16	43.68	3-20	–	–
R.J. Bright	5541	2180	53	41.13	7-87	4	1
D.R. Gilbert	1647	843	16	52.68	3-48	–	–
M.G. Hughes	1047	567	11	51.54	3-134	–	–
D.M. Jones	6	0	0	–	–	–	–
G.F. Lawson	8705	4420	145	30.48	8-112	10	2
C.J. McDermott	3346	1935	53	36.50	8-141	2	–
C.D. Matthews	421	233	6	38.33	3-95	–	–
G.R.J. Matthews	3500	1707	39	43.76	5-103	2	1
S.P.O'Donnell	940	504	6	84.00	3-37	–	–
B.A. Reid	2959	1368	41	33.36	4-64	–	–
G.M. Ritchie	6	10	0	–	–	–	–
P.R. Sleep	1405	697	13	53.61	5-72	1	–
P.L. Taylor	330	154	8	19.25	6-78	1	–
S.R. Waugh	1185	618	19	32.52	5-69	1	–

West Indies

Batting/Fielding	M	I	NO	HS	R	Avge	100	50	Ct/St
C.G. Butts	4	5	1	17	52	13.00	–	–	–
P.J.L. Dujon	43	57	4	139	2020	38.11	4	10	139/3
J. Garner	58	68	14	60	672	12.44	–	1	42
H.A. Gomes	60	91	11	143	3171	39.63	9	13	18
A.H. Gray	5	8	2	12*	48	8.00	–	–	6
C.G. Greenidge	77	128	14	223	5509	48.32	13	29	69
R.A. Harper	19	25	3	60	352	16.00	–	1	24
D.L. Haynes	65	108	12	184	4009	41.76	9	24	40
M.A. Holding	60	76	10	73	910	13.78	–	6	22
A.L. Logie	16	21	1	130	555	27.75	1	3	15
M.D. Marshall	51	62	5	92	1068	18.73	–	7	23
B.P. Patterson	6	7	4	9	18	6.00	–	–	2
I.V.A. Richards	88	131	8	291	6472	52.61	20	28	85
R.B. Richardson	26	41	4	185	1636	44.21	6	4	35
C.A. Walsh	13	16	7	18*	82	9.11	–	–	3

Bowling	Balls	R	W	Avge	Best	5wI	10wM
C.G. Butts	870	290	8	36.25	4-73	–	–
J. Garner	13169	5433	259	20.97	6-56	7	–
H.A. Gomes	2401	930	15	62.00	2-20	–	–
A.H. Gray	888	377	22	17.13	4-39	–	–
C.G. Greenidge	26	4	0	–	–	–	–
R.A. Harper	2997	1090	40	27.25	6-57	1	–
D.L. Haynes	18	8	1	8.00	1-2	–	–
M.A. Holding	12680	5898	249	23.68	8-92	13	2
A.L. Logie	7	4	0	–	–	–	–
M.D. Marshall	11278	5194	240	21.64	7-53	14	2
B.P. Patterson	895	527	22	23.95	4-30	–	–
I.V.A. Richards	3364	1208	22	54.90	2-20	–	–
R.B. Richardson	42	9	0	–	–	–	–
C.A. Walsh	2533	1111	45	24.68	5-73	1	–

New Zealand

Batting / Fielding	M	I	NO	HS	R	Avge	100	50	Ct/St
S.L. Boock	28	40	8	37	199	6.21	–	–	14
J.G. Bracewell	24	35	9	110	604	23.23	1	2	19
E.J. Chatfield	33	40	25	21*	142	9.46	–	–	6
J.J. Crowe	30	49	4	128	1323	29.40	3	6	35
M.D. Crowe	36	59	6	188	2162	40.79	7	6	42
E.J. Gray	8	12	0	50	208	17.33	–	1	4
R.J. Hadlee	70	111	16	151*	2622	27.60	2	13	36
P.A. Horne	2	3	0	16	25	8.33	–	–	1
A.H. Jones	1	1	0	38	38	38.00	–	–	–
D.N. Patel	3	6	0	21	73	12.16	–	–	–
K.R. Rutherford	11	18	2	65	191	11.93	–	2	5
I.D.S. Smith	37	49	10	113*	865	22.17	1	2	103/6
M.C. Snedden	13	13	2	32	154	14.00	–	–	3
J.G. Wright	52	92	4	141	2874	32.65	6	13	24

Bowling	Balls	R	W	Avge	Best	5wI	10wM
S.L. Boock	6022	2282	72	31.69	7-87	4	–
J.G. Bracewell	4774	1977	61	32.40	6-32	2	1
E.J. Chatfield	7749	3102	100	31.02	6-73	3	1
J.J. Crowe	18	9	0	–	–	–	–
M.D. Crowe	1239	607	13	46.69	2-25	–	–
E.J.Gray	1506	617	14	44.07	3-73	–	–
R.J. Hadlee	18091	7976	355	22.46	9-52	29	7
D.N. Patel	54	51	0	–	–	–	–
K.R. Rutherford	76	56	1	56.00	1-38	–	–
I.D.S. Smith	18	5	0	–	–	–	–
M.C. Snedden	2121	1053	29	36.31	5-68	1	–
J.G. Wright	30	5	0	–	–	–	–

India

Batting / Fielding	M	I	NO	HS	R	Avge	100	50	Ct/St
M.B. Amarnath	66	108	10	138	4322	44.10	11	24	45
B. Arun	2	2	1	2*	4	4.00	–	–	2
Arun Lal	5	9	0	63	286	31.77	–	4	5
M. Azharuddin	21	31	3	199	1461	52.17	6	4	18
R.M.H. Binny	27	41	5	83*	830	23.05	–	5	11
S.M. Gavaskar	125	214	16	236*	10122	51.12	34	45	108
Kapil Dev	88	126	12	163	3668	32.17	5	21	43
R.R. Kulkarni	3	2	0	2	2	1.00	–	–	1
R. Lamba	3	3	0	53	101	33.66	–	1	1
Maninder Singh	28	30	10	15	85	4.25	–	–	8
K.S. More	13	15	4	48	266	24.18	–	–	25/5
C.S. Pandit	3	5	1	39	140	35.00	–	–	4/1
C. Sharma	16	16	6	54	237	23.70	–	1	3
G. Sharma	4	3	1	10*	11	5.50	–	–	1
R.J. Shastri	54	79	11	142	2463	36.22	7	9	25
K.Srikkanth	28	44	1	123	1386	32.23	2	7	24
D.B. Vengsarkar	95	153·	20	166	5951	44.74	15	29	65
N.S. Yadav	35	40	12	43	403	14.39	–	–	10

Bowling	Balls	R	W	Avge	Best	5wI	10wM
M.B. Amarnath	3599	1740	32	54.37	4-63	–	–
B. Arun	252	116	4	29.00	3-76	–	–
Arun Lal	7	6	0	–	–	–	–
M. Azharuddin	6	8	0	–	–	–	–
R.M.H. Binny	2870	1534	47	32.63	6-56	2	–
S.M. Gavaskar	380	206	1	206.00	1-34	–	–
Kapil Dev	18547	9145	311	29.40	9-83	19	2
R.R. Kulkarni	366	227	5	45.40	3-85	–	–
Maninder Singh	6737	2568	77	33.35	7-27	3	2
C. Sharma	2586	1529	43	35.55	6-58	3	1
G. Sharma	1085	353	9	39.22	4-88	–	–
R.J. Shastri	12526	4683	119	39.35	5-75	2	–
K. Srikkanth	132	61	0	–	–	–	–
D.B. Vengsarkar	47	36	0	–	–	–	–
N.S. Yadav	8354	3580	102	35.09	5-76	3	–

Pakistan

Batting / Fielding	M	I	NO	HS	R	Avge	100	50	Ct/St
Abdul Qadir	48	56	5	54	724	14.19	–	2	12
Asif Mujtaba	2	4	0	12	32	8.00	–	–	1
Ijaz Ahmed	5	5	0	69	153	30.60	–	2	4
Ijaz Fakih	3	5	0	105	168	33.60	1	–	4
Imran Khan	70	101	17	135*	2770	32.97	4	11	24
Iqbal Qasim	44	50	14	56	446	12.38	–	1	39
Javed Miandad	86	133	18	280*	6251	54.35	15	34	71/1
Mansoor Akhtar	18	27	3	111	636	26.50	1	3	7
Manzoor Elahi	4	6	1	52	109	21.80	–	1	5
Mohsin Kamal	7	7	5	13*	31	15.50	–	–	2
Mohsin Khan	48	79	6	200	2709	37.10	7	9	34
Mudassar Nazar	65	99	8	231	3745	41.15	9	17	43
Qasim Omar	26	43	2	210	1502	36.63	3	5	15
Ramiz Raja	16	26	1	122	794	31.76	2	3	16
Rizwan-uz-Zaman	9	17	1	60	312	19.50	–	3	2
Salim Jaffer	3	4	1	9	17	5.66	–	–	–
Salim Malik	41	56	10	119*	1850	40.21	6	8	39
Salim Yousuf	16	21	3	91*	502	27.88	–	2	48/5
Shoaib Mohammad	13	18	1	101	472	27.76	1	2	5
Tausif Ahmed	22	23	12	23*	156	14.18	–	–	7
Wasim Akram	20	24	5	66	284	14.94	–	2	7
Younis Ahmed	4	7	1	62	177	29.50	–	1	–

Bowling	Balls	R	W	Avge	Best	5wI	10wM
Abdul Qadir	12041	5508	161	34.21	7-96	11	3
Asif Mujtaba	18	2	0	–	–	–	–
Ijaz Fakih	318	166	2	83.00	1-76	–	–
Imran Khan	16358	6903	311	22.19	8-58	21	5
Iqbal Qasim	11711	4362	149	29.27	7-49	6	2
Javed Miandad	1470	682	17	40.11	3-74	–	–
Manzoor Elahi	156	84	2	42.00	1-8	–	–
Mohsin Kamal	1024	597	17	35.11	4-127	–	–
Mohsin Khan	86	30	0	–	–	–	–
Mudassar Nazar	5217	2266	54	41.96	6-32	1	–
Qasim Omar	6	0	0	–	–	–	–
Rizwan-uz-Zaman	132	46	4	11.50	3-26	–	–
Salim Jaffer	432	205	4	51.25	2-115	–	–
Salim Malik	134	63	3	21.00	1-3	–	–
Shoaib Mohammad	72	40	1	40.00	1-19	–	–
Tausif Ahmed	5096	2049	70	29.27	6-45	3	–
Wasim Akram	4031	1677	63	26.61	6-91	4	1
Younis Ahmed	6	6	0	–	–	–	–

Sri Lanka

Batting / Fielding	M	I	NO	HS	R	Avge	100	50	Ct/St
S.D. Anurasiri	4	5	2	8	13	4.33	–	–	–
R.G. De Alwis	10	17	0	28	144	8.47	–	–	19/2
A.L.F. De Mel	17	28	5	34	326	14.17	–	–	9
E.A.R. De Silva	5	8	3	21	72	14.40	–	–	3
P.A. De Silva	13	24	2	122	626	28.45	2	1	5
R.L. Dias	20	36	1	109	1285	36.71	3	8	6
A.P. Gurusinha	7	12	2	116*	351	35.10	1	–	3
B.R. Jurangpathy	2	4	0	1	1	0.25	–	–	2
D.B.S.P. Kuruppu	1	1	1	201*	201	–	1	–	1/–
A.K. Kuruppuarchchi	2	2	2	0*	0	–	–	–	–
G.F. Labrooy	1	1	1	5*	5	–	–	–	–
R.S. Madugalle	19	35	4	103	993	32.03	1	7	9
R.S. Mahanama	3	5	0	41	79	15.80	–	–	1
L.R.D. Mendis	23	41	1	124	1252	31.30	4	7	8
A. Ranatunga	22	39	2	135*	1354	36.59	2	10	10
R.J. Ratnayake	14	23	4	56	272	14.31	–	1	5
J.R. Ratnayeke	18	31	5	93	514	19.76	–	2	1
S. Wettimuny	23	43	1	190	1221	29.07	2	6	10

Bowling	Balls	R	W	Avge	Best	5wI	10wM
S.D. Anurasiri	486	159	5	31.80	4-71	–	–
A.L.F. De Mel	3518	2180	59	36.94	6-109	3	–
E.A.R. De Silva	978	413	2	206.50	1-37	–	–
P.A. De Silva	30	22	0	–	–	–	–
R.L. Dias	24	17	0	–	–	–	–
A.P. Gurusinha	107	84	2	42.00	2-25	–	–
B.R. Jurangpathy	150	93	1	93.00	1-69	–	–
A.K. Kuruppuarchchi	272	149	8	18.62	5-44	1	–
G.F. Labrooy	210	164	1	164.00	1-164	–	–
R.S. Madugalle	84	38	0	–	–	–	–
A. Ranatunga	1305	576	9	64.00	2-17	–	–
R.J. Ratnayake	2825	1512	41	36.87	6-85	2	–
J.R. Ratnayeke	3102	1609	49	32.83	8-83	4	–
S. Wettimuny	24	37	0	–	–	–	–

Guide to Newcomers

Record in English First-Class Cricket 1987

Batting / Fielding		M	I	NO	HS	R	Avge	100	50	Ct/St
Derbyshire	M. Beardshall	8	8	3	25	47	9.40	–	–	1
	T.J.E. O'Gorman	2	4	1	11*	19	6.33	–	–	2
	M. Wakefield	1	1	0	4	4	4.00	–	–	1
Essex	M.G. Field-Buss	2	4	1	34*	56	18.66	–	–	–
	N. Hussain	2	3	0	18	32	10.66	–	–	2
	H.A. Page	15	20	4	60	266	16.62	–	1	5
	I.R. Redpath	7	12	1	46	128	11.63	–	–	2
Glamorgan	C.J.P.G. Van Zyl	8	5	0	35	85	17.00	–	–	–
Gloucestershire	D.A. Burrows	1	–	–	–	–	–	–	–	–
	V.S. Greene	8	11	4	62*	186	26.57	–	1	4
	K.B. Ibadulla	5	8	1	46*	145	20.71	–	–	2
	O.C.K. Smith	1	2	0	14	15	7.50	–	–	–
Hampshire	A.N. Aymes	1	1	0	58	58	58.00	–	1	1/-
Kent	P. Farbrace	5	7	3	75*	134	33.50	–	1	11/-
	S.C. Goldsmith	2	4	0	25	49	12.25	–	–	1
	D.J.M. Kelleher	12	12	1	20	81	7.36	–	–	1
	R.F. Pienaar	7	8	0	153	327	40.87	1	1	2
Lancashire	I.D. Austin	2	1	0	37	37	37.00	–	–	–
	D. Fitton	1	1	0	3	3	3.00	–	–	–
	K.W. McLeod	6	6	0	31	92	15.33	–	–	1
Leicestershire	C.C. Lewis	4	4	0	42	53	13.25	–	–	1
Middlesex	M.R. Ramprakash	8	14	3	71	321	29.18	–	2	6
Northamptonshire	S.J. Brown	5	5	3	20	25	12.50	–	–	1
	M.A. Robinson	7	6	2	2	4	1.00	–	–	1
Nottinghamshire	R.J. Evans	1	2	0	4	4	2.00	–	–	1
	P. Pollard	5	7	0	59	132	18.85	–	1	4
	A. Somani	1	1	1	26*	26	–	–	–	–
Somerset	R.G. Woolston	1	1	0	0	0	–	–	–	–
Surrey	D.J. Bicknell	12	20	3	105	600	35.29	1	4	5
Sussex	K. Greenfield	2	4	0	18	34	8.50	–	–	2
	P.A.W. Heseltine	18	18	3	26	172	11.46	–	–	3
	S.D. Myles	2	3	1	18*	19	9.50	–	–	1
	M.W. Pringle	1	1	0	12	12	12.00	–	–	–
	C.I.O. Ricketts	3	1	0	29	29	29.00	–	–	1
Warwickshire	A.A. Donald	11	10	3	37*	111	15.85	–	–	1
	T.A. Merrick	14	19	5	74*	220	15.71	–	1	5
	E.T. Milburn	3	4	2	24	37	18.50	–	–	2
	N.M.K. Smith	2	4	1	23	56	18.66	–	–	1
Cambridge Univ.	R. Bate	3	4	0	36	65	16.25	–	–	1
	R. Clitheroe	3	4	0	36	63	15.75	–	–	5/2
	R.J. Hart	6	9	1	12	46	5.75	–	–	1
	A.M. Hooper	3	4	0	89	112	28.00	–	1	–
	M.R. Middleton	2	1	0	6	6	6.00	–	–	–
	S. Palmer	1	1	0	18	18	18.00	–	–	–

Batting / Fielding (contd)		M	I	NO	HS	R	Avge	100	50	Ct/St
	J.N. Perry	4	3	0	21	31	10.33	–	–	1
	G.A. Pointer	8	11	3	33	104	13.00	–	–	1
	T.M. Verghese	1	1	0	2	2	2.00	–	–	–
CU & Lancashire	M.A. Atherton	21	35	4	110	1193	38.48	2	4	7
Oxford University	A.R. Beech	4	7	0	33	49	7.00	–	–	1
	M.A. Crawley	7	10	1	140	263	29.22	1	1	2
	P.G. Edwards	7	7	4	8	23	7.66	–	–	3
	T. Firth	7	7	0	10	33	4.71	–	–	1
	I.M. Henderson	6	7	1	14	33	5.50	–	–	2
	R.E. Morris	6	9	2	34	98	14.00	–	–	1
	J.D. Nuttall	1	1	0	3	3	3.00	–	–	–
	R.D. Sardesai	7	9	1	63*	222	27.75	–	1	2

Bowling		O	M	R	W	Avge	Best	5wI	10wM
Derbyshire	M. Beardshall	158.2	21	572	12	47.66	4-68	–	–
Essex	H.A. Page	340.2	52	1172	35	33.48	5-26	1	–
Glamorgan	C.J.P.G. Van'Zyl	172	37	511	14	36.50	3-35	–	–
Gloucestershire	D.A. Burrows	9	0	27	0	–	–	–	–
	V.S. Greene	216.5	32	819	29	28.24	7-96	1	–
	K.B. Ibadulla	54	8	156	4	39.00	3-37	–	–
Kent	S.C. Goldsmith	6	0	37	1	37.00	1-37	–	–
	D.J.M. Kelleher	301	72	878	34	25.82	6-109	2	–
	R.F. Pienaar	135.4	27	427	15	28.46	4-66	–	–
Lancashire	I.D. Austin	33.5	7	64	3	21.33	3-28	–	–
	D. Fitton	7	0	23	1	23.00	1-23	–	–
	K.W. McLeod	126.4	24	409	17	24.05	5-8	2	–
Leicestershire	C.C. Lewis	63	9	167	5	33.40	2-26	–	–
Middlesex	M. R. Ramprakash	1	0	1	0	–	–	–	–
Northamptonshire	S.J. Brown	82	23	216	9	24.00	3-67	–	–
	M.A. Robinson	150	25	501	13	38.53	3-45	–	–
Nottinghamshire	R.J. Evans	2	0	10	0	–	–	–	–
	A. Somani	4.3	0	7	2	3.50	2-7	–	–
Somerset	R.G. Woolston	43	10	107	2	53.50	2-70	–	–
Sussex	P.A.W. Heseltine	316.2	75	963	21	45.85	3-33	–	–
	S.D. Myles	4	0	28	0	–	–	–	–
	M.W. Pringle	16	4	45	2	22.50	2-45	–	–
	C.I.O. Ricketts	71.4	8	253	5	50.60	2-40	–	–
Warwickshire	A.A. Donald	301.4	36	1012	39	25.94	6-74	2	–
	T.A. Merrick	433.3	71	1439	57	25.24	7-45	4	1
	E.T. Milburn	36	6	128	2	64.00	1-26	–	–
	N.M.K. Smith	42	6	152	4	38.00	2-73	–	–
Cambridge Univ.	R.J. Hart	166.2	40	477	9	53.00	2-19	–	–
	M.R. Middleton	36	5	119	1	119.00	1-72	–	–
	S. Palmer	16	3	57	1	57.00	1-41	–	–
	J.N. Perry	66.5	12	193	8	24.12	3-56	–	–
	G.A. Pointer	176	25	568	10	56.80	3-52	–	–
	T.M. Verghese	22.2	1	110	1	110.00	1-36	–	–
CU & Lancashire	M.A. Atherton	162.5	16	544	9	60.44	3-72	–	–

Bowling (contd)		O	M	R	W	Avge	Best	5wI	10wM
Oxford Univ.	M.A. Crawley	161.1	32	516	6	86.00	2-30	–	–
	P.G. Edwards	172.4	42	500	14	35.71	4-93	–	–
	T. Firth	209.3	29	682	14	48.71	4-129	–	–
	I.M. Henderson	111	13	437	7	62.42	3-48	–	–
	R.E. Morris	2	0	11	0	–	–	–	–
	J.D. Nuttall	19	5	48	1	48.00	1-18	–	–

County caps awarded in 1987

Derbyshire: B.J.M. Maher, A.E. Warner
Glamorgan: S.R. Barwick, A.R. Butcher, M.P. Maynard, C.P. Metson
Gloucestershire: G.E. Sainsbury, A.J. Wright
Kent: C. Penn
Lancashire: I. Folley, B.P. Patterson, M. Watkinson
Leicestershire: P.J. Whitticase
Middlesex: J.D. Carr
Northamptonshire: W.W. Davis, D. Ripley, A. Walker
Nottinghamshire: M. Newell, R.A. Pick
Somerset: N.D. Burns, J.J.E. Hardy, A.N. Jones, N.A. Mallender
Surrey: I.A. Greig
Warwickshire: Asif Din, A.J. Moles, G.J. Parsons
Worcestershire: I.T. Botham, G.R. Dilley
Yorkshire: R.J. Blakey, P.J. Hartley

Deloittes Ratings
by Ted Dexter

Every good idea needs a little luck if it is to become a reality. When I first thought of a rating system for all Test cricketers, it was a daunting prospect for somebody who is only marginally computer literate, and that was where the luck came in. I telephoned friends at the *Cricketer* magazine in case they knew of anyone with cricket and computer knowledge in roughly equal parts, and so I came to meet Robert Eastaway and Gordon Vince. They had published details of a computerized Test cricket system, not the rating of players, but a ball-by-ball simulation of the real thing. It had no obvious application for what I had in mind, but convinced me that they knew their business.

An initial study of the problem was encouraging. Perhaps not everyone would agree that there was a problem. But for me the traditional averages had always been a very rough and ready measurement of player effectiveness, albeit that, by the end of a long career, they may well give a reasonable guide, particularly for batsmen.

Bowling figures, on the other hand, had always seemed unsatisfactory. Which is better, after 50 Test matches – 150 wickets at 21 or 220 wickets at 31? Only by going back through every scorecard can you start to build up a picture of real values. And this is precisely what it was agreed should be done once Robert Eastaway's employers, accountants Deloitte Haskins & Sells, took an interest in the planning and development of Deloittes Ratings.

How do the Deloittes Ratings differ from averages? Mainly in three areas. They are a more up-to-date form of measurement, because past performances are progressively discounted. So, Martin Crowe's increasingly good batting form is rewarded with a steep upward slope of his graph. By the same token, Ian Botham's bowling performance figures are no longer buoyed up by the wonder years in the early 80s.

Batting and bowling figures are remeasured in two ways, according to the quality of the opposition and according to the overall equation of runs

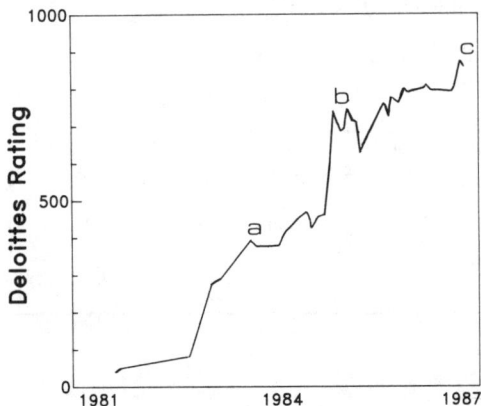

Martin Crowe (batting)
After a rather undistinguished start, Martin Crowe has grown in stature as a Test player to justify his 4th place in the world ratings. Notable landmarks in his rise were: (a) Rating reaches 392 at Christchurch against England in 1984, (b) passes 700 against Pakistan in 1985, and (c) reaches peak of 858 against West Indies at Christchurch in 1987.

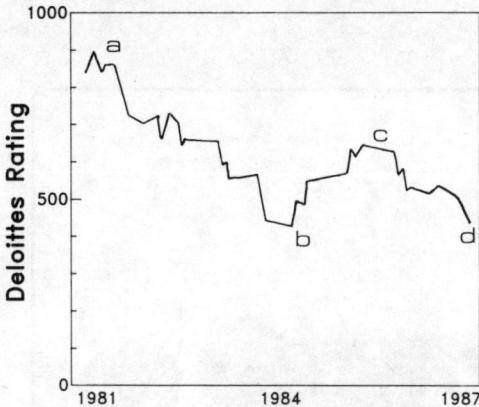

Ian Botham (bowling)
Since the golden year of 1981 Ian Botham's bowling has not lived up to his early successes. His rating dropped from a peak of 890 (a) to a low of 420 (b) against West Indies in 1984. A good series in 1985 saw a recovery in his rating to 646 (c), before it slid again to 446 (d) at the end of the 1987 series against Pakistan.

and wickets for the whole of a Test match. Once every batsman and bowler has a rating, it is easy enough to balance the performance figures accordingly, in much the same way that Sony Ranking in golf gives points for a tournament victory depending on the strength of the field.

The runs/wickets equation is computed against a researched Test average, approximately 31 per wicket. So, a high individual score at Adelaide, where the average may be nearer 50, is not rated so highly as at Headingley, where the average is in the 20s. To reach and maintain a very high rating, as Richard Hadlee has done, means taking wickets at reasonable cost against highly rated opponents on flat pitches as well as lively ones, and helping to win a few matches into the bargain.

At the time of writing, there have been only four Tests since the Deloittes Ratings were launched, before the England v Pakistan match at Lord's. During our winter, there are 19 more Tests scheduled, with England playing in seven of them. I don't think I am the only one who is looking forward to seeing how the world's players measure up to one another in the coming months.

Top 20 Deloittes Ratings

Batting		Rating	Bowling		Rating
1 Vengsarkar	(IND)	893	1 Hadlee	(NZ)	905
2 Greenidge	(WI)	875	2 Imran Khan	(PAK)	901
3 Jones	(AUS)	844	3 Garner	(WI)	835
4 Crowe, M.	(NZ)	838	4 Marshall	(WI)	813
5 Richards	(WI)	819	5 Holding	(WI)	795
6 Haynes	(WI)	818	6 Tauseef	(PAK)	684
7 Border	(AUS)	792	7 Qasim	(PAK)	678
8 Gatting	(ENG)	788	8 Harper	(WI)	675
9 Richardson	(WI)	784	9 Gray	(WI)	674
10 Miandad	(PAK)	762	10 Walsh	(WI)	654
11 Gower	(ENG)	725	11 Akram	(PAK)	639
12 Ranatunga	(SRI)	723	12 Lawson	(AUS)	635
13 Gavaskar	(IND)	714	13 Chatfield	(NZ)	609
14 Azharuddin	(IND)	698	14 Foster	(ENG)	602
15 Coney	(NZ)	693	15 Waugh	(AUS)	591
16 Gooch	(ENG)	683	16 Small	(ENG)	590
17 Mudassar	(PAK)	680	17 Reid	(AUS)	578
18 Imran Khan	(PAK)	678	18 Patterson	(WI)	577
19 Salim Malik	(PAK)	671	19 Ratnayeke	(SRI)	574
20 Broad	(ENG)	666	20 Sharma, C.	(IND)	572

Lending support
to British Sport

Obituary 1986-87

Sixteen Test cricketers come under notice this time, as against 17 last, several of enduring distinction and four who join the numerous band who did play for their countries but only once. The English list is headed by *W.E. Bowes*, whose name is bracketed with Hedley Verity's as the two chief architects of Yorkshire's dominance in the 1930s. With his control of the seam, late out-swing and steep rise, there was no more lethal opening county bowler in my time. He had his successes likewise in Test matches.

H.E. Dollery, always called Tom, is remembered, like Bowes, for county deeds, in his case for leading Warwickshire, in 1951, to the second Championship in their history. Tom was a popular and efficient captain at a time when only one other county (Sussex by James Langridge) was led by a professional. *J.W. Martin*, a once-only man, was the truest of amateurs in that as a fast bowler for Catford Wanderers he played for Kent (a mere 33 times) only on his annual holiday.

On to Australia: *A.G. Chipperfield* at Trent Bridge was c. Ames b. Farnes 99, poor fellow, in his first Test innings. He was a high-class slipper. *L.E. Favell*, 19 times capped, was a most attractive bat and personality and something of a legend in South Australia. Les led the state a record 95 times, scored most runs, 8,983, and on retirement made a successful transition to radio commentating until his death from cancer, aged only 57. *R.A. Saggers*, of NSW was an admirable wicket-keeper whose misfortune was that his career coincided with that of Don Tallon.

J.A.K. Cochran and *G.G. Hall* each played for South Africa, *R.L. Fuller* for West Indies. In August, *J.D.C. Goddard*, captain of West Indies in the years of their first supremacy just after World War II, died suddenly in London when over from Barbados as guest of MCC at the Bicentenary Match. John, in 1950, led West Indies to their first Test victory at Lord's. One of his side was *H.H.H. Johnson*, who at 40 was too old to fill the role of fast bowler. *E.E. Achong* of Trinidad was a member of that island's 'League of Nations' team. Ellis was a Chinaman, and he bowled them, often very well, before becoming a Test umpire. *M.L. Page*, nicknamed Curly, was prominent in New Zealand's early Test days and captain of the 1937 tour to England. He was also an All Blacks rugby footballer. The Indians *A.G. Kripal Singh*, *P.G. Joshi*, and *J.K. Irani* complete the Test casualty list.

Pride of place among the county cricketers must go to *J.E. Mercer*, whose service to cricket, delayed by the claims of World War I, nevertheless encompassed 65 years. From the Sussex staff he migrated to Glamorgan, being for many years the rock around which their flimsy attack was built. He was an inventive bowler of fastish speed who took 1,591 wickets. Jack coached and finally scored for Northants for 36 years, reluctantly giving up aged 88. He lived, this lovely fellow, to 92 – as he said, 'approximately'. *W.W. Timms* and *A.L. Cox*, both Northampton born and bred, served their native county well in the difficult inter-war years. *G.F. Hodgkinson* led Derbyshire in 1946. The fielding of *G.E. Hart* for Middlesex was much admired among the Lord's faithful. *T.H. Wade*, of Essex, was recruited in emergency to keep wicket for MCC in Australia in 1936-37, and was rewarded with the touring cap.

O.W. Herman, known as Lofty, was the pre-war mainstay of Hampshire's bowling (1,045 wickets) and in the 1960s a well-respected umpire. *D.D.S. Taylor* from Jamaica played a little for Warwickshire but made his real impact as the county coach. Derief was a smiling Edgbaston character. *W.R. Watkins* was MCC head coach in the 1930s and as such was specially proud of his star pupil, Denis Compton. *Admiral G.J.A. Miles* earns inclusion as having enjoyed 80 years of MCC membership, and being on his death aged 96 the senior of the 18,000 of us.

The deaths occurred of four Blues, *Dr. J.A. Nunn*, *W.H. Bradshaw*, and *R.Sale* of Oxford and *A.W.G. Hadingham* of Cambridge. John Nunn also won a rugger blue at stand-off half. Walter Bradshaw for many years ran the cricket at Stowe. Dick Sale, a left-hander who also opened the batting for Warwickshire and Derbyshire, was a long-serving headmaster of Brentwood.

I conclude with two men who in different ways rendered cricket devoted and distinguished service. *J.G. Dunbar* was an assistant-secretary of MCC for 25 years, and for the last five of them was also the first secretary of the National Cricket Association. His enthusiasm for boys' cricket – and for non-turf pitches – here had full outlet. An admirable club bowler, he was Hon. Sec of the Butterflies. *J.D.B. Coldham* was for the last 30-odd years of his life an utterly reliable historical researcher on the game. He wrote the only biography of Lord Harris, and was for 14 years editor of the *Journal of the Cricket Society*.

E.W. Swanton

Career Details

(b – born; d – died; F-c – first-class career)

ACHONG, Ellis Edgar; b Port of Spain, Trinidad, 16.2.04; d Port of Spain, 29.8.86. Trinidad and West Indies. F-c (1929-30 to 1934-35): 503 runs (14.37); 110 wkts (30.23); 20 ct.

BOWES, William Eric; b Elland, Yorkshire, 25.7.08; d Menston, Leeds, 5.9.87. Yorkshire and England. F-c (1929-47): 1,530 runs (8.59); 1,639 wkts (16.76); 138 ct.

CHIPPERFIELD, Arthur Gordon: b Ashfield, NSW, Australia, 17.11.05; d Sydney, 22.7.87. NSW and Australia. F-c (1933-34 to 1939-40): 4,295 runs (38.34), 9 hundreds; 65 wkts (39.72); 92 ct.

COCHRAN, John Alexander Kennedy; b South Africa, 15.7.09; d Johannesburg, 15.6.87. Transvaal, Griqualand West, and South Africa. F-c (1929-30 to 1931-32): 15 wkts (24.06).

DOLLERY, Horace Edgar; b Reading, Berkshire, 14.10.14; d 20.1.87. Warwickshire, Wellington, and England. F-c (1934-55): 24,413 runs (37.50), 50 hundreds; 0 wkt (0-37); 291 ct, 13 st.

FAVELL, Leslie Ernest; b Arncliffe, Sydney, 6.10.29; d Adelaide, 14.6.87. South Australia and Australia. F-c (1951-52 to 1969-70): 12,379 runs (36.63), 27 hundreds; 110 ct.

FULLER, Richard Livingston; b Kingston, Jamaica, 30.1.13; d Jamaica 3.5.87. Jamaica and West Indies.

GODDARD, John Douglas Claude; b Bridgetown, Barbados, 21.4.19; d London, 26.8.87. Barbados and West Indies. F-c (1936-37 to 1957-58): 3,769 runs (33.35), 5 hundreds; 146 wkts (26.33); 94 ct.

HALL, Glen Gordon; b Pretoria, 24.5.38; d Ramsgate, Natal, 26.6.87. NE Transvaal, Eastern Province, and South Africa. F-c (1960-61 to 1967-68): 306 runs (7.84); 110 wkts (29.66).

JOHNSON, Hophnie Hobah Hines; b Kingston, Jamaica, 13.7.10; d Miami, 24.6.87. Jamaica and West Indies. F-c (1934-35 to 1950-51): 316 runs (17.55); 68 wkts (23.36); 13 ct.

JOSHI, Padmanabh Govind; b Baroda, 27.10.26; d Pune, 1986-87. Maharashtra and India. F-c (1946-47 to 1964-65): 1,724 runs (17.06), 1 hundred; 0 wkt (0-13); 120 ct, 61 st.

KRIPAL SINGH, Amritsar Govindsingh; b Madras, 6.8.33; d Madras, 22.7.87. Madras, Hyderabad, and India. F-c (1950-51 to 1965-66): 4,947 runs (40.88), 10 hundreds; 177 wkts (28.41); 57 ct.

MARTIN, John William; b Catford, London, 16.2.17; d Woolwich, 4.1.87. Kent and England. F-c (1939-53): 623 runs (11.53); 162 wkts (24.00); 32 ct.

PAGE, Milford Laurenson; b Littleton, 8.5.02; d Christchurch 13.2.87. Canterbury and New Zealand. F-c (1920-21 to 1936-37): 5,857 runs (29.88), 9 hundreds; 73 wkts (32.39); 117 ct.

SAGGERS, Ronald Arthur; b Sydenham, NSW, 15.5.17; d Mar 87. New South Wales and Australia. F-c (1939-40 to 1950-51): 1,888 runs (23.89), 1 hundred; 147 ct, 74 st.

Their Record in Tests

Batting/Fielding	Career	M	I	NO	HS	R	Avge	100	50	Ct/St
E.E. Achong (WI)	1929/30-1934/5	6	11	1	22	81	8.10	–	–	6
W.E. Bowes (Eng)	1932-1946	15	11	5	10*	28	4.66	–	–	2
A.G. Chipperfield (Aus)	1934-1938	14	20	3	109	552	32.47	1	2	15
J.A.K. Cochran (SA)	1930/1	1	1	0	4	4	4.00	–	–	–
H.E. Dollery (Eng)	1947-1950	4	7	0	37	72	10.28	–	–	1
L.E. Favell (Aus)	1954/5-1960/1	19	31	3	101	757	27.03	1	5	9
R.L. Fuller (WI)	1934/5	1	1	0	1	1	1.00	–	–	–
J.D.C. Goddard (WI)	1947/8-1957	27	39	11	83*	859	30.67	–	4	22
G.G. Hall (SA)	1964/5	1	1	0	0	0	–	–	–	–
H.H.H. Johnson (WI)	1947/8-1950	3	4	0	22	38	9.50	–	–	1
P.G. Joshi (Ind)	1951/2-1960/1	12	20	1	52*	207	10.89	–	1	18/9
A.G. Kripal Singh (Ind)	1955/6-1964/5	14	20	5	100*	422	28.13	1	2	4
J.W. Martin (Eng)	1947	1	2	0	26	26	13.00	–	–	–
M.L. Page (NZ)	1929/30-1937	14	20	0	104	492	24.60	1	2	6
R.A. Saggers (Aus)	1948-1949/50	6	5	2	14	30	10.00	–	–	16/8

Bowling	Balls	R	W	Avge	Best	5wI	10wM
E.E. Achong (WI)	918	378	8	47.25	2-64	–	–
W.E. Bowes (Eng)	3655	1519	68	22.33	6-33	6	–
A.G. Chipperfield (Aus)	924	437	5	87.40	3-91	–	–
J.A.K. Cochran (SA)	138	47	0	–	–	–	–
J.D.C. Goddard (WI)	2931	1050	33	31.81	5-31	1	–
G.G. Hall (SA)	186	94	1	94.00	1-94	–	–
H.H.H. Johnson (WI)	789	238	13	18.30	5-41	2	1
A.G. Kripal Singh (Ind)	1518	584	10	58.40	3-43	–	–
J.W. Martin (Eng)	270	129	1	129.00	1-111	–	–
M.L. Page (NZ)	379	231	5	46.20	2-21	–	–

1988

LOOKING FORWARD

England on Tour 1987-88

Tour Party to Pakistan & New Zealand*

	P	NZ	Age†	Caps		P	NZ	Age†	Caps
M.W. Gatting, cap. (Mx)	●	●	30	58	B.N. French (Notts)	●	●	28	9
C.W.J. Athey (Glos)	●	●	30	17	G.A. Gooch (Essex)	●		34	59
B.C. Broad (Notts)	●	●	30	14	E.E. Hemmings (Notts)	●	●	38	5
D.J. Capel (Northants)	●	●	24	1	P.W. Jarvis (Yorks)	●	●	22	0
N.G.B. Cook (Leics)	●		31	9	M.D. Moxon (Yorks)		●	27	3
P.A.J. DeFreitas (Leics)	●	●	21	5	N.V. Radford (Worcs)		●	30	2
G.R. Dilley (Worcs)	●	●	28	30	C.J. Richards (Surrey)		●	29	6
J.E. Emburey, v-c (Mx)	●	●	35	46	R.T. Robinson (Notts)	●	●	28	21
N.H. Fairbrother (Lancs)	●	●	24	1	R.C. Russell (Glos)		●	24	0
N.A. Foster (Essex)	●	●	25	19					

Manager: P.M. Lush. Assistant Manager: M.J. Stewart. Physiotherapist: L. Brown. Scorer: P.W. Austin. Medical Assistant: Dr A. Hall.

* Including Bicentenary Test with Australia; † at 30.9.87.

Tour Itinerary – Pakistan

November	14-16	Three-day match (Rawalpindi)
	18	Pakistan (Hyderabad), 1st 1-day international
	20	Pakistan (Multan), 2nd 1-day international
	22	Pakistan (Peshawar), 3rd 1-day international
	25, 26, 27, 29, 30	**Pakistan** (Lahore), 1st Test
December	2-4	Three-day match (Sahiwal)
	7, 8, 9, 11, 12	**Pakistan** (Faisalabad), 2nd Test
	15, 16, 17, 19, 20	**Pakistan** (Karachi), 3rd Test

Tour Itinerary – New Zealand (and Australia)

January	18-20	Three-day match (Wellington)
	23-25	Northern Districts (Hamilton)
	29-31, 1, 2 Feb	**Australia** (Sydney), Bicentenary Test
February	4	Australia (Melbourne), 1-day international
	7-9	Shell XI (New Plymouth)
	12, 13, 14, 16, 17	**New Zealand** (Christchurch), 1st Test
	19-21	President's XI (Dunedin)
	25-29	**New Zealand** (Auckland), 2nd Test
March	3-7	**New Zealand** (Wellington), 3rd Test
	9	New Zealand (Dunedin), 1st 1-day international
	12	New Zealand (Christchurch), 2nd 1-day international
	16	New Zealand (Napier), 3rd 1-day international
	19	New Zealand (Auckland), 4th 1-day international

The 1988 Season

By the time the 1988 season in England begins much will have happened at international level. The World Cup, taking place while this Year Book is in production, will have been followed by England's tours of Pakistan and New Zealand and by that of West Indies in India. A full season in Australia will include a series with New Zealand and England's visit for a Bicentenary Test in Sydney. Before West Indies come to England, they will meet Pakistan in the Caribbean.

The hectic pace of it all and the growing signs of stress among leading players, positively expressed by Mike Gatting on his departure for the subcontinent, may well, one hopes, soon have a moderating influence. Meanwhile, how is the form-book likely to read when West Indies arrive in England next May?

Confidence ebbs and flows more frequently nowadays than in the days when the English winter could be spent by Test players in other pursuits and in conserving themselves and their enthusiasm for battles ahead.

The five-Test series with West Indies does hold one attraction for England next summer. Its outcome can scarcely be more disastrous than that of recent series between the two sides. Going backwards, the memory touches painfully on the last 5-0 defeat in the Caribbean, 5-0 in England in 1984, 2-0 in West Indies in 1980-81, 1-0 in England in 1980, 3-0 in 1976. You go back to Trinidad in 1973-74 for the last England victory in a Test over West Indies and to 1969 for the last series won by England.

On the favourable evidence of 1986-87 in Australia, where England recorded several one-day wins over West Indies, things are looking up. West Indies were showing some signs of disarray and were in transition. The snag is that their transition is likely to be less upsetting than that of most countries. England, moreover, have not been able to carry on the stirring recovery of last winter and have temporarily lost such as Gower and Botham, who in less strenuous times would still be fresh and at their peak.

England's recent home record of defeats by India, New Zealand, and Pakistan scarcely bodes well, but for West Indies the 1988 tour will be important for other reasons than success on the field. A growing feeling amongst spectators as well as administrators that endless fast bowling and sluggish over-rates are bad for the game makes it desirable for West Indies to show that they are good enough to win playing cricket of wider variety.

England, for their part, have another, rather special, goal in 1988, for Sri Lanka will play a Test match at Lord's in August, having previously played one against Australia in Perth. In Sri Lanka's only previous Test here, in 1984, the good cricket came to an embarrassing extent from the newcomers to the Test arena. England then were somewhat punch-drunk and short of confidence after a hammering by West Indies. It should be a matter of pride that the same thing does not happen again.

Fixtures 1988

Duration of Matches (*including play on Sunday)

Cornhill Insurance Tests	5 days	Texaco Trophy	1 day
Britannic Assurance		Benson & Hedges Cup	1 day
County Championship	3 days or as stated	NatWest Bank Trophy	1 day
Tourist matches	3 days or as stated	Sunday League or Cup	1 day
University matches v Counties	3 days	Other matches	as stated

APRIL 16, SATURDAY

Fenners	Cambridge U v Derbyshire
The Parks	Oxford U v Leics
Lord's	MCC v Notts (3 days)

APRIL 20, WEDNESDAY

Fenners	Cambridge U v Warwickshire
The Parks	Oxford U v Northants

APRIL 21, THURSDAY

Britannic Assurance Championship (4 days)

Derby	Derbyshire v Leics
Chelmsford	Essex v Kent
Bristol	Glos v Glamorgan
Southampton	Hampshire v Surrey
Old Trafford	Lancashire v Worcs
Lord's	Middlesex v Notts
Hove	Sussex v Somerset

APRIL 24, SUNDAY

Refuge Assurance League

Derby	Derbyshire v Leics
Chelmsford	Essex v Kent
Bristol	Glos v Glamorgan
Southampton	Hampshire v Surrey
Old Trafford	Lancashire v Worcs
Lord's	Middlesex v Notts
Hove	Sussex v Somerset

APRIL 26, TUESDAY

Benson & Hedges Cup

Bristol	Glos v Cambridge U
Chelmsford	Essex v Surrey
Leicester	Leics v Lancashire
Trent Bridge	Notts v Minor Counties
Glasgow Hamilton Cres.	Scotland v Derbyshire
Taunton	Somerset v Hampshire
Hove	Sussex v Kent
Headingley	Yorkshire v Northants

APRIL 28, THURSDAY

Britannic Assurance Championship (4 days)

Cardiff	Glamorgan v Somerset
Bristol	Glos v Sussex
Canterbury	Kent v Hampshire
Old Trafford	Lancashire v Warwickshire
Leicester	Leics v Northants
Lord's	Middlesex v Essex
Worcester	Worcs v Notts
Headingley	Yorkshire v Derbyshire

Other Match

Fenners	Cambridge U v Surrey

MAY 1, SUNDAY

Refuge Assurance League

Cardiff	Glamorgan v Somerset
Bristol	Glos v Sussex
Canterbury	Kent v Hampshire
Old Trafford	Lancashire v Warwickshire
Leicester	Leics v Northants
Lord's	Middlesex v Essex
Worcester	Worcs v Notts
Headingley	Yorkshire v Derbyshire

MAY 3, TUESDAY

Benson & Hedges Cup

The Parks	Combined Univ v Somerset
Derby	Derbyshire v Warwickshire
Southampton	Hampshire v Glamorgan
Lord's	Middlesex v Sussex
Swindon	Minor Counties v Worcs
Trent Bridge	Notts v Yorkshire
Glasgow (Titwood)	Scotland v Leics
The Oval	Surrey v Kent

MAY 5, THURSDAY

Britannic Assurance Championship (4 days)

Chesterfield	Derbyshire v Essex
Leicester	Leics v Kent
Northampton	Northants v Glos
Trent Bridge	Notts v Lancs
Taunton	Somerset v Worcs
The Oval	Surrey v Middlesex
Edgbaston	Warwickshire v Yorkshire

Other Matches

Fenners	Cambridge U v Glamorgan
The Parks	Oxford U v Hampshire

MAY 7, SATURDAY

Tourist Match

Hove	Sussex v West Indies

MAY 8, SUNDAY

Refuge Assurance League

Derby	Derbyshire v Essex
Southampton	Hampshire v Glamorgan
Leicester	Leics v Kent
Northampton	Northants v Glos
Trent Bridge	Notts v Lancashire
Taunton	Somerset v Worcs
The Oval	Surrey v Middlesex
Edgbaston	Warwickshire v Yorkshire

Tourist Match
Arundel   Lavinia, Duchess of Norfolk's
               XI v West Indies (1 day)

MAY 10, TUESDAY
Benson & Hedges Cup
Southampton	Hampshire v Glos
Canterbury	Kent v Essex
Liverpool	Lancashire v Derbyshire
Darlington	Minor Counties v Northants
Taunton	Somerset v Glamorgan
The Oval	Surrey v Middlesex
Edgbaston	Warwickshire v Scotland
Worcester	Worcs v Notts

MAY 12, THURSDAY
Benson & Hedges Cup
Chelmsford	Essex v Sussex
Cardiff	Glamorgan v Combined Univs
Bristol	Glos v Somerset
Canterbury	Kent v Middlesex
Old Trafford	Lancashire v Scotland
Leicester	Leics v Warwickshire
Northampton	Northants v Worcs
Headingley	Yorkshire v Minor Counties

Tourist Match
Southampton   Hampshire v W. Indies (1 day)

MAY 14, SATURDAY
Benson & Hedges Cup
Fenners	Combined Univ v Hampshire
Derby	Derbyshire v Leics
Swansea	Glamorgan v Glos
Lord's	Middlesex v Essex
Northampton	Northants v Notts
Hove	Sussex v Surrey
Edgbaston	Warwickshire v Lancashire
Worcester	Worcs v Yorkshire

Tourist Match
Taunton*   Somerset v W. Indies

MAY 15, SUNDAY
Refuge Assurance League
Chelmsford	Essex v Northants
Southampton	Hampshire v Middlesex
Canterbury	Kent v Lancashire
Trent Bridge	Notts v Glos
Hove	Sussex v Surrey
Edgbaston	Warwickshire v Glamorgan
Worcester	Worcs v Yorkshire

MAY 17, TUESDAY
Britannic Assurance Championship (4 days)
Northampton   Northants v Warwickshire

MAY 18, WEDNESDAY
Britannic Assurance Championship
Bournemouth	Hampshire v Glamorgan
Leicester	Leics v Middlesex
Trent Bridge	Notts v Glos
Worcester	Worcs v Somerset

Other Matches
Fenners	Cambridge Univ v Essex
The Parks	Oxford Univ v Kent

MAY 19, THURSDAY
Texaco Trophy (1st 1-day international)
Edgbaston   England v West Indies

MAY 21, SATURDAY
Texaco Trophy (2nd 1-day international)
Headingley   England v West Indies

Britannic Assurance Championship
Swansea	Glamorgan v Derbyshire
Canterbury	Kent v Yorkshire
Leicester	Leics v Worcs
Trent Bridge	Notts v Sussex
The Oval	Surrey v Northants
Edgbaston	Warwicks v Essex

Other Matches
Fenners	Cambridge U v Middlesex
The Parks	Oxford U v Lancashire

MAY 22, SUNDAY
Refuge Assurance League
Newport	Glamorgan v Derbyshire
Canterbury	Kent v Yorkshire
Leicester	Leics v Worcs
Trent Bridge	Notts v Sussex
The Oval	Surrey v Northants
Edgbaston	Warwickshire v Essex

MAY 23, MONDAY
Texaco Trophy (3rd 1-day international)
Lord's   England v West Indies

MAY 25, WEDNESDAY
Benson & Hedges Cup
Quarter-finals

Tourist Match
Bristol   Glos† v West Indies

†Will be replaced by another county if engaged in
B & H.

MAY 28, SATURDAY
Britannic Assurance Championship
Derby	Derbyshire v Notts
Chelmsford	Essex v Surrey
Swansea	Glamorgan v Glos
Old Trafford	Lancashire v Somerset
Lord's	Middlesex v Sussex
Northampton	Northants v Leics
Middlesbrough	Yorkshire v Hampshire

Tourist Match
Worcester*   Worcs v West Indies

MAY 29, SUNDAY

Refuge Assurance League

Derby	Derbyshire v Notts
Chelmsford	Essex v Surrey
Swindon	Glos v Warwickshire
Old Trafford	Lancashire v Leics
Lord's	Middlesex v Sussex
Northampton	Northants v Kent
Middlesbrough	Yorkshire v Hampshire

JUNE 1, WEDNESDAY

Britannic Assurance Championship

Southampton	Hampshire v Somerset
Dartford	Kent v Notts
Northampton	Northants v Yorkshire
The Oval	Surrey v Sussex
Worcester	Worcs v Lancashire

Other Match

| The Parks | Oxford U v Glos |

JUNE 2, THURSDAY

First Cornhill Test

| Trent Bridge | ENGLAND v WEST INDIES |

JUNE 4, SATURDAY

Britannic Assurance Championship

Cardiff	Glamorgan v Kent
Liverpool	Lancashire v Hampshire
Lord's	Middlesex v Worcs
Taunton	Somerset v Northants
Horsham	Sussex v Derbyshire
Edgbaston	Warwickshire v Notts
Harrogate	Yorkshire v Surrey

JUNE 5, SUNDAY

Refuge Assurance League

Merthyr Tydfil	Glamorgan v Kent
Old Trafford	Lancashire v Hampshire
Lord's	Middlesex v Worcs
Taunton	Somerset v Northants
Horsham	Sussex v Derbyshire
Edgbaston	Warwickshire v Notts
Headingley	Yorkshire v Surrey

JUNE 8, WEDNESDAY

Benson & Hedges Cup
Semi-finals

Tourist Match

| Edgbaston or | Warwickshire or Lancs |
| Old Trafford | v West Indies |

Other Match

| Harrogate | Tilcon Trophy (3 days) |

JUNE 11, SATURDAY

Britannic Assurance Championship

Derby	Derbyshire v Glos
Ilford	Essex v Sussex
Tunbridge Wells	Kent v Middlesex
Trent Bridge	Notts v Glamorgan
Bath	Somerset v Warwickshire
The Oval	Surrey v Leics
Worcester	Worcs v Hampshire

Tourist Match

| Northampton* | Northants v W. Indies |

Other Match

| Downpatrick* | Ireland v MCC (3 days) |

JUNE 12, SUNDAY

Refuge Assurance League

Heanor	Derbyshire v Glos
Ilford	Essex v Sussex
Trent Bridge	Notts v Glamorgan
Bath	Somerset v Warwickshire
The Oval	Surrey v Leics
Worcester	Worcs v Hampshire

JUNE 15, WEDNESDAY

Britannic Assurance Championship

Ilford	Essex v Glos
Basingstoke	Hampshire v Middlesex
Tunbridge Wells	Kent v Lancashire
Leicester	Leics v Glamorgan
Bath	Somerset v Sussex
Headingley	Yorkshire v Warwickshire

Other Matches

| The Parks | Oxford U v Notts |
| The Oval | Surrey v Cambridge U |

JUNE 16, THURSDAY

Second Cornhill Test

| Lord's | ENGLAND v WEST INDIES |

JUNE 18, SATURDAY

Britannic Assurance Championship

Derby	Derbyshire v Worcs
Southampton	Hampshire v Notts
Old Trafford	Lancashire v Glos
Leicester	Leics v Sussex
Luton	Northants v Middlesex
Edgbaston	Warwickshire v Kent
Sheffield	Yorkshire v Essex

JUNE 19, SUNDAY

Refuge Assurance League

Knypersley	Derbyshire v Worcs
Basingstoke	Hampshire v Notts
Old Trafford	Lancashire v Glos
Leicester	Leics v Sussex
Luton	Northants v Middlesex
Bath	Somerset v Surrey
Edgbaston	Warwickshire v Kent
Sheffield	Yorkshire v Essex

JUNE 22, WEDNESDAY

NatWest Bank Trophy (1st round)

Finchampstead	Berkshire v Yorkshire
Chester or Oxton	Cheshire v Northants
Torquay	Devon v Notts
Darlington	Durham v Somerset
Chelmsford	Essex v Wiltshire
Bristol	Glos v Ireland
Canterbury	Kent v Bucks
Old Trafford	Lancashire v Lincs
Leicester	Leics v Suffolk
Lord's	Middlesex v Hertfordshire
Edinburgh Myreside	Scotland v Glamorgan
Telford (St George's)	Shropshire v Hampshire
	Staffordshire v Surrey
Hove	Sussex v Derbyshire
Edgbaston	Warwickshire v Cambridge
Worcester	Worcs v Cumberland

JUNE 23, THURSDAY

Tourist Match

Fenners	Combined Univ v W. Indies (2-days)

JUNE 25, SATURDAY

Britannic Assurance Championship

Chelmsford	Essex v Middlesex
Swansea	Glamorgan v Lancashire
Gloucester	Glos v Leics
Trent Bridge	Notts v Northants
The Oval	Surrey v Derbyshire
Hove	Sussex v Yorkshire

Tourist Match

Canterbury*	Kent v W. Indies

JUNE 26, SUNDAY

Refuge Assurance League

Pontypridd	Glamorgan v Lancashire
Gloucester	Glos v Leics
Bournemouth	Hampshire v Essex
Lord's	Middlesex v Somerset
Trent Bridge	Notts v Northants
The Oval	Surrey v Derbyshire
Hove	Sussex v Yorkshire

JUNE 29, WEDNESDAY

Britannic Assurance Championship

Gloucester	Glos v Hampshire
Canterbury	Kent v Essex
Lord's	Middlesex v Yorkshire
Taunton	Somerset v Glamorgan
Nuneaton	Warwickshire v Lancashire

JUNE 30, THURSDAY

Third Cornhill Test

Old Trafford	ENGLAND v WEST INDIES

JULY 2, SATURDAY

Britannic Assurance Championship

Derby	Derbyshire v Middlesex
Northampton	Northants v Lancashire
Taunton	Somerset v Essex
The Oval	Surrey v Warwickshire
Hastings	Sussex v Kent
Worcester	Worcs v Glos
Headingley	Yorkshire v Leics

Other Match

Lord's	Oxford U v Cambridge U

JULY 3, SUNDAY

Refuge Assurance League

Repton School	Derbyshire v Middlesex
Canterbury	Kent v Notts
Tring	Northants v Lancashire
Taunton	Somerset v Essex
The Oval	Surrey v Warwickshire
Hastings	Sussex v Hampshire
Hereford	Worcs v Glos
Hull	Yorkshire v Leics

JULY 6, WEDNESDAY

NatWest Bank Trophy (2nd round)

Berks or Yorks v Middlesex or Herts
Cheshire or Northants v Sussex or Derbys
Devon or Notts v Worcs or Cumberland
Essex or Wilts v Staffs or Surrey
Kent or Bucks v Warwicks or Cambs
Leics or Suffolk v Glos or Ireland
Scotland or Glamorgan v Lancs or Lincs
Shrops or Hants v Durham or Somerset

Tourist Match

Derby†	Derbyshire v W. Indies

† Cancelled if Derby still in NatWest.

JULY 9, SATURDAY

Benson & Hedges Cup

Lord's	Final

Tourist Match

Trowbridge*	Minor Counties v W. Indies (2 days)

JULY 10, SUNDAY

Refuge Assurance League

Chelmsford	Essex v Glamorgan
Southampton	Hampshire v Glos
Canterbury	Kent v Middlesex
Old Trafford	Lancashire v Somerset
Northampton	Northants v Yorkshire
Trent Bridge	Notts v Leics
The Oval	Surrey v Worcs
Hove	Sussex v Warwickshire

JULY 13, WEDNESDAY
Britannic Assurance Championship

Southend	Essex v Derbyshire
Bristol	Glos v Northants
Old Trafford	Lancs v Leics
Trent Bridge	Notts v Middlesex
Guildford	Surrey v Hampshire
Edgbaston	Warwickshire v Worcs

Tourist Match

Swansea	Glamorgan v W. Indies

JULY 16, SATURDAY
Britannic Assurance Championship

Derby*	Derbyshire v Northants
Southend	Essex v Lancs
Bristol	Glos v Somerset
Lord's	Middlesex v Glamorgan
Trent Bridge	Notts v Worcs
Guildford	Surrey v Kent
Edgbaston	Warwickshire v Hampshire

Tourist Match

Leicester	Leics v W. Indies

JULY 17, SUNDAY
Refuge Assurance League

Southend	Essex v Lancashire
Bristol	Glos v Somerset
Lord's	Middlesex v Glamorgan
Trent Bridge	Notts v Yorkshire
The Oval	Surrey v Kent
Edgbaston	Warwickshire v Hampshire

Other Match

Dublin	
Castle Avenue	Ireland v Wales (3 days)

JULY 20, WEDNESDAY
Britannic Assurance Championship

Cardiff	Glamorgan v Warwickshire
Portsmouth	Hampshire v Essex
Southport	Lancashire v Surrey
Leicester	Leics v Derbyshire
Northampton	Northants v Kent
Hove	Sussex v Glos
Worcester	Worcs v Yorkshire

Other Match

League Cricket Conference v Sri Lanka (2 days)

JULY 21, THURSDAY
Fourth Cornhill Test

Headingley	ENGLAND v WEST INDIES

JULY 23, SATURDAY
Britannic Assurance Championship

Cardiff	Glamorgan v Yorkshire
Portsmouth	Hampshire v Derbyshire
Folkestone	Kent v Worcs
Leicester	Leics v Essex
Lord's	Middlesex v Surrey
Northampton	Northants v Sussex
Taunton	Somerset v Notts

Tourist Match

Old Trafford† or	Lancs or Warwicks
Edgbaston	v Sri Lanka

† Will include Sunday play if at Old Trafford.

JULY 24, SUNDAY
Refuge Assurance League

Cardiff	Glamorgan v Yorkshire
Portsmouth	Hampshire v Derbyshire
Folkestone	Kent v Worcs
Leicester	Leics v Essex
Lord's	Middlesex v Warwickshire
Finedon	Northants v Sussex
Taunton	Somerset v Notts

JULY 27, WEDNESDAY
NatWest Bank Trophy

Quarter-finals

Tourist Matches

	First-class county v W. Indies
Osterley	Indian Gymkhana v Sri Lanka (1 day)

JULY 29, FRIDAY

Arundel	Lavinia, Duchess of Norfolk's XI v Sri Lanka (1 day)

JULY 30, SATURDAY
Britannic Assurance Championship

Derby	Derbyshire v Warwickshire
Cheltenham	Glos v Surrey
Canterbury	Kent v Somerset
Worksop	Notts v Leics
Eastbourne	Sussex v Glamorgan
Worcester	Worcs v Northants
Headingley	Yorkshire v Lancashire

Tourist Matches

Chelmsford	Essex v West Indies
Lord's	Middlesex v Sri Lanka

JULY 31, SUNDAY
Refuge Assurance League

Derby	Derbyshire v Warwickshire
Cheltenham	Glos v Surrey
Canterbury	Kent v Somerset
Leicester	Leics v Middlesex
Eastbourne	Sussex v Glamorgan
Worcester	Worcs v Northants
Scarborough	Yorkshire v Lancashire

AUGUST 3, WEDNESDAY
Britannic Assurance Championship

Cheltenham	Glos v Warwickshire
Canterbury	Kent v Leics
Northampton	Northants v Essex
Weston-super-Mare	Somerset v Surrey
Eastbourne	Sussex v Hampshire
Sheffield	Yorkshire v Notts

Other Match

Swansea	Glamorgan v Rest of the World (1 day)

AUGUST 4, THURSDAY
Fifth Cornhill Test
The Oval   ENGLAND v WEST INDIES
Tourist Match
        Minor Counties v Sri Lanka
        (2 days)

AUGUST 6, SATURDAY
Britannic Assurance Championship
Swansea	Glamorgan v Surrey
Cheltenham	Glos v Yorkshire
Old Trafford	Lancashire v Middlesex
Leicester	Leics v Hampshire
Weston-super- Mare	Somerset v Derbyshire
Edgbaston	Warwickshire v Northants
Kidderminster	Worcs v Sussex

Tourist Match
Trent Bridge*   Notts v Sri Lanka

AUGUST 7, SUNDAY
Refuge Assurance League
Ebbw Vale	Glamorgan v Surrey
Cheltenham	Glos v Yorkshire
Blackpool	Lancashire v Middlesex
Leicester	Leics v Hampshire
Weston-super- Mare	Somerset v Derbyshire
Edgbaston	Warwickshire v Northants
Worcester	Worcester v Sussex

AUGUST 10, WEDNESDAY
NatWest Bank Trophy
Semi-finals

Tourist Match
Headingley   Yorkshire† v Sri Lanka

† If not in Nat West Bank semi-finals.

AUGUST 13, SATURDAY
Britannic Assurance Championship
Chesterfield	Derbyshire v Kent
Colchester	Essex v Notts
Abergavenny	Glamorgan v Worcs
Bournemouth	Hampshire v Northants
Lord's	Middlesex v Glos
Hove	Sussex v Lancashire
Edgbaston	Warwickshire v Leics
Scarborough	Yorkshire v Somerset

Tourist Match
The Oval*   Surrey v Sri Lanka

AUGUST 14, SUNDAY
Refuge Assurance League
Chesterfield	Derbyshire v Kent
Colchester	Essex v Notts
Swansea	Glamorgan v Worcs
Bournemouth	Hampshire v Northants
Lord's	Middlesex v Glos
Hove	Sussex v Lancashire
Edgbaston	Warwickshire v Leics
Scarborough	Yorkshire v Somerset

AUGUST 17, WEDNESDAY
Britannic Assurance Championship
Chesterfield	Derbyshire v Yorkshire
Colchester	Essex v Glamorgan
Bournemouth	Hampshire v Kent
Lytham	Lancashire v Notts
Uxbridge	Middlesex v Somerset
The Oval	Surrey v Worcs
Hove	Sussex v Warwickshire

Tourist Match
Bristol   Glos v Sri Lanka

AUGUST 20 SATURDAY
Britannic Assurance Championship
Bristol	Glos v Kent
Old Trafford	Lancashire v Derbyshire
Leicester	Leics v Somerset
Uxbridge	Middlesex v Warwickshire
Wellingborough School	Northants v Glamorgan
Trent Bridge	Notts v Surrey
Worcester	Worcs v Essex

Tourist Match
Southampton*   Hampshire v Sri Lanka

Other Match*
Dumfries   Scotland v Ireland (3 days)

AUGUST 21, SUNDAY
Refuge Assurance League
Lydney or Moreton-in- Marsh	Glos v Kent
Old Trafford	Lancs v Derbyshire
Leicester	Leics v Somerset
Wellingborough School	Northants v Glamorgan
Trent Bridge	Notts v Surrey
Worcester	Worcs v Essex

Cornhill Test
Lord's   ENGLAND v SRI LANKA

AUGUST 25, THURSDAY
Britannic Assurance Championship (4 days)
Neath	Glamorgan v Leics
Maidstone	Kent v Sussex
Northampton	Northants v Derbyshire
Taunton	Somerset v Hampshire
The Oval	Surrey v Lancashire
Worcester	Worcs v Warwickshire
Headingley	Yorkshire v Middlesex

AUGUST 28th, SUNDAY

Refuge Assurance League
Chelmsford	Essex v Glos
Llanelli	Glamorgan v Leics
Maidstone	Kent v Sussex
Northamton	Northants v Derbyshire
Taunton	Somerset v Hampshire
The Oval	Surrey v Lancashire
Worcester	Worcs v Warwickshire
Headingley	Yorkshire v Middlesex

Other Match
Edgbaston	Warwick Under-25 final

AUGUST 30, TUESDAY

Britannic Assurance Championship (4 days)
Southampton	Hampshire v Glos
Old Trafford	Lancashire v Yorkshire
Leicester	Leics v Notts
The Oval	Surrey v Essex
Hove	Sussex v Middlesex
Edgbaston	Warwickshire v Glamorgan

AUGUST 31, WEDNESDAY

Tourist Match
Derby	Derbyshire v Sri Lanka

SEPTEMBER 3, SATURDAY

NatWest Bank Trophy
Lord's	Final

SEPTEMBER 4, SUNDAY

Texaco Trophy (1-day international)
The Oval	England v Sri Lanka

Other Matches
Scarborough	Four Counties Knock-out Competition (3 days)

SEPTEMBER 5, MONDAY
Bain Clarkson Trophy Final (1 day)

SEPTEMBER 7, WEDNESDAY

Refuge Assurance Cup
Semi-finals

Other Match
Scarborough	Yorks v The Yorkshiremen (1 day)

SEPTEMBER 9, FRIDAY

Britannic Assurance Championship (4 days)
Chelmsford*	Essex v Leics
Cardiff*	Glamorgan v Hampshire
Bristol*	Glos v Worcs
Lords*	Middlesex v Kent
Trent Bridge*	Notts v Derbyshire
Hove*	Sussex v Surrey
Edgbaston*	Warwickshire v Somerset
Scarborough*	Yorkshire v Northants

SEPTEMBER 14, WEDNESDAY

Britannic Assurance Championship (4 days)
Derby	Derbyshire v Lancashire
Chelmsford	Essex v Northants
Southampton	Hampshire v Sussex
Canterbury	Kent v Surrey
Trent Bridge	Notts v Yorkshire
Taunton	Somerset v Glos
Worcester	Worcs v Glamorgan

SEPTEMBER 18, SUNDAY

Refuge Assurance Cup
Egbaston	Final